A Depth Psychology Model of Immigration and Adaptation

A Depth Psychology Study of Immigration and Adaptation: The Migrant's Journey brings current academic research from a range of disciplines into a 12-stage model of human migration. Based on Joseph Campbell's hero's journey, this depth psychology model addresses pre-migration reasons for leaving, the ordeals of the journey and challenges of post-migration adaptation. One-third of migrants return to homelands while those who remain in newlands face the triple challenges of building a new life, a new identity and sense of belonging. While arrivées carry homelands within, their children, the second generation, born and raised in the newland usually have access to both cultures which enables them to make unique contributions to society. Vital to successful newland adaptation is the acceptance and support of immigrants by host countries. *A Depth Psychology Study of Immigration and Adaptation* will be an important resource for academics and students in the social sciences, clinical psychologists, health care and social welfare workers, therapists of all backgrounds, policy makers and immigrants themselves seeking an understanding of the inner experiences of migration.

Phyllis Marie Jensen, PhD, is a Jungian psychoanalyst (ISAPZürich) and sandplay therapist in Vancouver, Canada. Also a social and behavioural science evidence-based researcher, she is an associate clinical professor in Family Medicine, University of Alberta. A second-generation Canadian, Jensen has experienced migration first-hand in England and Switzerland and three Canadian provinces. She is the author of *Artist Emily Carr and the Spirit of the Land: A Jungian Portrait* (Routledge, 2016).

A Depth Psychology Model of Immigration and Adaptation

The Migrant's Journey

Phyllis Marie Jensen

First published 2020

by Routledge

2 Park Square, Milton Park, Abingdon, Oxon OX14 4RN

and by Routledge

52 Vanderbilt Avenue, New York, NY 10017

Routledge is an imprint of the Taylor & Francis Group, an informa business

© 2020 Phyllis Marie Jensen

The right of Phyllis Marie Jensen to be identified as author of this work has been asserted by her in accordance with sections 77 and 78 of the Copyright, Designs and Patents Act 1988.

All rights reserved. No part of this book may be reprinted or reproduced or utilised in any form or by any electronic, mechanical, or other means, now known or hereafter invented, including photocopying and recording, or in any information storage or retrieval system, without permission in writing from the publishers.

Trademark notice: Product or corporate names may be trademarks or registered trademarks, and are used only for identification and explanation without intent to infringe.

British Library Cataloguing-in-Publication Data
A catalogue record for this book is available from the British Library

Library of Congress Cataloging-in-Publication Data
A catalog record has been requested for this book

ISBN: 978-1-138-33242-3 (hbk)
ISBN: 978-1-138-33246-1 (pbk)
ISBN: 978-0-429-44662-7 (ebk)

Typeset in Times New Roman
by Swales & Willis, Exeter, Devon, UK

*Dedicated to my migrating parents
Ella Katherine and Svend Aage Jensen*

Contents

Preface		viii
Acknowledgements		xiii
	Introduction	1
1	Phase 1: pre-migration	9
2	Phase 2: the journey	54
3	Phase 3: post-migration arrival	66
4	Phase 4: post-migration—home again	82
5	Identity and belonging	110
6	Generational differences	150
7	Host country	187
8	Summary and conclusions	229
	Bibliography	235
	Index	288

Preface

Five factors inspired this book:

1) Awareness of artist Emily Carr's migration complex. Often called "Canada's Van Gogh" and the "Mother of Modern Art in Canada," Emily Carr[1] had a classical art education in San Francisco, London and France. She deemed Aboriginal (First Nation) art as important as the ancient arts of other lands, and because it was believed to be disappearing, she vowed to document it. She made six camping trips along the Pacific Northwest coast by ferry, canoe and horseback with only her dog as companion. A hundred years later, her "wilderness" trips are seen as an "apprenticeship" in First Nation art and culture, that opened her eyes to a "fresh-seeing" of the land and its spirit energies and inspired her modernist paintings of the spirit of the land, forest, sea and sky. At the same time, in her writings is an underlying theme of the migration complex of self, family and community.
2) The art of the Canadian Group of Seven. Led by Lawren Harris (1885–1970) and J.E.H. Macdonald (1873–1932), these seven male artists known as the Group of Seven, asked: Who am I? Where am I? Where is here? Like Carr, they painted the outdoors fully determined to capture the spirit of the land.
3) American psychiatrist/psychoanalyst, Salman Akhtar, who migrated from India to New York and wrote extensively on migration. He noted "the reluctance of depth psychology to look at the social, historical and cultural factors of migration has forced us to fill the gaps with research from other disciplines."[2] Being a social and behavioural evidence-based researcher as well as a Jungian analyst, I took up the challenge. Thus, this book is an attempt to integrate the research literature of sister disciplines—anthropology, clinical and social psychology, economics, history, human geography, jurisprudence, linguistics, political science and sociology—into a depth psychology model of migration.

4) The heroic model appeared to me in a dream image. The research literature is segmented by discipline and I was seeking an inclusive model for depth psychology's clinical and research work. I had a dream of an ancient scroll on which was written: "Migration is a heroic act." This led to my use of the hero archetype as the organizing principle for this integrative work.
5) Joseph Campbell (1904–1987), a professor of mythology found a repeating theme in world literature, the Hero Archetype, the "will and capacity to undergo repeated transformations."[3] In *The Hero with a Thousand Faces*,[4] he describes the hero as leaving a known order to enter a journey of chaos before a new order emerges.[5] The twelve stages of the heroic archetype are organized in this depth psychology model of migration: pre-migration, the journey and post-migration arrival and adaptation.

Awareness of Emily Carr's migration complex led me to explore my own migration experiences as a "2.5-generation" Canadian who has lived in several provinces, travelled extensively and been a sojourner student in two countries. This is not unusual in Canada. In fact, it's actually rare to meet a "stayer," born and living in the same place. One in five Canadians is a naturalized citizen (born outside the country), a figure predicted to rise to one in three persons in 20 years.[6] Toronto, the most multicultural city in the world, reports over half of its population was born outside the country.[7] Internal migrations within the country are a constant feature. "Modernity implies mobility,"[8] says Duyvendak. "The motif of modern culture … is being rootless, displacement between worlds, living between a lost past and fluid present [and] a metaphor for the journeying modern consciousness."[9] Because worldwide, one in 30 people is a migrant,[10] it's important to have a workable depth psychology model of migration.

In C.G. Jung's *Collected Works*, there are eleven references to migration. Transcribed below, the most relevant passages relating to human migration are italicized.

Jung on European Migration

Because we still can and will wander, we imagine that we can live more or less anywhere. Not yet convinced that we ought to be able to get along with one another in closely packed families, we feel that we can afford to quarrel, for there is still good open country "out West" if things come to the worst. At least it seems so. But it is no longer quite true. Even the Englishman is not settled in India; he is really condemned to serve his term there and to make the best of it. Hence all these hopeful, jolly, eager, energetic, powered voices issue from people who are thinking and dreaming of spring in Sussex.[11]

Jung on Migration Motifs/Symbols, Archetypes

Even dreams are made of collective material to a very high degree, just as, in the mythology and folklore of different peoples, certain motifs repeat themselves in almost identical form. I have called these motifs "archetypes," and by this I mean forms or images of a collective nature which occur practically all over the earth as constituents of myths and at the same time as autochthonous, individual products of unconscious origin. *The archetypal motifs presumably derive from patterns of the human mind that are transmitted not only by tradition and migration* but also by heredity.[12]

As the products of imagination are always in essence visual, their forms must, from the outset, have the character of images and moreover of typical images, which is why, following St. Augustine, I call them "archetypes." Comparative religion and mythology are rich mines of archetypes, and so is the psychology of dreams and psychoses. The astonishing parallelism between these images and *the ideas they serve to express has frequently given rise to the wildest migration theories,* although it would have been far more natural to think of the remarkable similarity of the human psyche at all times and in all places. Archetypal fantasy-forms are, in fact, reproduced spontaneously anytime and anywhere, without there being any conceivable trace of direct transmission. The original structural components of the psyche are of no less surprising a uniformity than are those of the visible body. The archetypes are, so to speak, organs of the pre-rational psyche. They are eternally inherited forms and ideas which have at first no specific content. Their specific content only appears in the course of the individual's life, when personal experience is taken up in precisely these forms.[13]

Jung on Myth and Migration

Every endeavour has been made to explain the concordance of myth-motifs and symbols as due to migration and tradition ... [which is] contradicted by the fact that a mytholgem can arise anywhere at any time, without there being the slightest possibility of any such transmission ... [I] investigated the dreams of pure-bred [Africans] living in the southern United States. I found in these dreams, among other things, motifs from Greek mythology and this dispelled any doubt that I had that it might be a question of racial inheritance.[14]

> The customary treatment of mythological motifs ... was not exactly a help to us in recognizing their universality; and the psychological problems raised by this universality *could be easily shelved by hypothesis of migration* ... [making us conclude that] "myth forming," structural elements must be present in the unconscious psyche.[15]
>
> fantasies-images (including dreams) of an impersonal character ... have their closest analogue in mythological types ... *Although tradition and transmission by migration certainly play a part*, they are, as we have said, very many cases that cannot be accounted for in this way and drive us to the hypothesis of "autochthonous revival."[16]
>
> It has previously been *supposed that mythological symbols were disseminated by migration.* But I have found that *the occurrence of the same symbols in different countries and continents does not depend on migration*, but rather on the spontaneous revival of the same contents.[17]

Jung also speaks of migration metaphorically as the loss of roots:

> it is the body, the feeling, the instincts, which connect us with the soil. If you give up the past you naturally detach from the past; you lose your roots in the soil, your connection with the totem ancestors that dwell in your soil. You turn outward and drift away, and try to conquer other land because you are exiled from your own soil. That is inevitable. The feet will walk away and the head cannot retain them because it is always wandering over the surface of the earth. Always looking for something. It is exactly what Mountain Lake, the Pueblo chief said to me. "The Americans are quite crazy. They are always seeking, we don't know what they are looking for ..." Well, there is too much head and so there is too much will, too much walking about, and nothing rooted.[18]
>
> is a disaster not only for primitive tribes but for civilized [hu]man[s] as well ... The life of instinct—the most conservative element in [hu]man[s]—always expressed itself in traditional usages. Age-old convictions and emotions are always deeply rooted in the instincts. If they get lost, the conscious mind becomes severed from the instincts and loses its roots, while the instincts, unable to express themselves, fall back into the unconscious and reinforce its energy causing this in turn to overflow into the existing contents of consciousness. It is then that the rootless condition of consciousness becomes a real danger. The secret *vis á tergo* (pushing from behind) results in a hubris of the conscious mind which manifests in the form of exaggerated self-esteem or

an inferiority complex. At all levels a loss of balance ensues, and this the most fruitful soil for psychic injury.[19]

Marie-Louise von Franz writes:

> the rootless person is liable and in danger of losing his values and inner strength. In folktales certain features are common to practically all the stories ... loneliness, being alone, being separated from the village group or the tribal group. Loneliness in nature opens the door to the powers of evil, as does being in a foreign country. You need the protective ring of human beings and also of your beloved objects. They protect one from the complete exposure to the terrifying forces of the unconscious ... If you live alone for a very long time, then the tribe, the other people project their shadow onto you.[20]

Jung speaks briefly about migration and has given us the means to construct a depth psychology model of migration in an adaptation of the hero archetype. An archetype is a primordial image of "basic and universal experiences of life" comparable to Plato's Ideals, Kant's *a priori* categories and Schopenhauer's prototypes linking body and psyche, instinct and image.[21]

Notes

1 Jensen, 2016.
2 Akhtar, 1999/2004:154.
3 Samuels et al, 1986/2000:66.
4 Campbell, 1949/1973.
5 Vogler, 1998/2007:188.
6 Torstar News, 2017, Jan 26.
7 Ngabo, 2016, May 16.
8 Duyvendak, 2011:7.
9 Duyvendak, 2011:7.
10 Hill, 2018.
11 Jung, CW10:1001
12 Jung, CW11: 88
13 Ibid.: 845
14 Jung, CW8: 228
15 Jung, CW9i:259
16 Ibid.:262
17 Jung, CW 18:1286.
18 Jarrett, 1997:373.
19 Jung, CW16: 216.
20 Von Franz, 1995:173.
21 Samuels et al, 1986/2000:26–27.

Acknowledgements

In Canada, The Multiculturalism Act (1988)[1] is public policy, making it a privilege to have been called to write this book.

Many people need to be thanked for their encouragement. Top of the list is the University of Alberta library and librarians for the many systematic reviews that comprise the work. The Vancouver Jung Library, the Vancouver Public Library and inter-library loan program also played important roles. I want to acknowledge the unnamed clients whose migration discussions inspired and illustrate the work. Many colleagues and friends have been open with their thoughts and suggestions: David and Terre Arscott, Heige Boehm, David and Guadalupe Buchwald, Sue Card, Maryan Cernia, Michael Coulis, Ruth Jensen, Gail Lyons, Lisa McConnell, Ana Mozol, David Roomy, Jane Murphy-Taylor, Malcolm Timbers, Leslie Turner, Inge Sardy and Barbara Shannon as well as those at the Writer's Union of Canada and the Canadian Authors Association. Very special thanks are given to my sister Dr Ruth Jensen for her editing, and British editor Susannah Frearson and associate editor Heather Evans at Routledge who guided the process.

NB: In the chapter endnotes, citations of Jung's Collected Works (CW) are followed by the volume and the § numbers, i.e. in Jung, CW10:23, '23' is not a page number; it is the § number.

Note

1 https://en.wikipedia.org/wiki/Canadian_Multiculturalism_Act.

Introduction

Immigration, a "transformative force"[1] also carries the potential for psychological problems.[2] In depth psychology, there has been little focus on migration "despite of—or perhaps because of the fact many pioneers of psychoanalysis were themselves emigrants."[3] Erik Erickson (1902–1984) spoke of the diaspora of peoples and psychoanalysis due to 20th-century European wars.[4] Today, we need to "fill the gaps with research from other disciplines."[5] This describes *The Migrant's Journey*.

Research methods

The objective of the literature review was to explore, survey, synthesise and critically evaluate the literature on migration (emigration, immigration) to inform depth psychology and enhance understanding and clinical practice. The design includes scholarly publications and government documents published between 2000 and 2019: research papers, reviews and meta-analyses in anthropology, economics, human geography, health sciences, history, political science, social psychology, psychology, psychoanalysis and sociology. Key article references were searched to follow "the trail of footnotes" for works outside the time-frame. The electronic data base of the University of Alberta Library was used: Medline, Embase, Cochrane, CINAHL, science citation index and the national research register. Inclusion criteria were: English-language quantitative studies (demographic, experimental, statistics and survey) and qualitative studies (interviews, historical analysis and observational) addressing incidence and psychology of migration plus identity and belonging, generational issues and host-country reception. Relevant titles and abstracts sought: 1) Provenance: Is the discipline appropriate and the author qualified? 2) Methods: What approach is used, questions examined, sample size, data sources and how are results interpreted? 3) Objectivity: Is the text biased or open-minded? 4) Standards: Does the work meet accepted research standards? 5) Credible: Do the findings and conclusion logically follow the data? Are they convincing? 6) Value: Do findings contribute to greater understanding? 7) Inclusion: Should the work be included?

Data analysis was qualitative since the range of disciplines and variety of methods used made quantitative synthesis difficult to impossible. Attempts were made to enumerate the frequency of certain observations and to report statistics. Concepts were abstracted to provide descriptive details of each issue historically and current situations. The 12-action steps of the heroic journey were used as a model and report format. Special acculturation issues included identity and belonging, generational differences and host-country responses.

The Migrant's Journey is not a definitive work—that would be an encyclopaedic task. This is an exploration and integration of published research—international and interdisciplinary—about the outer and inner experiences of migration. The approach is pragmatic. Philosopher Mary Daly describes such work as leaping over the walls of knowledge to spin and weave threads of research.[6] It's how Joseph Campbell[7] undertook his review of world literature and discovered the hero archetype.

Migration literature is segmented by discipline, with the primary focus on adaptation, yet the pre-migration period and the circumstances leading to a decision or need to migrate are important. The nature of the physical journey is also important—whether it is simple, harrowing and/or traumatic. In fact, pre-migration and journey experiences can overshadow and hamper later adaptation and settlement[8] and foster psychopathology. This is especially true of forced/involuntary migration and exile with traumatic journeys causing post-traumatic stress disorder (PTSD). Later, it may manifest as locked-in loss and living in the past (psychologically trapped) in homeland social, religious and political battles. "We can only improve our understanding of migration if we understand the broader change processes of which it is a constituent part,"[9] says de Haas at the International Migration Institute in Oxford. And "to understand society is to understand migration, and to understand migration is to better understand society."[10]

Chapter précis

Chapter I, Phase I: pre-migration

Stage 1, "The homeland" (or "the ordinary world"), where situations may be dire as people do not uproot easily from the known and dear. Stage 2, "Call to adventure," explores voluntary/chosen migration for adventure, self-development, opportunities and economics. Stage 3, "Refusal of the call," refers to "stayers" or those who don't or can't migrate, and involuntary (forced/tied) migrations. The latter are often caught in nostalgia, and, like the biblical Lot's wife, face forever backward with salty tears.[11]

Chapter 2, Phase 2: the journey

Stage 4, "The mentor," may be family, friends or relatives. Some villages sponsor an "anchor migrant" to leave, who sends home remittances to finance others to follow in "chain migrations." Today, cell-phones and websites act as mentors, guiding and advising migrants about passage, detours and dangers. Stage 5, "The crossing," is classically a descent into the chaos of the unknown—for migrants, crossing waters and borders embody the unknown. Stage 6, "Tests, allies and enemies," are situations and encounters with people that demand thinking on one's feet. In myths, birds and animals are allies: psychically, this can be interpreted as acting on instinct. Classically, enemies include shape-shifters and tricksters who may test, cheat and entrap, or can be psychological complexes that frustrate and impede the journey. Stage 7, "The approach," is the final step before arrival, which may represent a limbo of laws, physical walls, transit camps and statelessness.

Chapter 3, Phase 3: post-migration arrival

Stage 8, "Arrival," is a series of tasks and ordeals calling for heroic action while enduring threats of harm and the risk of death. For migrants, it can be rejection of entry or psychological challenges, like an initial euphoria that flips into its opposite of disappointment and despair. Stage 9, "Possession of the treasure," emphasizes that the reward is not given but must be seized or won. For migrants, this may represent opportunities or resolution of losses, with positive feelings and gratitude towards the host country and willingness to adapt. Unresolved grief, the *Ulysses syndrome*, prevents seizing the gift of the newland, whereas its opposite, denied grief, can result in indiscriminate merging or *cultural localitis*.

Chapter 4, Phase 4: post-migration, home again, or adaptation

Stage 10, "The road back," is classically the hero's return. This may be true for migrants, as one-third of migrants return to their homelands. For stayers, it may be an unrequited desire for homelands and replication of homelands in newlands. Stage 11, "Resurrection," is regaining former status and position. For migrants, this may be the recognition of homeland credentials with equivalent status plus adaptation. This is neither simple nor inevitable. To explore adaptation, theories of assimilation are contrasted with theories of acculturation and Jung's model of psychic transformation. Stage 12, "Return with the elixir (treasure)," in migration can be interpreted as growth, wisdom, knowledge and understanding. Many tribal groups recognize that those who leave experience psychic changes, so they undergo a ritual cleansing before re-entry into the home society. For migrants remaining in the newland, the elixir or treasure is to become a contributing citizen with a sense of belonging.

Chapter 5, Identity and belonging

The psychoanalytic concepts of persona, ego, self, identity and belonging are important in migration. The ability to adapt and belong is explored via theories of psychic development: John Bowlby's attachment theory, Donald Winnicott's transitional object, time and space, Daniel Stern's emerging sense of self and Erik Erickson's Stages of Life. Identity, self-development and adolescent separation theories are discussed along with the special issues of exile and diaspora. Religion plays an important role in adaptation, with churches and temples offering migrants solace, resources, community and a sense of belonging.

Chapter 6, Generational differences

Much is written about the migration challenges for émigrés (1st generation). Many claim to have migrated for the sake of their children (2nd generation) born in the newland. Whether true or a rationalization, this creates debts of gratitude in children for their parents' sufferings, hardships and sacrifices of migration. The 2nd generation, born, raised and educated in newlands, usually embrace newland attitudes, values and beliefs that may clash with those of their émigré parents from traditional societies. They can be caught "betwixt and between" cultures and struggle with their parents' symbolic and diasporic identities. Both 1st and 2nd generations face the task of reconciling cultural differences. Case studies and biographies illustrate the search for roots, authenticity and belonging. Much migration literature is fiction, but may also be thinly disguised (auto)biography that iterates difficult truths.

Chapter 7, Host country

Concepts of nation states and citizenship are based on 1) "rights of blood" (*jus sanguinis*), 2) "rights of soil" (*jus soli*), and 3) rights of citizenship under rule of law. Migrants coming to newlands may evoke mixed emotions in residents, ranging from idealization to paranoid anxiety. There are three levels of migrants' reception: government, society and community, and three possible responses: exclusion, passive acceptance and active encouragement. Successful adaptation depends to a large degree on the host-country reception. This includes attitudes, values and beliefs towards migrants. Studies of personality, prejudice and xenophilia are explored. Societal expectations of migrant adaptation range from assimilation (becoming identical) to multicultural celebration of differences. Issues particular to women include marriage practices, reproductive rights, motherhood, and special labour conditions, such as employment in private homes as domestics and childcare workers who are vulnerable to exploitation.

Chapter 8, Summary and conclusions

Jung speaks briefly about migration. His concepts of archetype and complexes give us the means to construct a depth psychology model of migration. Here it's represented by the heroic 12-step journey, along with the special issues of identity and belonging, generational differences and host-country responses.

Migration is ancient history

Scientists studying archaeology, DNA[12] and fossil records report human ancestors emerged as a nomadic species in sub-Sahara Africa about 200,000 years ago. Living off the land, they foraged for fruits, vegetables, tubers, seeds and eggs; caught birds and fish and hunted animals as they followed seasonal migrations. About 70,000 years ago, a sudden cooling of the earth's climate reduced ancestral populations to near-extinction. Later, as the climate improved and greater numbers survived, some left Africa. The *National Geographic*'s genographic map[13] of human migrations shows one group went to present-day Yemen on the Arabian Peninsula and along the Arabian Sea to India and South East Asia. A few reached Australia about 50,000 years ago. Others went to the Middle East, to Europe and South Central Asia. About 15,000 years ago, during the last glacial period, Polynesians in Australia and Tasmania crossed the sub-Antarctic islands to South America. There's evidence of Polynesian water migrations to the west coast of the Americas and crossings of the Atlantic sea ice. About 20,000 years ago, during an ice age when sea levels were lower than today, a widened Alaska land-bridge permitted travel to and settlement in the Americas. In 2018, on Canada's Pacific Northwest coast, 29 human footprints were found, dating from 13,000 years ago in three sizes suggestive of a man, woman and child.[14]

Reasons for early migration are population pressures, conflicts over land, politics and religious differences that led to forced migrations, escape and exile. In an exploration of one of Socrates' dreams, Von Franz says it tells of his decision not to escape Athens to avoid trial, but to be obedient to its laws.[15] In contrast, Dante Alighieri the Florentine poet exiled in 1302 AD to Rome for supporting the losing political power tells of the pain of exile in Canto XVII of the *Paradiso* of *The Divine Comedy*.[16]

> You shall leave everything you love most:
> this is the arrow that the bow of exile
> shoots first. You are to know the bitter taste

of others' bread, how salty it is, and know
how hard a path it is for one who goes
ascending and descending others' stairs.[17]

During the European medieval period, most people were serfs and feudal tenants who belonged to the land and were not permitted to leave. In recent days, some nation states have attempted to control out-flows of citizens, especially the highly skilled. In 1948, the United Nations' *Universal Declaration of Human Rights* enshrined the freedom to leave one's birthplace. Article 13 states: "Everyone has the right to freedom of movement and residence within the borders of each State," and "Everyone has the right to leave any country, including his own, and to return to his country." Article 14 states: "Everyone has the right to seek and to enjoy in other countries asylum from persecution." Article 15 states: "Everyone has the right to a nationality," and "No one shall be arbitrarily deprived of his nationality nor denied the right to change his nationality."[18]

Despite universal rights to mobility and nationality, the right to enter another country lies with nation states.[19] Some are open to migrants: other countries force migrations to "solve" social and political problems by "dumping" and/or requiring the departure of surplus populations and "undesirables," like convicts, paupers, orphans, unmarried women and certain ethnic groups.[20] Before World War I (WWI), surplus population was defined by class, gender and occupation (or lack thereof), and afterwards was defined in terms of national, religious and racial minorities.[21] Dumping and ethnic cleansing has been supported by ideologies and "dreams of homogeneous nation-states."[22] The reality is individual migrants' interests and those of nation states do not always align. A 20th-century example was the Soviet Union's Iron Curtain, erected to "uphold state sovereignty in the face of globalization,"[23] and giving that country a tight grip on preferred citizens—the highly skilled and professionals needed to fill demographic gaps brought about by wars. From earliest times, a shadow or dark side to migration has existed, of traffickers who capture, trick, imprison, sell and export people; today, traffickers also engage in organ harvest for personal profit.

Migration statistics

The most recent year the UN[24] provided global statistics for migration was 2013, when 244 million people were living in countries other than their birthplace. Half were Asian migrants with a 41% increase in migration over the previous 15 years, at a rate greater than global population growth. Two out of every three migrants went to Europe or Asia, and the remainder to North America (20%) and Africa, South America, the Caribbean and Oceania (Australia, New Zealand, Micronesia). In 2016 in Europe, asylum claims were made by 1.3 million migrants;[25] for unknown reasons this number dropped by half in 2018.[26] In 2017, the UN reported that the world's displaced population hit a record high of 68.5 million, an increase of 3 million over the previous year; this translates into one person fleeing every two seconds and becoming one of 25.4 million refugees.[27] Developing countries are host to 86% of the world's refugees, with the poorest nations providing asylum to 25% of the global total.[28] Also in 2017, the UN estimated that 258 million people were living in a country other than their birthland, representing a 49% increase since 2000,[29] translating into one in 30 persons (52% male, 48% female, and 72% working age).[30] The International Organization for Migration (IOM) predicts globally by 2050 there will be 405 million international migrants.[31] In the West for the past 50 years, the United States (US) has been a primary destination and the number of foreign-born has quadrupled from less than 12 million in 1970 to 46.6 million in 2015. Until its dissolution, the USSR was the second largest host country of international migration, but recently Germany has replaced the USSR.[32] It is predicted that if migration continues at the present rate, attitudes towards migration will be a central issue of the 21st century.[33]

Reflections

Depth psychology may have lacked a model of migration because the discipline's focus has typically been on the inner self, and migration seen as an external event. Yet, migration is central to human history—it is ancient and instinctual, and often has been necessary for survival. Jung says migration has been taken for granted: "Because we can and will wander, we imagine that we can live more or less anywhere."[34] Still, migration presents psychological challenges that need understanding. Often a person has a reasonably functioning personality until migration, when underdevelopment and unresolved issues become paramount, such as attachment and separation issues, ego development and psychic strength to make one's own decisions. On top of this are adaptation challenges, such as acquiring a new language and culture, and learning to live "in the now" instead of the past or an imagined future.

Depth psychologists Papadopoulos and Hulme, who work in London with refugees ask, "How many Britons faced with a seemingly unending prospect of poverty and a future with no hope would seek to make their way to other lands?"[35]

Notes

1 Portes & Rumbaut, 2006: xv.
2 Mehta, 1998:149.
3 Grinberg & Grinberg, 1989:1.

4 Erikson, 1968/1994:227.
5 Akhtar, 2007b:165–190.
6 Daly, 1978:xii–xiv.
7 Campbell, 1949/1973.
8 Heptinstall et al, 2004:373–380.
9 de Haas, 2014:16.
10 Ibid.:6.
11 Wikipedia, 2019n: Lot's wife.
12 Reich, 2018.
13 National Geographic Partners, 2018.
14 Smart, 2018.
15 Von Franz, 1996:42.
16 Scott, 1996.
17 Dante, 1909–14:14
18 United Nations, Human Rights.
19 Dummett, 2001.
20 Zahar, 2016:10.
21 Ibid.:17.
22 Ibid.:18.
23 Ibid.:21.
24 United Nations, 2017b: Sustainable Development.
25 Connor, 2017; British Broadcasting Company, 2016.
26 Deutsche Welle, 2017.
27 Keung, 2018.
28 Hollenbach, 2016:14–17.
29 United Nations, 2017b: On Migration.
30 McAuliffe & Ruhs, 2018:17.
31 Ibid.:2.
32 Ibid.:8.
33 Esses et al., 2006:653–669.
34 Jung, CW10: 1001.
35 Papadopoulos & Hulme, 2002:139–166.

Chapter 1

Phase 1
Pre-migration

Phase 1 of the heroic migrant's journey begins at home. Stage 1, 'The ordinary world', discusses the archetype of land and home. Stage 2, 'Call to adventure', explores reasons for migration. Stage 3, "Refusal of the call", looks at "stayers," those who choose not to go and/or lack choice—the involuntary migrants and exiles who don't want to but are forced to leave.

Stage 1: the ordinary world

Archetypes defined

Swiss psychiatrist/psychoanalyst, Carl Jung, initially defined archetypes as primordial images of basic and universal experiences of life comparable to Plato's Ideals, "Kant's *a priori* categories, and Schopenhauer's prototypes that link body and psyche, instinct and image."[1] Later archetypes are described as innate structures of perception that link body, mind, psyche, instinct and image[2,3,4,5,6] visible in myths, arts and dreams.[7] Archetypes are instincts of the *collective unconscious*,[8] our inherited psyche that patterns and influences our *personal unconscious* of perception and experience. The direct experience of an archetype is overwhelming and numinous, an awesome, peak experience never fully understood nor integrated,[9] and the essence of religious belief.[10]

Everyone also has the potential for numinous, transcendent archetypal experiences of land with the power to enlighten and transform psyche.[11] Forester Rowe tells of a repeated childhood numinous dream of land that he then stumbled upon as an adult in uncharted territory and is now protected: Riding Mountain National Park.[12] Space is integral to land and psyche.[13] Historically, tribes established themselves in a territory that became their ancestral land and with the help and blessings of gods or spirits, it became a sacred place:[14] "When land is local, bounded, and personal, it becomes a place. We have experiences in places, build memories of them, and become emotionally attached to them."[15]

All of us hold an imprinted archetype of home and land. Initially, imprinting or psychic stamping was thought to be rapid and restricted to a critical early period of life. Now imprinting is perceived as a cumulative process, deepening with experience and accompanied by positive feelings with the release of endorphins (feel-good hormones)[16] that give a sense of connectedness. We are imprinted with the land of our origin, that becomes a personal experience of the archetype of land. There is too an unconscious ideal of land, known as "Arcadia." Art studies report landscapes as the universally preferred subject, especially Arcadian bluish scenes with trees, water, humans and animals.[17]

In classical Greek mythology, Gaia, goddess of the land represents fertility and nourishment necessary for survival: she arouses feelings of awe and devotion. The dark side of Gaia is the Hindu goddess Kali, the Terrible Mother representing hidden, as well as dark and destructive forces: fire, flood, earthquake and wind.[18] Jung speaks of the earth having a soul and the spirit of the land living in us. Our present danger, he cautions, is alienation from nature and not honouring our inner nature. He advises spending time in nature and connecting with the soul of the earth.[19] Likewise Thoreau, in *Walden* offers wilderness as a prescription for the discontents of civilization.[20] Studies of "Japanese forest bathing" show that phytocides —essential oils emitted by trees and plants as protection from microbes and insects—have significant benefits for humans. They improve immune function, lower heart rate and blood pressure, reduce stress hormones and promote general feelings of well-being.[21,22]

The archetype of migration

The migration archetype is experienced as a strong desire to leave. Often this desire arises with growing awareness of disparities between one's needs and interests and the deficiencies of home. An inner stress is relieved when imagining different worlds that then diminish the importance of attachments and feelings of loyalty to home. Peterson recalls growing up with migration as the norm for youth, the expected next step. As early as age 12, he remembers wanting to leave home.[23] The desire and decision to migrate arises from a "complex interplay of intra-psychic and socio-economic factors".[24] "We now know from ancient DNA that the people who live in a particular place today almost never exclusively descended from the people who lived in the same place far in the past."[25]

In anticipation of leaving, migrants create "mental maps" full of projections and expectations that often differ from reality.[26] These mental maps guide decision making which is often "intendedly [sic] rational, rather than actually so."[27] Intent to migrate, to be realized, requires "access to economic, social and human capital."[28] Youth may migrate for studies, along with an embedded "psychological need to separate from their parents, to prove their independence and coming-of-age and to satisfy their curiosity,"[29] and many countries issue youth work-travel and study visas.[30]

In early migration studies, typically migration was portrayed in a "deficiency" model—social/economic/political deficiencies in the homeland *versus* ideal images of newlands and the personal desire for better situations.[31] Voluntary migrants[32] with papers to cross borders, legally enter another country though the "front door," while those without papers are known as "backdoor" migrants. Generally, these are not the desperately poor: to leave requires resources. Many backdoor migrants are ambitious, educated, urban-based and motivated by persistent generalized violence. Because of local chaos and/or power politics, they are unable to secure border-crossing papers and without these, for example in the Mediterranean, they cannot book passage on ferries.[33] Backdoor migration is more expensive than regular transport, costing a minimum of $2,000 to board overcrowded, unseaworthy vessels.[34] The Central American walking "caravan" to the United States is different: "They say they are fleeing persecution, poverty and violence in their home countries of Honduras, Guatemala, and El Salvador."[35]

Historian McInerney questions assumed knowledge regarding the Irish migrations. From 1845–1900, migration was blamed on the potato famine due to "Landlordism and British misrule."[36] From 1940–1946, migrants were blamed for being "psychologically inadequate," and from 1946–1956 a full 10% of Ireland left, it is said, for "economic reasons." But for many Irish migrants, it was a "flight from restrictive familial and cultural mores, a form of self-banishment,"[37] with conflicts of deep attachment and unresolved dominance and subjugation. Migration has also been touted as a response to government policies to stabilize the country socially and economically through reductions in population.[38] Miller and Boling say Irish images of the US arose from religious ideas of "Paradise" with Uncle Sam promoted to secular "saviour."[39] The imagined US created hope and a sense of adventure, whereas the reality was often bitter disappointment and humiliating exile.[40] Zahar says the "American mirage incites people."[41] Knafo and Yaari see the American dream and archetypal migration fantasies as "influenced by a political, economical and cultural images of America"[42] as a "superpower, a big brother" and "economically the land of opportunity and abundance" representing the potential for education, "jobs, wealth and career advancement."[43] Hollywood films portray the US as an archetypal land of freedom where everyone realizes their own personal goals and lives happily ever after. After World War II (WWII), a "haemorrhage of Europe's best talent" chose the "gate of escape from the bondage of the past."[44] Migration can be a substitute for revolution: "Why raise your voice to contradiction and get yourself into trouble as long as you can always remove yourself entirely from any given environment should it become too unpleasant?"[45]

During the Cold War (1947–1962), the US symbolized a great land of unlimited possibilities: "Czechs and Slovaks came to America seeking prosperity and freedom from oppression during Nazi German occupations and later during the communist regime."[46] The US carried the promise "of upward social mobility, of being better off by moving elsewhere than by staying put."[47] However, the true reality, Bauder says, is that migration has been encouraged by western industrial economies dependent upon a skilled adult workforce.[48] Still, migration is not without benefits. The World Bank reports "migrants from the poorest countries, on average, experienced a 15-fold increase in income, a doubling of school enrolment rates and a 16-fold reduction in child mortality after moving to a developed country."[49]

Stage 2: the call to adventure of voluntary migrants

The heroic legend, *Search for the Holy Grail*[50] by Chrétien de Troyes begins with Percival, a young boy living in the forest with his mother. She chose the forest intentionally to shield her son from the "ways of men" or becoming a knight. Her view of the knight's heroic role is certain death as befell her husband and elder sons. At age 15, fate intervened. On the edge of the forest, Percival encountered a group of knights. Impressed with their heroic bearing and stories of adventure, he found a horse and left home to become a knight.

The forest in the myth symbolizes the ordinary world of home. The edge of the forest is a place of transition. Percival's youthful mindset is an emerging sense of self, of independence and is future-focused. Glimpsing the knights is symbolic of information and global communications (news, films, books, the Internet) that captivate and create desire for adventure as well as inform. Despite attachment to the known place (home) and persons (mother), the voluntary knight (Percival) glimpses the potentials of a new life in another place (Camelot) with new relationships (King Arthur's Court) and a greater purpose (a Quest). The horse symbolizes resources (energy/education/skills/credentials/finances) that enable departure. The Holy Grail, the focus of the search, is symbolic of individuation and fulfilment, as well as making a contribution to society.

Desire and the intent to migrate

Imagining,[51] considering and desiring migration emerges after hearing of other places from others' travels, the media, books, and the internet. In the developing world, the affluent first-world countries act as "siren calls"[52] welding "magnetic forces"[53] of temptations called a "Columbus complex"[54] with the "twin beacons of political liberty and economic prosperity."[55] A 2010 Gallup Poll in 134 countries found 16% of the world's adults (700 million) expressing a desire to migrate internationally and permanently.[56] The first choice of 165 million is the US—a number equal to half that country's current population. The second choice of 45 million is Canada—a number 1.2 times greater than its current population. The choice of another 25 million is Britain, France, Spain, Germany, Saudi Arabia and Australia. Since migration on this scale would overwhelm host countries, it's not surprising that a 2012 *International Social Survey* of 25 host countries reports their citizens favouring reductions in migration.[57] In 2017 in Poland, an estimated 60 million people marched on Independence Day shouting: "Pure Poland, White Poland; Refugees Get out!" even though very few refugees live there.[58] Still, the five primary countries of immigration—Argentina, Australia, Canada, New Zealand and the United States continue to actively recruit skilled economic migrants in a points-selection system,[59,60] and they provide asylum to refugees. The city-state of Singapore has a "4M entrance policy" of "multi-racial, multilingual, multireligious and multi-culturalism."[61]

Existential migration is voluntary. Not motivated by social, economic or political need, it addresses fundamental issues of existence: "seeking greater possibilities for self-actualising, exploring foreign cultures in order to assess their own identity, and ultimately grappling with issues of home and belonging in the world generally."[62]

A psychological *task-value model* of migration is defined as intrinsic determination, flow, interest and goals[63] with futuristic mindsets of adventure and achievement.[64,65] However, aspiration, ability and/or capability are not sufficient for migration; opportunity and resources are necessary. When social, cultural and political environments do not permit or support migration, it's impossible.[66] De Jong and Fawcett argue for a *value-expectancy model*, which they define as a psychological/cognitive cost-benefit model of action dependent upon calculations of the expectation of realization of specific values and goals:[67] wealth, status, comfort, stimulation, autonomy, affiliation and morality.[68] Still, this is not the whole picture. Personality traits, like risk-taking, efficacy and adaptability, are important.[69] Ten values in the universal values theories of Schwartz[70] and Rokeach[71] are predictive of migration: power, achievement, hedonism, stimulation, self-direction, universalism, benevolence, tradition, conformity and security.

Beyond desire and motivation, the intent to migrate is a function of freedom of choice.[72,73,74] To explore this, de Hass uses Isaiah Berlin's concept of liberty,[75] where negative liberty is the absence of obstacles or constraints and positive liberty is mastery, the potential to take control of one's life towards realization of one's purpose. Here, aspirations, expectations and preferences are seen as arising through a combination of "culture, education, personal disposition, identification, information, and images,"[76] while personal capabilities and situations are theorized as enabling and/or preventing migration. Important are *instrumental* and *intrinsic* values, where the former are the means to achieve the goal—finances, social status and education—and the latter are attached to the goals themselves: joys and pleasure of exploring new societies.[77] The *"bright lights" theory* of migration—seeking urban environments—is viewed as potentially corrupting due to the potential of crime and prostitution.[78] Today, de Hass says, social prestige is derived from the suffering of migration (and travel) as a *rite of passage* in being modern, sophisticated and having knowledge and experience of the world.[79]

Migration decision making

Two books, *The Age of Migration*[80] and *Migration Theory*[81] cover most aspects of migration but neglect individual psychology and decision making. The same is true of most theoretical models of migration.[82,83,84,85,86] While they help us to understand the action of migration, post-migration and settlement,[87] questions remain regarding the inner world of migrants. Why do people migrate? How do they make the decision to go?[88]

People feel they have a "right to be mobile," says Bauman.[89] The migration concept should be replaced by a "mobilities model,"[90] says Urry. Castles agrees, saying that the 21st century is an "era of fluidity and openness in which changes in transportation, technology and culture are making it normal for people to think beyond borders and to cross them frequently."[91] Other researchers insist people are socialized to migrate, making it normative and acceptable: it's described as a fever facilitated by family and networks of friends in chain migrations.[92] However, cautions de Haas, in Africa and Asia the decision to migrate legally is the "prerogative of elite groups who have the right diplomas to qualify for a work or study visa and the financial means to pay. Those without papers may be involuntary stayers or are pushed into irregular and illegal migration."[93] In some cultures, migration is valued and prescribed:[94] exogamy—leaving home upon marriage (mostly women)—while men are expected to leave temporarily for work and send home remittances. In Nepal, the survival of one in three persons depends upon seasonal migration and remittance monies.[95]

Macro-level migration decision making

Macro-level studies of situational factors are important in understanding migration decision making. They use aggregate data (like census) and large-large survey data to look at:

1) Personal values—wealth, status, comfort, stimulation, autonomy, affiliation and morality;
2) Place utility—characteristics of origin and destination that facilitate values;

3) Factors that affect accurate perception of place—sources, quantity and quality of information;
4) Objective constraints and facilitators—attachments, demographics, distance, cost of relocation, social approval and family obligations and importantly government policies, and
5) Accurate perceptions of constraints and facilitators.[96]

Still, migration is not just a factor of origin and destination; ideas of other lands are a motivation.

Meso-level decision making

Meso-level decision making takes place at the level of households and small groups. Haug says migration may seem to be an individual's decision, but more often it's a family strategy with temporary departures of individuals who send back remittances. This diversifies the survival risk of those at home.[97] Here, migration decision making involves the whole family "weighing up the costs versus benefits."[98] Important in these decisions are age, gender, economics, social expectations, cultural norms and personality (risk taking and adaptability), opportunities and assistance.[99] It is not only the primary earner or head of household who benefits from migration; indeed, whole families gain.[100] A 2005 French study of migration decision making of dual-earning couples found compromise solutions respected occupational and family roles and the couples' relationship.[101]

A 2012 UK Household Panel Survey looked at dual migration decision making where interests of both partners are considered. They found "only 7.6% of couples move if only the man wants to move, and 20.1% of shared moving desires led to a subsequent move."[102] The NELM (New Economics of Labour Migration) views migration decision making at the meso-household-level as maximizing family incomes, and minimizing risks in the face of the limitations of national market failures. But families do not always migrate together. Often one or more are sent ahead as anchor or pioneer migrants to establish a foothold and send remittances.[103,104,105] In 2006, remittances were estimated to exceed $100 billion annually and accounted for the largest source of foreign capital in some countries.[106]

In a review of Third World migrations, Hugo identified six meso-migration hypotheses:

1) *The Affinity Hypothesis* examines emotional attachment and loyalty to kin and friends. Here compromises are made for circular or intermittent migration and commuting to maintain bonds.[107] Hugo defines migrants from rural areas to towns as bicultural because they retain home cultures and participate in city and national cultures. Few

migrants leave rural areas without intent to return. Usually, they maintain a stake in the village, a sort of rural insurance policy if things don't work out in the city. Middlemen also play a two-way role in securing employment for migrating rural villagers and supplying labour to local city businesses.[108]

2) *The Information Hypothesis* is related to network theory, where pioneer "anchor" migrants encourage the migration of family and friends through sharing of information about conditions and employment opportunities. In the developing world, the most common and trusted information sources are personal ones.[109]

3) *The Facilitating Hypothesis* refers to chain migrations that inform and assist arrivals.

4) *The Conflict Hypothesis* arose from research in Africa and the Pacific where intra-family and intra-community friction was found to be a significant push-factor for migration. Currently in Western Uganda, there's little economic incentive to migrate, but family friction and a desire to see the world prompt leavings. Evidence for this can also be found in Korea and Papua New Guinea suggesting migration is one way to get away from pressures and obligations of family and community organizations.[110]

5) *Required Migration* is of several types. One is exogamous marriage, where the bride relocates to the husband's family home. Sometimes couples of different religions will migrate in order to marry.[111] Some families fund education for a child (usually the eldest son), and in return expect city employment with remittances sent home and chain-migration assistance for others.

6) *Economic bondage* can be a motivator for migration. In Zimbabwe due to high bride prices, a husband is often in bondage to his father-in-law after marriage and sent off to the city to pay off the debt. In other countries with primogeniture (where only the eldest son inherits the family land or business), the permanent migration of later-born children is both expected and a necessity for survival.

Micro-level or individual decision making

Micro-level decision-making studies are at the individual level and explore intent to migrate. Often using economic models of maximizing net benefits, they assume rational choice. Though useful, they fail to capture the decision-making process, just the outcome.[112] In a five-stage model, Janis and Mann argue to consider real conditions:[113] 1) *appraising* the challenge with feedback about risks; 2) *surveying* alternatives; 3) *weighing* alternatives including: canvassing alternatives, surveying objectives and values, evaluating consequences, searching for information, unbiased assimilation of information, careful re-evaluation, and through plans of action and possible contingences;[114] 4) *deliberating* about commitment may include conformity, since autonomous behaviour is more often a myth than reality as many actions are done for social approval; and 5) *adhering* to personal decisions despite internal or external negativity resulting in compromise, defensive attitudes, rationalization and psychosomatic, psycho-pathological and antisocial actions.[115]

Sly and Wrigley say micro-level decision-making studies often fail to distinguish between decision making and leaving itself. In a study of rural Kenyan youth, they found 34% used an identifiable migration decision-making process, but later were only slightly more likely to migrate than those without an obvious decision-process.[116]

Montero interviewed 400 migrants to Canada before 1977 and found 15 different reasons given for migration.

1) *Need:* "We wouldn't come, you know, if there was enough bread in our own countries ... only hunger drives us here."[117]
2) *Renewal:*

   It was very hard in Europe after the Second World War. My family was destroyed ... I felt that if I should make a new life, it should be on soil far away in a new land ... it seemed a way of ensuring something different, something to wipe away all the pain of the years before.[118]

3) *Change:* "I was 30 years of age. We had been married for seven years and had two boys. I had a feeling I was stagnating. I thought maybe there was a better place somewhere else. I was right."[119]
4) *Safety:* "As Asians (in Kenya) we felt very insecure because of the political climate. After the Uganda experience we felt it was time to leave."[120]
5) *Work:* "There was no work in Ecuador. No future for the children: we had to come."[121]
6) *Family:* "I came because my daughter is here. I wanted to be close to her ... it was exciting when I arrived."[122]
7) *Future:* "We came because a travel agent in Colombia convinced my husband that it was a good idea ... there was no future in our own country. In Canada, the children could go to a good school and we could earn good money."
8) *Economics:* "My life before was not very nice. If it was, I wouldn't be here. I'd much rather be in my own country, but the economic situation is so bad there. It's terrible."[123]
9) *Over-population:* "I came ... for the one and only reason that Germany was over-populated. With all the destruction of the war there was little future there."[124]

10) *Adventure:* "I was the first in my family to go to sea. I wanted to travel ... After a few years on the ships, I came into Canada—dock strike—couldn't leave so decided to stay."[125]

11) *Marriage:*

My mother always said: "you're not cut out to work in the field ... if you're a good girl somebody will come from America and will want to marry you" ... It was a dream I grew up with. So when my husband came along, I said to my mother she had got her wish.[126]

12) *Tied Migrant:* "I was just a kid—13 years old. Things were tough in Italy ... but my family came and I really didn't have much choice. My mother has relatives here, that's why she came here."[127]

13) *Anchor Migrant:*

Friends in America sent us the money to come ... As the older girl I would have to come. I didn't want to ... but my parents said that if I wouldn't, then my younger sister must come ... it was my duty to my family ... I was 19 years old.[128]

14) *Land:*

Landholding and inheritance patterns ... left peasants with a tiny plot of land that could not sustain a family. The farm had been in the family for eight or nine generations and had continued to be divided among the sons..there was not much left. I decided to come here to earn enough money to pay off my brothers and sister and at least accumulate a bit more land.[129]

15) *Return home:* Many of the 4,000 Japanese Canadians "repatriated" (exiled) to Japan in 1946 after WWII, chose to return to Canada.[130] Kage, who studied the Japanese returnees, says one wanted his children to "grow up in a country with more physical space" and compares their returning to "a salmon swimming back to its birthplace."[131]

In a 2012 review of life-cycle models of migration decision making,[132] Schultz uses an economic model of "investment in human capital."[133] DaVanzo rejects this idea, saying most people don't migrate, and many who do leave later return home.[134] Kennan and Walker write that "migration decisions should be viewed as a sequence of location choices where the individual knows there will be opportunities to modify or reverse moves that do not work out well."[135] They propose an economic decision-model of choices subject to informed costs including financial, social, cultural and emotional plus moving costs and estimated potential payoffs.

They note this incorporates Mincer's research on married-couple migration decision making that maximizes combined incomes[136] and doesn't limit migration to standard economic factors. It also takes into account family and household determinants,[137] and speaks to "tied-movers" and "tied-stayers," reminding us that both situations increase the potential for divorce.[138]

In a 2016 review of migration models of micro-level decision-making, Gok and Atsan define "bad migration decisions" as due to stress, "information overload, limitations of human information-processing, group pressure, blinding prejudice, ignorance, organizational constraints, and bureaucratic politics."[139] They list five common decision-making patterns: one is good and four are defective, which result in "bad" actions: 1) *unconflicted adherence* and/or ignoring information on risks and loss, 2) *unconflicted change* or uncritical adoption of new courses of recommended action, 3) *defensive avoidance* from procrastination, shifting responsibility (blaming) and/or wishful rationalizations with selective inattention to relevant information, and 4) *panic or hypervigilance* which entails drastic searching and impulsively seizing on what seems like immediate relief with excitement and repetitive thinking. The only "good" or optimal decision-making process is 5) *incorporating vigilance* in search for relevant information, and careful appraisal and analysis.[140]

Reichlová proposes a micro-level decision-model based on Abraham Maslow's hierarchy of needs[141] that takes into account attitudes, income, perceived safety (risk) and social needs.[142] Wasuge says situations are important: Somalian youth, for instance, are not deterred by risk. They freely admit preferring "to die in the seas or deserts trying to reach Europe rather than sitting at home and doing nothing ...'I wanted to leave, because I wanted to help myself and my family.'"[143] However, they argue, their ideas may be simply group influence on individual decision-making due to homeland deficiency and destitution.

Ajzen and Fishbein say the *theory of reasoned action* takes into account situational influences including persuasion and the probability of negative outcomes from inaction.[144] For Somalian youth, the latter are the prime motivators of migration decision making. Ajzen's Theory of Planned Behaviour (TPB)[145] has been used to explore migration decision making. It holds intention as a function of attitudes toward expected consequences, social norms and expectations of possibilities of occurrence. TPB models were used in a 2011 study of climate-driven migration in Burkina Faso,[146] and a 2014 study of rainfall-induced migrations in Tanzania.[147] In these two studies, age, gender, marital status and situation played strong roles in migration decision making, and in terms of "when" to leave and when migration is seen as impossible.[148]

A 2016 French study of elderly migration during 2003–2008 (12.67 million dataset) found at retirement many decide to leave large cities, such as Paris and old industrial areas, in favour of socially and environmentally attractive places with good climates, collective services and low crime rates.[149] In other regional studies, the gravity model of spatial interaction has been used to describe close rather than distant human migration flows.[150]

Agent-Based Models (ABMs) predict small group and individual behaviour in terms of values, socio-cultural physical environments and decision-feedback. A 2016 review of 27 ABMs of human migration decision making found "the most prominent behavioural theories used as decision rules are the random utility theory, as implemented in the discrete choice model, and the theory of planned behaviour."[151] The latter assumes people are likely to leave when they expect to be better off somewhere else—a value-expectancy model—and when they see possible barriers to migration as manageable. At the same time, life-course events (graduation, marriage, birth and death), the economy, employment and anchor migrants are known to greatly influence migration decision making. Thus, psycho-social -economic models have five major dimensions: 1) *the actors*—demographics and life course; 2) *information* that forms expectations; 3) *evaluation* of alternatives; 4) *decision-process models* where "economists often use utility maximisation models, other social scientists are more likely to employ theories from cognitive psychology, and physicists tend to prefer minimalistic models,"[152] and 5) *migration networks* and their contents and methods of transmissions.[153]

A 2018 review of 15 ABMs focused on environmental migration[154] in terms of four decision-factors. 1) in- and/or out-migration and return; 2) environmental, economic and social influence factors; 3) social and ecological systems, like environmental consequences of migration: and 4) conceptual gaps of modelling.[155] They concluded ABM models taking into account environment-migration are scarce; and that nine of the 15 models lacked any social-ecological feedback. It points to a need for interdisciplinary research between social and natural scientists to develop standards for creation and analysis that include environmental issues.[156] In support of this, a 2018 World Bank study reports by 2050 an estimated 140 million people across sub-Saharan Africa, Latin America and South Asia may be forced into internal migrations due to the consequence of climate change: "sea level rise, water availability, and crop productivity decline."[157]

Western decision making

In contrast to developing world migration decision-making studies is western decision making. A 20-year Geneva study of sojourner families found differences in democratic and autocratic families. In *high-cohesive* democratic families, migration was agreed upon by all members. In *low-cohesive* autocratic families, one person (usually the father) made decisions, with members agreeing or becoming "tied migrants."[158] It points to the importance of influence and power in the expression of personal interests and conscious choices.[159] An example of high-cohesive family decision making is related by Bickerton who was offered jobs in two countries. He says: "A family conclave took place; the issue was examined from every angle."[160]

A 2014 study of 127 English retirees who moved to Wales[161] found three distinct stages of joint decision making: *whether*, *where* and *when*. "Whether" and "where" took "a long time," and emerged from discussions and joint agreements. "When" depended upon external factors—the availability of housing and land—and was described as accidental and lucky.[162] The conclusion was that partner migration decision making has its own dynamics with issues of place, family, friends, work, finances and health status.[163]

A 2015 New Zealand study of international migration decision making of skilled migrants from the UK/Ireland, India and South Africa interviewed 20 before departure and 26 after arrival. They too found three pivot points of decision making: *whether*, *where* and *when*. "Whether" was a combination of intra-personal and social environmental issues: "where" led to New Zealand as the top choice because of its quality of life, safety, environment, cultural similarity, job opportunities and welcoming attitude. "When" was described as negotiated within nuclear and extended families. All three decisions took "a long time."[164]

A 2015 study of *urban-urban* migration from North America to Israel found three decision-factors. "Whether" lasted for an unidentifiable time, while "where" and "when" took from two to ten years. The strongest influence on "when" was age, gender, education, reasons to migrate, social capital and economic status.[165] Influence of community leaders was also explored. Over half did not see any one person as having a real significance. Yet, they agreed that opinions and role modelling of several influential Israeli and Jewish organizational figures played a part in their decision to migrate.[166]

Developing world migrators: "anchor", "pioneer" and "seed" migrators

In Somalia and other African countries, some families and villages pool their resources to subsidize or invest in one or more young men to go north as pioneers to become "seed" or "anchor" migrants for the chain-migrations of others who follow. Their journeys entail unsafe overland travel, delays in ports, sometimes capture and, if lucky, passage in smuggler boats in the Mediterranean which are launched into the sea regardless of conditions and are abandoned for rescue within the territorial waters of the nearest country. Such village decisions and agreement by selected lads are motivated by lack of hope and no work, low quality of local education, poor access to technology, and belief in increased security overseas. Strong smuggling networks assist. "Many of the migrants are from poor families, and they migrate with the aim of helping those left behind ... some parents think migration is economically good for the family."[167] They expect financial reimbursement with regular remittances and an anchor or "on-site" person to assist others in migrations. Differences exist between pioneer migrants who "strike out to new and little-known destinations," and later migrants who migrate in an "atmosphere of almost complete certainty along an established path."[168] The shadow-side of pioneer migration is: 1) lack of quality information about realities of migration, 2) travel dangers, 3) the need to revert to illegal means to actually migrate, 4) use of unscrupulous smugglers, and 5) social discrimination upon arrival.[169]

Thirty middle-class Bangladeshi men, pioneer migrants to Italy, were interviewed and later, their spouses.[170] The men arrived first and after becoming established, those who were married sent for wives and children; the unmarried went home for a bride. The arrival of the families was seen as an antidote to the men's loneliness and suffering of migration. Some wives experienced migration as emancipation from the domination of in-laws; for others, it represented a forced removal from relational networks, deep losses and life as a tied migrant. For women used to communal living in Bangladesh who in Italy were living in nuclear family settings, the religious and cultural restrictions made life difficult—they were either restricted or not permitted to go outside. After 15 years in Italy when citizenship was granted with European Union (EU) privileges, the wives pushed for onward migration to established Bangladeshi communities in the UK. The men, established at work and socially bonded, didn't want to leave Italy.[171]

Birth tourism in countries with *jus soli* or birthright citizenship has come under criticism. In 2017 in Canada, 3,628 "passport babies" were born to birth tourists.[172] Recently, other "countries have ended or modified their birthright-citizenship laws, including the UK, Australia, Ireland, New Zealand, India, the Dominican Republic, Thailand and Portugal."[173]

Sojourners: students and healthcare workers

The demographics of nations—a who's who of citizens, their age, gender, education, finances and occupation—are important to governments, especially the numbers of skilled workers and professionals. Thus, intent to migrate studies focus on students and the highly skilled. A 2013 survey of European and Latin-American students found economics to be the main reason for migration, fostered by a belief life was better elsewhere.[174] In New Zealand, 623 international students expressed intent to migrate after graduation. Important too was their intent to return to homelands for lifestyle, family ties and the opportunity to use their skills.[175] A 20-year follow-up of Icelandic youths' intent to migrate found their early desire to leave was strongly predictive of migration from remote communities, but not from central ones. Stated intent-to-leave from rural areas was predictive only when more than half the youth said they would leave.[176] A 2001 Taiwan analysis of population-level data found educational level highly related to intent to migrate.[177] An intent-to-migrate survey of engineering students (349 in Hong Kong and 82 in the UK) found education abroad enables migration, but doesn't always lead to staying in newlands.[178]

That migration is related to education is not surprising. Jung speaks of the importance of education in the development of consciousness and ability to discriminate.[179] In this view, education is not just a "ticket to ride," but a skill-set of information gathering, evaluation and decision making. Professionals are trained in this: to observe, examine, evaluate and create and/or act, to diagnose, treat and improve. Standards are both individual- and professional-level responsibilities. Seeking excellence requires continuing education and improvement-process action plans applied to self, profession and society. When the homeland doesn't measure up in terms of professional standards of practice, opportunities for further education and development, and quality work environments and delivery of service, it's not surprising professionals look further afield. In 2018 in Hungary, 31% of radiography graduates expressed interest in migrating; 42% saw it necessary because of lack of career potentials and poor wages at home.[180] In contrast, graduate ophthalmologists in Ethiopia, Cameroon and Kenya (n=106) in 2015 spoke of their intent to stay at home. They cited family ties, commitment to their country, and praised local working conditions and home possibilities for further training and income. They also gave detailed reasons to leave: better incomes, technical equipment and lack of homeland security.[181]

Healthcare workers are an important national resource and their departure represents a huge loss for developing countries. Although professionals are seen as having responsibilities to homelands, countries are also charged with the responsibility to ensure sufficient opportunities, good working conditions and benefits to keep professionals at home. The World Health Organization (WHO), in an attempt to stem recruitment of healthcare workers from fragile health systems, drafted the *Global Code of Practice on International Recruitment of Health Personnel*.[182] While it discourages recruitment, it respects individual rights to pursue personal values: justice, wealth creativity and cleanliness.[183] Questions have been raised about the ethics of countries signing the WHO agreement and continue recruiting in the developing world. Today, receiving countries are asked to compensate donor countries for their "brain-gains."[184]

A British review of studies on the intent to migrate of African healthcare workers found six major reasons.

1) Struggle to realise unmet material expectations; 2) Strain and emotion, interpersonal discord, and insecurity in workplace, 3) Threats to personal or family safety, 4) Absence of adequate professional support and development, 5) Desire for prestige and respect, 6) Conviction that hopes and goals will be fulfilled overseas.[185]

South Africa remains "an epicentre for out-migration exporting more healthcare workers to high-income countries than any other African country."[186] To fill gaps, it imports healthcare workers from lower-income neighbours. In 2014, South African physicians and nurses surveyed in the UK said they didn't leave for better salaries, careers, or working conditions because they have first-class private health systems. They left because of political insecurity, high crime levels and racial tensions. Working in the UK in the underfunded National Health System (NHS), they fear becoming "de-skilled," making it doubly difficult to return.[187]

In Nepal in 2018, 93% of nursing students expressed intent to migrate, citing poor working conditions, insufficient postgraduate education and lack of professional autonomy.[188] In Korea in 2013, 70% of graduating nurses expressed intent to migrate—more men than women. Reasons given were economic (30%) and professional development (28%). Almost two-thirds said they would return after achieving higher education and professional development unavailable at home. Half believe the US has better working conditions and 71% cited language as a barrier to imminent departure.[189] A 2011 Israeli survey of 132 graduate and student nurses reported 55% intent to migrate for better salaries and working conditions elsewhere.[190]

Physicians

An early intent to migrate study of physicians in Colombia, Nigeria, India, Pakistan and the Philippines reports they saw using their highly specialized skills as possible only in developed countries. They also expressed the desire for increased income, greater access to enhanced technology, a stable social atmosphere of general security and improved prospects for their children. Although they didn't see leaving the homeland as causing shortages in private city practices, they agreed it would cause shortages in rural areas and publicly funded healthcare systems.[191] Today, the situation is relatively unchanged. A 2005 study in Pakistan, India, Nepal, Bangladesh, Kenya, Nigeria, South Africa and Brazil found reasons given by physicians for intent to migrate were economics, job satisfaction and social issues.

In 2013 in Ireland, 37 non-EU doctors who were recruited to fill junior hospital doctor "service posts" unpopular with local physicians were interviewed. They had come to Ireland expecting career progression and postgraduate training, but found these were not possible in their lowly service posts. They feared becoming de-skilled and spoke of onward migration.[192] A 2016 Irish on-line survey of 345 non-EU physicians (94% response) found 16% were Irish-trained and 30% planned to stay; 23% planned to return home and 47% planned onward migration. Differences in intent to migrate were explained by country of origin and a complex mix of personal and professional expectations: opportunities for further professional training and supervision, employment, citizenship status, and satisfaction with life in Ireland.[193] In 2017, another on-line Irish survey of 893 trainee physicians (58.6% response) with 50 follow-up interviews found high levels of dissatisfaction with working conditions, training and career opportunities in the Irish health-care system. Researchers say these must be addressed because physicians, even the Irish-born, are free agents and not blind to better opportunities abroad.[194]

In 2008, the major reason Middle East medical graduates gave for intent to migrate was poor work environments. Over 50% cited poor salary structure, poor work environment and lack of rigour in teaching. Over 95% of Aga Khan University and 65% of Baqai University final-year medical students said access to postgraduate training was their main reason to leave.[195] In Belgrade, Serbia, 938 medical students surveyed in 2014 during their 1st and 5th years of study, (94% response) found 81% considered migrating. Most (82%) would leave immediately after graduation and 42% would work abroad permanently and 53% temporarily. Half had firm migration plans already in place in Germany, Switzerland and Italy. Reasons given were better working conditions, quality of life, higher salaries, professional advancement, and lack of positions in Serbia, as well as the need for additional training, and the desire to work and live elsewhere. The likelihood of actual migration was increased for those speaking two other languages and knowing someone living abroad. Perceived barriers to migration were separation from family, language skills, complex migration procedures, risk of failure and demands of acculturation.[196]

A 2008 study of French doctors in the UK found they came for personal and professional reasons.[197] More than half (59%) had studied in France; 29% had come to join a spouse and 12% came because they were disappointed with the French hospital system—specifically the lack of professional recognition, poor pay and limited career prospects. A 2015 comparative survey of French doctors (n=244) in the UK and British doctors in France (n=86) found the French had come to the UK for better working conditions and 84% were satisfied. The UK physicians had gone to France for career advancement, to join a spouse, or the desire for more favourable social and physical environments and 58% were satisfied.[198]

Post-migration recall of reasons for leaving

Post-migration studies of reasons for leaving are criticized for being rationalizations after the fact and reconstructed narratives to justify stresses, traumas and adaptation challenges of migration.[199] Below, these studies are grouped in classical "push-pull" models that assume rational decision making.

Push factors prompt leaving, like unsatisfactory economics, employment and lack of social-cultural-political freedoms, security and natural environments.[200,201] Accidental push-migrations occur when events in the homeland make return impossible and the person is given the right to stay in the newland.[202] It is not as simple as "the grass is greener on the other side of the fence"; the "capacity to leave everything behind and move to another country" is part of the British identity, says Bruillon.[203] Recent migrations from the UK are motivated by "deep attachment to the traditional values"[204] no longer part of British life. "The environment has deteriorated and there are no more open, uncluttered spaces, unlike in France," where they experience liberty and no social pressures.[205] For Mexican youth, migration is an accepted, familiar and normative path.[206,207]

Pull factors draw and motivate voluntary migrations: education, economics, labour market demands, political issues and over-population as well as desire for adventure, marriage and a better life "for the children."[208] Also cited for migration to the US are personality and self-fulfilment.[209]

Post-migration reasons for leaving do not always fit neatly into push/pull categories because migration is a complex mix of both. Push/pull migration models are criticized for assuming people react in "similar, automatic and predictable ways to external stimuli,"[210] or are simply objects lacking their own will.[211] Yet, it's never clear-cut:

> Many migrants, if not most, are torn by conflicting emotions before they leave. There is the 'pull' of friends and family to remain, the 'push' of dullness and boredom, there is the 'pull' of possible excitement and freedom in the city, the 'push' of fear of the unknown.[212]

Early Irish emigration was largely an "involuntary flight from famine and severe economic oppression, it was easily viewed as reluctant exile."[213] Not surprisingly, "poverty and exile are the major themes of Irish literature— the one driving them out, the other maintaining emotional and sentimental links with home,"[214] and exile dominating the Irish psyche.

A 2013 American review of post-migration reasons for leaving found three main push/pull factors: 1) economic cost-benefit analyses seeking the American dream, 2) family unification and marriage migration, and 3) unsatisfactory social and political climates. Although Biles and Frideres note official statistics usually report voluntary migrations for family reunifications as pull factors, the idea of push factors is used for displaced persons, asylum seekers and refugees.[215,216] Employment is a primary push/pull factor.[217] When work opportunities appear better somewhere else, it's a pull factor. When the homeland is work deficient, it's a push factor. But employment is rarely the whole picture.

A 2016 study of Turkish nationals in Germany and Canada found social-cultural-political issues—migrant-friendly environments, liberal migration and citizenship policies—to be more important reasons for migration than higher wages.[218] For Turks, Germany was the preferred country for education and its large Turkish community was deemed important, whereas multicultural Canada was seen as the preferred country for employment and settlement.[219] A 2009 study of Brazilians migrating to the US found they left for financial and work reasons. Underlying the given objective reasons lay significant and complex issues seldom admitted: curiosity, family, escape and strong web of transnational Brazilian social and religious communities in the US.[220] A 2017 study of the high numbers of elderly Hawaiians migrating to mainland US and Alaska found their primary reasons were racial discrimination in Hawaii, and the challenges of ageing and care-giving. Important too, was the desire to maintain their cultural traditions and values which for them was seen as more possible on the mainland than in their Hawaiian homeland.[221]

A 2014 Ghanaian study of persistent "brain-drain" of African healthcare workers attributed it to a search for better living and working conditions in better-resourced and better-governed healthcare systems with more educational and career opportunities. Yet, these migrations are not always permanent: many shuttle back and forth between countries and after meeting their personal, career and financial goals, they return home. With them, they bring new ideas, values and skills and they establish clinics, diagnostic centres and charity organisations.[222]

A 2018 study of media reports asked: what does the media say about migrants and migration? How does this affect policy makers and the public, the role of journalism itself in this discourse? What are the implications of recent reporting? They found among Mexican and Salvadoran women, US media images of good childhoods had strong effects: "Mothers' decisions to migrate were strongly influenced by ideals of a childhood free from want, ideals they construed as diametrically opposed to their own experiences of childhood in their countries of origin."[223]

A 2015 Norwegian study of the "feminization of migration" looked at Eastern European women migrating alone to the EU and further abroad. The women came to improve their own lives and that of their families via remittances from their work in the home and healthcare sectors. While they saw migration as an act of sacrifice for the family, the media criticizes them for enjoying the good life abroad and abandoning their children to the care of grandparents.[224]

In 2009, Singapore economists tested the neoclassical micro-economic theory of migration defined as attempts of individuals to maximize the future. Using data from the South African national migration survey, they found the concept of maximizing futures held true for migrating, never-married men and women. For married persons, duration of migration was an important determinant of whether or not they left. The goal of short-term migration was to maximize household income: for longer migrations, the intent was to reduce household risk (via remittances and singles' migrations).[225]

In the past, migrations usually meant the end of relationships, but today telecommunications, social media and rapid transportation permit ongoing connections. A 2014 British study of Palestinian migrants found distances no longer foreclose familial intimacy; instead it leads to reworking of family relationships and re-imagination of the family as a smaller unit. Visits (regular, crisis, duty and tourist) re-establish proximity, relatedness and intimacy.[226] New media of email, instant messaging, social networking and webcams are integral to maintaining family relations around the globe.[227,228] In Canada, people tell of daily contact with family in distant homelands and across the country via Skype or Zoom. In fact, new media permits more frequent contact than being in the same place: distance reduces tensions and increases appreciation.

Types of migration: internal, turn-around, external

Internal migration, relocating within one's homeland is known as the "geographic cure" in Canada: "From 2006 to 2011 close to 3% of the Canadian population moved to a different province or territory."[229] This does not account for shorter moves within provinces, rural-to-urban, urban-to-urban, or urban-to-rural moves. The US has a mobile population too, with the average person moving 11.7 times during a lifetime.[230] "Fluidity" is a "millennial or entrepreneurial trait,"[231] says Duyvendak. It represents a "dislike of being locked into one place."[232] Mobility includes capital, information and people:[233] "The motif of modern culture ... is being rootless, displacement between worlds, living between a lost past and fluid present ... a metaphor for the journeying modern consciousness."[234] The American ideal of "rootless and restless man,"[235] is seen as an attempt to "define their identity by their lack of place."[236] Many who migrate for employment, and those in the international development community, see their "roots as going around the outside of the globe rather than down into the earth in one location which makes it possible to be at home anywhere."[237]

Americans "move, on average, at least every five years, Europeans move, at most, every ten years (and often not as far away),"[238] and

> the very ideals of restlessness and rootlessness have helped Americans to feel at home in their country since these notions have become *patriotic* emblems. The 'self-made man,' the American dream, the Western

frontier, the melting pot and the classless society are all ideals held nation-wide.[239]

Still, a small decline in internal US migration in 2013 was attributed to dual-earning couples who can't always easily relocate two careers.[240]

Young people desire new situations, people and places. They seek the social, economic and cultural potentials of big-city life while they also want to connect with nature. In fact, nature is as important to youth as the imagined social, educational and economic opportunities of cities.[241] Many migrants to Canada come, they say, for its vast unspoiled nature. In the rural Anglo-Scottish Borders area, 45 young people interviewed in 2000 saw migration as necessary to get a "good job." In fact, middle-class youth are "socialized" into migration, and are most likely to leave; yet they retain local ties and plan to return.[242]

Migration is the norm in many places,[243] but this does not make leaving easy. Sabelli recalls his family migrating from rural Argentina to "Rosario, the 'Chicago' of Argentina, its second city and industrial center."[244] It felt like a foreign migration: "we were immigrants in our own country,"[245] a form of self-exile: "Sooner or later, the sin of having left our family and our culture comes back to haunt us."[246] Sabelli equates it with dying: "if emigration is like dying, immigration is living anew, loving anew."[247] In Brazil, rural migrants flock to the capital seeking meaningful, rewarding work and/or for "love" (defined as partner or family). They come voluntarily and speak of hardship, emotional costs and never-ending adaptation challenges.[248]

In Taiwan, migration from rural to urban areas was normative for many decades and justified by the "poor quality" of rural life, especially the lack of opportunities in education and economics and public services.[249]

In Western Russia, four types of internal migration are described:

1) *Survival migrants* from depressed/remote regions escaping poverty, unemployment;
2) *New opportunity migrants* seeking improvement in income and life quality;
3) *Hope and prosperity migrants* seeking to avoid environmental crises and progressive degradation of environment, unemployment and poor economic opportunities, and
4) *Economic migrants* seeking housing, employment and socio-cultural opportunities.[250]

Migration from rural and depressed regions is so common that it seems that only the elderly and incapacitated remain. Although out-migration is easily blamed on individuals, it's argued that societies have responsibilities to develop comfortable and cherishable environments to retain rural youth.[251]

In India, deterioration in the quality of life in 12 mega-cities in the 1990s was blamed on the arrival of rural migrants whose numbers were greater than the cities' ability to supply housing, water and transportation. Rural migrants were also "blamed" for urban crises. Only later and reluctantly did the government admit that migrants were necessary for development. Paradoxically, while rural migrants were looked down upon, they had higher than average literacy and educational status than urban residents.[252]

Licensed Practical Nurses (LPNs) who left eastern Canadian cities for western provinces said it was for greater educational opportunities, professional advancement, recognition and greater respect, as well as more chances to maximize their skills and to be full members of health teams.[253] This is a good example of internal migrants' belief in upward social mobility, and being "better off by moving away rather than staying."[254] Also in Canada, in 2003 a variation on the "bright lights" hypothesis occurred when natural resource wilderness workers moved into regional urban centres and commuted back to rural areas for work in resource industries. The common push factors were "stress over economic uncertainty and instability in resource industries, the vulnerability of local employment, and concern over a lack of services" in the bush,[255] and the social isolation and extreme climate of resource-industry towns. For families, the pull factors to regional "bright lights" towns are housing, schools, medical services, shopping, recreational facilities and employment opportunities for spouses.[256]

Historically, in Africa internal migration has been the norm. Recently, this has been dominated by rural-area residents' movement to urban centres of administration, industry and commerce which had been developed under colonial rule. These contrast sharply with traditional homeland areas which lack housing, roads and sanitation. While migration of tribal peoples into urban areas is explained by the bright lights theory, researchers say it's neither bright lights nor youthful rejection of traditional values that draws migrants to the cities; it's the "serious and persistent underdevelopment in the rural communities that draws youth away from home."[257]

The opposite of bright lights migration is *"turn-around migration,"* a "back-to-the-land" movement of urban-to-rural migration in pursuit of quality of life in the countryside.[258] In China, urban-to-rural migration has become common for returnees with dual citizenship.[259] Those returning from Sydney, London, San Francisco and Boston seek cleaner air and safer food in remote areas, like Yunnan, Tengchong and Lijiang.[260]

External migration is leaving the homeland for another country. Approximately 50 million Chinese live outside China (88% in South East Asia). In an historical analysis, Zhu says from early days to the 17th century, migration was seen as spontaneous. During the colonial period, migration was forced under contract-labour systems, while more recent migration has been "provoked" by political and social upheavals. In 1985, the Emigration and Immigration Law allowed people to return to China or join relatives abroad.[261]

Migration into Europe from southern and eastern countries has taken place for many years,[262] in response to demands for cheap agricultural labour and jobs in the service industry and hospitality sectors. Historically, seasonal workers could come and go, but since *revolving-door migration* is no longer allowed, migrant workers are forced to enter illegally. If they have visas, they over-stay to work the next season and then can't return home because they may not get back in, and their families rely on financial remittances. However, it's not just migrants into Europe for seasonal work who are affected: "one in three persons in Nepal depends upon seasonal migration [to India] for family survival,"[263] and now Malaysia is the number one destination country for Nepalese migrants, followed by Qatar, Saudi Arabia, the UAE and Kuwait.[264] Recently, the annual seasonal flow of migrants into Europe became a flood of Mediterranean boat people escaping from areas of poverty and generalized violence. At the time of writing (2018), a mass migrant "caravan" was also under way from Central America to the US. Though the caravan is not a new phenomenon, the massively increased numbers of participants have gained attention. For many years, only individuals and some families attempted to make their way to the US, but now they're leaving en masse "fleeing persecution, poverty and violence in their home countries of Honduras, Guatemala, and El Salvador."[265]

For many years, the financial remittances of Algerian worker migrants in France were the "only source of disposable monetary income in rural areas," says Sayad. "At the national level ... it was the main source of Algerian budgetary resources (equal to and sometimes greater than the income from petroleum products)."[266] Remittances also gave legitimacy to migration. Only after it was no longer possible to migrate was the illegitimacy of prolonged absences suddenly denounced.[267]

Collective behaviour theories explore mass actions. *Contagion theory* asserts that crowds have a hypnotic effect that leads individuals to abandon personal responsibility and control over their actions.[268] *Convergence theory* proposes that those with similar thoughts and beliefs come together to form a critical mass for action.[269] *Emergent-norm theory* sees crowds as non-homogeneous, but gradually developing new norms for the purposes at hand.[270] *Value-added theory* sees collective behaviour as a release valve for built-up strains within society that under certain conditions leads to action.[271] *Complex adaptive systems theory* builds on all the above while proposing that, under specific conditions, synergetic aspects can bring all of these together.[272] Still, historians theorize that past collective migrations were driven by need, attitudes and beliefs. North American examples include: 1) the Gold Rushes of California and British Columbia/Yukon; 2) the Western land rushes; 3) the 1930s Depression migration to California and in Canada "riding the rails" 4) Blacks in the US going north for freedom after the American Civil War, and 5) religious groups' migrations to attain freedom of worship. Other countries' mass migrations include Ireland during the 1845–1849 potato famine, and the 1947 Partition of India from West and East Pakistan (later Bangladesh).

Australian demographers found 95% of skilled, temporary workers came with an intent to apply for permanent status. Those from less-developed countries were most likely to stay:[273] Asians attracted by better employment opportunities and higher salaries stayed for their children's futures as did Africans who were unhappy with homeland social, economic, or political conditions. The least likely to stay were Europeans, North Americans and Japanese, but those who did stay said it was for the Australian lifestyle.[274]

In Israel, there are mixed feelings towards those who migrate to the US. They are envied, and criticized as defectors who have abandoned the Promised Land: they're labelled as selfish, weak traitors. The migrants express anger and guilt about having to carry the burden of 2,000 years of diaspora. They complained about Israel's unrelenting political strife, compulsory military service and highly saturated competitive job market. In an early study,[275] three major reasons were found for emigration: 1) population pressure and extreme competition for education and jobs, 2) discrimination, social stigma and isolation of homosexuals, and 3) the desire for privacy, which is seen as impossible in cooperative Israeli community structures with powerful cultures of collective social values. The latter was seen as conflicting with modern healthy adult identities leading to the solution of escape through migration.[276] In contrast, women footballers migrating to Scandinavia claim to come for the "love of the game," secondary was careers and economics.[277]

Onward, twice, secondary and serial migrations

Migrating and staying for a while—long enough to get "papers" or citizenship—then moving within the country or to another country is known as *onward migration*, twice migration and secondary migration. A variant is *serial migration* of trans-nationalists who move freely about the world living in many places where each move becomes a chapter in a life.[278] Primary reasons for onward migration are life-course events: marriage, childbirth and family reunification, relationship break-ups, and educational or career changes. In the EU in 2011, there were 33.3 million foreign-born residents and nearly two-thirds were non-EU-27 citizens.[279] Many émigrés to Canada in their first year migrate onward to another province or city,[280] explained by port of entry, social status, search for community,[281] and employment opportunities.[282]

A study of onward migration from Spain to London in 2018 describes three types: 1) *mature* reluctant migrants; 2) *mid-life*, career advancement migrants; and 3) *young*, independence-seeking migrants.[283] A 2000 UK study of the effects of a policy of compulsory dispersal of refugees to "spread the burden" of housing asylum seekers and to discourage settlement in London and the South East found dispersed refugees are more likely to move many times after being granted status.[284] Many Iranian refugees in Sweden upon receipt of EU status migrate onward to London.[285] They explain that Swedish refugee-processing camps were socially satisfying with "a strong sense of community" and "optimism about the future."[286] But after being given permission to stay, they were dispersed. This made some feel very isolated. Others said it fostered their language skills and social integration. Iranian-Swedes who migrated onward to London were mostly highly educated and personally familiar with the multiculturalism of London and the social, cultural and economic opportunities in the UK. They left Sweden, they said, because of the homogeneity of its culture.[287]

A 2015 UK study of naturalized EU citizens from Somalia, Iran and Nigeria identified six types of onward migration.[288] 1) *Career movers* overcoming employment barriers in the first EU country they entered.[289] 2) *Student movers* studying English.[290] 3) *Family movers* coming for their children's future who saw positive ethnic role models as important for aspirations and opportunities.[291] 4) *Political movers* voted "with their feet" against discrimination and the lack of integration policies in their first country of residence. As one German-Nigerian said, "I know that there is discrimination everywhere, but there are places that are worse. In this place because of the human rights here [in UK] you can stand up for yourself and then they will judge it."[292] 5) *Diaspora movers* left for sociocultural reasons—wanting to be closer to family, friends and ethnic communities.[293] and 6) *Cosmopolitan movers* or "global citizens" moved to live in multicultural environments in order to improve careers and lifestyles.[294]

Chain migration is defined as joining family, friends and villagers in newlands. Reasons given are: opportunities in education, employment, marriage, land availability, wealth, and cultural, religious and political freedom and climate. They are especially important when countries are not accepting migrants, since chain migrations permit people to cross closed borders for family reunification. Once in the newland, they are provided housing and assistance in adaptation. Yet, not all established migrants are eager to help: "Studies show excessive demands on 'network assistance' in chain migrations can shift them from facilitating bridgeheads into reluctant gatekeepers."[295]

A story of chain migration was related at the Vancouver Museum of Migration[296] by a former senior medical student from Syria. Arrested for filming a mass political student protest with his phone and alleged to be a terrorist, he was imprisoned and tortured. After release two years later, he sought asylum in a Canadian community of Syrian refugees. Fluent in English, within a year he was hired as a refugee counsellor for Syrians seeking asylum. As a landed immigrant, he was able to initiate sponsorship of his mother and sisters who had fled to Turkey and his brothers in Germany. Two days after being granted citizenship, his family arrived; at the time of writing, they had been in the country for several months.[297]

Stage 3: refusing the call—stayers and involuntary migrants

Stayers choose to remain where they are born and don't live elsewhere for any appreciable time.[298] The freedom to stay is ignored in major theories of migration, says Arango: "The usefulness of theories that try to explain why people move is in our day dimmed by the inability to explain why so few people move."[299]

Voluntary stayers choose to stay. In the US, Vermont stayers are happy to be at home, citing attachments to place, the landscape, community and family.[300] A special 2018 issue of the journal, *Population, Space & Place*[301] was devoted to rural stayers. Mobility is the norm, say the editors; it's the zeitgeist[302] in "response to the functional demands of neoliberal capitalism."[303] Staying is confused with being stuck or left behind.[304] This is not always true. Stayers choose to stay, and are important to the sustainability of communities.[305] In an early study, stayers were described as having deep roots in the community with strong kinship ties, large social investments and a lack of interest in assimilating into new social environments.[306]

Swedish stayers were interviewed in 2014. Those 60 years and older who had lived their entire lives in the same place found it harder to articulate reasons for staying than those giving reasons to leave. Hjälm says staying is complex, multi-layered and often stigmatized. Yet staying is rarely a one-time, never-renegotiated decision. Staying is the result of repeated decisions taking into account intertwined lives of family and friends of several generations. It's a conscious choice with its own dynamics.[307]

Involuntary stayers or involuntary immobile are those who would like to migrate, but lack the means. They feel trapped by social and political situations, like refugees in transit camps.[308,309] A 2006 Beijing study found many stayers had strong desires to change their residence, but lacked the means to relocate.[310] In 2012, data from a 1994 Canadian National Population Health Survey of those 65 years and older (n = 2,551) found mobility is the norm. Nearly one in ten self-identified as an involuntary stayer, citing lack of socio-economic resources, poor health and need for assistance, and low social activity. Involuntary stayers reported more distress and low self-rated health than migrants.[311]

Involuntary migrations

Reasons for involuntary migration vary from not having a voice in decision-making processes to being forced by circumstances to relocate. In 1994, Cubans on rafts paddled to Miami for liberty,[312] and 2,100 Haitians in 2015[313] "escaped high levels of violence by the coup government."[314]

Tied or trailing migrants

Family migration decisions often lack consensus. Those who accompany a primary migrator, spouses, children and elderly, are called "tied" or "trailing" migrants. In an historical review of research into family migrations, Cooke says the earliest studies of migration are of human capital. Now seen as gendered research, because they presumed women were tied migrants or trailing spouses/wives,[315] this was a reasonable assumption at the time as only a small percentage of married women were employed full-time outside the home and some countries forbade women employment. Recent research reveals when couples have egalitarian gender roles, both have a voice in decisions. Couples are less likely to move when the wife is employed and more likely to move when she is unemployed and wants to work. In contrast, couples with traditional gender roles show that migration is not affected by the employment status of the woman.[316] Today, there are cases of migration where the woman has higher or more desirable qualifications under the entry points system and the husband is the trailing spouse.[317] In the US in 2012, almost all (94%) of international migrations were family reunifications.[318] In contrast, in Canada, reasons for immigration in 2009 show high-skill economic categories exceeded humanitarian or family reunification and refugee asylums.[319]

In the light of two-career families, some researchers challenge the asymmetry and inadequacies of early economic migration models. They ask if migration maximizes the human capital of the husband or wife, or both. A unique study in 1991 using macro-level administrative Canadian data[320] found 67% of family migrations were motivated by the husband moving for employment, with his wife accompanying. In 2008, just 2% of migration was for the wife's employment with an accompanying husband.[321] This has led to questions about the importance of gender roles in migration decision making. In the UK, Stockdale found when couples practice traditional gender roles; the husband has a greater voice in decision making regardless of who has the greater salary. In egalitarian gender roles, the effects of migration on employment of both spouses is considered, regardless of who has the greater salary.[322]

Family migration research went through a lull for many years until 2008 when Clark and Withers introduced the life-course approach to cross-national studies of migration. They found migration decisions were "gendered" in many countries, but over time changes emerged in dual-income families with the advent of birth of children and other life-course events. The effects of migration on fertility and divorce are not as big as the effects of fertility and divorce on migration.[323] In Sweden in 2011, Åström and Westerlund report: "The greatest income gains from migration are accrued by highly educated males married to or cohabiting with lower-educated females."[324] A 2004 literature review of highly skilled scientists moving within the EU, found young, single women were as mobile as their male counterparts until the doctoral and post-doctoral levels. Because scientific careers demand a high level of international mobility, huge tensions emerged in dual science-career couples that led to women "exiting" from science careers or failing to progress,[325] or succeeding in another field.[326]

In 2002, Magdol decided not to assume that work and migration experiences were similar for men and women and explored self-reported well-being. The "survey research indicates that about 15% of corporate wives whose husbands have been relocated report psychological problems, about 5% report substance abuse problems, and about 5% report physical health problems."[327] It's "not clear if these rates are substantially higher than those of non-mobile women."[328] In 2013, Cooke argued the "trailing" wife has been a myopic obsession of researchers, whereas in US migration statistics from 1997 to 2007, it was a relatively rare phenomenon and not limited to women. "Tied staying" is more common than tied migration and experienced equally by men and women.[329] *Tied staying* is an individual's desire to move but is unable to and is related highly to divorce actions.

Displaced people and refugees and exile

Scientific American's special 2016 issue on migration[330] defines involuntary migrants as persons "pushed out" by violence, violations of human rights and freedom, and military conscription, war, expulsion (exile) and disasters: flood, drought, earthquake, cyclones and overpopulation. The result is millions of internally displaced migrants (IDPs) and international refugees (IRs).[331] Although there is no official definition of IDPs, UNESCO defines this as the forced movement of people due to armed conflict: war, civil conflict, political strife, and gross human rights abuse, as well as natural disasters, such as famine, and development and economic changes:[332] "Women and their children make up nearly 80% of the forcibly displaced."[333,334,335]

Most countries assist cross-border migrants, but IDPs often don't attain help.[336,337] Globally in 2009, there were 740 million IDPs. India had the greatest number with 3.7 million forced to leave their homes due to flooding and cyclones. In the same year, "official statistics placed the number of internal migrants in China at one-tenth of the country's 1.3 billion people."[338,339]

The construction of the Three Gorges Project in China displaced 1.27 million people. When promises made for homes and land were not honoured, increased rates of mental depression were reported.[340] Not surprisingly, internal displacement affects physical and mental health.

By 2050, it is predicted worldwide one in every 45 persons or 200 million people—a number higher than current global migrant populations—will be displaced by two types of climate change. *Climate processes* are rising sea-levels, land salinization, desertification and increasing water scarcity. Often those most in need of migration lack the resources to leave. *Climate events* are natural disasters: fire, floods, landslides, storms, glacial lake outbursts, among others.[341] Today with early-warning systems,[342] people can act quickly and hopefully save lives, but they lose everything else. The 2004 Boxing Day Sumatra–Andaman earthquake and tsunami was the third largest quake ever recorded and caused the planet to vibrate. It created immense destruction and deaths of 227,898 people.[343] Yet there exists political resistance to expand the definition of asylum for refugees to include climate causes.[344] Other events also challenge the definition of refugee. The "new wars" waged in Asia, Africa and parts of Eastern Europe do not take place in rural battlefields as of old, but in dense, urban spaces where whole cities and towns can be displaced in a matter of hours.[345] Most people see "no other option but to run away."[346] It's the brightest, best resourced and most mobile who leave, sometimes forever.[347]

Refugees

A *refugee* is officially defined as a displaced person outside their own country who is unable or unwilling to return due to fear of persecution based on race, religion, nationality, political views, or group membership.[348] Refugee status arises from "arbitrary political or administrative decisions."[349] *Asylum* or protection sought by refugees includes the right not to be forcibly returned.[350] *Refugee law for asylum seekers* arose during and after WWII with the Geneva Conventions[351] of rights of combatants and civilians. The UN's 1948 *Universal Declaration of Human Rights* guarantees the right to asylum.[352] The International Justice Center lists 16 charters and international and regional conventions related to legal protection of refugees.[353] Although refugee status is defined by the 1967 UN Protocol on Refugees, most countries have their own statutes. The US Refugee Act of 1980 states under the circumstances outlined by the UN Protocol, the US will allow a certain number of individuals entrance as refugees.[354] There's a ceiling determined by the President and Congress.[355]

Before 1980 when the US Congress passed the US Refugee Act, "immigrants from Communist states had automatically been accorded refugee status in the US," but afterwards they did not qualify.[356]

"Historically, attitudes towards refugees fall along a continuum of compassion to rejection and dehumanization" says Varvin. "In times of insecurity and collective anxiety, refugees represent something alien and frightening," and "have come to represent the Freudian Uncanny/*das Unheimliche*."[357] In a review of British ideals and tradition of giving refuge, Ibrahim and Howarth argue that the concept of refugee has been repeatedly challenged by new policies in immigration and asylum, securitization of border controls and controls on entry. Following 9/11, the fear of terrorism "delegitimized refugees" and created "tighter barriers to entry" with refugees portrayed increasingly as dishonest "economic migrants,"[358] or "scheming asylum seekers."[359] A Rohingya woman in a refugee camp in India protests: "We have come all the way here not just because we were trying to escape poverty and find a way to earn a better living ... but because it was the only option to save our lives."[360]

Most countries' policies on asylum are in states of flux. For instance, in Canada, since 1976 there have been four major policy modifications and many minor ones.[361] In studies of post-war violence, Gartner and Kennedy argue that wars not only harm and kill people, they damage and destroy social and economic institutions, political legitimacy and group relations. Because institutions are not part of negotiated peace treaties, during the peace-building processes, policies often emerge that fuel violent behaviour and crime. Although the external war may be over, an internal one may be happening with the same need for fight and flight that is not always recognized under refugee laws.[362]

Since international refugee laws were enacted, millions of people have been given asylum, but the original concept of socio-political dangers that defined the right to asylum left gaps in refugees' protection. This remains true today for those fleeing from generalized violence (ongoing civil strife), which is more prevalent than full-scale war but just as dangerous for civilians, and creates the need to broaden the framework of displaced persons and refugees.[363] Since 1992, approximately 18 million displaced civilians fled from indiscriminate generalized violence of bombardments of mortar and aerial assaults, but these situations don't qualify under the old terms of refugee status of individual and purposeful persecution. Compounding the problem are mass rapes and killings of civilians that do not meet the definition because the victims are not individually targeted due to race, religion, nationality or group membership—as the Geneva Convention requires—but are targeted because their existence hinders military actions. Mass violence is often justified by perpetrators in accusations of civilians harbouring enemies.

Generalized violence persists, Chow says, because countries shirk their duty or lack the capacity to protect their citizens. An appeal is made for an expansion of the definition of refugee to account for today's realities.[364] Manchandra concurs: "In modern conflicts there is no segregated battlefield. The home front is the war front. Today's armed conflict—particularly internal wars ... produce conditions of generalized violence and terror that target women and children."[365] Usually, men and young boys flee to escape conscription by the enemy, leaving the most vulnerable: women, children, the elderly and disabled. "Internally stuck," often with no means to escape, they are left to face increasing deprivation and violence.[366] When they *are* able to flee, there are reports of women being sent back first "to test if it is safe to return."[367]

Zahar notes during the Balkan War in 1992, "both Serbian and Croatian forces engaged in ethnic cleansing."[368] The West feared "offering asylum to Yugoslav refugees would 'reward' ethnic cleaning" and thought having them standing nearby in refugee camps would make it easier for them to return home when the conflict ended. But "on July 11, 1995 the Serbian general [Ratko Mladić] entered one such 'safe haven' in Srebrenica and slaughtered 7,400 men and boys, in the worse massacre on European soil since the Second World War."[369]

Refugee health status

In assessment of refugee health status, the timing, nature and extent of violence are important. Many escapees experience traumas prior to or during hazardous flights of exile—a "profound identity transforming and disturbing process."[370] The conditions of the refugee camps must be taken into account too, as some border on sub-human conditions: too little space, no privacy, scarcity of water and sanitation, with inadequate rations and no health care and extended waiting periods. In West Bengal, refugees are "prisoners of the past," neither rehabilitated nor resettled with lives "frozen" in camps for five decades.[371] Those held longest are passed over by resettlement countries and develop the highest rates of psychopathology. In realization of losses suffered, "some of them become apathetic and helpless; the others become maniac and aggressive."[372]

A 2008 Canadian study of refuge risk assessment and response, Cameron reports it's believed by adjudicators of refugee status that when people decide the situation is dangerous, they will leave immediately for safety and will not return, but this is not always the case.[373,374] Usually they find the thought of leaving as risky as staying and they reluctantly leave only when staying carries a higher risk. Assessment of risk is compounded by 13 factors of underestimations:

1) *Familiarity* with the danger—when danger is a regular feature, it tends to be discounted;
2) *Outcome history*—what happened in the past colours assessment of present:
3) *Desire to stay* at home may be strong;

4) *Place attachment* is an emotional bond along with commitment to religion, culture and ethnicity that can hinder leaving;
5) *An unreal sense* of ability to "control" situations leads to unrealistic assessments of dangers;
6) *High risk tolerance* leads to underestimated present risks;
7) *Optimism bias* lowers risk ratings;
8) *Non-physical risks* or ideological/political/cultural risks affect assessment of physical risks;
9) *Low knowledge of options* leads to inaction from simple ignorance;
10) *Passivity* is a feature of those who have suffered as post-traumatic stress that leads to indifference and minimizes risk or relinquishes initiatives in the face of new risks;
11) *Defiance* or attitude and belief of ability to stand up to risks underestimates dangers;
12) *Strong religious faith* that the situation is in God's hands or "God's will," and
13) *Pace of decision making* regarding risk is slowed when trauma has occurred or fear rules.[375]

Not all refugees' situations, context, or experience are the same, nor are their journeys or arrival obstacles and challenges, says Dow.[376] *Anticipatory refugees* are usually wealthy, educated, well connected and have good information sources. They "sense the danger and leave when this move is still possible ... the whole family moves, brings resources with it,"[377] and are prepared for a new life. *Acute refugees* flee when the situation becomes too dangerous to remain. Generally,

> they have not planned nor prepared for the journey because they lack resources to do so. Many suffer from severe psychological stress as a result of experiencing and/or witnessing torture, rape or murder of others, inability to protect their own spouses or children, and uncertainty for the future.[378]

They reach places of asylum in states of shock and the degree of trauma experienced may affect them for many years.[379] Children

> under war-time duress are largely a voiceless population whose rights and needs are often subordinate to those of soldiers, and the necessities of war. Children have been murdered, raped, maimed, starved, exposed to brutality, and subject to lack of control and chaos.[380]

According to UNICEF, "In the past ten years, approximately two million children have been killed in war zones, and six million injured or permanently disabled."[381]

A Scandinavian study found that, because of the lack of specialized services, refugees seek health care from general practitioners. Yet many suffer from complex medical and psychological conditions due to persecution and exile; they avoid discussing traumatic experiences, escape and exile due to differences in language and culture.[382] But this may not be entirely negative, as "frozenness"[383] is a common refugee psychological state of constriction, contradiction and retrenchment that permits them to concentrate on the bare essential functions and processes for survival. In fact, it's a necessary stage of recovery that helps to "minimize the damaging effects of multiple losses"[384] and helps them to conserve energy and to "develop a reflective state" that permits them to move forward.[385]

The Konstanz Psycho-trauma Research and Outpatient Clinic for Refugees conducted a repatriation study of refuges in 2008 where, under pressure from immigration authorities, two-thirds were returned after 13 years of exile. Using standardized psychological tests in Germany, 53% showed psychiatric disorders and were still experiencing traumatic stress from the war, flight and seeking refuge. After repatriation, this number increased to 88% as they were still vulnerable and poorly equipped to cope with the stress of repatriation. "Living conditions after return (such as housing, work, and health care) were poor and unstable"[386] and after living abroad, for many years, they had difficulty re-adapting to their original cultural environment.[387]

What about failed asylum seekers, asks a Swiss psychiatric team? They note that asylum applications rely on personal accounts but since many are suffering from PTSD which affects memory and performance, they have difficulty recounting and arguing their case. The more stressed they are, the more likely they are to be rejected. They conclude decision-making processes for accepting refugees may be failing to identify those most in need of protection.[388]

Abuse and torture

The United Nations Convention against Torture and Other Cruel, Inhuman or Degrading Treatment or Punishment[389] defines "torture" as any act of physical or mentally inflicted severe pain or suffering to obtain information or confession, or punishment for suspected of commission of an act, or for purposes of intimidating or at the instigation of or consent or acquiescence of another in an official capacity.[390] A 2005 review of literature on survivors of politically motivated torture at the Centre for Torture Victims states the numbers are high: "Either torture has increased worldwide or the exposure of torture events has improved."[391] A South African study of tortured exiles living on the streets found they face double challenges: one was recovery from torture, while the second was the mixed blessing of exile: "Torture damages bodies, psychological functioning and the capacity to trust others; exile uproots people from their social, linguistic and cultural worlds, leaving them without the means to provide for themselves or their families."[392]

Few refugee studies of torture exist because of a reluctance of researchers to face the subject; exiled people may hide or minimize it for social and political reasons: expectations of other's disbelief, fears of reprisals, shame, stigmatization and humiliation, and cultural prohibitions about talking about oneself or about sexual acts such as rape.[393] Speaking of refugee trauma, Papadopoulos says there is a need to recognize differences of refugees as persons in terms of culture, experience, traumas and to assess the four phases: 1) *anticipation* of leaving, 2) *devastating* events, 3) *survival* physically and psychologically, and 4) *adjustment* to a new place. Most important is *not* seeing the person primarily in terms of the trauma experienced since this privileges trauma and trauma does not always happen.[394] Further, we tend to confuse three sets of discourses: moral/ethical and clinical/pathological with social/political history.[395] Also "we tend to confuse the justified abhorrence of the atrocities (which are considered the 'cause' of the trauma) by pathologizing the very persons who survived them."[396] The reality may differ.

A 1998 Danish study of 311 refugee children, aged 3–15 years, from the Middle East, who had experienced many types of organized violence reports: 67% were assessed as clinically anxious:

> The most important risk indicators for anxiety were having "lived in a refugee camp outside the home country," being "part of a torture-surviving family," "lack of opportunities for play with other children," being "beaten/kicked by an official," and "loss of father."[397]

The "worst experiences these children had were during the Survival Phase and not during the Devastating Events stage."[398] The survival period is multi-dimensional and may include abduction, captivity and abuse. Human Rights Watch quotes a young Nepalese woman who escaped and was seeking asylum in India: "I was 13 ... They raped me three or four times a day for seven days. I was taken from my home along with two other girls: my aunt's daughter and daughter-in-law. After that, we didn't feel like staying there."[399]

Criminal migrations: abductions, kidnapping, smuggling, trafficking

At the International Policy Institute for Counter Terrorism, Israeli director Shay classifies criminal abduction in terms of the identity of the hostages and the goal of the perpetrator. Hostages may be members of security forces (soldiers, police force, intelligence, etc.) or government personnel and civilians who may be a chance or planned target or "botched up abduction."[400] Abduction may be an act of war or a criminal action with intent to bargain for money, weapons, or to make political demands.[401] While terror abductions and kidnappings for ransom and forced conscription are beyond the scope of this book, they need to be mentioned as some refugees are survivors of these actions.[402,403,404,405,406]

Abductions: India's 1947 Partition following independence resulted in the "largest human migration known to history" in order to reduce religious persecutions.[407] Behera asks, "What did this mass migration of five to six million people mean to the women who had no choice in the decision to leave and faced rape, abduction or death by family men for their safety and to maintain their honour?"[408] An estimated 100,000 women were abducted on both sides with a Central Recovery Operation of 7,981 women in Pakistan and 16,168 in India by 1954. Abducted and recovered, the women twice crossed the border, but neither crossing was of their own free will making it difficult to define them as migrants, refugees, or dislocated women.[409] Recovered women lacked support, and many families considered them dishonoured and refused their return. Today, raid and rescue operations of women and children abducted into the sex industry are attractive to donors, say Australian social workers: "It caters to stereotypical assumptions about human trafficking, produces measurable outcomes and relies on the concepts of a hero, victim, and villain."[410]

Child abductions and kidnappings: the unlawful taking of children is unfortunately not rare. Parental abductions occur during marriage break-ups, while kidnapping is the theft of children by strangers for criminal purposes, such as extortion, illegal adoptions, or human trafficking for the purposes of forced labour, slavery, sexual abuse, organ "harvesting" and murder. The 2005 Hague Convention is an international treaty to assist children taken across borders. Since its inception, Canadian journal *Foreign Affairs* reports over 400 Canadian children have been returned.[411] Today, as a preventative action, all Canadian children have their own passports:

> If parents are separated or divorced, a child will not be issued with a passport unless the application is supported by evidence that the issuance of the passport is not contrary to the terms of a custody order or a separation agreement.[412]

Smuggling is the illegal border crossing of persons—intent is the important distinction. The United Nations Convention against Transnational Organized Crime (2000) adopted The Protocol against the Smuggling of Migrants by Land, Sea and Air (2004).[413] The headline of a 2010 news report of smuggling of Haitians following the earthquake summarizes the problem: "Thousands try, hundreds die: they Prey on the Desperate."[414] After a motorboat overturned seven miles from Miami Beach, the Chief of Enforcement for the US Coast Guard in Miami, warned:

> The immigrant smugglers don't choose to run up nice and soft onto the beach and let the people off gently. They'll stop 20, 30 yards off the rocks and literally force the people out of the boat to swim for it ... you have some folks who might not swim at all. You have children that are in these boats and they're trying to swim across rough water in surf conditions onto a rocky out-cropping. It's a recipe for disaster.[415]

It's not only dangerous, it's expensive, and costs $1,000 to $2,000 per passenger.

Trafficking is defined by the UN as 1) *the act or recruitment*, transportation, harbouring or receipt of persons; 2) *through threat*, force, coercion, abduction, fraud, deception, abuse of power or vulnerability, or giving payments or benefits to a person in control of the victim; 3) *for exploitation*: prostitution, sexual exploitation, forced labour, slavery and removal or harvesting of organs.[416,417] Trafficking is rooted in poverty, family violence, marginalization and lack of education. Women and girls are the primary victims (70%), forced into the sex trade or exploited in domestic servitude and forced labour. Children (<18 yrs) are also exploited for forced labour, petty crime and begging, child pornography and sex.[418] Young boys are taken as soldiers.[419]

Trafficking does not always involve border crossings, but may include irregular crossings and/or smuggling and *harbouring*—defined as holding with the knowledge of or intent to participate in organized crime. Unlike smuggling, border crossings of trafficked persons may appear regular. The persons may seem to have genuine travel documents that permit crossing. What's important is the intent of others to exploit them,[420] which is outlined in the 2003 Protocol to Prevent, Suppress and Punish Trafficking in Persons, especially Women and Children.[421]

Historically, more than one state has trafficked its own citizens. After WWII, "East Germany began to sell its citizen to raise foreign currency ... dissidents were allowed to leave permanently for the West in exchange for hefty ransoms paid by the West German government."[422] The "Deputy Chancellor ... called it 'trafficking in human beings ... very close to a slave trade,' echoing decades of rhetoric linking emigrant to slavery."[423] Between

> 1969–1974 Romania ransomed Jews and Germans for profits..The price of exit could go up to $50,000 depending on the migrant's age, education, profession family status and political importance.. the ransom scheme expanded to include ethnic Germans, sold to West Germany for suitcases stuffed with US dollars.[424]

After the break-up of Eastern Europe, there was a boom of human trafficking in the transnational sex industry, as well as an increase in mail-order brides and gay sex tourism. Zahar notes estimates are that "about half of the 17,000 migrant women working as prostitutes in the UK are from Eastern Europe."[425] It's difficult to detect the line between voluntary and forced prostitution when "victims are young, impoverished, dependent, and unable to speak the local language."[426]

Notes

1. Samuels et al., 1986/2000:26–27.
2. Jung, CW9i:6.
3. Jacobi, 1959/1974:37.
4. Hillman, 1975.
5. Jacobi, 1959/1974:37.
6. Samuels, 1985.
7. Jung, CW9i:6.
8. Ibid.:3.
9. Otto, 1917/1923/1970.
10. Samuels et al., 1986/2000:100.
11. Merritt, 1991.
12. Rowe, 2002.
13. Wolman, 2007:23.
14. Eliade, 1959:30–32.
15. Walck, 2003:205–219.
16. Hoffman, 1996.
17. Dutton, 2009.
18. Husain, 1997:60–61.
19. Sabini, 2002:6–7.
20. Livni, 2016.
21. Ibid.
22. Wohlleben, 2016.
23. Peterson, 2018:71.
24. Akhtar, 1999/2004:15.
25. Reich, 2018:pxii.
26. Brown & Sanders, 1981:151.
27. Ibid.:151.
28. de Haas, 2014:17.
29. Ibid.:17–18.
30. https://global-goose.com/working-holiday-visas-for-canadians/
31. Bauder, 2011:116–117.
32. Tartakovsky & Schwartz, 2001:88.
33. Ibid, 88.
34. Saunders, 2018.
35. BBC News, 2018b.
36. McInerney, 1997:118, 123.
37. Ibid.:123.
38. Ibid.:137.
39. Miller & Boling, 1990–1991:16.
40. Ibid.:16.

41 Zahar, 2016:246.
42 Knafo & Yaari, 1997:225.
43 Ibid.:225.
44 Hirschman, 1970:107.
45 Ibid.:108.
46 Marlin, 1997:142.
47 Krahn & Gartrell, 1981:307–324.
48 Bauder, 2011:116–117.
49 McAuliffe & Ruhs, 2017.
50 De Troyes, 1996.
51 Van Blerk & Ansell, 2006:256–272.
52 Kundu, 2016:101–107.
53 Groody & Campese, 2008:247.
54 Bauman & Tester, 2001:41.
55 Zahar, 2016:268.
56 Esipova et al., 2010.
57 Jedwab, 2012:276.
58 Fukuyama, 2018b:121.
59 Spoonley & Tolley, 2012:7.
60 Duncan, 2018.
61 Spoonley & Tolley, 2012:9.
62 Madison, 2006:238.
63 Eccles & Wigfield, 2002:109–132.
64 Brym, 1992:387–395.
65 Carlson & Nilsen, 1995:179–186.
66 Carling, 2002:5–42.
67 de Jong & Fawcett, 1981:47.
68 Ibid.:49–50.
69 Ibid.:55.
70 Schwartz, 1992:1–69.
71 Rokeach, 1973.
72 de Haas, 2014:23–24.
73 Sen, 1988:269–294.
74 Ibid.:269–294.
75 Berlin, 1969.
76 de Haas, 2014:23–24.
77 Ibid.:23–24.
78 de Jong & Fawcett, 1981:38.
79 de Haas, 2014:23.
80 Castles et al., 2014.
81 Brettell & Hollifield, 2007.
82 Massey et al., 1995:431–466.
83 Hirschman et al., 1999.
84 Boswell & Mueser, 2008:519–529.
85 Goldin et al., 2012.
86 Smith & King, 2012:127–133.
87 Koikkalainen & Kyle, 2016:761.
88 Haug, 2008:585–605.
89 Bauman, 1998.
90 Urry, 2007.
91 Castles, 2010:1567.
92 de Jong & Fawcett, 1981:42.

93 de Haas, 2014:10.
94 Gardner, 1981:65.
95 Manchandra, 2006:209.
96 Gardner, 1981:84.
97 Haug, 2008:587, 591.
98 Hagen-Zanker, 2008:20.
99 Haug, 2008:591.
100 Mincer, 1978:749–773.
101 Challiol & Mignonac, 2005:247–274.
102 Coulter et al., 2012:16–30.
103 Taylor & Fletcher, 2001.
104 Maphosa, 2007:123–136.
105 Hagen-Zanker, 2008:11–12.
106 Özden & Schiff, 2006.
107 Hugo, 1981:96–199.
108 Ibid.:211.
109 Ibid.:200–201.
110 Ibid.:202–204.
111 Jensen R, 2019.
112 Haberkorn, 1981:252–278.
113 Janis & Mann, 1979.
114 Haberkorn, 1981:254–255.
115 Ibid.:252–276.
116 Sly & Wrigley, 1985:78–97.
117 Montero, 1977: frontispiece.
118 Ibid.:21.
119 Ibid.:43.
120 Ibid.:54.
121 Ibid.:68.
122 Ibid, 69.
123 Ibid, 134–135.
124 Ibid, 139.
125 Ibid, 145.
126 Ibid, 150.
127 Ibid, 153.
128 Ibid, 200–204.
129 Ibid, 213–214.
130 Ibid, 213–214.
131 Kage, 2012:130.
132 Kennan & Walker, 2012.
133 Schultz, 1961b:1–17.
134 DaVanzo, 1983:552–.559.
135 Kennan & Walker, 2012.
136 Mincer, 1978:749–773.
137 Kennan & Walker, 2012:17.
138 Gemici, 2011.
139 Gok & Atsan, 2016:39.
140 Ibid.:39.
141 Maslow, 1954.
142 Reichlová, 2005.
143 Wasuge, 2018:8.
144 Ajzen & Fishbein, 1980.

145 Ajzen, 2014:438–459.
146 Kniveton et al., 2011:S34.
147 Smith, 2014:77–91.
148 Ibid.:77–91.
149 Schaffar et al., 2016.
150 Poot et al., 2016:No.10329.
151 Klabunde & Willekens, 2016:73.
152 Ibid.:88.
153 Ibid.:84.
154 Thober et al., 2018:41.
155 Ibid.:41.
156 Ibid.:41.
157 Rigaud et al., 2018.
158 Haour-Knipe, 2002.
159 de Jong & Fawcett, 1981:45.
160 Bickerton, 2008:75.
161 Stockdale, 2014:161–171.
162 Frank, 2016.
163 Stockdale, 2014:169.
164 Tabor et al., 2015:28–41.
165 Amit & Riss, 2010:51–67.
166 Amit et al., 2016:371–389.
167 Wasuge, 2018:8.
168 Ibid., 2018:8.
169 Ibid., 2018:8.
170 Puppa, 2018:358.
171 Ibid.:358.
172 Grauer, 2018:3.
173 CBC News, 2018 Birth tourism.
174 Mihi-Ramirez & Kumpikaite, 2013:351–359.
175 Soon, 2012.
176 Bjarnason, 2014:500–515.
177 Liao, 2001:435.
178 Li et al., 1996:51–67.
179 Jung CW12j30; j32.
180 Sipos et al., 2018:1–10.
181 Nentwich et al., 2015:429–434.
182 http://www.who.int/hrh/migration/code/practice/en/
183 Tartakovsky & Schwartz, 2001:88–99.
184 Aluwihare, 2005:15–21.
185 Blacklock et al., 1982:99–106.
186 Bidwell et al., 2014:24,194.
187 Ibid.:24,194.
188 Poudel et al., 2018:95–102.
189 Lee & Moon, 2013:1517–1522.
190 Hendel & Kagan, 2011:259–262.
191 Astor et al., 1982:2492–2500.
192 Humphries et al., 2013:63.
193 Brugha et al., 2016:45–54.
194 Clarke et al., 2017:1–12.
195 Syed et al., 2008:61–68.
196 Santric-Milicevic et al., 2014:173–183.

197 Duverne et al., 2008:360–373.
198 Abbas et al., 2015:21–28.
199 McHugh, 1985:585–589.
200 Kniveton et al., 2008.
201 Bardsley & Hugo, 2010:238–262.
202 Elovitz, 1997b:67.
203 Brouillon, 2007:132.
204 Ibid.:133.
205 Ibid.:133.
206 Tucker et al., 2013a:61–84.
207 Kandel & Massey, 2002:981–1004.
208 Biles & Frideres, 2012:304, 308.
209 Zalinsky, 1974/2016:144.
210 de Haas, 2014:17.
211 Ibid.:17.
212 Duffy, 1995:29.
213 Ibid.:22.
214 Ibid.:22.
215 Biles & Frideres, 2012:299.
216 Yok-Fong, 2013:403–412.
217 McHugh, 1985:585–589.
218 Ozcurumez & Aker, 2016:61–72.
219 Ibid.:61–72.
220 Marcus, 2009:481–498.
221 Browne & Braun, 2017:395–411.
222 Adzei & Sakyi, 2014:102–120.
223 Allen et al., 2018:191–208.
224 Guri, 2015:56–71.
225 Gubhaju & de Jong, 2009:31–61.
226 Long, 2014:243–252.
227 Madianou & Miller, 2011.
228 Leander & de Haan, 2015.
229 Statistics Canada, 2016.
230 Warnick, 2016:254.
231 Duyvendak, 2011:19.
232 Duyvendak, 2011:19.
233 Cresswell, 2011:550–558.
234 Rapport & Dawson, 1998b:7.
235 Duyvendak, 2011:19.
236 Rapport & Dawson, 1998b:7.
237 Jensen, 2019.
238 Rapport & Dawson, 1998b:7.
239 Ibid.:20; original emphasis.
240 Cooke, 2013:818.
241 Vilhelmson & Thulin, 2016:276–287.
242 Jamieson, 2000:203–224.
243 Tucker et al., 2013b:963–970.
244 Sabelli, 1997:169.
245 Ibid.:168–169.
246 Ibid.:168–169.
247 Ibid.:170.
248 Carvalho & Martins, 2016:216–224.

249 Pei-Shan, 2001:435.
250 Gurieva et al., 2015:61–73.
251 Ibid.:61–73.
252 Srinivasan, 1990:21–27.
253 Harris et al., 2013:70–78.
254 Krahn et al., 1981:307–324.
255 Halseth & Sullivan, 2003:138, 144.
256 Ibid.:138,144.
257 JRank Articles http://science.jrank.org/pages/10217/Migration-Africa-InternalMigration
258 Campbell & Carkovich, 1984:89–105.
259 Falk, 2013|.
260 Roberts, 2013.
261 Zhu, 1990:229–246.
262 Saunders, 2015.
263 Manchandra, 2006:209.
264 www.ilo.org/kathmandu/areasofwork/labour-migration/lang–en/index.htm
265 BBC News, 2018b www.bbc.com/news/world-latin-ameria-45951782
266 Sayad, 2004:129.
267 Ibid.:129.
268 Le Bon, 1895/2009.
269 Allport, 1920:159–182.
270 Turner & Killian, 1987.
271 Smelser, 1962.
272 Van Ginneken, 2003.
273 Khoo et al., 2008:193–226.
274 Ibid.:193–226.
275 Knafo & Yaari, 1997:221–223.
276 Ibid.:221–223.
277 Botelho & Agergaard, 2011:806.
278 Ossman, 2013.
279 Vasileva, 2012.
280 Newbold, 1996:728–747.
281 Nogle, 1994:31–48.
282 Ostrovsky et al., 2008.
283 Ramos, 2018:1841–1857.
284 Stewart & Shaffer, 2015.
285 Kelly, 2013.
286 Ibid.:69.
287 Ibid., 2013.
288 Ahrens et al., 2016:86.
289 Ibid.:89.
290 Ibid.:90.
291 Ibid., 2016:91.
292 Ibid.:92.
293 Ibid.:93.
294 Ibid.:96.
295 Collyer, 2005:699–718.
296 Pacific Canadian Heritage Centre.
297 Alsaleh, 2018: email.
298 Haug, 2008:585–605.
299 Arango, 2000:283–296.

300 Morse & Mudgett, 2018:260–269.
301 https://onlinelibrary.wiley.com/doi/10.1002/psp.2124
302 Barcus & Halfacree, 2018:98.
303 Stockdale & Haartsen, 2018: e2124.
304 Looker & Naylor, 2009:39–64.
305 https://onlinelibrary.wiley.com/doi/10.1002/psp.2124
306 Uhlenberg, 1973:297–311.
307 Hjälm, 2014:569–580.
308 Carling, 2002:5–42.
309 Lubkemann, 2008:454–475.
310 Fang, 2006:671–694.
311 Strohschein, 2012:735–751.
312 University of Miami, 2018: http://balseros.miami.edu/
313 Potter, 2015.
314 Campisi, 2016:27, 59.
315 Cooke, 2008b.
316 Cooke, 2008a.
317 Jensen, 2019.
318 Cooke, 2013:818.
319 Boyd & Pikkov, 2009.
320 Shihadeh, 1991:432–444.
321 Cooke, 2008:257.
322 Stockdale, 2017:e2022.
323 Clark & Withers, 2008:260.
324 Åström & Westerlund, 2011:19–20.
325 Ackers, 2004:189–201.
326 Jensen, 2019.
327 Magdol, 2002:554.
328 Ibid.:554.
329 Cooke, 2013:817–836.
330 Graphic Graphic Science, 2016:88.
331 Erhabor et al., 2013:17–27.
332 UNESCO, 2018 national-migration/glossary/displaced-person-displacement/
333 Manchandra, 2006:206.
334 Keely, 1992:14–18.
335 Martin, 1991.
336 Fischetti, 2016.
337 Oliver-Smith, 2009:3–24.
338 Scheineson, 2009.
339 Zheng, 2017.
340 Ng et al., 2011:245–256.
341 Brown, 2008:9–10.
342 https://en.wikipedia.org/wiki/Early_warning_system
343 https://en.wikipedia.org/wiki/2004_Indian_Ocean_earthquake_and_tsunami
344 Brown, 2008:9–10.
345 Rajasingham-Senanayake, 2006:172.
346 Behera, 2006:31.
347 Ibid.:176.
348 Zieck, 2018:19–116.
349 Loisos, 2002:41.
350 Hollenbach, 2016:4–17.
351 Geneva Conventions.

352 United Nations, 1948.
353 International Justice Center, 2018.
354 US Census Bureau, 2005: Refugee status.
355 Wroughton, 2018: www.reuters.com
356 Zahar, 2016:266.
357 Varvin, 2017:359.
358 Ibrahim & Howarth, 2018:348–391.
359 Glenn, 2002:169.
360 Manchandra, 2006:209.
361 Zambelli, 2018:228.
362 Gartner & Kennedy, 2018:1–68.
363 Chow, 2018:28–69.
364 Ibid.:50.
365 Manchandra, 2006:210.
366 Ibid.:210.
367 Ibid.:212.
368 Zahar, 2016:272–274.
369 Ibid.:272–274.
370 Varvin, 2016:825–855.
371 Raychaudhury, 2006:157–158.
372 Dow, 2011:212.
373 Cameron, 2008:567–585.
374 Hébert et al., 2018:45–58.
375 Papadopoulos & Hulme 2002.
376 Dow, 2011:210.
377 Ibid.:210.
378 Ibid.:210.
379 Ibid.:210.
380 Barenbaum et al., 2004:41.
381 Ibid.:41.
382 Grut et al., 2006:1318–1320.
383 Papadopoulos & Hulme 2002:149
384 Ibid.:149.
385 Ibid.:149.
386 Von Lersner et al., 2008:88.
387 Ibid.:88.
388 Mueller et al., 2011:84–89.
389 United Nations, 1984: https://treaties.un.org
390 https://en.wikipedia.org/wiki/United_Nations_Convention_against_Torture
391 Quiroga & Jaranson, 2005:1–96.
392 Higson-Smith & Bro, 2010:14.
393 Ibid.:24.
394 Papadopoulos, 2002a:163–188.
395 Papadopoulos, 2002b:29.
396 Ibid.:29.
397 Montgomery, 1998:1–152.
398 Papadopoulos, 2002b:29.
399 Human Rights Watch, 2003:Nepal.
400 Shay, 2017.
401 Ibid., 2017.
402 Hanna & Aris, 2017.
403 Walzer et al., 2009.

404 Pham et al., 2007.
405 https://data.colombiareports.com/colombia-kidnapping-extortion-statistics/
406 Neistat, 2008.
407 Behera, 2006:32.
408 Ibid.:32.
409 Ibid.:32.
410 Jones et al., 2018:231–255.
411 Foreign Affairs Canada, Rev 2005:6.
412 Ibid.:6.
413 United Nations www.unodc.org/
414 Potter, 2015.
415 Ibid., 2015.
416 United Nations www.unodc.org/
417 Guild, 2009:172.
418 https://sherloc.unodc.org/cld/en/v3/htms/index.html
419 Stor, 2014.
420 Guild, 2009:170–172.
421 Wikipedia, 2019n: Protocol to Prevent, Suppress and Punish Trafficking.
422 Zahar, 2016:260.
423 Ibid.:260.
424 Ibid.:261.
425 Ibid.:284–285.
426 Ibid.:284–285.

Chapter 2

Phase 2
The journey

Myth, the natural language of psyche speaks in images, says Jung: "No intellectual formulation comes near the richness or expressiveness of mythical imagery."[1] The myth of the Journey is that of the hero, Odysseus and his ten-year voyage as he encounters archetypal characters and situations potentially part of any "journey": 1) The mentor, 2) Threshold guardians, 3) The crossing; 4) Allies and enemies, and 5) The inmost cave, just before arrival.

Mindsets during migration journeys depend upon the pre-migration situation, if the journey has been consciously chosen and planned, involuntary, or an emergency flight to save one's life. Journeys differ in degree of risk and time of travel: Odysseus travelled homeward for ten years; early settlers to the Americas often took three months by ship followed by long overland journeys. In comparison, today's travels by car, ship and airplane seem miraculous. Still, for refugees, the time prior to departure is often stressful, with many challenges described as a "social earthquake"[2] when leaving arises from "push" factors of survival, rather than "pull" factors of desire and opportunity.

A 2012 American study explores the difficulty of distinguishing between and comparing types of migration including leaving, return and transit journeys. "Over a five-year period, about one in 80 people around the world migrate to another country"[3] and "more than a quarter of that movement is down to people returning to their country of birth."[4] So, "roughly one of four migration events is a return to a homeland, particularly large return migration flows from the United States to Central and South America and from the Persian Gulf to South Asia."[5]

Since the 18th century, many migrators have been reluctant travellers, "urged by hunger or fear, hunted or pushed out, ordered about."[6] Some of the most unfortunate were Africans at the height of the Guinea slave trade. The Scottish clearances and Irish famine saw people forced onto the ships to North America; in England the Poor Laws offered subsidized emigration or jail, while "In France some rebellious characters were offered either jail or the colonial armies."[7] Historians Poirier and Piquet ask, was there ever any real choice?[8] Recently, Munich's main train station saw the arrival of thousands of exhausted migrants who had fled through Eastern Europe from desperate situations in Syria and Iraq.[9] Approximately 4,000 to 5,000 left their homeland, not by choice but in desperation, and were held in refugee centres. They started with the goal to get to Europe and begin a new life; faced with barriers, they found alternate routes, and were not opposed to using well-connected and organized smugglers.[10]

Since 9/11, the Mexican border has proved to be ten times more deadly than the Berlin Wall during its 28 years of existence, notes Italian theologian Campese.[11] With its constant nearness of death,[12] it's a reminder of how dangerous are some migrations.[13] The ongoing, persistent demand for unauthorized immigrant labour means the steadily escalating American spending on border enforcement has been a weak deterrent. The increased challenges of border crossing and quadrupled financial cost of irregular entry have resulted in increased numbers of undocumented migrants choosing to stay in the US, resulting in surges of anti-immigrant vigilante activities.[14]

In *The New Odyssey*, Kingsley relays stories of migrants walking into Europe. These are "as epic as the classical heroes, such as Aeneas and Odysseus who fled a conflict in the Middle East and sailed across the Aegean."[15] In telling today's stories of migrators crossing the Sahara, the Balkans and the Mediterranean, Kingsley reminds us there are commercial and government-owned ferries criss-crossing the Mediterranean, but because migrants from the developing world often lack the necessary "papers" (entrance visas and passports) to board them, they must find clandestine passage. They travel overland to the Mediterranean, catching rides on the backs of land cruisers when they can, before finding illegal passage in the holds of wooden fishing boats or on open vessels and rafts. Odysseus' ancient enticing Sirens today are smugglers and entrepreneurs eager to make money from those seeking work and asylum: "Violent border guards are the contemporary equivalent of Odysseus' Cyclops."[16] *The Penguin Dictionary of Symbols*[17] describes Cyclops as having one eye in the middle of his forehead, suggestive of single-mindedness, ebbing of intelligence and rule by emotions. Cyclops as a master of thunder and thunderbolts is also symbolic of the brute force and fear elicited by border guards operating from the dictates of rule, rather than human sensibilities of thought and compassion.

Using focus groups, in-depth interviews and surveys, Sačer and colleagues studied migrants passing through refugee transit camps in Eastern Croatia.[18] Of the 137 who participated, 51% were Afghans, 32% Syrians and 18% Iraqis, who reported an average of five years to save enough money to pay for the journey: "The vast majority of those attempting this dangerous crossing are in need of international protection, fleeing war, violence and persecution in their country of origin."[19] Of the 856,723 people surviving the journey in 2015, almost a third (29%) were children, 17% women and 54% men. From 2010 to 2016, more than 13,389 persons died en route.[20] A study of Zimbabwean refugees in South Africa (10 women and 10 men) in 90-minute focus groups, followed by detailed semi-structured interviews, reports that all had witnessed and experienced threats and physical violence on the journey, and many had to engage in "survival sex."[21]

A decade ago, migrant boat tragedies occurred mostly on two routes, the West African Route passing from West Africa to the Canary Islands, and the Western Mediterranean Route crossing the strait between Morocco and Spain.[22] By 2005, more than 30,000 people were crossing annually, with many tragedies ensuing, until agreements were negotiated between the countries to end illegal migration. By 2018, this resulted in migrants simply finding more difficult routes to their destination: the Central Mediterranean Route from Tunisia, Libya and Egypt across to Italy, Malta and the local islands. This crisis-prone route was halted after Italy and Arab countries began to police the beaches. But the real drop in the number of travellers followed a series of economic crises, which reduced the number of jobs available to migrants. Finally, the conflict in Syria forced migrants to negotiate passage via smuggler networks, illegal boats and rafts that cost around $2,000 per person.

Ramji-Nogales says today's "migration emergencies"[23] are the result of international migration law that doesn't address systemic inequality or provide an adequate structure for the global migration system. At the International Organization on Migration (IOM), McAuliffe reports each day people set off from fragile countries wracked by civil conflict, persecution and disasters. The migrants' journeys are uncertain, long, dangerous and known to carry the risks of abuse, exploitation and even death. Many lack travel documents because their countries have no means of issuing them, and they tend to have only a general idea of where to go, who can be relied upon and what things cost. Still, these are the lucky ones. IOM's Missing Migrants project reports "more than 46,000 migrants have died during migration journeys since 2000."[24]

In 2018, Rabin studied 38 migrant youths who left Mexico with their parents, but were separated due to the enforcement of immigration policies.[25] Of this group, 19 ended up living with aunts, grandmothers, or cousins; six were with grandparents, or aunts and uncles, and three were with brothers, grandfathers, or cousins. Although all of them describe childhoods filled with trauma and hardship, Rubin found, they show remarkable resilience and are "on track" to graduate from high school.[26] Their resilience is demonstrated in optimism, perceptions of control, self-efficacy and positive emotional support systems.[27] Most have chosen to stay in the US because of its greater economic potential. One said:

I mainly take on my culture from Mexico, like the traditions and the religion. But I'd much rather stay here for the opportunities like a good job, in something that I would love to do ... I like Mexico ... I just don't see myself getting anywhere with my dreams.[28]

Stage four: meeting the mentor

In traditional hero stories, the mentor is an elder possessing magical power and/or wisdom.[29] "Mentor was the loyal friend of Odysseus,"[30] Voglar says. Although "Mentor has given his name to all guides and trainers; it's really Athena, the goddess of wisdom, who works behind the scenes."[31] The mentor guides, advises, motivates and sometimes saves the hero's life. Mentor gives gifts to the hero that s/he earns by passing tests or making a sacrifice or commitment.[32] For migrants, the mentor is important:

> A trustworthy person who can take over or neutralize the anxieties and fears he feels toward the new and unknown world can be compared to that of a child who is left alone and separately searchers for the familiar face of his mother or a mother-substitute.

There's a parallel to childhood imprinting and attachment processes: "the immigrant needs to find in the external world other persons who represent 'godfathers' or substitute fathers."[33]

Historian Montero reminds us that migration is costly: one form of mentorship is financial. She recounts how friends financially mentored her family's migration to Canada. They said: "whenever we had the money we could pay him for it, even if it took a year."[34] Ramanujam tells of having a son born in the US before returning to India. When the child was 16, they returned to New York City and were mentored by three families who "smoothed our re-entry into American life."[35]

Knafo and Yaari, coming to the US from Israel, tell of arriving "equipped with an impressive supply of telephone numbers of friends and friends of friends [with a] focus on forming a network."[36] The newcomer does not discriminate in choice of social contacts, but neither does the community—there is a commitment to "always do their best to aid and abet their fellow countrymen."[37] These mentoring communities function like Winnicott's *transitional object* or a mother-substitute: "In a familiar ethnic community, the process of separating from one's motherland and adaptation to a new country is facilitated and rendered less painful."[38] Historian Petschauer recounts when two aunts made a visit home to Germany from the US and invited him to come back with them. Despite his mother's advice, he agreed and an uncle in the US became his mentor.[39]

Smuggling/trafficking mentors

Migration mentors may be smugglers, who for a fee guide irregular, clandestine crossings. Trafficking is defined as *"attempting, participating* (accomplice), *organizing* or *directing* others to recruit, transport, transfer, harbour or be in 'receipt of person'"[40] for the purposes of exploitation. It includes

> threat or use of force or other forms of coercion, of abduction, of fraud, of deception, of the abuse of power or a position of vulnerability or of the giving or receiving of payments or benefits to achieve the consent of a person having control over another person.[41]

Threshold guardians

Many guardians appear in Greek myths. One is the three-headed monster, Cerberus—who can see past, present and future—and who guards the entrance to the underworld. Charon the Ferry-man guides souls across the River Styx, the boundary between the living and the underworld. The "Herald" is a special ally whose role is to call to action and motivate. Guardians may be people, objects, or natural occurrences and they may be positive, negative, or neutral. In contemporary migrations, a border guard or police may act as a herald. A 2017 Human Rights Watch report cited eleven cases of Turkish police torturing and abducting migrants[42]—heralds are not always positive figures.

The classical primary role of a Guardian is to test heroes and strengthen them for the tasks ahead, but a guardian can also be antagonistic, friendly, or a secret helper. One way to get around threshold guardians is to adopt their skin or their language and/or persona, the way they present themselves to the world. Child migrants do this well, with a great facility in acquiring new languages and adopting new customs. Following India's independence and the Partition of Pakistan with the largest mass migration known, there were many threshold guardians on both sides. An estimated 100,000 women were abducted and later (guardian) police assisted families in relocating them.[43] Some families acted as negative threshold guardians, refusing to permit the women to return home, seeing them as defiled and made unclean by living with the enemy.

Marlin defected from Eastern Europe during the Cold War era while attending professional psychiatry meetings in Vienna and tells of the police and army taking on the role of threshold guardians: "Many of us while growing up in a totalitarian state, cherished and idealized freedom."[44] At the time, the US "symbolized a great land of unlimited possibilities and freedom ... Czechs and Slovaks came to America to seek prosperity and freedom from oppression during Nazi German occupation and later during the communist regime."[45]

Stage 5: the crossing

Migrant crossings begin with a leap of faith, as the reality of crossing deserts, mountains and seas is fraught with dangers and rough landings. This is especially true of clandestine smugglers' boats, as death is always a potential. Robert Press interviewed 60 African migrants in Italy and France who fled homeland persecution and/or poverty between 2014 and 2016. Their crossings of the Sahara and Mediterranean speak to resilience, courage and strategic decision making that diverges sharply from media images of migrants as helpless. Their stories suggest a need to re-examine migrant networks as migrants face huge challenges that arise on these journeys and as statuses blur. A person can shift easily from being free to becoming a slave, and simply surviving clandestine crossings can be seen as lucky because tens of thousands drown.[46]

Behera recounts mass migrations from the former East Pakistan to Bengal following Partition. As a widow, in the accepted cultural tradition, she rarely left her room but one night hearing great noises outside, she peeped out and saw nearby houses aflame. It was apparent they would have to flee: "So many people of our village ran away from their own ancestral land!"[47] She travelled by boat steamer and train before her father died: "My mother and me know nothing as to where to go."[48] At the border, they registered as refugees and were there two years before being brought to the refugee camp where many decades later they were interviewed.[49]

Kage, a Japanese-Canadian tells of his family's expulsion during WWII. After arrival in Japan by ship, they went about 1,000 km south by train to Hakata. Today, by super-express train, it is a 14-hour-long journey. In 1946, the trip was unbearably long; the train cars were jam-packed. Passengers had to sleep on the floor and hang from the handrails. Having grown up in Canada, Kage found the "hardships in Japan wrought by war were beyond anything he could have imagined."[50] There were food shortages and their house was robbed.

Modarressi recalls being on the plane from Iran to the US thinking, "most immigrants, regardless of their familial, social or political circumstances causing their exile, have been cultural refugees all their lives. They leave their home because they have always felt like outsiders."[51] Beltsiou tells of a similar awareness emerging when she was "on an airplane, between places, leaving the past, moving into an unknown future."[52] She thought of how today, we are literally up in the air.

> We move through luminal spaces like airports and airplanes, hotels and waiting rooms…the crossing of borders is both exciting and

frightening as we transgress by separating from the familiar and entering into new relations. We cross internal boundaries, into a netherland/twilight zone, toward an unknown place.[53]

Also on an airplane, this time from Brazil, Marcus says he had always thought of the distance between countries as physical, but when American coffee was served he realized the distance was cultural too: "The coffee on the airplane was the wake-up call that I was leaving behind everything I was familiar with."[54]

Campisi interviewed Cubans who had escaped to the US. One man had windsurfed 110 miles from the Cuban coast to Marathon Key in Florida, but mostly they came across the open seas by raft, in a great deal of physical danger and uncertainty. They were emotionally awash with grief and loss, struggling with confrontation with death, physical discomfort, hallucinations, extreme fright, and having to face the fact of not going back.[55]

Such clandestine journeys are defined as nested experiences of mobility and immobility. They may require being physically hidden in a compartment, or detained and held by authorities with periods of waiting for financial remittances from home to enable continuing the journey. Some involve being marooned in a drifting boat at sea: "Migrants themselves view this fragmentation—the stopping, waiting and containment—as part of the journey to be endured."[56] An increasing problem with today's escapes are the risks and need to forfeit agency at crucial moments.[57]

Letters of Scottish Highlanders (approximately 16,000) who migrated to Canada in the 19th century (1846–1854) show recurring themes.[58] One was the attempts to dispel common fears of crossing the Atlantic and fears of bad weather. Though the country is described as "magnificent, the climate much better than in the Highlands, the grass of better quality, the firewood plentiful, the cattle well fed and well looked after, and there was land as far as the eye could see,"[59] some report less satisfying experiences with ship conditions described as inhuman.

> The emigrant is shewn [sic] a berth, a shelf ... in a noisome dungeon ... airless and lightless, in which several hundreds of both sexes and all ages are stowed away, on shelves ... still reeking from the ineradicable stench left by the emigrants on the last voyage ... filth, foul air and darkness.[60]

Stage 6: tests, allies, enemies

On the journey, the hero encounters tests where allies may appear, but tests may also be set by enemies, shape-shifters and tricksters. The Shadow (unseen energy) may help, dazzle, or confuse—it just depends upon whose side Shadow is on. Sometimes enemies are animals. Fleeing after the

Partition of India, one woman told of reaching Cooper's refugee camp[61] (now in West Bengal) and having to stay for a whole day on the railroad platform packed with people. The next day they were sent deep into the camp where refugee families of four were given one tent. Sanitation was poor and children were dying of dysentery. Wild hyenas surrounding the camp appeared after sunset and stole children from overcrowded tents.[62]

Tests may come in the form of laws and government policies, which have led to calls for the free movement of people across borders because increased migration controls have been shown to lead to greater numbers dying on the journey. Today, North African migrations are often "odysseys of horror towards which most of the world remains indifferent."[63] Although believed to be underestimated, current reports are "at least one migrant dies every day at the US-Mexico border, mostly because of hypothermia, dehydration, sunstroke or drowning."[64] Similar data is reported regarding migrations into Europe, with "more than 4,000 deaths between 1992 and 2003 crossing the straits of Gibraltar" and similar numbers of deaths off the coasts of Australia, the borders of Mexico and Guatemala, and the Sahara.[65] These stressful, often traumatizing journey experiences are risk factors for later mental health problems. They may include detention or reclusion, and/or deportation "racial discrimination, urban violence, abuse by law enforcement officers, forced removal or separation from their families."[66] Modern information communication technologies (ICTs) have become the new *modus operandi* of criminals, including those involved in human and organ trafficking of Eritrean refugees.[67]

Robert Press tells of one lad's escape story in 2014 from a village in Sudan's Nuba Mountains. When government and allied Arab militias began genocidal repression of black Arabs, Toto and his family fled overland to Libya. At the best of times, this is a dangerous journey as many die and others are captured, bought and sold as slaves. It happened to Toto who was held servant/prisoner in a Libyan home. He described it as "a most horrible time."[68] His captors treated him like an animal and always shouted in his face. Yet his resilience enabled him to exercise survival skills and to make strategic decisions that allowed him to escape nine months later.[69]

Observations on current migrant caravans from South and Central America to the US describe it as "simply the latest manifestation of a crisis that's really affecting the entire Americas."[70] The underlying causes are the absence of democracy, organized crime, drug trafficking and corruption. Climate change has begun to fuel even more migration, as drier conditions in some areas have decimated crops.[71] The migrant caravan is described as spontaneous because "it's absurd to think that someone can convince all these people [to migrate] … the government doesn't want to recognize that we have a human tragedy that people no longer can bear,"[72] says former Honduras congressman Fuentes. Likely, there were "thousands of people in Honduras who were considering going sometime in the next few months, or in the next year or two. [The caravan] just changed their calculation about when [was] the best time to go."[73]

The Regional Mixed Migration Secretariat reports 92% of potential Ethiopian migrants are well aware of the risks associated with irregular travel to Yemen and Saudi Arabia. Yet 42% feel the benefits to be worth the risks of the journey and dangers upon arrival. Reports of abuse vary from 1% (sexual abuse) to 44% (social/psychological/verbal abuse).[74] A high awareness of risk was found in European interviews with 500 people who had crossed the Mediterranean. They admitted choosing to embark on the irregular sea passage because it was the only possibility for escape from intolerable conditions. Fully aware of the dangers, they tell of using psychological mechanisms to succeed—like avoidance and discrediting negative information to minimize the harms and resignation to pain. The authors note that "abuse, exploitation and trauma during migration journeys remain an under-researched, and perhaps not well understood, facet of irregular migration."[75]

One of the world's busiest migrant corridors is the Mexican transit route from Central America through Mexico to the US.[76] In 2017 *Médecins Sans Frontières* (MSF) found 68% of refugees and migrants reporting violence on this route,[77] ranging from gangs extorting migrants for passage to officials boarding trains engaging in physical and verbal abuse and detaining undocumented migrants.[78] Not surprisingly, there's talk about creating a safe corridor, with Mexico's National Human Rights Commission working with federal and state authorities and civil organizations. Amnesty International says it's important that the focus is on protection and not opportunities for increased persecution of migrants.[79]

The Darién Gap is an example of extreme risk of passage. On the Colombia/Panama border in Central America, the Gap runs though the world's most dangerous and lawless wilderness jungle teeming with the world's most deadly snakes and guerrilla militias. With traditional migration pathways being closed, Cubans, Somalis, Syrians, Nepalis, Bangladeshis and others have been going to South America to travel northward through the Darién Gap's roadless jungle. Every year hundreds never reappear, but are killed and/or abandoned by coyotes (migrant smugglers) on ghost trails. Researchers say it's difficult to imagine how they end up "half a world away from home, without the faintest idea of the grueling trials. Not only is their willpower amazing, the Gap's shadowy depths have swallowed travelers far more prepared."[80]

Stage 7: the approach or inmost cave, prior to arrival

In classical myth, upon arrival at their destination, but before leaping into the great unknown of the newland, there's a period of reflection upon one's progress and a gathering of courage to continue—a brief respite before meeting the great ordeal. Today, the inmost cave is characterized by border guards and laws with interdictions or measures designed to prevent entrance of non-citizens. It includes visas to board vessels and interception during travel.[81] British historians explored the reality and mind-states of 500 anarchists who fled prosecution in France (1880–1914) for exile to England. Exile became an important rite of passage of generations of continental political activists, who organized themselves into a group to preserve their identity.[82] Without the possibility of returning to France, their attitudes, concerns and expectations were marked by a new collective identity, a new cosmopolitan idealism and sociability.[83] For instance, Moreau, Flaubert's hero, who left France following the December *coup d'état* in 1851, is described as knowing "the melancholy of ships, the cold of tents in the morning, the dullness of landscapes and ruins, the bitterness of interrupted friendships."[84]

Kage, in his personal account of childhood deportation during WWII from Canada to Japan tells of the arrival of 10,000 people per day who were systematically processed on a mass production assembly line of inoculation, delousing, customs examination, payment, discharge and bathing. He speaks of 12 hellish days after arrival, of being confined like a prisoner without food except for "dried army biscuits crawling with insects, and soup with unidentifiable floating objects."[85] Although it was hot midsummer, the water was not potable and there were realistic fears of widespread cholera. Only one pleasant memory exists—the entertainment of music and dancing.

In 2018, the EU countries reached an agreement about processing migrants rescued at sea and the need to establish control centres outside Europe, where migrants deemed eligible would be distributed among member states agreeing to take them. The intention is to stop a reoccurrence of uncontrolled migrant flows, and to break the smuggler's business-model which is seen as responsible for the tragic loss of life on existing and emerging routes.[86] The use of migration control centres outside a country's territory is an existing model of countries with external visa offices. What's needed, the EU countries say, is to find new ways to respond to "illegal" (irregular) migrations.

In summary, the Journey includes meeting and responding to, and sometimes having to outwit, Threshold Guardians who control entrance to the newland. Mentors have the opposite role, to assist migrants to adjust and survive. The Crossing is the physical process which may entail stopping and starting, hiding and encountering many physical and social dangers including capture, enslavement and even death. The classic Inmost Cave is translated as the arrival. In US films, it's portrayed as Ellis Island, the landing and processing centre just outside New York City. The Cave also refers to the migrant's reflecting and taking stock of the situation before stepping onto the newland and into the new culture.

Notes

1 Jung, CW12:28.
2 Idemudia et al., 2013:19.
3 Azose & Raftery, 2018.
4 Ibid., 2018.
5 Ibid., 2018.
6 Poirier & Piquet, 2007:207.
7 Ibid2.:07.
8 Ibid2.:07.
9 Rath, 2015.
10 Cornish, 2015.
11 Campese, 2008:277.
12 Guerra, 2008:250.
13 Campese, 2008:271.
14 Cornelius, 2005:775.
15 Kingsley, 2016:10.
16 Ibid.:1.
17 Chevalier & Gheerbrant, 1969/1996:270–271.
18 Sačer et al., 2017:48–60.
19 Ibid.:48–60.
20 Ibid.:48–60.
21 Idemudia et al., 2013:1, 17–27.
22 Saunders, 2018:1.
23 Ramji-Nogales, 2017:609–655.
24 McAuliffe et al., 2018:171.
25 Rabin, 2018:1–40.
26 Ibid.,14.
27 Tak et al., 2012:390–450.
28 Rabin, 2018:30.
29 Vogler, 1998/2007:118.
30 Ibid.:120.
31 Ibid.:120.
32 Campbell, 1949/2008:17–63.
33 Grinberg & Grinberg, 1989:76–77.
34 Montero, 1977:84.
35 Ramanujam, 1997:141.
36 Knafo & Yaari, 1997:227–228.
37 Ibid.:227–228.
38 Ibid.:227–228.
39 Petschauer, 1997:35–36.
40 Guild, 2009:168; original emphasis.
41 Ibid.:168.
42 Human Rights Human Rights Watch, 2017.
43 Butalia, 2006:41.
44 Marlin, 1997:242–433.
45 Ibid.:242–433.
46 Press, 2017:3–27.
47 Raychaudhury, 2006:163.
48 Ibid.:163.
49 Ibid.:163.
50 Kage, 2012:54.
51 Beltsiou, 2016:94.

52 Ibid.:94.
53 Ibid.:94.
54 Marcus, 2009:488.
55 Campisi, 2016:25,45.
56 Brigden & Mainwaring, 2016:407.
57 Ibid.:407.
58 Auer, 2007:43.
59 Ibid.:43.
60 Ibid.:48.
61 https://en.wikipedia.org/wiki/Cooper%27s_Camp
62 Raychaudhury, 2006:165.
63 Harris, 2007:56.
64 Pécoud & De Guchteneire, 2007:4.
65 Ibid.:4.
66 Bustamante et al, 2018:220–221.
67 www.africanbookscollective.com/books/human-trafficking-and-trauma-in-the-digital-era
68 Press, 2017:3.
69 Ibid.:3.
70 BBC CBC News, 2018:30 Oct.
71 Ibid.:30 Oct.
72 Shoichet, 2018:Nov 4.
73 Ibid.:2.
74 Horwood et al, 2018:16.
75 McAuliffe et al., 2018:181.
76 Laventure, 2017: Feb 22.
77 MSF, 2017.
78 International Crisis Group, 2018: May 9.
79 Amnesty International, 2017: June 15.
80 McAuliffe et al., 2018:182.
81 Baglay & Jones, 2017:274.
82 Geoffroy & Sibley, 2007:5.
83 Ibid.:16.
84 Sylvie, 2007:34.
85 Kage, 2012:24 &104.
86 DPA & Reuters, 2018:1.

Chapter 3

Phase 3
Post-migration arrival

This chapter introduces the migration complex. Stage 8, "The ordeal," at arrival carries threats of harm and risks of death as well as the potential for peak experiences;[1] and thus, is classically defined as the "mainspring of heroic action," the key to magical powers.[2] Stage 9, "Possession of the treasure," tells us the treasure is not freely given, but must be won or seized. Metaphorically in migration, this may be resolution of loss of the homeland[3] with the treasure being acceptance of the newland,[4,5,6] openness to adaptation and belonging. Unresolved grief, the *"Ulysses syndrome,"* prevents the migrant from seizing the gift of the newland. The opposite is denied grief, which can then result in indiscriminate merging or *cultural localitis.*[7]

Migration complexes

Complexes are psychic seizures of extreme feelings with "a collection of images and ideas, clustered around a core derived from one or more archetypes and characterized by a specific emotional tone."[8] Complexes can become patterned ways of experiencing the world. Jung says, "Where the realm of complexes begins the freedom of the ego comes to an end."[9] Complexes can split off, act autonomously and dominate the personality, resulting in a split personality. One aspect of maturity is the defusing of complexes with awareness and integration that enriches the inner life and strengthens the ego, the mover of psyche.[10] Working with dream images and through the arts—drawing, painting, music, theatre and dance—we can bring consciousness and understanding to complexes and their underlying archetypes. A first step in psychoanalysis is depotentiation of the polarized and seizing energies of complexes (good/bad, love/hate) with recognition of the transcendent function of the complexes. It's the "linkage between real and imaginary, or rational and irrational,"[11] conscious and unconscious; in Buddhism, this is called the "middle path."

Migration embodies the great allegory of life: leaving a familiar past for an unknown future. Even when migration is a free choice, followed by successful adaptation, the geographic dislocation and loss of family, friends and culture can prompt feelings of isolation and alienation. Morais identifies this homesickness as the loss of sacred space and reminds us that the stress of migration can be transmitted through the generations.[12] In Psalm 137 of the Bible, the captive Israeli people ask: "How shall we sing the Lord's song in a strange land?"[13] Jung concurs:

> It is the body, the feeling, the instincts, which connect us with the soil. If you give up the past you naturally detach from the past; you lose your roots in the soil, your connection with the totem ancestors that dwell in your soil.[14]

Today, migration has become normative. British writer Stuart Hall speaks of growing up in anticipation of leaving Jamaica: "it was a sort of *rite de passage*, a coming of age or growing up."[15] Nevertheless, imprinted geographies of homelands have deep psychic importance. In the initial excitement and challenges of migration, often there's a lack of awareness of separation and dislocation until loss and alienation emerge.[16] Sometimes places differ so much we cannot even replicate homeland experiences in newlands.[17,18] Geographic dislocation is poetically described as the "laceration of the waking screen."[19] Akhtar recounts the initial excitement of coming from India to the US before reality set in accompanied by pain, regret and feelings of unbelonging. As a result, émigrés may begin to idealize their homelands with unrequited love. In the East, Akhtar says, the past, present and future merge into each other in a "time of the heart"; whereas in the West, the past, present and future are discrete periods, literally "time of mind and money."[20]

In *Longing for Paradise*, Jacoby captures nostalgic longings for the homeland,[21] and warns that even chosen migration can be more than loss of roots; it can herald psychic disaster, as can exile. Jung says the psychic injury of migration and its accompanying loss of environmental instincts can result in exaggerated self-esteem, or inferiority complexes.[22] Von Franz says the danger of loss of roots is the loss of one's own values and inner strength experienced as existential loneliness: it opens the door to evil and the projection of the other's shadow.[23]

Stage 8: ordeal at arrival

Classically, Stage 8, the "Ordeal at arrival," carries the risk and the "taste of death."[24] The ordeal also carries the potential for peak experiences[25] and euphoria that can flip into its opposite of disappointment and despair.[26] In the myth of Perseus, his ordeal at arrival required the slaying of the enthroned Gorgon/dragon, Medusa, "a winged human female with living venomous snakes as hair."[27] Her throne is symbolic of entrenched power to which one must yield and bend the knee. One heroic task is overcoming resident power. In ancient times, gods were believed so powerful that they could not be looked upon directly without destroying mortals. In the Bible, to remedy this problem, God appears to Moses as a burning bush and a voice in a cloud.

Medusa's hair of writhing snakes symbolizes venomous ideas. To slay her and avoid sudden death from her direct gaze, Perseus was advised to use a mirror. Symbolically, mirrors represent a different perspective. Cutting off Medusa's head is symbolic of over-throwing entrenched power and venomous ideas. For involuntary migrants, venomous ideas may be waves of debilitating homesickness. For voluntary migrants, they may be unrealistic expectations of the newland which in the face of reality need to be "cut off." Hall cites Albert Camus[28] and Frantz Fanon[29] as mentors in his process of shattering illusions and "inaugurating a process of protracted disenchantment."[30]

Perseus in slaying the dragon, is accidentally exposed to a drop of dragon's blood which has magical powers: 1) the bird's-eye view, or wide perspective; 2) the ability to understand the language of birds, with vast knowledge of many places, and 3) the ability to see through deception, including self-deception. Migrants, like classic heroes, need new perspectives, knowledge and power. They must confront the power of newlands: here success may be as simple as gaining permission to enter the country, or a clandestine overcoming of the border and unauthorized arrival. Medusa's head and other dragons may symbolize conquering new languages, and gaining new perspectives and self-realizations, with epiphanies as well as new evaluations regarding the homeland. Hall admits he learned Jamaican history only by leaving and seeing it from afar. Migrators may need to slay illusions about both homelands and newlands, and recognize their limitations. At this stage of the heroic ordeal, psychic distortions can emerge, such as ego inflation, arrogance, cockiness or abuses of power and privileges of new life, says Vogler.[31] There's also the possibility of underestimating the psychological after-effects of the ordeal of arrival, and thus falling into denial of loss and/or inconsolable grief along with anger and contempt for the newland.

Arrivées

Each migrant carries psychic and emotional baggage from the homeland—values and personal limitations which include: 1) despair over homeland situations which prompted leaving; 2) degree of choice to leave; 3) journey experiences; 4) right to enter newlands, and 5) personal characteristics of age, gender, health, race, religion, ethnicity and profession. Migrants are "travellers in unfamiliar territory, puzzled about what the future held, fearful about whether we would survive, unsettled by how different everything seemed and worried by how much the experience would change us."[32] Especially important is the legal right to enter a newland or as a refugee seeking asylum. Irregular/illegal/undocumented entrance carries special dangers and potential for exploitation.

Legal migrants

Legal migrants are non-citizens who satisfy bureaucratic requirements for visas, with the right to stay in the newland to study and/or work and perhaps seek citizenship through naturalization.[33] In 2016, the UN General Assembly adopted the *New York Declaration for Refugees and Migrants*; it was officially ratified in 2018 and cited 23 objectives to manage safe, orderly and regular migration locally, nationally, regionally and globally.[34] One objective is for homelands to "mitigate the adverse events and factors that hinder people from building and maintaining sustainable livelihoods in countries of origin."[35] Another is to reduce risks at various stages of migration and to acknowledge the impact of migration on destination countries. A third is to create conditions that enable migrants to enrich adopted societies.[36]

The media often stereotypes migrants as poor, criminal, uneducated, desperate and violent persons. The reality is most migrants are not from the world's poorest and most destitute regions, because people have to be able to afford to leave homelands.[37,38,39] Immigration specialists Portes and Rumbaut argue the new economics of migration are not driven by absolute need, but relative deprivation.[40] A family sends a member abroad—an anchor or seed migrator—to "generate sufficient income to 'catch-up' with the levels of consumption and lifestyle that are already present and visible among others nearby."[41] Today, in the US, most migrants are from middle-income nations and issued visas only if they have investment capital and/or higher educational credentials. In 2003, "the proportion of the foreign-born with a college degree, 26.5% was essentially the same as native-born."[42] Compared to US-born citizens, most migrants have better health,[43] higher education levels,[44,45,46] work longer hours,[47] have strong moral values,[48] and carry the desire to return home someday.[49,50,51] It's suggested that migrant xenophobia may arise from envy and resentment. In contrast, in France, the legal, temporary Algerian migrant workers are mostly pauperized peasants who have resorted "to the extreme, or even desperate, solution of emigration."[52] Their arrival experience is one of astonishment in encountering a world so profoundly different from their rural homeland culture. Through waged labour, they are "depeasantified," and transformed into the sub-proletariat with a "new temporal consciousness and a new social consciousness."[53] Consequently, in the homeland, they no longer fit in. Their realities of arrival and return are social-psychological ordeals comparable to facing Medusa and other dragons.

Montero interviewed 400 people who arrived in Canada before 1977. One recalled an arrival ordeal as utter loneliness, of missing people and homeland culture.[54] Another who stayed behind to save money so she and the children could afford to join the husband and father in the newland faced an unexpected dragon upon arrival—the discovery of his having taken a new wife. Without money to return home, they had to stay.[55] One couple described their arrival ordeal as over-crowded housing. Due to lack of monies, they shared a one-bedroom apartment with eight others. Their son's ordeal, a tied involuntary migrant, was going to school in a new language. He found the whole thing so stressful, he began to stutter.[56] Another admitted to instant assimilation or *localitis:* "When I first came here I wanted to be absorbed. It was almost an act of amputation. I needed so much to be accepted."[57] In contrast was an arrivée's ordeal of homesickness described as a year of crying,[58] culture shock and disillusionment,[59] discussed in detail in *The Psychology of Culture Shock*.[60] The concept of culture shock is explored in many dimensions: acculturative stress, cultural knowledge, host-culture relations, personal resources such as self-efficacy and skills, situational variables and social support.[61]

Most arrivées do not receive settlement help, but in the US some labourers are given resettlement assistance.[62] In chain migrations, arrivées are helped by family or homeland community members who are established in the newland. Many social services are provided by religious and ethnic organizations in Canada,[63] Europe,[64] and the US.[65,66,67,68,69] In New York's Chinatown, "churches provide housing, food, employment, and a safe haven to Chinese recently arrived from the Fuzhou region of China."[70] And "in addition to direct assistance, religious centers also foster networks that often lead to mortgages, housing, jobs, and business opportunities that facilitate social and economic adaptation."[71]

In summary, for voluntary, legal migrants, the primary arrival ordeals and heroic tasks are settlement issues: housing, employment and health services, and facing inner attitudes, expectations and disappointments that put them at risk for physical and mental health problems.[72]

Involuntary migrants: refugees and exiles

Refugees encounter bureaucratic arrival ordeals. Being a "refugee is not a matter of personal choice or definition, but a government decision based on legal guidelines and political expediency."[73] Refugee status was defined after WWII in the 1951 United Nations Refugee Convention,[74] which outlines official criteria for eligibility and asylum.[75] Two models of refugee criteria exist: 1) a security model, where refugees are perceived as threats to national security; and 2) an individual rights model, where asylum seekers are seen as having potentially justifiable claims for protection determined upon merits.[76] Yet there's little international agreement and cooperation about what a refugee is, and few "fair, efficient and expeditious procedures for the determination of refugee status/entitlement."[77] Across Europe, there's great variation in the definition of "refugee," and acceptance rates. What's important, says Goodwin-Gill, is the capacity to mediate, intervene and share responsibility for the protection of refugees, with flexible policies that permit "moving between immediate protection, longer-term asylum and third country resettlement."[78] Other issues are "national and international institutional mechanisms competent to deal with and promote migration and migration management,"[79] and "integration of human rights doctrine into legislation, administration and policy making."[80]

Internationally, a new framework is needed for the better management of migration-based human rights law and international obligations, as well as cooperation and the right of refugees to return to their homelands.[81] Proposals have been made to expand the eligibility criteria for refugees to include persons fleeing war and civil strife, since irregular (illegal) migration is now the primary reason that so many migrants are in refugee camps.[82]

Although the number of refugees entering the US is seen as high, it actually "pales in comparison to that of regular immigrants ... and temporary workers."[83] An applicant for refugee status must establish and prove the fear of homeland persecution in one of five protected rights: race, religion, nationality, political opinion, or social group.[84] In Canada, asylum can be sought: 1) upon arrival (Persons in Need of Protection) with the establishment of reasonable fear of being subjected to torture, risk to life, risk of cruel treatment or punishment if sent back, or 2) from residing outside the homeland in a transit camp (Convention Refugees).[85] Researchers say that during escape rape, forced "survival sex" and other physical abuses are common for women.[86] But this abuse is notoriously difficult to prove when seeking asylum.[87,88] And it's not just on the journey: survival sex is for many the dragon or primary arrival ordeal. And later, it's often the only work available.[89,90]

Refugees are defined in terms of their homeland exit[91] as "anticipatory" or "acute."[92] Anticipatory refugees are first to arrive. They are usually wealthy and educated and have access to information prompting the whole family to prepare to leave in anticipation of a new life elsewhere. Acute refugees flee when their situation is too dangerous to stay. Usually they lack resources to leave earlier and flee only when there are no other options. During their escape, they may suffer severe psychological or physical harm and stress, as well as the stress of being unable to protect family members and/or witnessing torture, rape, or murder of others. Not surprisingly, they often arrive in a state of shock and face uncertain futures. The most common stressful events witnessed or endured during leaving are the death or imprisonment of a family member, fleeing alone, negotiating exit bribes, being physically assaulted, fears of being killed, being in a refugee camp for more than two years, and being unable to communicate with family left behind and not knowing what has happened to them or where they are.[93] Depending upon the social-cultural distance between country of origin and host country, culture shock upon arrival may be extreme.[94,95] Studies of refugees from Vietnam, Laos and Cambodia report their "experience prior to and during escape emerged as the most powerful predictor" of later stress levels and demoralization as measured by the General Well-Being Scale.[96,97]

The context of reception of the host country is important, especially for refugee children who have special needs.[98] Children who arrive alone may be placed with a foster family that speaks an unfamiliar language and has a different culture. Children who arrive with family may struggle from family fragmentation and/or loss of members. Many child refugees on the journey experience violence and torture, or witness atrocities. Child psychiatrist Hodes notes that even for refugee children not exposed to war "the rate of psychiatric disorder was found to be almost twice as high as among peers of the same age."[99] He postulates that the rate is likely higher for those who are exposed to war and have experienced other negative situations, and concludes "many refugee children are impaired with a range of psychological problems and disorders, and benefit from mental health intervention."[100] At the London Medical Foundation for the Care of Victims of Torture, Burnett and Peet report some refugee children have previously been "abducted to become child soldiers and forced to commit violent acts themselves."[101] So, while it's not surprising that refugee children may seem mature beyond their years, they may be deeply traumatized and psychologically immature. School is therapeutically recommended, but many are unfamiliar with school and struggle with the student role itself.[102]

Zahar studied documents left by 50 million refugees to the US between 1846 and 1940. At arrival, disillusionment was common: "It wasn't the America we knew from movies and books ... I was deeply, deeply disappointed. To me, America was behind. We lived better in Czechoslovakia."[103] In *Ignorance*, Kundera[104] tells of his personal migration experience, the ordeals of arrival and the emotional costs of being a refugee, including repeated nightmares of hell-escaped and paradise-lost.[105] In *Love and Exile*, Singer describes his arrival ordeal and feelings of being uprooted. It was "as if we had dropped down here from another planet."[106]

Refugees with pre-existing mental health issues, anxiety or depression, and those who suffered persecution in their homeland[107] do not suddenly recover upon arrival. Compared to voluntary migrants arriving with optimistic expectations, language competency and social supports, refugees and exiles are vulnerable. They carry the emotional stresses of homeland rejection, of being pushed out and the experience of delays in gaining status papers, independence and a new life.[108,109,110] Although locations and conditions of transit and refugee camps may vary, their effects are similar. While there, people begin to realize their losses, leading some to become apathetic and helpless; others may become manic and aggressive. Those in camps the longest show the highest rates of psychopathology.[111]

For many countries today, the rising number of refugees seeking asylum is a pressing issue. In Canada, for instance, the number crossing from the US at clandestine border sites often rises beyond the country's ability to process them efficiently.[112] During the two-year wait-time for processing, refugee claimants are literally "in limbo,"[113] without passports or the right to work: "According to an internal report from the Canadian Immigrant and Refugee Board, if these rates of border crossing continue, the wait could be as long as eleven years by 2021."[114] A similar situation exists in the UK where

> the government has been accused of leaving thousands of people in a "state of limbo" ... people who have lived in the UK for more than a decade say they have been made suicidal by the delays, unable to visit dying relatives or apply for jobs.[115]

Some UK asylum seekers have waited twenty years for decisions,[116] a situation described as "barbaric" because "asylum seekers are not allowed to work,"[117] given a bare "allowance of £37.75 a week,"[118] and often live in shared rooms described as slum-like. In 2018 in the US, depending upon the entry state, wait-times for refugees to *apply* for citizenship (*getting* it is another step) range from 10 to 26 months.[119] Thus, time and number are modern monsters of the ordeal of arrival.

Irregular or undocumented (illegal migrants)

Carens, in *The Ethics of Immigration*, reminds us the terms "illegal" and "undocumented" migrant are not correct. Officially, they're "irregular" migrants, a more accurate and less pejorative term that carries awareness of their human rights regardless of status.[120] Irregular migrants who are victims of crime and/or in need of medical care have difficulty seeking help, because it exposes them to discovery and deportation.

In 2018 in the US, there were an estimated 11 million irregular migrants.[121] Some had entered legally and then overstayed their visas. Others, guided by smugglers, had clandestinely crossed borders without valid passports or visas.[122] Of these, some were pushed from homelands without valid papers due to social, political and financial conditions that made it impossible to procure them. Others who experienced difficult escapes suffer from PTSD, but don't meet the outdated and limited criteria for asylum.

Many countries set limits on the number of refugees permitted annually. When the number has been reached, it leaves late-year arrivals with no alternative but that of becoming subterranean irregular migrants, who live in fear for their safety and survival.[123] Irregular migrants are especially vulnerable to exploitation and discrimination. When they're suffering with a mental or physical illness, they are less likely to receive entrance and assistance, and at the same time are "more vulnerable to stress and psychopathology as compared with the legal immigrants."[124] Lacking employment rights, sheer necessity forces them into the irregular labour force of underpayment and overwork. "Fractured self-esteem, irritability, regressive daydreaming and bad tempers are rampant in this sub-population."[125] It's only with the assurance of civil status that important intra-psychic work of mourning and adaptation can truly begin, says Akhtar.[126] However, not all irregular migrants are innocent victims of economic and political situations. In 2017, at the US/Mexican border, 100,000 irregular migrants arrived in 60 days.[127] Many came via paid smugglers who had coached them on how to pass border tests. Single arrivées were paired with children because by law children cannot be held longer than 20 days. At one border in 2017, there were "600 fraudulent families" and "alleged fathers" arrested for "multiple felony offences of rape, oral copulation, forcible sexual penetration, and endangering or causing injury to a child."[128]

Migration officials

It's important to acknowledge the difficult and strenuous work of migration officials who play important roles in migrant journeys. More than a hundred years ago, on 17 April, 1907, the Ellis Island reception centre in New York City showed a record-breaking day of almost 12,000 people being processed.[129] The work carries high interpersonal and emotional costs, with vicarious trauma and high levels of burn-out of legal advocates and adjudicators.[130,131,132,133] British intake workers experience vicarious trauma: "The need to negotiate the personal, emotional consequences of the persecution stories of 'others' is one that affects all professionals working in the asylum arena."[134] "Applicant accounts of fear, trauma, violence and persecution are central to their claims of asylum. These narratives are, at a human level, primed to provoke emotional responses, not only in the narrator but also in those to whom the account is relayed."[135]

Stage 9: possession of the treasure

After the ordeal of arrival with its risk and taste of death, the hero is free to claim the treasure.[136] In myth, Campbell reminds us, the treasure is not given—it must be won or seized.[137] This may require engaging one's inner trickster, a psychological state that carries with it the potential to self-intoxicate and lose one's boundaries.[138] Examples are Prometheus stealing fire from the gods, and Adam and Eve tasting the apple and gaining the treasured knowledge of good and evil. Possession of the treasure may require an initiation—a death-and-rebirth rite—and renaming, that signifies a new person has been born. In an earlier era, some émigrés to the West anglicized their names or simplified the spelling. US President Trump's family, for example, shortened their Germanic name, Trumpf.[139] Ellis Island migration officials are said to have imposed name changes, but Ault found if name changes occurred, they happened at departure in the homeland when clerks wrote the passengers' names on the ships' manifests. Officials at Ellis Island simply matched names of arrivées with those on the manifests. Because many émigrés did change their names within the first five years after arrival, in 1906 the American Naturalization Act was passed, requiring documentation of name changes.[140]

Arrival challenges

A Seventh Man: A Book of Images and Words about the Experience of Migrant Workers in Europe, written forty years ago by Berger with photographs by Mohr,[141] explores temporary legal migrant workers who left homelands in the hope of transforming the futures for self and families. Usually the most enterprising of their generation, within days migrants had learned unskilled labour jobs. In the homeland, their "lost labour" led to "ghost villages" and under-developed economies. Because local land-owning and moneyed classes weren't interested in industrial development or agricultural mechanization, when the migrant worker returned, there was still no work for him or her and their foreign experience was "not applicable to the village."[142] It belonged elsewhere which meant "an assured place for him no longer exists in his village."[143] The only choice was to return to Europe as temporary migrant workers.[144] Not being eligible for citizenship, some still remained as irregular migrants and in *jus soli* countries, their children were eligible for citizenship.

Possession of the treasure depends, to some degree, upon the host-country's reception and if adaptation is enabled, as well as migrants' willingness to acculturate. When Berger wrote about migrant workers in 1975, they were already important to Europe's economy and comprised 25% of the industrial labour force in France, Switzerland and Belgium.[145] In fact, migrants' temporary-employment status had become an economic necessity for European countries and their homeland families.[146] The situation is unchanged today: "governments and multi-national corporations plan their policies on a global scale, and the advantages for capitalism of worker migration being temporary are considerable."[147] The economics of temporary migrant workers makes them desirable employees because they bear the costs and risks of the journey, are motivated, diligent and willing to work for low wages with few benefits, and are "prevented or discouraged from settling permanently in the country in which they work."[148] In the US and Canada, temporary migrant workers are a much-wanted resource and not an "alien invasion"[149] as they are often portrayed. "A 2002 study of entrepreneurial activities among Latin American immigrants in the US found up to 58% of firms ... relied on transnational ties for their continued viability and growth."[150]

The situation of foreign professionals differs from that of labourers. Professionals whose credentials are accepted may find comparable work and need only to adapt. Those with non-recognized credentials face educational and employment challenges and disappointment that become social and financial ordeals. An early study of Sri Lankan migrants and refugees to Australia reports that despite good language skills and professional qualifications, more than half of the newcomers held positions of lower status than they had in the homeland.[151] Recognition of the credentialling problem of migrants has led some countries to establish credentials referral offices in foreign countries and on-line programs.[152]

Acute refugees are often unable to adapt, says family therapist Dow. The sudden unexpectedness of migration along with "experience of profound losses and cultural shock can lead to extreme adjustment problems on both the individual and family levels and may even throw them into chaos and disequilibria."[153] Other involuntary migrants may fall into clandestine and dangerous situations[154] and descend into psychological hells of anger and loss after arrival.[155]

Involuntary migration is related directly to later depression and indirectly to the weakening of social and psychological resources.[156] Thus, it's no surprise, says Akhtar, that psychological outcomes are better for legal migrants pulled from homelands with expectations of opportunity and psychological readiness to seize the treasure of newlands. PTSD impairs adaptation, since the aftermath of traumatic events and economic hardship often result in "poor social networks (e.g. loneliness and boredom, weak social integration), poor access to counselling services, socioeconomic/political instability,"[157] and no legal status and/or unemployment, detention and language difficulties. "The prevalence of post-traumatic stress disorder (PTSD) among migrants is very high (47%), especially among refugees, who experience it at nearly twice the rate of migrant workers."[158]

The *Selective Migration Hypothesis* attributes the increased rate of PTSD and migrant mental disorders to predisposition in migrants, yet a Dutch/Swedish team[159] found no such evidence. An alternate theory, *Migration Stress*, describe it as a "chronicity with a tendency to overwhelm the human adaptive capacity resulting in mental and/or physical illness."[160] This includes feelings of "not belonging to a single place"[161] and weak social conditions such as status documentation insecurity, work exploitation and poor housing, as well as "linguistic and cultural changes, loneliness, failure of one's migration project, and the everyday struggle to survive."[162]

Migration has been compared to mourning and as a risk factor for mental illness.[163] Seen as moving away from family, friends, language, culture, country, social status and social groups to enter a situation of insecurity,[164,165,166] it's also known as the "Ulysses syndrome"[167] described as a "U-shaped curve."[168] It starts at the top of the "U" with leaving and the lower curve representing a crisis stage of acute stress disorder characterized by "rejection or isolation, sadness, crying, sleeplessness, irritability, distrust, recurrent and intrusive thoughts, psychosomatic symptoms (headaches, fatigue, musculoskeletal pain), dissociative and somatoform symptoms. Stress reactions can occur with cognitive fatigue, role and personal shocks."[169] If migration stresses are not resolved, there's a high risk of mental illness, especially among those traumatized during migration and/or suffering from PTSD. The second prong of the "U" is adaptation. Health professionals are cautioned to distinguish between experiential reactions, like the Ulysses syndrome, that call for psychosocial support, and real mental illness, in order to avoid "psychiatrization and therapeutic nihilism."[170]

At the British Medical Foundation for the Care of Victims of Torture, physicians advise the use of arrival screening protocols to identify physical illnesses and psychological problems that hinder adaptation.[171] In refugee populations, there are high rates of tuberculosis, parasites, and lack of immunizations, dental disease and psychological problems: depression, anxiety, panic attacks and agoraphobia. Psychological issues usually arise from negative homeland events, escape experiences, or current social isolation and poverty accompanying refugee status. Host-country hostility and racism can also have negative effects on refugee mental health. Some refugees may want to tell their story—this can be cathartic—but it should not be assumed, as every culture has its own ways of help-seeking and coping with crisis. Mozambican refugees describe forgetting as their usual cultural means of coping with difficulties. Ethiopians call this "active forgetting."[172] For children, re-telling isn't always the best approach: it may re-traumatize them.[173]

Women refugees need special attention because their situations are often more precarious. They are more "vulnerable to physical assault, sexual harassment and rape,"[174] yet their experiences and fears are not always taken seriously. After arrival, women may have to take on new and unfamiliar roles and responsibilities. Migrant training and employment programs are usually targeted for men and can leave women unable to financially care for themselves and children. If the husband is unemployed and the wife gets a job (usually menial), this can create stress in the marriage based on traditional gender roles. So, it's not surprising divorce and domestic violence are common in refugee populations. When a woman's refugee status is tied to her husband's and he abandons her, then she and the children can lose their migrant status. Since women from some cultures are less likely to be literate or fluent, they are often not seen or heard or personally assessed, despite some having been mutilated and having experienced other harms.[175]

Summary

Archetypes are primary structures of perception linking body, mind, psyche, instinct and image with their polar aspects manifesting as complexes, or autonomous emotional seizures of feelings, images and ideas. Psychological complexes exist about land and migration. The context of homeland exit (voluntary or forced); timing (anticipatory or acute), and context of reception (acceptance or rejection) are fundamental to adaptations. All migrants face degrees of ordeal at arrival and status at entrance is especially important. For legal migrants, there are social, psychological and organizational factors. For refugees seeking asylum, there are additional bureaucratic factors and irregular migrants face discovery. Assessment of health status at arrival and the often precarious situations of women refugees' status, rights and living situations need to be ascertained. Refugees and irregular migrants are at risk for higher rates of family violence and divorce.

Notes

1. Williams, 2007.
2. Vogler, 1998/2007:155.
3. Eisenbruch, 1991:673–680.
4. Van Oudenhoven et al., 2006:637–651.
5. Sakamoto & Zhou, 2005:209–229.
6. Ndeti, 1981:264–277.
7. www.merriam-webster.com/dictionary/localitis
8. Young-Eisendrath, 1992:159.
9. Jung, CW8:¶216.
10. Samuels et al., 1986/2000:49–50.
11. Ibid.:150.
12. Morais, 1986.
13. King James Bible, 2014.
14. Jung, 1998:373.
15. Hall & Schwartz, 2017:135.
16. Williams, 2007:xvii–xx.
17. African foreign-exchange students in Canada on mountain trips usually slept. Being used to the deserts, they said they were unable to bear the green vastness of forests and mountains.
18. Denford, 1981:325–333.
19. Akhtar, 2007b:167.
20. Ibid.:173.

21 Jacoby, 1985.
22 Jung, CW16:216.
23 Von Franz, 1995:188.
24 Vogler, 1998/2007:160.
25 Ibid.:155–156.
26 Williams, 2007.
27 Wikipedia, 2018: Medusa.
28 Wikipedia, 2019n:Albert Camus.
29 Wikipedia, 2019n: Frantz Fanon.
30 Hall & Schwartz, 2017:149.
31 Vogler, 1998/2007:182.
32 Hall & Schwartz, 2017:153–154.
33 Mulder et al., 2001.
34 UN Refugees and Migrants, 2018.
35 Ibid., 2018.
36 Ibid., 2018.
37 Dixon & Linz, 2000.
38 Espanshade & Calhoun, 1993.
39 Pew Hispanic Center, 2006.
40 Portes & Rubens, 2006:16.
41 Ibid.:16.
42 Ibid.:15.
43 Reuters Health Information, 2018.
44 News News Desk, 2018.
45 *The Economist*, 2018.
46 Grant, 2009/2018.
47 Vickers, 2017.
48 Fuller & Guerrero, 2018.
49 Admin, 2016.
50 Guarnaccia, 1997.
51 Portes & Rumbaut, 2006.
52 Sayad & Macey, 2004: 99.
53 Ibid.:91.
54 Portes & Rumbaut, 20016: FP.
55 Ibid.:28.
56 Ibid.:47–49.
57 Montero, 1977:Frontspiece.
58 Ibid.:87.
59 Ibid.:125.
60 Ward et al., 2001.
61 Ibid.:40.
62 Portes & Rumbaut, 20016:20.
63 Bailey-Dick, et al., 2015.
64 Schär & Geisler, 2008.
65 Alba et al., 2009b.
66 Campion, 2003.
67 Ebaugh & Pipes, 2001.
68 Menjívar, 2001.
69 Min, 1992.
70 Cadge & Ecklund, 2007:363.
71 Ibid.:363.
72 Dow, 2011:211.

73 Portes & Rumbaut, 2006:31.
74 United Nations High Commissioner for Refugees, 2018.
75 Rousseau et al., 2002.
76 Goodwin-Gill, 2001:15.
77 Ibid.:15.
78 Ibid.:15.
79 Ibid.:15.
80 Ibid.:15.
81 Ibid.:16.
82 Gunning, 1989:85.
83 Portes & Rumbaut, 2006:32.
84 Wikipedia, 2018.
85 LegalLine.ca, 2018.
86 Wikipedia, 2019n.
87 Baillot et al., 2014.
88 Amnesty International, 2016.
89 Rosenberg, 2016.
90 Wikipedia, 2019n.
91 Portes & Rumbaut, 2006:179.
92 Dow, 2011:211.
93 Portes & Rumbaut, 2006:182.
94 Dow, 2011:211.
95 Ward et al., 2001.
96 Portes & Rumbaut, 2006:181.
97 Longo et al., 2017.
98 Pine & Drachman, 2005.
99 Hodes, 2001:229.
100 Ibid.:229.
101 Burnett & Peel, 2001.
102 Ibid., 2001.
103 Zahar, 2016:236.
104 Kundera & Asher, 2003.
105 Zahar, 2016:253.
106 Singer, 1984:265.
107 Yakushko, 2008.
108 Escobar & Gara, 2000.
109 Hondagneu-Sotelo, 1994.
110 Salgado de Snyder et al., 1996.
111 Dow, 2011:211.
112 Statistics Canada, 2018: Immigration.
113 Zilo, 2018.
114 Hopper, 2018.
115 Bulman, 2018.
116 Chambers, 2018.
117 Lyons, 2018.
118 Lyons, 2018.
119 The Associated Press, 2018.
120 Carens, 2013:129–130.
121 Passel, 2018.
122 Dow, 2011:211.
123 Akhtar,1999/2004:33.
124 Dow, 2011:211.

125 Akhtar,1999/2004:33.
126 Ibid.:33.
127 Cuthbertson, 2018:1.
128 Ibid.:3.
129 Ault, 2016.
130 Zimmerman, 2002.
131 Jaffe et al., 2003:1–9.
132 Levin & Greisberg, 2003:245.
133 Surawski et al., 2008:16–29.
134 Baillot et al., 2014:509.
135 Ibid.:509.
136 Sayad & Macey, 2004:175.
137 Campbell, 1949/1973:155.
138 Vogler, 1998/2007:179.
139 Blair, 2015.
140 Ault, 2016.
141 Berger & Mohr, 1975:221.
142 Ibid.:221.
143 Ibid.:221.
144 Ibid.:78.
145 Ibid.:12.
146 Ibid.:18.
147 Ibid.:111.
148 Portes & Rumbaut, 2006:38.
149 Ibid.:24.
150 Ibid.:31.
151 Iredale & D'arcy, 1992.
152 Tilson et al., 2009.
153 Dow, 2011:210.
154 Akhtar, 1999/2004:33.
155 Von Franz, 1999.
156 Dow, 2011:211.
157 Bustamante et al., 2017:223.
158 Ibid.:220.
159 van der Ven et al., 2015.
160 Bustamante et al., 2017:221.
161 Ibid.:221.
162 Ibid.:221.
163 Serrano Diaz de Otalora et al., 2011.
164 Ibid., 2011.
165 Achotegui, 2002.
166 Shelley, 2002.
167 https://en.wikipedia.org/wiki/Ulysses_syndrome
168 Serrano Diaz de Otalora et al., 2011:476.
169 Ibid.:476.
170 Ibid.:476.
171 Burnett & Peel, 2001.
172 Ibid., 2001.
173 Dyregrov et al., 2002.
174 Burnett & Peel, 2001.
175 Ibid., 2001.

Chapter 4

Phase 4
Post-migration—home again

Chapter 4 explores the final three stages of the migrant's journey from arrival to new order in newlands. Stage 10, "The road back," may be a return to the homeland or a psychological return with persistent longing and replication of the homeland in the newland. With Stage 11, "Resurrection," the emergence of a new self in the newland is neither a simple nor a linear process.[1,2] Although today's modern multicultural societies encourage dual citizenship, some countries still require relinquishing homeland citizenship.[3,4] Regardless, both require inner changes,[5,6] and several models are discussed here. Stage 12, "Return with the treasure," represents a psychological shift where the newland becomes a new homeland and the migrant a citizen.[7] The role of organized religion in adaptation is also discussed.

Stage 10: the road back

In Homer's *Odyssey*, when Odysseus left for the Trojan wars to release captured Helen, he always intended to return home—it just took longer than expected.[8,9] Many migrants arrive in newlands with the intent to return,[10,11,12] and one-third *do* return.[13] This is known as the "migration paradox," and in Canada in earlier days was often called "the $1,000 immigrant ticket," which represented the cost for the return voyage home. Iraqis in Helsinki and Rome who arrived with the intent to return were interviewed—this expectation was interpreted as a cultural fantasy that impairs integration.[14] Migrant nurses in Italy from India also planned temporary stays, but most settled. Although reported to be happy, they considered leaving for their children's education arguing that Italy was "not a good place to acquire competencies for the international market and the future employment opportunities for their descendants."[15]

Not all migrants want to return.[16] For many academics, diplomats and professionals in medicine, military and missions, relocation is a way of life,[17] and often they're "never quite sure where home is."[18] Some see themselves as internationalists,[19] whose roots span the globe—home is where they are.[20] Grass-roots internationalism ranges in degree:[21] known as "globalization from below,"[22] it can be prompted by "globalization from above."[23] Transnationalism empowers migrants: it invests them with a sense of purpose and self-worth and acts as "an effective antidote to the tendency towards downward assimilation":[24] "Migrants may mobilize around a whole host of issues: immigrant politics (to better their situation in the receiving country, homeland politics, emigrant politics, and diaspora politics) and trans-local politics."[25] Homeland organizations engage with migrant nationals.[26] Migrants are most likely to engage in homeland politics when newlands don't allow settlement, but only permit labour migration and foreigner enclaves.[27]

In the myth, when Odysseus arrived home by ship he was sound asleep, so the captain left him in a safe haven on Ithaca's shore. Being asleep is symbolic of a lack of consciousness. For voluntary migrants, the equivalent may be unrealistic expectations, and for involuntary migrants and exiles, it may be negative emotions, culture shock and/or anger, confusion and loss. Caught in PTSD trauma or the distress of homeland politics, migrants are easily recruited to participate in transnational politics and may not be fully present or awake in the newland.

Stuart Hall recounts arriving in Oxford as a student "possessed" by thoughts of returning home.[28] In the "ambiguous pleasures of exile"[29,30] and caught in disavowal, he postponed the decision to return. Disavowal, Hall defines as a "complicated psychic maneuver" allowing migrants to "'know' and 'not know' at the same time."[31] Disavowal suppressed his inner issues, he says, concealed them and "let him sleep suspended between two worlds"[32] until the decision to stay emerged. "I'm not conscious," he says "when or for what particular reason the decision to stay was finally made."[33] It took the "form of a long postponement. By the time I thought I really had to decide, I discovered the decision had already been made."[34] After deciding to stay in England, Hall admits disavowal protected him from "shattering of illusion ... a process of protracted disenchantment ... a bewildering farrago of reality and fantasy."[35]

Migrants often resort to "dissociative mechanisms"[36] such as idealizing the newland and devaluing the homeland as persecutory. These permit them to avoid "mourning, remorse, and depressive anxieties which would otherwise be aroused and intensified by the migration, especially if it was undertaken voluntarily."[37] Differences exist in attitudes of voluntary and involuntary migrants. Voluntary migrants mourning for homelands may be caught in idealizations, accompanied by depressive anxieties and guilt. Involuntary migrants, especially those who have suffered persecution, may mourn their loss accompanied by anxiety and paranoia.[38]

The loss of homelands is compared to mourning loss of a loved one, says Levy-Warren: "Bit by bit, the mental representations of people, places, and various kinds of symbols associated with the culture are brought to mind. The representations are first invested with great emotional intensity and gradually diminish in their emotional significance."[39] She distinguishes between culture shock—a function of lack of ego strength—and culture loss—where migrants with strong egos encounter cultural impoverishment in the newland and experience a sense of loss.[40]

Life-stage timing of migration is important. "A move made with parents within the first five years of life is only a geographical move for the young child,"[41] says Levy-Warren. At this age, culture "is almost entirely associated with the primary caretakers, so that the 'culture' for the child moved with the family."[42] And when young children experience upset and anxiety during migration, it's primarily a reflection of the caregivers' mindset.[43] Adolescents and adults with strong egos and an established sense of culture may experience culture loss.[44] The degree of choice in migration and amount of time available to prepare physically and psychologically for migration affects the sense of culture loss as does the duration of the move as temporary or permanent and degree of cultural distance between the lands. When there is cultural consonance of one's values and self-esteem, "the experience of culture loss or culture shock is, then, dependent on the stability and differentiation of the individual's mental representation of culture."[45]

Common psychological coping mechanisms for the losses of migration are disavowal and persistent longing or dwelling in homeland fantasies and politics. Compulsive television watching or video gaming are also common. Still, longing for homelands may be driven by more than emotional attachment, loss, or nostalgia; it may arise from guilt over leaving and feelings of disloyalty[46] or survivor-guilt syndrome. Juni says migration-guilt includes a range of phenomena, such as personal guilt for what one did or thought or "passive guilt (for what one failed to do), guilt without culpability, guilt for the implications of one's survival, and inequity guilt."[47] Guilt may function as "damage control, as a rationale for victimization, as a form of punishment, as a tool to gain a sense of control or mastery over chaos."[48] Guilt may also be a "maneuver to preempt further punishment, as a method to avoid facing harsher emotional implications, or means of maintaining a relationship not otherwise feasible."[49] Disavowal, survivor-guilt and PTSD all present with symptoms of being "on edge," hyper-vigilance with anxiety, obsessive thoughts or actions, and depression.[50]

Montero's interviews with 400 migrants to Canada before 1977 tell of nostalgic longing. A boy who arrived from Italy at age 2 had no memory of ancestral lands, but said his father "would shoot off all the time about his village back home and how great it used to be and what a big shot he was there ... It was almost like he didn't live here at all ... wasn't living in the present."[51] When he turned 18, the family visited the homeland: "We get to my father's village and it's like nobody's ever seen him before ... this village is really, really small ... his big farm he had with his brother, it was like a big garden."[52] He describes the trip as a disastrous disappointment. It was "like his memory was playing a dirty trick on him."[53] This is not uncommon: revised memories can easily become part of one's identity, especially when facing the reality of homeland loss and giving up nostalgia leads to disillusionment and depression. "When we came back" he recalls his father being "sort of older, quieter, even smaller in a way. It was as if he didn't care anymore."[54]

Hron explores migrant psychology in works of literature and reports they are often "conflated with the stranger, exile or émigré."[55] Generally, at departure, migrant suffering is silenced and arrival in the newland is "greeted with a mixture of suspicion, resentment, and hostility."[56] Return can break "the spell of home:"[57] be it a village, town, province, or country. Writer Atwood recalls the family's internal migration: "My parents were both from Nova Scotia, a province from which they felt themselves in exile all their lives."[58] Dahlie says the lamentations of the Roman poet Ovid are the earliest written expressions of exile and bear striking resemblance to migrant literature. He quotes Ovid: "No interchanges of speech have I with the wild, and of the people: they hold intercourse in the tongue they share: I must make myself understood by gestures. Here ... I am a barbarian, understood by nobody."[59]

In a literature review of thought processes, Bluedorn explains thoughts occur simultaneously in the past, present and future[60] in patterns of "temporal focus"[61,62,63] and "time attitudes."[64] The Zimbardo Time Perspective Inventory describes these. 1) *Past Negative* or pessimistic thinking is suggestive of past trauma; 2) *Past Positive* is sentimental; 3) *Present Hedonistic* is desire for pleasure without regard to risk or consequences; 4) *Present Fatalistic* is lack of hope and belief in fate; and 5) *Future* is oriented towards achieving long-term goals.[65] Many psychologists see Future thinking as the healthiest, representing: goal setting, motivation, performance,[66,67] learning and self-regulation,[68] sense-making,[69,70] and psychological well-being.[71] Negative past-thinking[72,73] is linked to aggression, anxiety, low self-esteem, depression, perceived stress,[74,75,76,77] and suicidal ideation.[78] Other studies report homesickness[79] and/or rumination about past mistakes and regrets as well as diminishing current well-being.[80,81]

Knafo and Yaari see the migrant's progress as having four phases: 1) Planning, 2) Adjustment, 3) Mourning, and 4) Acceptance or assimilation.[82] Social suffering, they claim, is the most significant and "most pervasive and overlooked form of 'damage' inflicted on immigrants."[83] Because "there's no definition of 'structural social violence,' a multi-axial model of migrant social class, gender and culture is needed to study the dynamics of social suffering ... [which] results in alienation, racism, poverty and/or violence."[84] Portes and Rumbaut agree: "most of the suffering associated with immigration is psychological [producing] profound stress even among the most motivated and well prepared individuals, and even among the most receptive circumstances"[85] The primary suffering is loss of "home, familiar food, native music, accepted social customs, maternal language, childhood surrounding, and loved ones [and] lost aspects of their old selves."[86] And gender roles, a "central organizing principle of migrant life"[87] can be enormously altered by migration.[88]

The *Persephone Syndrome* is described as the long-term distress of married migrant Greek women in the US due to an overly strong and unresolved separation of the emotional attachment to their mothers.[89] Dunkas and Nikelly say the Greek family unit encourages an almost pathological mother-daughter loyalty and dependency, resulting in superficial interest in marriage. After migration, the fantasized return to mother results in resistance to adaptation. Although mother-daughter dependency-attachment in the homeland may not be pathological, in the newland with the stress of migration, geographic separation and differing cultural demands, it can emerge as overt pathology.[90]

In the West, talking about and expressing negative emotions about difficult events are seen as assisting in healing and recovery. Yet, at the Kent State Emotion, Stress & Relationships Lab, Coifman and associates report evidence for repressive coping or non-bereaving, which is seen as directing attention away from negative experiences, producing a sense of psychological protection that promotes resilience. One study of repressive coping, supported by neuroimaging, found the non-bereaved had fewer physical and psychological symptoms, and were rated better adjusted by close friends.[91] Related is Meaders's research contrasting eastern and western cultural attitudes towards resignation. In the West, resignation carries a negative connotation of lack of self-assertion; whereas in the East, resignation (in Japanese, *akiramenai*) is defined as adjustment and acceptance and is promoted as a virtue to be cultivated.[92] A leadership paper speaks to the importance of the capacity to think in the present rather than being caught in the past or future.[93] Simpson and French quote Bion, a former president of the British Psychoanalytical Society, who argues for being present in the moment without memory, desire, or even understanding;[94] as well as the importance of receptivity,[95] and the ability to tolerate ambiguity and the unknown. This perspective enables the emergence of new thought.[96]

When Odysseus, in the ancient tale, awakens in the hut where he was left sleeping, he discovers that, having been away for ten years and presumed dead, his wife Penelope has been pressured to remarry. To investigate, he disguises himself as a wandering beggar and goes to his home. Only his old dog, Argos, recognizes him. Not being seen or recognized upon return is common among migrant returnees and causes social suffering. Like many returnees, Odysseus is shocked to discover that what he remembers of home and the people are not the same as what he encounters. Called the *wound of return*, it arises from the lack of fit between memories and reality, and from not being recognized. This happened to Canadian artist Emily Carr's parents, who returned to England and found disappointment and disillusionment. "Everything seems different to what I expected," her father says. "But the change is in me, twenty-five years absence makes things appear different even in one's native country."[97] Like many returnees, they missed the newland and its newfound freedoms and decided migrate onward to the colony of British Columbia, now Canada.

Kulu says return migration is seen as "counter-stream" behaviour and not adequately studied.[98] As neither macro nor micro migration theories account for return migration, he proposes using Anthony Giddens's structuralist model which distinguishes between knowledge and beliefs.[99] Within this framework, Kulu explored the 1990s return migration of descendants of Russian Estonians who in the late 19th and early 20th centuries had been forced-marched to Russia. There, they lived with an "unconscious norm of homeland return" that awakened when their land was confiscated for collectivization and better-off peasants (*kulaks*) like themselves were liquidated as a class, and sent to the underdeveloped northern areas. Accompanying these deportations were purges of Estonian culture, education and language. During WWII when the Soviets occupied their ancestral homeland of Estonia, they sent the Soviet Army's Estonian Rifle Corps, who spoke the language. After demobilization, many stayed, triggering the return migrations of Estonians socialized to homeland return.[100] However, recent generations educated in Russian schools didn't want to go to their ancestral lands; they wanted to migrate internally to Russian cities for education and jobs.[101] The lack of shared generational desire to return to ancestral Estonia acted as a wedge between the generations.[102] Kulu concludes: nurturing ethnic identity acted as the carrier for return migrations of later generations.[103]

Sayad says the migrant is always suspect, seen as running away and betraying the homeland in an "original sin."[104] Brown explored the return migrations of thousands of Czech exiles following the fall of communism and the 1989 Velvet Revolution. The returnees who had escaped or were exiled were hurt and disillusioned by the resentment, xenophobia and discrimination they faced, and few stayed.[105] The unexpected inhospitality, illwill and resentment towards returnees was attributed to beliefs that émigrés had betrayed the state and exiles were deserters and traitors. Because of this, relatives who remained had been punished by authorities. Upon return, many exiles who had nurtured a fantasy of a "triumphant, happy homecoming"[106] were guilt-ridden since in post-communist Czech Republic, emigration carried a moral judgment. Although "the returnee was either a traitor or a faithful patriot, either a self-indulgent charlatan entrepreneur or a do-good humanist intellectual,"[107] they were seen as having abandoned the homeland and as a result, deserved to remain emigrants.[108] Further, the suffering of those who stayed was evidence of their political "legitimacy, national rights, and the key to national belonging."[109] Frohlick speaks of migration trajectories where after time, émigrés have stayed away too long to return.[110]

Eastern Europe historian Zahar tells Anna's story. Born in Czechoslovakia, as a child she escaped with her family to Vienna and her life was dominated by the desire to return. When political changes made it possible, the family did return and encountered so much hostility and rejection for having escaped years of local hardships that they went back to Vienna, their adopted home.[111] Hron describes Czech émigrés in 1989 following their dream of an exultant return home that was "shattered in the face of stereotyping, hostility and discrimination."[112] At issue was collective suffering, the ideological and "mythic charter for belonging in the Czech Republic."[113] Although émigrés had suffered the pain of loss and exile, they had not expressed it to protect the people at home. Because it was unseen, they were seen as not having suffered.[114] Hron cites Czech writer Linhartová, who lived in Paris and Japan. She describes exile as a cathartic, transformative process and recommends that everyone should try it.[115]

The *Lord Jim guilt complex*[116] is named after a character in a Joseph Conrad novel, and refers to the crew abandoning a sinking ship and not drowning. Those who escape homeland conflict can have a Lord Jim complex. Exiles may feel "shorn of the ritualization"[117] of departure. When this is compounded by loss and a Lord Jim guilt complex, newland adjustment is inhibited. Exiles fleeing for their lives may feel "bitter, resentful, and frustrated"[118] and as a defence may deny the present. The mindset is that of being "imprisoned between a past mythologized life (converted into the 'only thing worthwhile') and the future, represented by the illusion of being able to return home," yet "impossible to act upon."[119] In response, they "may reject everything the new country has to offer—anything that is different from their own customs, language, work, and culture."[120] Wanting to believe their exile is temporary, they put little effort into newland adaptation and/or regaining social and professional status. Often the resulting lower social standing in the newland may increase their feelings of insecurity and sense of persecution.[121] Anger and disappointment may be misdirected against the newland that gave them refuge.

In a documentary film, *My Mother's Village*, director Paskievich interviews Canadian descendents of Ukrainian refugees who are saddled with the responsibility to free ancestral lands from 500 years of occupation.[122] The Ukraine existed only in the imaginations of descendants. Because they were born in the newland and unable to visit their homeland under Soviet rule, they speak of survivor guilt and intergenerational transmission of PTSD, experienced as indefinable grief, feelings of homelessness and yearnings to return. They had a sense of belonging to the ancestral homeland, and an obligation to complete unfinished business. They had learned the language, practiced the culture and had engaged in repeated political actions to free the ancestral homeland. In fact, descendants are described as holding a holy reverence towards the Ukraine: "It lived inside your soul." One woman admitted being liberated and escaping the deep obligation by marrying an Anglo-Canadian and changing her name. When the Soviet Union broke up and Ukraine was freed, for some the desire to return was freed. When film-maker Paskievich visited his mother's village, he joined in the Ukrainian freedom songs and dances he had been taught in Canada. A Ukrainian elder offered him hard-won, survivor-wisdom: "Life stops us in our tracks, it's better to laugh than to cry."[123]

Historian Montero says the desire to return arises from lack of choice in leaving, i.e., exile, tied and other involuntary migrations. Caught in loss and resentment, they experience adaptation issues. Examples include Carmen who migrated from Spain for work and admitted it was the first time she had ever been alone. Filled with terrible loneliness, the idea of returning home became an obsession until she achieved a greater degree of personal independence and realized it was impossible to return to her old life. In fact, she didn't want it.[124] One man said: "after half a year, if we had been able to go back to Norway, we would have,"[125] then added, "no, I don't think so. I still had my pride. I wouldn't have gone back."[126] Another said he'd always thought of himself as a hard man, an emotionless sort of guy and was shocked migration was such a big challenge. "I used to cry," he said:

> Tears would roll down my face. I was feeling sorry for myself. I used to get drunk every day. I used to want to drown this damn situation [but] there was no going back [you'd be] a social outcast if you went back—a guy who couldn't make it.[127]

He admitted the desire to return remained for a long time, but because going back would be demeaning, he couldn't do it and didn't do it.[128]

Historian Petschauer tells of leaving Germany and migrating to the US at age 17 with his family. He felt a persistent nagging desire to return. Years later, while visiting extended family, he realized that migration had fostered his personal growth. He felt enormous debt to his newland mentors, who had helped him overcome outsider feelings and encouraged "independence of thought and action."[129] With his new perspective, he openly accepted "the impossibility of fully returning to my past,"[130] and was able to be fully present in the newland.

Scheutz who studied WWII homecoming soldiers was the first to identify the wound of return. Soldiers recounted emotional, psychological and physical distress in attempts to fit into home communities which had changed during their absence. They felt isolated because none at home could relate to the emotional and cultural challenges they had faced in war or their deep trauma.[131] More recent studies of *re-entry distress* look at cross-cultural aid workers, missionaries and sojourner students. Almost 50% of returning aid workers report re-entry distress due to the loss of sense of self and community.[132] Although returnees report creative thinking is a cognitive benefit of multicultural experience,[133] returning creates a need to "integrate disparate experiences"[134] that makes re-entry difficult. Janoff-Bulman explains: often such feelings arise from shattered assumptions and beliefs that the world is benevolent and meaningful.[135] Nearly half a million aid workers overseas will potentially experience re-entry distress of "disenfranchised grief,"[136] due to community expectations for them to be happy to be home.

"It's always more difficult to return and re-integrate than it is to go out,"[137] says Dr. Ruth Jensen, who worked in India and Nepal for twenty years. "One expects challenges on the outbound due to culture and language issues. When we return, we forget that people at home have moved on and changed too." She advises returnees to recognize that "you'll be a one-day wonder and those at home have stories to tell and we need to listen to them too."[138] Madison agrees: returnees often feel exotic and superior despite being envious of the material gains of those who remained at home.[139] A study of returning missionaries to Australia found links between re-entry resilience and "flexibility, expectancy, self-determination, denial using minimisation, mental health, social support, reintegration and personal spiritual connection with God."[140]

Reverse migration is sending newland children to parental homelands. Reasons given for sending American infants "home" range from their mother's need to work (69%), to lack of childrearing experience (33%), and inability to afford childcare costs.[141] The benefits are seen as better retention of ancestral language and culture, and support of family and friends. Yet, 81.5% of mothers said if they had reliable, affordable childcare in New York, they would have liked to have kept their children.[142]

The U-shaped migration model arose out of Oberg's 1955 US study of Norwegian scholarship students.[143] The first stage (arrival to six months) is adventurous; the second (six to eighteen months) is loneliness characterized by need for friendships made difficult by language deficiencies; and the third (eighteen months plus) is integration and becoming part of social groups. Oberg named the stages: "honeymoon," "crisis" and "recovery," and called the whole process "culture shock."[144] It arose, he said, from the loss of familiar cultural signs and symbols, and was an occupational emotional disease of students, missionaries and aid workers who idealize homelands and, feel fear and frustration in newlands, with which they refuse to engage . The period of greatest shock was just before adjustment began. In 1963, the U-shaped culture-shock model was expanded to a W-shape to include re-entry distress.[145] But neither U or W-shaped culture-shock models have shown firm research results because they describe some, but not everyone's experience.[146,147,148,149] In 2001, Kohls found that culture shock is lessened with language fluency and cultural preparation.[150]

The *Homecomer Culture Shock Scale*[151] and *Reverse Culture Shock Scale*[152] measure the wound of return and re-entry distress in explorations of work problems, host-culture attachment, culture, social withdrawal, alienation, insecurity and home-culture attachment. Studies show younger people and those with a spousal buffer exhibit lower distress scores on these scales.[153,154] Re-entry distress can be lessened with preparation, social resources and positive welcomes.[155] A study of 44 American managers returning from abroad reports those least prepared to return experienced the most cultural identity change and most severe repatriate distress.[156] The *Cultural Quotient* (CQ) measures cultural intelligence and adaptability[157] as a function of motivation, knowledge, strategy and behaviour,[158,159] and seen as important in today's globalized world.[160,161]

Stage 11: *resurrection*

In Homer's story, Odysseus was away for ten years and presumed dead. His wife, Penelope, was unwilling to accept this, and resisted the pressure to remarry with delaying tactics. When Odysseus had left, she began a new needlework project, saying if he was not home by the time she had finished, she would remarry. To ensure it would remain unfinished, each night Penelope would unpick that day's work. As the pressure to remarry increased, along with her rising fears of being murdered for her vast lands, she mounted a competition and agreed to marry the winner. In this way, she felt the decision was left to fate. Luckily, Odysseus had arrived home and entered the shooting contest, but instead of aiming at the target he shot the other suitor-competitors. Still, Penelope did not recognize the winner and set an impossible task. She asked him to move the marital bed, knowing it was impossible because Odysseus had built it using a living olive tree as one of the bedposts. When he said her request was impossible and why, Penelope recognized Odysseus and, it is said, accepted him in like-mindedness.

Hall describes like-mindedness as cultural adaptation arising through "a process of protracted disenchantment" that's "painful as well as exciting."[162] He admits like-mindedness "changed me irrevocably, almost none of it in ways I had remotely anticipated."[163] He says cultural adaptation is a formidable piece of psychic work that's not completed until there's a continuity of personal character between homeland and newland personalities.[164]

Cross-cultural psychologist Triandis notes: "certain virtues are universal —wisdom and knowledge, courage, love and humanity justice, temperance, spirituality and transcendence."[165] Cultural adjustment requires critical evaluation of these and conscious decision about changes.[166] Triandis lists ten social-cultural values:[167] 1) political freedom, 2) justice, 3) trust in fellow citizens, 4) brotherhood, 5) security, 6) social equality, 7) low rates of lethal accidents, 8) few environmental disasters, 9) individualism, and 10) peace.[168] He also calls attention to individual factors: a person should strive for a happy cooperative personality with a purpose and clear goals for personal growth and self-acceptance. Important too is good physical health, a good job, a good marriage, enough education and a wide circle of friends and acquaintances. Being conscientious, optimistic, open to others, and developing mastery are important, along with laughter which promotes good health and happiness.[169]

Kivisto, director of the American research laboratory on Transnationalism and Migration Processes defines multiculturalism as an analytic concept and normative precept.[170] He uses Parks' Chicago School of four stages of race relations as the model for multiculturalism: 1) contact, (2) conflict, (3) accommodation, and (4) assimilation.[171] He draws attention to the strong affinity of this model with modernization theory and its assumptions that change is inevitable yet occurs only gradually. Then, he turns to Taylor's Canadian idea of multiculturalism defined as the politics of recognition, where ethnic identities are preserved, and at the same time one has citizenship within a larger polity.[172] Important also in multiculturalism, Kivisto says, is national consciousness and refers to Marshall in Britain,[173] and his concept of the same, which ranges from a rigid perception of the nation as unchanging and exclusive whose members who refuse to embrace a British identity (Scotland, Ireland and Wales), to the new marginalized diaspora and fundamentalists who "view themselves as exile peoples, residing in a society whose liberal values are seen as antithetical to their own religious beliefs."[174]

Several change models describe migrant adaptation to multiculturalism. Dabrowski's *Positive Disintegration* model has five levels.[175,176] 1) Primitive integration is the ground zero of physical, social and cultural inheritance. 2) Unilevel disintegration describes a series of crises of emotional ambivalence justified by specific situations. 3) Spontaneous multilevel disintegration refers to a period of great "dis-ease" with inner conflicts arising from comparisons with what could or should be with the newland reality. Dabrowski says some migrants get caught at this third stage with challenges and potential for personal growth, increased autonomy and choice of a higher path. 4) Directed multilevel disintegration is a conscious review of oneself psychologically with reductions in reactivity and automatic conditioned responses replaced by conscious choices towards an authentic self. 5) The final level is integration and inner harmony heralding decision making relative to personal values with the creative expression of deep empathy.[177] Dabrowski's model has been equated to Maslow's hierarchy of needs, which was influenced by the transcendentalism of Emerson and Thoreau. Both Maslow's hierarchy of needs and Dabrowski's crisis-change model have an antecedent in Jung's model of psychic change and are highly relevant to migration (see Section 4.3 below).

Maslow's hierarchy of needs has physical and psychological aspects: food, water, sleep, safety and security, belonging and love, self-esteem and self-respect. All these must be met, Maslow says, before it's possible to reach the goal of self-actualization or creative self-growth and meaning in life.[178,179] It's illustrated in a Turkish study of effects of migration on illiterate children. With an average age of 13 years, they had been denied education and "made to work so as to meet the economic needs of families."[180] Unqualified and holding illegal jobs in unsavoury environments; they were pushed into delinquency and crimes of property to meet their families' basic physical needs.

Migration challenges are especially hard on fragile personalities who might have maintained a psycho-physical balance if they stayed in their homelands: migration can cause dissociation.[181] Some may have an initial conflict-free period, but then later collapse.[182] Halperin explains: "immigration challenges the stability of the individual's psychic structure and family organization and it has significant transgenerational implications. Its psychodynamics includes interrelated processes of mourning, discontinuity of identity and imbalance of self-esteem."[183] It's not unusual to meet refugees who "hold it together" during ordeals of escape and difficult journeys and show leadership within families or larger cultural groups, but after reaching safety they "collapse," mentally or physically. An Eritrean woman who escaped a war-torn homeland spent several years in an Israeli refugee camp and emerged as a leader. After being granted asylum and arrival in Canada, she "fell apart," challenged by severe PTSD.

A British team explored the higher rates of psychosis in migrant and minority populations in the UK, the Netherlands, Denmark, Sweden, Australia and the US.[184] In research reports, they found a diverse range of explanatory factors. 1) Selective migration claims those with vulnerability for schizophrenia are more likely to migrate. 2) Genetic evidence suggests an interaction between environmental factors and latent risk. 3) Neurodevelopment models show maternal viral infections, obstetric complications and natal vitamin D deficiency are linked to schizophrenia. (d) Substance use (cannabis) associated with psychosis. 4) Psychosocial factors of cumulative disadvantages of unemployment, living alone, and childhood separation from a parent and social environment including discrimination, isolation and social disadvantages lead to psychotic breaks.[185] They conclude, "there is now robust research linking urbanicity,[186] childhood trauma,[187,188] and social adversity (social defeat) over the life course with the onset of psychosis."[189]

A Hong Kong team noted the city has always been a society of migrants. In a comparison of the mental health status of mainland (migrants) and local adolescents, they found, contrary to their expectations, that migrant youth had better mental health than the local youth.[190] In another Chinese study of adult migrant workers, 25% of the men and 6% of the women could be classified as having poor mental health, attributed to financial and employment difficulties and interpersonal tensions and conflicts.[191]

The developmental psychology models of British paediatrician/psychiatrists, John Bowlby and Donald Winnicott, shed light on individual variation in migration. Bowlby's attachment theory[192] argues that infant psychological attachment with caregivers is an evolved survival mechanism. When alarmed by strange situations—representing survival threats—the securely attached infant will seek proximity and comfort with trusted caregivers. Secure attachment fosters psychological resilience. Infants who lack trusted caregivers are insecurely attached and to protect themselves, they respond to strange situations with anxiety, alienation and confusion and withdrawal. The Grinbergs suggest attachment differences may explain why some migrants "disintegrate" after arrival: "When the person loses the fantasy that the migration is temporary with the hope of prompt return, and it gradually dawns on him—for some it is a wrenching realization—that the loss and separation are definitive and irreversible."[193]

Winnicott's theory of the holding environment[194] begins with the premise that no parent is perfect and being "good enough," or generally reliable and loving, is sufficient to create a positive "holding environment" necessary for development of emotional cohesiveness that permits integration of current experiences. The security of positive holding environments permits expression of the "true" self. A lack of positive holding environments leads to development of a "false self" oriented towards meeting expectations of others. This is also known as a *Figure-Ground Gestalt* or perception of an object in relation to another.[195] In migration, a true self has an inner reference, whereas the false self has only an unknown other-as-reference and becomes confused and alienated, making adjustment and adaptation difficult or nigh impossible. The psychic transformations following migration require strong ego function, patience and perseverance to scrutinize, understand and bring to consciousness the "True Self."

In-depth interviews with British men, aged 40–45 years, who had lived in another country for more than three years, found that all had felt compelled to travel, that travel idealized and represented adventure.[196] Travel for those with fragile home attachments appeared to be attempts to heal childhood issues that held the potential for psychosis, perversion, delinquency and/or drug use.[197] Men with secure home bases reported fewer difficulties in migration adaptation and returning home.[198]

Cultural adaptation requires double consciousness, an awareness of belonging to more than one world, of being both here and there, of thinking about there from here and vice versa, and of being at home—but never wholly—in both places, neither fundamentally the same, nor totally different.[199] A primary characteristic of migration is that it requires an ongoing "cultural translation"[200] and is the price of psychic survival. A high level of internal migration in North America is the norm. In Canada the incidence is 8/1000,[201] and in the US it is 14/100.[202] Internal migration is hypothesized as a substitute for European revolution and the tendency to fight:[203] "Why raise your voice to contradiction and get yourself into trouble as long as you can always remove yourself entirely from any given environment should it become too unpleasant?"[204] Hirschman says when Europeans adopted newland mobility to solve problems, there was a haemorrhage of the best talent to newlands.[205] James Joyce insisted: "No one who has any self-respect stays in Ireland, but flees afar."[206]

Culture is defined as visible artefacts: food, clothing, tools, architecture and behaviours based on system codes: language, roles, rituals, values, beliefs and attitudes. Rudmin says:

> the presumption is that the strangeness of a new culture causes stress at time of contact (T1), which motivates the minority to have an orientation to be assimilated by the new culture, or to be separated from it, or to become bi-culturally integrated, or to just endure the stress of marginalization.[207]

This is not always true: the second culture may be embraced enthusiastically. Rudmin proposes a positive model of acculturation or second-culture learning,[208] requiring four things: "(1) information about the second-culture, (2) instructions, (3) imitation of second-culture behaviors, and (4) mentoring by persons competent in the new culture and caring enough about the acculturating person to be personally supportive."[209]

A review of research for measures of intercultural mobility and adaptation found four separate measures translated into measurement scales, showing "good reliability and adequate structural equivalence across languages":[210] 1) Brief Sociocultural Adaptation Scale (BSAS), 2) Brief Psychological Adaptation Scale (BPAS), 3) Brief Perceived Cultural Distance Scale (BPCDS), and 4) Brief Acculturation Orientation Scale (BAOS).[211] These show that the greater the adaptation of the migrant or sojourner (sociocultural or psychological), the lower the level of stress and anxiety and the higher the measures of self-esteem and satisfaction with life.[212] For migrants who fall into homeland replication in the newland, the evidence is "the greater the importance placed on maintaining the home culture, the poorer the sociocultural and psychological adaptation,"[213] and "the more importance placed on embracing the host culture, the better the adaptation."[214]

Cultural distance is defined in terms of climate, natural and social environments, ease of living, practical aspects—such as transportation, shopping and food, family life (closeness and time together)—social norms, including humour, values and beliefs (religion, politics, right and wrong);

the people (friendliness and stress levels), ease of making friends and language. The higher the score of social distance, the poorer is the adaptation.[215] Although some research reports benefits in migrants maintaining homeland culture, students who "downplayed the importance of the home culture while strongly endorsing the host culture, reported higher levels of adaptation."[216]

Stage 12: the hero's return

For the Hero archetype, the Return is the final stage. In migration, this implies consciousness of self and citizenship in the newland.[217] In the *Odyssey*, after shooting his wife's suitors, Odysseus was accosted by the citizens of Ithaca who wanted revenge, but the goddess Athena intervened, and persuaded them to make peace. In migration, this represents inner peace, which is achieved through a process of psychological transformation.

Jung[218] saw the ancient opus of alchemy changing base metal into gold as representing unconscious projection onto matter and a model of psychic transformation.[219] Edinger in *Anatomy of the Psyche: Alchemical Symbolism in Psychotherapy*[220] outlines the seven stages of alchemical-psychic transformation: *calcinatio, solutio, coagulatio, sublimatio, mortificatio, separatio,* and *coniunctio.*

1. *Calcinatio* is heating to drive off moisture and attain the essence. Psychologically, it symbolizes driving off emotions to find the basic mindset.[221] In migration, it may represent dissatisfaction with homeland situations or awareness of a lack of goodness of fit between the self and the homeland. A friend said by age 8, she had decided to leave for "America." Peterson says by age 12, he knew he had to leave his north-western frontier town.[222] *Calcinatio* may also be the fires of violence and war that desiccate the ruling principles of a land and forces citizens to flee. Today, it may be climate change and desertification that forces migration. What remains after *calcinatio* is "salt," which may symbolize the "bitter as salt" thoughts and memories of homeland circumstances that led to migration.
2. *Solutio* means to dissolve. In alchemy, *calcinatio* salt is the substance to be dissolved. Water is the universal solvent. Water symbolizes the womb and rebirth.[223] Psychologically, water represents questioning of ego attitudes and practices. In migration, *solutio* refers to recognition of differences in social-cultural practices and questioning of homeland attitudes, beliefs, values and practices. Water also represents baptism and purification. Edinger says psychological cleanliness suggests being aware of one's own dirt and expectations and not projecting them on to others.[224] In migration, it means not projecting homeland

expectations onto the newland. "The solutio experience 'solves' psychological problems by translating the issue to the realm of 'feeling' ... it answers 'unanswerable questions'."[225]

3. *Coagulatio* is coming together, or integration. It symbolizes ego and earth and "is often equated with creation."[226] Having become concretized, *coagulatio* represents "active, responsive, and participating,"[227] and can lead to further transformation. In migration, *coagulatio* is both attitudes and actions needed to adapt and integrate.

4. *Sublimatio* from the Latin means air and upward movement. Psychologically, it refers to dealing with concrete problems by rising above, and viewing them from a distance.[228] This requires ascent: the higher we go, the grander and more comprehensive is the perspective, but also the more remote we become and less able to have an effect on what we perceive.[229] In migration, often it's not until we leave families and homelands that we have a clear view of self, origins and situation. Following migration, it refers to the newcomer's detached, distant perspective of the homeland and the newland. Unconsciously, it implies judgement and being remote from the reality of the situation, including longing for the homeland.

5. *Mortificatio* means killing and death: "It has to do with darkness, defeat, torture, multination, death and rotting," and the "colour black."[230] Psychologically, it refers to the Shadow, or the part of ourselves that we don't see without effort. Recognition of the Shadow is important in the change process, because "out of darkness is born light."[231] And "outbursts of affect, resentment, pleasure and power demands—all these must undergo *mortification* if the libido tapped in primitive, infantile forms is to be transformed."[232] This stage holds potential for new beginnings. In migration, it requires emotional leaving of the homeland and giving birth to a newland psyche: "Just as evening gives birth to morning, so from the darkness arises a new light, the *Stella matutina*, which is at once the evening and the morning star."[233]

6. *Separatio* is division into component parts: "Order is brought out of confusion in a process analogous to that in which cosmos is born out of chaos in creation myths."[234] Pythagorean discovery of the opposites was psychologically important because it ushered in conscious existence through "separation of subject from object, the 'I' from the not-I."[235] In migration, *separatio* is decision making about what to retain from homelands and what to embrace in newlands.

7. *Coniunctio* is the final step, the culmination of the change process. There's a difference between the lesser and greater *coniunctio*: the former is the union of those things not yet differentiated.[236] In migration, these may be attitudes, values, or cultural beliefs not yet recognized that need transformation. The greater *coniunctio* is extreme

accomplishment, variously called the "Philosopher's Stone, Our Gold," and "Wisdom."[237] It's the remedy of the psychological state of one-sidedness.[238] Classical images are marriage,[239] miraculous growth of flowers,[240] the Biblical Song of Songs[241] and the New Jerusalem—"a beautiful, bejeweled city in the shape of a mandala [where] the process of civilization takes place."[242] Love is an ancient image of *coniunctio*: "Transpersonal love is at the root of all group and social loyalties, such as allegiance to family, party, nation, church and humanity itself," and is that "which holds things together."[243] In migration, the greater *coniunctio* represents cultural adaptation, respect and transpersonal love[244] with a sense of feeling at home and belonging in the newland, and becoming a contributing citizen.

Migration, seen metaphorically as an alchemical change process, can also be seen as the resurrection of a new self in a newland: "Adaptation to a strange (new) culture is a formidable piece of psychic work."[245] It calls for individual identity and continuity of personal character or personality and character that are stable and not split by homeland regressions. It enables a transcultural identity that represents the creative internal synthesis of true adaptation.[246] This is more difficult for involuntary migrants and exiles, so it's not surprising they speak of mixed feelings and of being betwixt and between in the newland.[247] Adaptation is not a process that can or should be hurried. In Israeli, 68 migrants from the former Soviet Union were interviewed one year after arrival. Those who made early attempts to resolve psychic splits between homelands and the newland initially showed lower levels of symptoms, but one year later their symptom levels were higher than those who did not adapt so quickly. Taking time to change is important, as precocious resolution is more likely to lead to later adaptation difficulties.[248]

Some migrants never fully adjust. Singer in *Love and Exile* admits: "I can't seem to become adjusted. I'm here over twenty years and I'm still torn between America and Russia. In the meantime, Russia has changed too and if I went back, I surely wouldn't recognize it."[249] Similar feelings were expressed by India's First Prime Minister, Jawaharlal Nehru who studied in Cambridge England.

> I have become a queer mixture of the East and the West, out of place everywhere at home nowhere. I am a stranger and alien in the West. I cannot be of it. But in my own country also, something, I have an exile's feeling.[250]

Migration research has borrowed from anthropology the concept of acculturation which now has become central in cross-cultural studies: acculturation signifies changes in behaviour, attitudes and cognitions.[251] Three acculturation styles have been identified: 1) Assimilation or superficial adoption of the dominant culture, 2) Integration or acculturation, and 3) Separation or marginalization or lack of adaptation.[252] In early stages of migration, "the exile may feel like a hero and the recipient of admiration and sympathy, but this may be difficult to integrate when it is experienced as betrayal of those they left behind or have died."[253] Attempts to reduce survivor-guilt may lead exiles to reject the newland, especially things that differ from homeland customs, language, work and culture.[254] This suggests that successful adaptation depends on symbolic *sublimatio* with the reduction of cultural distances between homeland and newland. While it's known that the greater the cultural difference, the more difficult and demanding is adaptation, multicultural integration also leads to the highest levels of individual and social satisfaction.[255]

In *The Psychology of Culture Shock*, four adaptation responses are noted:[256] 1) *Passing* or *localitis* is rejection of a "lower culture" of origin and uncritical adoption of the higher culture of the newland;[257] 2) *Chauvinism* is rejection of newland culture which is seen as alien, along with a retreat into homeland culture, militant nationalist and chauvinistic stances;[258] 3) *Marginalism* is vacillating between two or more cultures and not feeling at home in any,[259] and in 4) *Mediating* migrants are able to synthesize and acquire a genuine bicultural or multicultural personality.[260] An Australian cross-cultural relations team[261] referencing Argyle's[262] research on social skills training in interpersonal behaviours, calls for a cultural learning approach to migration to reduce culture shock.[263] Successful adaptation and acculturation are defined as "learning the culture-specific skills required to negotiate the cultural milieu"[264] to survive and thrive in newlands.[265]

Transnationalism was rare in the past and is possible today due to "technological innovations in transportation and communications and strength of sending nation-states, and their new attitude towards their respective immigrant diasporas."[266] For migrants, transnationalism is daily contact by telephone, email, Facebook and national news, as well as rapid travel. Transnational communities are emerging, with members having residences in more than one place: they travel back and forth and have influence in all of them.[267] An increasing shift towards "globalist and strong transnationalist perspectives"[268] challenges modern nations with the creation of a "mismatch between territorial and personal boundaries and citizenship,"[269] says Bauböck. This requires reorientation because democracy requires participation, and "citizens will only vote responsibly with a view towards the implications of their choices for the common good if they know that they will have to bear the consequences of the outcome."[270]

Differences between assimilation (replication) and integration (respect of cultural differences) in relation to ethnicity, race and religion, have been explored.[271] European countries can learn from the US and Canada where, at the individual level, there is a desire to belong and to feel like an insider, while at the collective level there's a desire to participate and make a contribution:[272] "Policies can seek to reduce the racial and religious barriers confronting immigrants and their descendents [with a focus on] citizenship and legal status."[273] Adelman's biography of philosopher Hirschman says he "detached himself from his family and city, but he never defined himself against them; neither did he mourn the loss or carry his displacement like a badge, a familiar default for exiles."[274] Like others, "he was a willing Odysseus, [and] an antecedent to our more 'globalised' intellectual types. The key is to be open to possibilities."[275]

Organized religion and cultural adaptation

Historically, religions have provided solace to migrants, facilitated adaptation and helped them to maintain links with homelands.[276] Ethnic enclaves are often intent on religious retention and transplanting religious heritages into the newlands.[277] Religious beliefs assist migrant adaptation by instilling "an important sense of identity and purpose,"[278] as well as maintaining social rituals, practices and networks, and setting up organizations that help migrants to "gain power and influence and combat prejudice and discrimination in their new society."[279] Religious practice can be private within the family or public in an organized community setting. Religions can marginalize migrants in tight-knit enclaves and lead the host society to acknowledge that what migrants bring to newlands is valuable and legitimate.[280] In the US, where 60% identify as Christians, migrants are said to be transforming religious life. "While millennials are walking out the front door," says Granberg-Michaelson, "immigrant Christian communities are appearing right around the corner, and sometimes knocking at the back door. And they may hold the key to vitality for American Christianity."[281]

In North America, religion is seen as a bridge to integration, whereas in Europe religion is seen more often to be a barrier to integration, especially the patriarchal religions, such as Islam, because of their social practices: arranged marriages, women's dress codes (hijab/niqab) and honour killings.[282,283] Europeans are seen as more secular than Canadians, who are seen as more secular than Americans of whom 60% identify religion as very important.[284]

Early American books, *Protestant-Catholic-Jew*[285,286] and *The Uprooted*,[287,288] claim Americans are more accepting of religious diversity than ethnic diversity, making it easier to construct a newland identity and create community via religion than via ethnicity.[289,290] In this process, churches, temples and synagogues play vital roles in providing physical, emotional, psychological and spiritual refuge, as well as settlement help, economic opportunities and social recognition.

In a literature review, the Canadian *Centre for Community Based Research*[291] found 91 studies exploring the roles of the church in migration settlements. They speak to: 1) vision, beliefs, values and attitudes that guide religious groups in acculturation; 2) the necessary structures to enable it, such as rituals, programs and organizational partnerships, and 3) processes or how the work is accomplished. Indeed, religious organizations provide the "three Rs" to migrants: refuge, respectability and resources.[292]

Refuge is provided by the religious community with networks of mutual support with co-ethnics offering fellowship and friendship in a familiar cultural environment and language. They act as "a source of solace and shelter from the stresses, setbacks, and difficulties of coming to terms with life in a new country."[293] They provide recognition for migrants who have suffered loss and downward mobility. And they act as community centres facilitating fellowship with their own, reducing traumas of migration and shielding and buffering negative experiences.[294] Functioning as comfort zones, they are bridges between homelands and newlands where migrants meet and "worship in their own languages; enjoy the rituals, music, and festivals of their native lands, share stories from their homeland."[295] The Lutheran Church in the US recently declared itself a "sanctuary church body" for undocumented migrants.[296]

Respectability is offered to migrants by religious groups. This is especially important for those denied social recognition or who have suffered downward mobility from migration. Being a good Christian, Muslim, or Buddhist brings respect within religious and ethnic communities and provides opportunities for leadership and service. Immigrant women's groups play central roles in religious groups in reproducing traditional ethnic cultures: food, decorations and social activities. The recent decrease in Catholic priests with increases in women's education and professional status has permitted women to compete with men for lay positions and honorific roles within the Church. Women's "involvement in the women's movement has mobilized Catholic women to demand and obtain greater participation in formal roles."[297] The numbers of women participating in religious organizations has increased in recent years, while the number of men has declined, a situation that is believed to be related to a loss of male status and authority through migration.[298]

Resources of religious communities assist migrants: "lawyers, financial planners, health-care providers, and others offer on-premises advice and services. Several have formal mechanisms, and all have informal ones, to help newcomers."[299] Religious institutions recreate and reassert homeland cultures with "worship in their own languages, enjoy the rituals, music, and festivals of their native lands, share stories from their homeland, and pass on their religious and cultural heritage to the next generation"[300] through language and history classes and ethnic celebrations.[301] A US study of Vietnamese children found church attendance and activities protect youth from neighbourhood gangs and perceived negative and immoral influences of American culture. The children's attendance strengthened ties in ethnic communities and reinforced educational achievement.[302]

Constructing ethnic identity is an important role played by religious organizations in light of Americans being more accepting of religious than ethnic diversity. Religious communities provide refuge and replicate ethnic cultures in newlands and help in construction of newland identities.[303,304] Many religious leaders appeal to ethnic identity to encourage political action on behalf of the homeland and defence of migrant rights. Paradoxically, while worship groups support ethnic identity and reinforce a sense of difference, it's through their civic actions that migrants build democratic skills[305] that help them to integrate into civic and political life.[306] Although migrants' religious practices and beliefs undergo changes in the newland, worship still gives expression to homeland cultures that nurtures and strengthens ethnic identity.

For Koreans in the US, religion has become a training ground for adjustment and acculturation. Although traditionally a Buddhist country, 70% of Koreans in the US identify as Christian: 40% convert after migrating.[307] Those who don't convert are often marginalized within the ethnic community that sees Buddhism as a relic of the past and devil-worship because "Buddhism denies the ultimate existence of God."[308] Within the Korean community, this has led to struggles over their authentic identity and values. Some claim Buddhism is more than a marker of Korean identity, that it enables adaptation since Buddhism fosters psychological strength, open-mindedness, self-knowledge, independence and high self-esteem—all of which are American values. Some see adoption of Christianity as a marker of successful American identity and adaptation; while others see Korean Christians as duped by western culture,[309] becoming westernized, weak-willed and dependent.[310] They argue Buddhist-fostered wisdom and independence produces the mindset needed to make it in the new world, whereas "Christianity symbolizes blind faith in ministers and God to make life more fruitful."[311] Advocates of Christian conversion recognize the importance of churches in building community with praying and singing and social activities,[312] which contrast with Buddhist temples where people sit and meditate silently and don't create community.[313]

Religious communities are seen as training grounds for democracy because it's where people stand for election long before they enter local or state politics.[314] Catholic and Muslim refugees in the state of Maine use churches and mosques to bond and to build social capital. And religious centres act as a bridge from former nationalist identities to becoming hyphenated-Americans.[315]

Migration to the West has also led to the adoption of new religions. Although Christians, Jews and Muslims all recognize Abraham as a founding prophet, over history, rather than their common ancestry binding them together, it has led them to ostracizing, punishing and battling one another.[316] Haddad points to the dual *religious and cultural identities* of Arab Muslims in the US. As *Arabic speakers, they can find "ethnic and geographic commonality with others of Middle Eastern and North African origins, Christians and Jews as well as Muslims."*[317] New generations of Arabs and Muslims express uncertainty about the degree the US can become their new homeland.[318] They "identify with a wider Islamic religious community, or *umma* whose members derive from various cultural, geographic and national origins, including not only Arabs, but also Pakistanis, Indians, Africans and American-born Muslims, the largest percentage of whom are African Americans."[319] New generation issues are different for American Jews: 1) the religion believed and practiced by their migrant parents is unappealing which has led to modernization, and 2) the question is how to "remain apart *from* American society and culture at the same time they have moved to become a full part *of* it."[320]

The increasing number of studies on migrants and religion reaffirm what Herberg asserted more than 50 years ago: it is through religious membership that migrants and their descendants have found a place in American life.[321]

Notes

1 Portes & Rumbaut, 2001:45.
2 Hua, 2005:191–208.
3 Fischer & McGowan, 1995:39–56.
4 Bauböck, 2003:703.
5 Wikipedia, 2019n: Positive Disintegration.
6 Lewicka, 2014:49–60.
7 Scarpa, 1995:141–161.
8 Homer, 1946.
9 Wikipedia, 2019n: Homer.
10 Admin, 2016.
11 Guarnaccia, 1997.
12 Portes & Rumbaut, 2006.
13 Admin, 2016.
14 La Vecchia-Mikkola, 2013:12.
15 Stievano et al., 2017:4242.
16 La Vecchia-Mikkola, 2013:12.
17 Gordon & Jones, 1999.
18 King et al., 1995:xiv.
19 La Vecchia-Mikkola, 2013:13.
20 Jensen, 2019.
21 Østergaard-Nielsen, 2003:761,764.
22 Portes et al., 2017:1489.

23 Ibid.:1489.
24 Østergaard-Nielsen, 2003:777.
25 Ibid.:762.
26 Ibid.:767.
27 Sayad & Macey, 2004: 67.
28 Hall & Schwartz, 2017:170.
29 Ibid.:200.
30 Lemming, 1992:50.
31 Hall & Schwartz, 2017:187.
32 Ibid.:203.
33 Ibid.:203.
34 Ibid.:203.
35 Ibid.:149.
36 Grinberg & Grinberg, 1989:8.
37 Ibid:8.
38 Ibid.:27.
39 Levy-Warren, 1987:305.
40 Ibid.:306.
41 Ibid.:305.
42 Ibid.:305.
43 Ibid.:306.
44 Ibid.:306.
45 Ibid.:307.
46 Hall & Schwartz, 2017:184.
47 Juni, 2016:335.
48 Ibid.:335.
49 Ibid.:335.
50 Wilson & Raphael, 1993.
51 Montero, 1977:218–219.
52 Ibid.:218–219.
53 Ibid.:218–219.
54 Ibid.:218–219.
55 Hron, 2009:6.
56 Ibid.:208.
57 Ibid.:208.
58 Atwood, 2002:6.
59 Dahlie, 1985:1.
60 Shipp et al., 2009.
61 Bluedorn, 2002.
62 Shipp et al., 2009.
63 McKay et al., 2017.
64 Andretta et al., 2013.
65 Zimbardo & Boyd, 1999.
66 Bandura, 2001.
67 Fried & Slowik, 2004.
68 Sanna et al., 2003.
69 Weick, 2015.
70 Langerberg & Wesseling, 2016.
71 Bandura, 2001.
72 Weick, 2015.
73 Langerberg & Wesseling, 2016.
74 Andretta et al., 2014.

75 McKay et al., 2017:283.
76 Zimbardo & Boyd, 1999.
77 Drake et al., 2008.
78 Laghi et al., 2009.
79 Morais, 1986.
80 Holman & Silver, 1998.
81 Sanna et al., 2003.
82 Knafo & Yaari, 1997:221–240.
83 Ibid.:221–240.
84 Farmer et al., 2006.
85 Portes & Rumbaut, 2001:56.
86 Hron, 2009:29.
87 Levitt et al., 2003:568.
88 Ibid.:2003:568.
89 Dunkas & Nikelly, 1972.
90 Ibid., 1972.
91 Coifman et al, 2007.
92 Meaders, 2018.
93 Simpson & French, 2006:245.
94 Bion, 1970/1984: 43.
95 Vanstone, 1982.
96 Eisold, 2000: 65.
97 Jensen, 2016:24.
98 Kulu, 1998:314.
99 Giddens, 1979:57.
100 Ibid.:320.
101 Ibid.:323.
102 Ibid.:323.
103 Ibid.:324–325.
104 Sayad, 2004:137.
105 Brown, 2002:187–188.
106 Ibid.:198.
107 Ibid.:198.
108 Ibid.:198.
109 Ibid.:198.
110 Frohlick, 2009:402.
111 Zahar, 2016:231.
112 Hron, 2007:52.
113 Ibid.:52.
114 Ibid.:52.
115 Ibid.:61.
116 Ibid.:202.
117 Grinberg & Grinberg, 1989:158.
118 Ibid.:158.
119 Ibid.:158.
120 Ibid.:157.
121 Ibid.:160.
122 Paskievich, 2008.
123 Ibid.:2008.
124 Montero, 1977:40.
125 Ibid.:49.
126 Ibid.:49.

127 Ibid.:126.
128 Ibid.:126.
129 Petschauer, 1997:30.
130 Ibid.:46.
131 Scheutz, 1945.
132 Lovell, 1997.
133 Lee et al, 2012.
134 Mirksy & Kaushinsky, 1989.
135 Janoff-Bulman, 1992.
136 Selby, 2011b.
137 Jensen, 2019.
138 Ibid.:2019.
139 Madison, 2010:178.
140 Selby et al, 2009.
141 Kwong et al, 2009.
142 Ibid.:2009.
143 Lysgaard, 1955.
144 Oberg, 1960.
145 Gullahorn & Gullahorn, 1963.
146 Black & Mendenhall, 1991.
147 Church, 1982.
148 Nash, 1991.
149 Ward et al, 1998.
150 Kohls, 2001.
151 Fray, 1988.
152 Seiter & Waddell, 1989.
153 Akhtar et al, 2018.
154 Pritchard, 2010.
155 Sussman, 2001.
156 Ibid.:109.
157 Wikipedia, 2019n: Cultural Intelligence.
158 Ang & Van Dyne, 2008.
159 Livermore, 2011.
160 Earley & Ang, 2003.
161 Linderman & Brayer-Hess, 2002.
162 Hall & Schwartz, 2017:149.
163 Ibid.:149.
164 Ibid.:16.
165 Triandis, 2009:20.
166 Ibid.:9.
167 Ibid.:15–18.
168 Ibid.:15–18.
169 Ibid.:18–19.
170 Kivisto, 2002:36.
171 Ibid.:27.
172 Ibid.:36.
173 Marshall, 1964.
174 Kivisto, 2002:153.
175 Mendaglio, 2008.
176 Dabrowski, 1964/2016.
177 Hall & Schwartz, 2017:16.
178 Maslow, 1954/1987.

179 Maslow, 1962/2010.
180 Firat et al, 2017:82.
181 Grinberg & Grinberg, 1989:89.
182 Ibid.:89.
183 Halperin, 2004.
184 Morgan et al, 2010: 655.
185 Ibid.:655.
186 Krabbendam & van Os, 2005.
187 Morgan & Fisher, 2007: 3–10.
188 Fisher et al, 2009: 319–325.
189 Morgan et al., 2010:662.
190 Wong et al, 2003:85.
191 Wong & Song, 2008:138.
192 Bowlby, 1969/1997.
193 Grinberg & Grinberg, 1989:144–145.
194 Winnicott, 2016.
195 Smith, 1988.
196 Mason & Lelitro, 2018.
197 Ibid.:2018.
198 Ibid.:2018.
199 Hall & Schwartz, 2017:140.
200 Ibid.:93.
201 Statistics Canada, 2018b.
202 Sauter, 2018.
203 Hirschman, 1970:107.
204 Ibid.:108.
205 Ibid.:108.
206 O'Brien, 1968.
207 Rudmin, 2009:107.
208 Ibid.:109.
209 Ibid.:118.
210 Demes & Geeraert, 2014:91.
211 Ibid.:94.
212 Ibid.:99.
213 Ibid.:102.
214 Ibid.:102.
215 Ibid.:103.
216 Ibid.:103.
217 Scarpa, 1995:141–161.
218 Jung, 1953/1993:41–47.
219 Edinger, 1985/1996:5.
220 Ibid.:14.
221 Ibid.:17.
222 Peterson, 2018.
223 Edinger, 1985/1996:48.
224 Ibid.:73.
225 Ibid.:76.
226 Ibid.:83.
227 Ibid.:99.
228 Ibid.:117.
229 Ibid.:118.
230 Ibid.:148.

231 Ibid.:150.
232 Ibid.:150.
233 Ibid.:180.
234 Ibid.:183.
235 Ibid.:187.
236 Ibid.:211.
237 Ibid.:215.
238 Ibid.:215.
239 Ibid.:217.
240 Ibid.:220.
241 Ibid.:220.
242 Ibid.:220.
243 Ibid.:222.
244 Ibid.:224.
245 Elovitz & Kahn, 1997:16.
246 Ibid.:16.
247 Petrič, 1995:162–171.
248 Walsh & Shulman, 2007.
249 Singer, 1984:265.
250 Nehru, 1936/1956:596.
251 Ward et al, 2001:331.
252 Berry, 1997.
253 Ibid.:7.
254 Ibid.:7.
255 Berry, 2001.
256 Ibid.:331.
257 Stonequist, 1937.
258 Tajfel & Dawson, 1965.
259 Park, 1928.
260 Bochner, 1982/2013:31.
261 Ibid.:5–44.
262 Argyle, 1969:72–79.
263 Ward et al., 2001:337.
264 Ibid.:337.
265 Ibid.:446.
266 Portes & Rumbaut, 2006:130–131.
267 Ibid.:130–131.
268 Bauböck, 2003:702.
269 Ibid.:702.
270 Ibid.:713.
271 Alba & Foner, 2015:219.
272 Ibid.:197.
273 Ibid.:245.
274 Adelman, 2013:2.
275 Ibid.:2–3.
276 Kivisto, 2014.
277 Kivisto, 2002:149.
278 Lin, 2009:273.
279 Ibid.:273.
280 Ibid.:293–294.
281 Granberg-Michaelson, 2013.
282 Alba & Foner, 2015.

283 Foner & Alba, 2008: 360–392.
284 Bejan, 2017:164.
285 Herberg, 1955/1985.
286 Stahl, 2015.
287 Handlin, 1951/2002.
288 Rothman, 1982.
289 Foner & Alba, 2008.
290 Karpathakis, 2001:390.
291 Centre for Community Based Research, 2013–2014.
292 Hirschman, 2004:1228.
293 Foner & Alba, 2008: 360–392.
294 Akresh, 2011:645–647.
295 Ebaugh & Chafetz, 2000:141.
296 Miller, 2019.
297 Ebaugh & Chafetz, 1999:587.
298 Ibid.:585–613.
299 Ibid:599.
300 Ibid.:141.
301 Kim & Min, 2001.
302 Zhou & Bankston, 1998.
303 Herberg, 1955/1985.
304 Karpathakis, 2001:390.
305 Foley & Hoge, 2007:188–189.
306 Ibid.:214.
307 Suh, 2009:166.
308 Ibid.:167.
309 Ibid.:167–168.
310 Ibid.:189.
311 Ibid.:185.
312 Ibid.:189.
313 Ibid.:189.
314 Eck, 2019:336.
315 Allen, 2010:1051–1052.
316 Alba et al., 2009b:191.
317 Haddad, 2009:247.
318 Ibid.:193.
319 Ibid.:247–248.
320 Eisen, 2009: 224,226.
321 Herberg 1955/1985:27–28.

Chapter 5

Identity and belonging

Chapter 5 focuses on identity and the sense of belonging following migration. Both self and identity are socially constructed concepts emerging through being and doing[1] in relation to others.[2] Identity is the container for the contained.[3] The universal human need for recognition and unconditional acceptance[4] is true too for those who migrate. In the five multicultural countries of immigration—Argentina, Australia, Canada, New Zealand and the United States—migrants are permitted dual citizenship. It enables both a sense of self, identity and belonging in a newland, and staying connected to the homeland.

Persona, ego, self and migration

Jung introduced the concept of Persona to psychology. "Persona" in Latin means "theatre mask" and "the face presented to the world,"[5] the "part of consciousness that 'negotiates' with the outer world on the ego's behalf."[6] Persona is "a mask of the collective psyche, a mask that *feigns individuality* only, making others and one's self believe that one is individual, whereas one is simply acting a role through which the collective psyche speaks."[7] Recently in a Sandplay—a psychotherapeutic art technique using a sandtray and miniatures[8]—a woman discovered her cultivated Persona of innocent lamb was a cover for a hungry inner wolf whose needs she had never seen nor met, but were evident to others.[9] Persona is "the place in the personality where public and private meet; where who we are collides with who we are told we should be."[10] A person identified with their Persona is caught in a false self where the self is treated as an object to be manipulated for political gain as opposed to being a subject and the true self of psychic wholeness.

A healthy ego carries the true self and creates and manages an "appropriate" Persona or outward portrayal of self:[11] "A healthy ego balances conscious and unconscious elements of psyche. A weakened ego leaves a person 'in the dark' in danger of being swamped by chaotic unconscious images."[12] Jung defined the relation of the self to the ego as "the mover to the moved."[13]

In childhood, the ego is merged in *participation mystique* with primary caregivers. Psychic separation is needed to become truly one's self: "A person's becoming him/herself, whole, indivisible and distinct from other people or collective psychology (culture) ... is the key concept in Jung's contribution to the theories of personality development."[14] Jung saw the Self as the archetype of higher inner authority,[15] and the Individuated Self as the unifying and "ordering principle of the entire personality, [and] destiny of the individual."[16]

Existentialist Heidegger[17] defined conscious awareness of self and identity as the phenomenological experience of being that occurs in relation to family and community.[18] His philosophy underlies Jung's theory of individuation as an unfolding of the self in a differentiation of consciousness where inner authority shifts from the ego to self.[19,20] "Individuation is practically the same as the development of consciousness out of the original state of *identity*,"[21] says Jung.[22] Although almost a given, "many people ignore it, repress it, and distort themselves in convoluted attempts to avoid acknowledging its presence out of fear of appearing nonconformist or being seen as 'different.'"[23] Wanting to belong, people become followers or fall into passive people-pleasing lambs until a crisis occurs that challenges the sense of self. Migration is one of these situations prompting the great questions of life: Who am I? Where am I? Where is here? What should I do?

Jung's writings influenced Erikson's life-stages model where he renames individuation "ego integrity" and defines it as a sense of coherence, wholeness and wisdom.[24] Maslow called individuation "self-actualization" and defined it as "becoming fully human."[25] Rogers argued that self-actualization is only possible in open social environments with acceptance, recognition and unconditional positive regard: "The good life is a process, not a state of being. It is a direction not a destination."[26]

Identity and developmental theories

When Odysseus arrives home in Ithaca, he's surprised and shocked that it's not how he remembers it and that no one recognizes him.[27,28] His disappointment, his wound of return, underscores the importance of "mutual recognition"[29] and meaningful relationships supporting a sense of self, identity and belonging. Migrants need "navigation skills, diplomacy, strength, persistence to negotiate the external dangers and obstacles"[30] of newlands; they also need inner psychological resources of "stamina, containment, insightfulness and resilience."[31] Psychological theories of development provide a guide to understanding migrant adaptation and acculturation: Bowlby's attachment theory, Winnicott's transitions, Stern's sense of self and Erikson's life stages.

Bowlby's attachment theory

During WWII, British paediatrician and psychoanalyst John Bowlby (1907–1990) was responsible for children evacuated from London during bombing raids. The observed difference in children's responses led him to the hypothesis of secure attachment, where children feel they can depend upon caregivers. Later research[32,33,34] led to the discovery of three types of insecure attachments due to undependable caregiver relations that manifest psychologically in children as preoccupied, fearful and/or dismissive.[35] Attachment patterns have been shown to persist in adulthood[36] and are related to personality profiles.[37]

Many languages use parental terms to refer to nations as "motherland" and "fatherland." Attachment to parents and nations play a role in migration. Securely attached migrants are able to identify with both homeland and host countries, which implies an "integrated acculturation strategy."[38] Insecurely attached migrants are negatively associated with both, which implies a "marginalised strategy of acculturation."[39] Migrants with secure nation-attachment are more likely to maintain homeland cultural beliefs, values and traditions, to report subjective well-being,[40] and a sense of "flourishing"[41] in the newland.[42] Four different patterns of migration and attachment are observed.[43] *Circular migrants* go back and forth between countries and show weak attachment to the newland. *Bi-nationals* show strong attachments to both homeland and newland. *Footloose* migrants show weak attachments to any lands: *Settlers* in newlands have weak attachments to the homeland. Yet, a European survey of 654 labour migrants found successful newland integration to be unrelated to strong or weak attachment to homelands. This suggests it's important to take into account if migration is actually chosen, or forced.

Winnicott and transitional time, object and space

Bowlby's colleague, British paediatrician and psychoanalyst Donald Winnicott (1896–1971) saw *transitional objects* or caregiver substitutes, like security blankets, as important in infant development, enabling infants to distinguish between "me" and "not-me."[44] In social interactions, *transitional space* permits infants to distinguish between "self" and "not-self."[45] Winnicott also found *attunement* or shared feelings across transitional spaces and between objects and/or persons is where fantasy and reality overlap and creativity emerges. It's essential to a child's exploratory play and later adult cultural life.[46,47] In Bowlby's theory, secure attachment is important because it permits the child to return to play regardless of separation crises: play is the essential work and learning process of childhood.

Applying Bowlby's and Winnicott's developmental concepts to migration suggests migrants need secure attachment and security objects (persons or cultures), which allow for an attitude of openness and creativity that enables a sense of new self to emerge in relationship to the newland. In contrast, those who are insecurely attached face the newland and peoples with preoccupation with the homeland, as well as fear and dismissive attitudes towards the newland self and others.

Stern's sense of self

Infant researcher, Daniel Stern (b. 1957) presents a time-model of psychic development and emergent sense of self. During the chaos of birth and afterwards, the infant begins to organize sensory stimuli and integrate these into an *emergent sense of self*. A parallel for migrants is the chaos of travel and arrival in the newland that needs to be integrated into an emergent sense of self in newlands. This migrant hypothesis is supported by research on arrival and adaptation in Australia,[48] Canada[49] and the US.[50] (See Chapter 3 "Arrival Challenges" and Chapter 4, "Stage 11: Resurrection.")

At two months, Stern found infants show qualitative changes in perception with direct eye contact, visual scanning and motor patterns, plus stabilization of diurnal hormonal and sleep pattern and emergence of the *core self*.[51] A parallel in migration exists as, after two months, migrants generally find increased skill in finding one's way and meeting one's needs. The infant's *core self* has two aspects: *core self I* refers to recognition of self *versus* others in four distinct realms: 1) self-agency or the sense of having caused something to happen, 2) self-coherence or the sense of being a physical whole, 3) self-affectivity or feelings related to experience, and 4) self-history or the sense of continuity.[52] For migrants, the parallels are increasing sense of self-agency, self-coherence, self-feelings and self-history in newlands.

Core self II is a sense of self *with* others and attachment styles firmed with primary caregivers. It's mutually created and reinforced with subjective attunement (sharing of feeling and emotion) and a growing awareness of being the focus of attention.[53] This speaks of secure attachment, whereas lack of mutuality leads to insecure attachment with preoccupied, fearful and dismissive responses. The parallel in migration points to the importance of a positive host-country response and cultural enclaves that provide positive regard and support of migrants. (See Chapter 7 "Host Country").

Seven to eight months after birth, Stern found quantum leaps in infant perception, along with a growing sense of the subjective self. *Subjective self I* refers to an emerging discovery of his/her own mind with realization of desires, wants and feeling states. An increasing ability to focus attention permits infants to develop a theory of mind of self and of others as distinctly separate entities.[54] *Subjective self II* refers to attunement and relatedness where "feeling states within one person can be knowable to another and that they both sense, without using language that the transaction has occurred."[55] In other words, the infant experiences feeling connected to others. A migration parallel is sense of relatedness and attunement to newland others. This is an important step for migrants, especially those from obedience-cultures where personhood is not encouraged. At this stage, migrants form separations between their fantasies and raw realities of newlands. They may begin to take responsibility for meeting and relating to newland people.

In the second year, the *verbal self* emerges with language and symbolic thinking. According to Stern, the child opens to a new sense of relatedness with others and inter-subjectivity that makes experiences and feelings shareable. It allows for constructed narratives of one's life.[56] It's also described as the socially constructed self in terms of relatedness and sameness of being and doing.[57] A migration parallel is that usually by the second year, the migrant gains increased language competence and knowledge of the newland, permitting wider actions, activities and interactions. Verbal competence is important to social agency in migration:[58] it enables independent action in meeting needs, maintaining health[59] and workforce participation.[60,61] Some avoid full fluency, feeling that a base capability in language is sufficient, while others experience lack of access to advanced language training.

Erikson and life stages

Erikson's (1902–1994) theory of eight life stages provides useful parallels to migration. Each stage requires a healthy ego and personality, which enables individual thought and action. Each requires strength and resilience to meet inner and external changes and to respond to differences in collective values of the homeland and the newland. Each migrant stage refers to a western model of psyche and individuality which may not be experienced in other cultures:

Life Stages

1) Infant to 1 month—Trust vs mistrust (manifesting as anxiety/fear);
2) Age 18 months to 3 years—Autonomy vs shame/doubt (leading to low self-esteem);
3) Age 3–5 years—Initiative (self-confidence and purpose) vs obedience (with thwarted sense of self and guilt);
4) Age 5–13 years—Industry (action-oriented) vs inferiority (non-action and development of an inferiority complex);
5) Age 13–21 years—Identity (sense of self) vs role confusion (uncertainty with apathy and conformity);
6) Age 21–39 years—Intimacy (closeness to others) vs social isolation (leading to a negative self-concept);
7) Age 40–65 years—Generativity (growth) vs stagnation (and lack of meaning), and
8) Age 65 and older—integrity (unique self) vs despair (with sense of failure and bitterness about what should or could have been).[62]

The parallel developmental stages can be seen in migration as part of an inner psychic process of newland adaptation: trust, autonomy, initiative, industry, new identity, social intimacy, self-growth and integrity. Difficulties in meeting expected psychological competencies in newlands can lead to feelings of being trapped, unhappiness, despair and neuroticism. It can lead to grief and an unrelenting desire to return to the homeland. Former Governor General of Canada, Adrienne Clarkson, who emigrated from China, advises:

> What matters is whether you define your life by what you have been able to recreate out of the past or whether you define it by what you have lost. And like the unexamined life, the life defined by loss is not worth living.[63]

Erikson's eight life stages are western *rites de passage* that unfold differently for men and women in different cultures and historic periods.[64] Some cultures do not encourage these stages and western adaptation can result in rifts within and between families and homelands. Some migrants are surprised after adapting to the West; they no longer fit in their homelands. This is more common for women who migrate to the West and discover freedoms they are unwilling to give up, which creates inner conflict in their desire to stay or return home. The opposite is also possible. In the newland, some cultural enclaves reinforce homeland cultural identity and prevent adaptation: "In the attempt to valorize the tradition, it is not uncommon for community leaders to objectify women and girls as the preservers of a true tradition, religion or ethnic culture—often expressed in opposition to modernity."[65] Such expectations placed on women and girls makes adaptation and acculturation difficult, especially those conditioned to collectivity rather than individuality.

A Canadian survey of migrants four years after arrival compared the self-reported mental health of three types of newcomers: 1) refugees, 2) family unification migrants and 3) economic migrants. Almost a third (29%)—more women and refugees from South and Central American and those in the lowest income quartile—"reported emotional problems and 16% reported high levels of stress."[66] Those satisfied with the settlement process were less likely to report emotional problems.[67]

Identity and migration

For Jung, identity is an archetypal capacity—an inherited "structured psychological pattern linked to instinct"[68] that emerges from the attachment-separation drama of mother and child.[69] This makes identity a central part of the socially constructed self-theory of self,[70] including biological, social-cultural, geographic/political and psychological aspects. Integration and coherence of identity is a maturation objective related to belonging.[71] A multidimensional understanding of identity requires identifying the different nuances and meanings of identity in each discipline.[72]

Historically, identity was ascribed at birth in terms of social roles of gender, family origins, class and occupation. For many, there was little choice. The modern idea of identity arose out of 18th-century American pragmatism. Individual identity was uncommon until the 1950s, when questions arose of individual survival in mass society.[73] More recently, with globalization, questions of identity have resurfaced with reference to *alterity* or otherness.[74] It's often said that modern ideas of individualism have eroded traditional identities and social bonds,[75,76] making it more difficult to have a sense of continuity and consistency of self.[77] In fact, in modern western society, especially for youth,[78] the forming and sustaining of a sense of identity is a dynamic struggle of definition amongst constant cultural changes.[79,80]

Jung defines *identity* as an unconscious phenomenon emerging from identification with others and "psychological conformity,"[81] which is a relic of early infancy and *participation mystique* or merging with caregivers and non-differentiation of subject and object.[82] It assumes an *a priori likeness* based on assumptions of similarity. It's possible for identity to emerge from a psychic infection and/or paranoia. Conscious *collective* identity and social *attitude* differ and for Jung, the highest expression is "the Christian ideal of brotherly love."[83] A healthy identity is a realistic and coherent sense of self.

The modern idea of identity was proposed in 1919 by Victor Tausk, a colleague of Freud. Since then, identity has "occupied an ambiguous place in psychoanalysis and psychiatry [with its] intrapsychic and social or interpersonal aspects."[84] Erikson defines "ego identity" as sameness-of-self that one feels internally as an inner solidarity, and "a persistent sharing of some kind of essential character with others."[85] Akhtar lists four psychoanalytic aspects of identity:

1) *Temporal continuity of identity* is based on the tree metaphor where "rings accumulate around a central core without altering its shape."[86] Likewise, "individuals with a consolidated identity can both change and remain the same."[87]
2) *Authentic or crystallized identity* is a constructed "ideology that has as its credo the experience of being true toward oneself and others."[88]
3) *Gender identity* is "concordant with one's biological sex and shows harmony between identity, role and sexual partner orientation."[89]
4) *Ethnic identity* includes cultural values and a "sense of history, modes of expression and patterns of interpersonal behavior" that give rise to "a sense of historical depth to the adult identity."[90]

Taylor sees the idea of identity arising in a complex evolution of moral philosophy about human dignity, and the rights of self and others over the past four centuries with ideas of human agency, inward focus, freedom and individuality.[91] Identity is also about "rational mastery and control [and] the transformation of the will"[92] along with human vision, creativity and expressive power.[93] Taylor speaks of the influence of ideas of self on identity and individualism in the American "human potential movement," and the evangelical Protestant revival of "the Great Awakening."[94] He argues this late-modern perspective of identity means that identification with an ancient cosmic order is no longer possible:[95] "Significant others are not simply external to me: they help to constitute my own selfhood."[96]

Identity is neither innate nor a matter of choice, says Lawler.[97] Identity is socially created in relation to collectivities (groups) and is not an individual odyssey.[98] It is in micro-worlds of personal interaction where the freedom lies in self-agency and identity construction,[99] but the deeper and yet more practical question is how to achieve personal identity within the constraints of a specific context.[100] Rattansi takes a different perspective, saying most people lack knowledge about their inner selves and project their "inner fears and bad feelings about the self onto the others."[101] And he insists it's true too in construction of their personal identity, and is why people behave inconsistently and in contradictory manners.[102] He cautions against group identities because groups lack inner coherence.[103] And he advises vigilance against the essentialization of collective categories and identities, arguing that it's "impossible to find a single 'essence' or core in a collective identity."[104] Bauman affirms this, saying identity is by its very nature, elusive and ambivalent.[105]

Psychologists speak of *personal identity*; sociologists speak of *social identity*.[106] In an attempt to integrate these two perspectives, Côté[107] and Arnett[108] speak of numerous ways that modern mass-culture and profit-driven globalization have weakened social relations and replaced traditional identities with individualistic atomized lives. Turkle describes it as being alone together in a world of technology that leads us to expect more from it and less from people.[109] She points to today's young "tethered to cell-phones with everyone a call away,"[110] and missing the *rite of passage* of being perfectly alone and responsible for themselves.[111] Some even construct false identities online.[112]

Identity and migration are a separate issue. "Psychoanalysis has not yet developed a coherent theory about immigrant subjectivity,"[113] says Lobban. He proposes borrowing Black Americans' idea of double consciousness to conceptualize the migrant's experience; however, it's not a parallel situation. One cannot erase colour and sense of alterity, even in newlands "that genuinely welcomes its otherness and believes that 'otherness' is a vital and important addition to culture, like salt and spice in cooking."[114] Still, migrants struggle with the double consciousness[115] of cultural identity. Newlands "revel in a panoply of selves of all makes, shapes, and sizes, some grown at home and some grown in their host county, all mixed up in a glorious multicultural, multihued, hybrid 'me-ness.'"[116] At the same time, migrant identity is often assigned otherness that erodes self-esteem with a sense of second-class citizenship. While a reinterpretation of self is needed in the newland;[117] it's not always possible. Identities are imagined, necessary fictions,[118] and "the identity of person and place is always continuously being produced,"[119] says Connell.

Biological identity is called "animalism,"[120] but philosophy has never clarified if humans are biological organisms, spatial or temporal parts of organisms, or simply bundles of perceptions.[121] In fact, from Locke to Descartes, says Schechtman, philosophers have seen human identity as a psychological matter.[122] He defines three identity spheres. 1) *Biological identity* includes age, gender, ethnicity, race and body height, weight, colour of skin, hair and eyes and today, DNA. 2) *Social-cultural identity* includes family, education, nationality, language, occupation, religion, social status and wealth. 3) *Geographic/political identity* refers to birthplace, town or country, continent, nation state and one's status: legal and documented (temporary/permanent) or undocumented.[123] All are used as markers of self and to justify prejudice and discrimination.

After migrating, the struggle with identity can be so stressful that it triggers psychic collapse. Migration also carries positive potential for a new identity with freedom and an expanded sense of self. "It is precisely in America that the dream of leaving your working class roots and reinventing yourself takes on mythological proportion. America is the iconic place where repudiation of your origins becomes the catapult to success,"[124] says González. Identities today are fluid, multiple and cross-cut many domains. While we develop core identities, we adopt values and norms appropriate for specific situations.[125]

Migration has the potential to clarify identity. Haitian migrants to the US find their "sense of race pride has begun to form broader senses of identity,"[126] not only as Haitian-Americans, but as "part of an African diaspora,"[127] and they have begun to "respond publically to political movements that identified them as African people."[128] Similarly, "many Chinese began to be aware of their Chinese identity only after leaving China to live overseas."[129] Collectively, "Chinese identity in Canada has ranged from the model of the sojourner to the assimilationist depending on historical circumstances and how welcoming the policies of the Canadian government are at the time."[130] (See Chapter 7, "Host Country.")

Migration and social-cultural identity

"Identity formation is a crucial normative task of adolescence,"[131] especially the anchoring of self in a cultural identity. Successful identity is "experienced as a sense of psychological well-being."[132] The adolescent four-process identity-challenges model has application to migration:[133]

1) *Identity foreclosure* is where life commitments (career, partner, country) are made without considering other options. The parallel with migration is the decision to migrate without considering all options, while for tied-migrants and exiles, there's a lack of choice. It blocks creative thinking and adaptation.
2) *Identity diffusion* signifies lack of exploration of possibilities and an inability to make a commitment. The migration-parallel is a *diasporic complex* that prevents or hinders adaptation and where adaptation is seen as betrayal of the homeland.
3) *Identity moratorium* is exploration and playing the field without commitment, where the sheer number of possibilities can produce high anxiety. The migration-parallel is multiple possible newlands that precludes commitment to one.
4) *Identity achievement* is full exploration of possibilities with clear decision making and commitment. Identity is self-defined rather than other-defined. The migration-parallel is successful newland adaptation where sense of self includes dual-identity and dual-citizenship.

The Grinbergs define identity as "born of the continuous interaction among spatial, temporal, and social integration links"[134] comprising an unconscious fantasy of different "pieces of the self."[135] Here, *spatial integration* refers to physical aspects of being, and differences between self and non-self.[136] *Temporal integration* refers to continuity over time and recognition of "sameness."[137] *Social integration* refers to relations between self, objects and others, and feelings of "belonging."[138] Migration presents great challenges to identity—everything is new, all is unknown and one is a stranger:

> The immigrant loses most of the roles (s)he once played in his/her community as family member, member of a profession or the workforce, member of a circle of friends, political activist, and so on. "In the new country no one will know me; no one will know my family. I'll be nobody."[139]

To counteract fears of loss of homeland identity, "often immigrants decorate their homes profusely with objects typical of their original cultures. The art and handiwork, folk music, paintings, or wall hangings"[140] anchor identity by providing evidence of their past, maintaining relations with the absent, and helping "to bear the sorrow of being in a place where [s]he has no roots, no history, no older generation (ancestry), and no personal memories."[141] However, there's a shadow side to cultural objects that reaffirm one's homeland identity in the newland: they take over psychic space, and prevent adaptation and facing the reality that the past is past.[142] At the same time, "oppositional tugs of the home and newland"[143] may not be wholly detrimental; they may assist migrants to live more creatively.[144]

Identity crises and creative illness

Psychological crises affect identity formation. Homans brings our attention to the intellectual and psychological crises of Freud that "had the effect of consolidating a new sense of personal identity."[145] In the Jungian model of psyche illustrated by mythology, identity crises are seen as the *Nekyia*, the night-sea journey[146] and descent to the underworld,[147] where survivors "return, full of knowledge and wisdom, equipped for the inward and outer demands of life."[148] For migrants, especially exiles, the *Nekyia* may represent difficult escapes or limbos of uncertainties and dangers of refugee camps.

In the Jungian perspective, creative illnesses signal the need for new attitudes. Dabrowski calls it positive disintegration, defined as "a progression from an initial primitive integrated mode of experience, followed by three forms of disintegration, and culminating in a re-integrated mode of experience that includes the attainment of personality."[149] It moves from egocentrism to altruism embodied in an authentic and personally responsible individual.[150] Creative illnesses show "spontaneous and rapid recovery accompanied by a feeling of elation."[151]

Adolescent developmental identity crises and adult identity disorders have three distinct forms: 1) *identity diffusion* of narcissistic, schizoid, hypomanic, antisocial, and paranoid and schizotypal personalities; 2) *identity dissociation* of multiple personalities, and 3) *identity fragmentation* or a breakdown of the boundary between social identity and psychotic states.[152] Veterans discharged from armed forces before the end of WWII had unique identity crises. Worn out by too many changes, Erikson says, they experienced loss of "ego synthesis,"[153] and suffered from s*omatic (body) tension* and *social panic* and *ego anxiety*: "The men felt that they did not know any more who they were: there was a distinct loss of ego identity. The sense of sameness and continuity and the belief in one's social role were gone."[154]

Identity instability is a theme in immigrant novels where some claim not to know anymore who they are: "Others feel as if they are hiding a secret, a different identity or special knowledge. Some dissociate, to counteract their anxiety or confusion, while others respond in a manic way harming others or themselves."[155]

Diasporic identity

For exiles, the "defilement" of identity occurs in three phases: "First is the destruction of land, houses and towns ravaged by war, as well as the broken trajectories of lives and the irreducible mark of physical and moral wounds."[156] Second is "confinement—months of waiting, years or whole life-cycles spent in transit on the fringes of cities in camps."[157] Third is action or "the search for a right to life and speech which, in the disturbed contexts of war and exodus, often emerges in a context of illegality but may eventually give birth to new forms of political commitments."[158]

The UN estimates today that 50 million people are exiled refugees and another 25–30 million are internally displaced in their own countries.[159] With loss of place comes loss of identity,[160] which is replaced by a virtual home[161] with the "gated identity" of a refugee camp.[162] A primordial identity is replaced by a stigmatized identity[163] as "victims, illegal and defenseless,"[164] and "undesirable survivors suspected of being guilty, accomplices, disease or marked by dirty wars."[165]

The word "diaspora" comes from ancient Greek, meaning "to sow" or "to disperse seeds." Applied to humans in the past, diaspora referred simply to migration, until "for Jews, Africans, Palestinians and Armenians it acquired a more sinister and brutal meaning. Diaspora began to signify a collective trauma, a banishment where one dreamed of home but lived in exile."[166] Today, diaspora is used to describe migrant communities replicating homeland cultures in newlands with strong identities and bonds of solidarity.[167] Diasporic identities emerge from forced migrations with "displacement, exile, and longing for the homeland."[168] Diasporic thinking accounts for loss and suffering, and carries hope for salvation.[169] "In search of economic and political support,"[170] many homeland governments reach out to diasporic citizens in newlands.

Stuart Hall describes diaspora as the loss of roots along with longing for return and a consolatory dream of freedom: "To think of yourself as diasporic, as I now do, has therefore become a sort of substitute for identity [where] the diasporic challenges the idea of whole, integral, traditionally unchanging cultural identities."[171] A New Zealand colleague living in the US for more than twenty years describes herself as diasporic, as "living in the land of longing." She explains: "leaving home, I lost two generations, my parents and grandparents; if I return, I'll lose two other generations—my children and grandchildren. I don't really belong anywhere."[172]

In his memoir, *Out of Place*, Said speaks of the differences between Middle Eastern philosophy and American psychology. The latter he criticizes as unreflective and lacking memory.[173] He tells of missing Cairo, of persistent longing to be back there, and keeping a bedside clock set on Cairo time. Over the years, letters from home "deepened the wound of abandonment and separation."[174] He recalls pulling out suitcases from under his bed filled with mementos and leafing through picture albums and letters; he'd begin to cry before remembering his father's advice during childhood: "Buck up boy don't be a sissy."[175] Coming from a warm climate to unfamiliar and unwanted change of seasons, he says migration makes one face environmental challenges: "I have never gotten over my feeling of revulsion for snow."[176]

Looking beyond the official legal definition of *de jure* statelessness of those in legal limbo who number more than ten million people;[177] Tas expands the definition to *social statelessness* or those with official nationality who are unable to return to their homelands because of political views and actions. He says millions experience double and even multiple diaspora. They "do not feel that they belong either to their country of origin or to the country in which they now live."[178] They left when their homeland was no longer comfortable or homely: it was de-territorialized and the people de-nationalized, marginalized and labelled as foreigners. Undocumented, they became invisible and *de facto* stateless.[179] One does not "have to leave their country of birth to lose their nationality."[180] The Kurds in Syria and Iraq are an example.[181] Granted citizenship in western states, they still feel stateless, other and insecure.[182] High levels of alienation and depression are reported. Not surprisingly, they reshape the past with selective memories that may be inaccurate, exaggerated and transformed into mythical, mystical places reconstructed and endowed with political meaning. This leads to a new nationalism of "their own independent, or at least autonomous, region with cultural, linguistic and legal rights, much like their Kurdish brethren in northern Iraq."[183]

Many stateless people "have been subjected to forced migrations, displacement, and social and political marginalisation in the many places they have lived [and] do not feel fully in control of their lives."[184] Because the "socially stateless live in double or even multiple diasporas [they] feel that they need to mobilize against the dominant, majoritarian regime so that their stateless condition can be addressed. They do not feel safe or have a sense of belonging."[185] For stateless people the two most difficult questions to answer, even in polite, casual conversations are: "Where are you from?" and "Where is home?"[186] A Kurdish refugee says: "I hate my birthday because it reminds me of where and in which condition I was born. It reminds me how powerless I was, without my own identity and without my own language."[187] Another says:

> My homeland is ruled by others, so it can't be a homeland for me. Today my identity is forced. My nationality too: I am even not allowed to speak my own language and give my own child the name of my choice in my own land.[188]

For the stateless, the feeling is loss, marginalization, oppression and depression. In fact, "it can be hard to establish where diaspora or exile begins or ends."[189] As people relocate more than once, they begin to inhabit psychologically double and even multiple diaspora. "A common perception amongst Kurds is that, since they don't have a strong religious or linguistic identity, they need to strengthen their nationalism;"[190] with the result that "unity through nationalism [is seen as the] only way to end their statelessness."[191] Thus, diaspora politicalizes, it's "seen as a safe environment within which to organise [and to create a] future Kurdish 'virtual' state."[192]

Diasporic people express victim psychology, citing alienation, sadness and anger.[193] Stateless orphans of the world, many are born and die in diaspora: "Everywhere is diaspora for them. It doesn't make any difference where they are."[194] Collective memory is presented as not being inert and passive, but "where selective homeland 'memories' and myths are important in mobilizing political activity."[195] For diaspora to gain cultural meaning, "the consciousness of those dislocated from their origins must exhibit at least a minimal shared history, and at least some conception of a common destiny."[196] In the Netherlands, rather than developing new Dutch identities, Moroccan and Turkish male youths live socially and culturally segregated lives; their low economic status and limited future has led them to seek alternate, religious identities.[197] Within ethnic cultural enclaves, women face dual challenges. They are "both tradition bearers and integration proponents, cultural and generational mediators,"[198] facing the need for dual compromises.

Psychologist Kohut escaped the Nazis and was interred in an English refugee camp before joining an uncle in Chicago. It created, he says, a split identity: "two totally different, perhaps, *unbridgeable* lives."[199] Brown says, the psychic pain and woundedness can lead to diasporic identity. It can awaken or lead to a desire for institutionalized protection promised by totalitarian regimes. In contrast, a true democracy requires sharing power and freedom and not seeking totalitarian protection.[200] The emotional pain of the loss of one's homeland can motivate political action. Mahatma Gandhi cautioned care that political action not be just retaliation.[201]

Sayad speaks of Algerian migrants caught in a collective illusion which is an existential problem rooted in colonialism. It's described as a tragedy of intense suffering of double absence[202] where the past is lost, shattered and irrevocable:[203]

> Always torn between his permanent present, which he dare not admit to himself, and the "return" which, whilst it is never resolutely ruled out, is never seriously contemplated, the immigrant is doomed to oscillate constantly between, on the one hand, the preoccupations of the here and now and, on the other, yesterday's retrospective hopes and the eschatological expectation that there will be an end to his immigration.[204]

Reding accused France of being a whore and enchantress that took away his Algerian self-autonomy.[205] Bauman cautions that refugees and exiles often become an underclass. Since they lack the power to create their own identity, labels are imposed upon them—as undocumented and illegal immigrant, economic migrant and even terrorist.[206] Economic immigrants are criticized for being too obviously self-seeking.[207] However, historically, chosen migration was motivated primarily by economic opportunity. In Eastern Europe, many who chose to migrate were pejoratively called economic opportunists and Volkswagen Germans.[208] Only when Eastern bloc countries entered the EU did they "secure the privileges of 'white' Europeans."[209]

Diasporic complex resolution

The diasporic complex manifests as grief and yearning for the homeland and desire for return—whether or not the homeland still exists. To resolve a diasporic complex, Hall suggests we rethink and reinterpret "roots" as "routes" of change, transformation and adaptation.[210] He counsels "no identities survive the diasporic process intact and unchanged or maintains their connection with their past undisturbed."[211] Resolution of wounded diasporic identity is a "shift from 'I am' to 'I want.'"[212] Meaders recounts at age 25 when she chose to migrate from Japan to New York, she noticed an inner three-stage process towards a transcultural self: 1) survival of identity after immersion in a new culture, 2) bicultural identity and, finally, 3) transcultural identity.[213]

Before the transcultural self emerges, she says, there's an identity crisis with three possible responses:

1) *Rapid adjusters* imitate normative behaviours, roles and identities that fit with the host culture. While this may appear painless, they deny their own culture and their newland adjustment is often fragile and doesn't stand the migration tests of disappointments and disillusionments and later can result in disintegration of self.
2) *Isolationists* withdraw into homeland cultural groups, or internally into themselves. Unable to explore the newland and unwilling to adapt, they hold rigidly onto homeland culture and find themselves at odds with the newland. Over time, they become rigid, aloof and fearful.
3) *Dualists* despise the disorientation of migration and express their own culture while being open to the newland. They try to avoid extremes and make room for new input and direction. Relying on their own integrity, they "make the most lasting and flexible adaptation."[214]

Social psychologists speak of five life-course identity strategies of adolescence which are part of an ongoing inner struggle that can be chaotic or consciously constructed.[215] The model has application to migration and the diasporic complex.

1) *Adolescent refusers* fail to become adult and develop defences or "self-defeating cognitive schemes that lock them into child-like behavior patterns of dependence."[216] Defences can be parents, government benefits, crime or an underground economy, or similar friends caught in alcohol/drug abuse. Adolescent refusers lack the inner structures necessary to develop social, emotional and vocational skills and may be the outcome of too permissive parenting. *Migrant refusers* lack the competencies necessary to gain entrance to newlands through regular channels. Tied migrants and/or forced migrants can become refusers and live in a state of exile with diasporic complexes: they usually fail to adapt and become independent citizens.

2) *Adolescent drifters* are similar to refusers but have more personal resources—higher education, family wealth, or occupational skills—but are unable to consistently utilize them. Cognitively, they are caught in a chronic pre-adult or puerile mindset, with poor impulse control and have shallow relationships with low commitment.[217] The *migrant drifter* may gain entrance to a foreign country through official channels, but once there, lacks the ability to utilize opportunities.

3) *Adolescent searchers* achieve adult competencies, but their difficulty lies in relationship: "Unable to find perfection in themselves, and unable to find perfection in a community, the searchers are locked into a perpetual journey for which there can be no end."[218] Likewise, *migrant searchers* may have sufficient competencies to gain entrance to newlands, but newlands do not meet their high standards of perfection. Whether migrant searchers stay or return home, they carry a grudge, a sense of anger and contempt for both newlands and homelands.

4) *Adolescent guardians* have a well-structured childhood with internalized values and resources, but may be overly identified with parental values or traditional authorities and lack the flexibility needed for modern life.[219] *Migrant guardians* do not leave the homeland by choice, and in newlands they are caught in a diaspora complex of perpetual longing and, unable to adapt, they may become politically active for the homeland.

5) *Adolescent resolvers* actively engage in "forming an adult identity [and] developing intellect, emotional maturity and vocational skills rooted in one's general competencies and interests."[220] If they're held back, they "find themselves yearning to grow in certain ways and will likely do so with whatever means are at their disposal."[221] Likewise, *migrant resolvers* have sufficient qualities and competencies to gain entrance through official channels to newlands. If they come up against barriers, they pragmatically adapt and find a way forward. An example is a former oil executive who in the newland works as a supermarket cashier. While searching for a better job, he sees the current one as opportunity for cultural adaptation and improving his language skills.

Successful adaptation

Successful adaptation following migration is function of several factors: 1) the health of the pre-migration personality, 2) motivation for migration, 3) the host country providing a good-enough holding environment, and 4) accepting the mourning necessary for psychological adjustment. Winnicott's[222] concept of "good-enough" parents who meet most of the infant's needs is a good model for newlands. Parental imperfections promote growth through disillusionment, anger and frustration that forces the child to confront reality, instead of resting in fantasies of perfection and omnipotence. In migration, "it is unclear whether the migration identity that emerges as a result of the mourning-liberation process is a reasonably solid hybrid entity or a loose, albeit, well-functioning confederacy of diverse selves."[223] For adolescents, the stability and harmony of the parental relationship and the family itself and the compatibility of the values of family and peers puts "an extra burden upon the adolescent's ego, rendering identity consolidation difficult. Such a child has to create 'a third reality' neither the parent's homeland nor the adopted land but uniquely and historically different."[224] There's also the push-pull of homeland culture: "A mild culture hunger is cultural, while more intense forms of it are the result of deeper unresolved conflicts."[225]

Said describes his migration experience and identity challenge as chaotic transformation[226] that left him with a basic split in ethnicity and language,[227] accompanied by a sense of a "buried second self."[228] He says "I was beginning again in the US, unlearning to some extent what I had learned before, relearning things from scratch, improving, self-inventing, trying and failing, experimenting, cancelling, and restarting in surprisingly and frequently painful ways."[229] Despite living in the US for 37 years, he says: "To this day I still feel that I am away from home ... there is still some measure of regret..a sense of provisionality."[230] At the same time, there's a sense of freedom.[231] He prefers his self-image symbolized by "a cluster of flowing currents,"[232] rather than "the idea of a solid self, the identity to which so many attach much significance."[233] His modern sense of self as a flowing current is what Bauman calls "liquid modernity."[234] Said says self and identity require no central theme, no reconciling and no harmonizing; and "with so many dissonances in my life, I have learned actually to prefer being not quite right and out of place."[235]

Born in southern France, philosopher Foucault speaks of a similar experience. As a young adult, he found reading Nietzsche broke his comfortable life and made him decide to migrate to Algeria. Years later in France, he couldn't identify fully with the country: "I'm still not quite integrated within French social and intellectual life."[236] Migration, he says, opened his eyes and taught him: "You don't have to have a homogenous intellectual and cultural life. As a foreigner, I don't have to be integrated."[237]

The opposite is also true. After migrating, "many expatriate South Asians in the west have become more aggressively traditional, and more culturally exclusive and chauvinistic."[238] And "as their children begin to show symptoms of integration into their adopted land, they become more protective about what they think are their faiths and cultures."[239] Some migrants disapprove of naturalization seeing it as alienation from one's own culture, as "adulteration and denial of one's basic being."[240] Sayad explains: "You live in a country, work in a county and even work for that country, but you are from a homeland."[241] These attitudes can "coexist in contradictory fashion within the same individual, with one or the other reaction becoming dominant depending on the context and need and customs of the moment."[242]

Migrants report dreams of buying furniture, which are interpreted as a dream of commitment. One dreamer said: "that image to me represents such a clear complexity between finding a fulfillment in a new surrounding (relatively speaking) while slowly detaching oneself from everything one was familiar with or believed to be."[243] British migrants in Aquitaine France for more than thirty years, some of whom were married to locals, were interviewed. They admitted their sense of humour remained an area of difference—an "inability to capture the nuances of foreign humour and to express one's own identity through this medium."[244] One said: "I don't really feel connected to the UK any more ... but I feel English generally, culturally."[245] Others spoke of cultural ambivalence and of feeling part of both cultures, but not fully integrated in either: "The longer one stays in France, the more one feels that one will never be totally accepted into the culture and, at the same time, the more one feels alienated from one's original culture."[246] Several admitted the British are "not allowed to feel similar" and "are confronted, on a daily basis, by their own otherness."[247] The challenge of identity and otherness is dynamically important. The French categorization of them as British feels disorienting, and at the same time, it "forces the migrant to take refuge in a familiar cultural environment for a more positive reflection of self."[248] It also "reinforces the cultural bonds of the group."[249] Although the British in France become defensive and console themselves in cultural alterity, they also regard British culture as superior. They have an almost colonialist verve of having collectively improved the area. They take credit for kick-starting the local economy: "Without us this region would be dead." "All these houses were falling to pieces and the people were just peasant farmers." "We come and do up the houses and the French see it and think 'they look good' and so they do it as well and the whole village looks better now since we got here."[250]

In multicultural countries, it's often easier to identify with the newland. Montero cites a new citizen: "I feel as much as Canadian as anyone around here. We found a new country and we really like it now."[251]

However, some find the relocation difficult, citing lack of history and visible coherent culture:

> The trouble with a lot of immigrants is that they seem to think it is possible to have a dream world where they can become more or less, Canadian, but where they can retain the best part of their old life too. That would be beautiful if it were possible, but it's not. I know because I tried it.[252]

She explains having suffered delayed culture shock after her baby was born when she wanted to give her child a Polish name and speak Polish. Although her husband was also from Poland, she says he was resentful of what he saw as her psychological regression. In response, she surrendered to his wishes and concluded that for her "integration equals annihilation"[253] of her homeland identity.

In multiculturalism, Sen says, there's a need to distinguish between "cultural liberty—the freedom to preserve culture—and valuing of cultural conservation."[254] In contrast, Sayad sees migration as liberation, saying securing a European passport transformed him: "It gives me the freedom to be me. It means freedom: life. It's not an abstraction ... you are free from the allegiance that comes from belonging to any particular national territory, or in other words a nation or a nationality."[255] This idea is supported by clinical observations: "Migration does not necessarily destabilize one's sense of identity,"[256] note the Grinbergs, even when it puts "one's psychic and emotional stability to the test."[257] Good inner psychic relations permit the acceptance of losses and a working-though the mourning process with integration of "two countries, two time periods, and two social groups in a discriminatory way ... the person reorganizes and consolidates his sense of identity as someone who remains himself despite changes and restructuring."[258]

Migration and identity politics

Nations are described as "historically, geographically, socially, politically, and culturally grounded constructions,"[259] with identities arising from a "dialectical movement of self-discovery and identity formation."[260] Nations are also imagined communities created for political and economic ends.[261] They're products of the imagination, Anderson says, because "members of even the smallest nation will never know most of their fellow members, meet them, or even hear of them, yet in the minds of each lives the image of their communion."[262] History or "collective memory is not an inert and passive thing, but a field of activity in which past events are selected, reconstructed, maintained, modified, and endowed with political meaning."[263] National identity is based on multiple self-categories;[264] and identification with land, history, culture, race and religious and political beliefs.[265]

Billig coined the term "banal nationalism" to describe identification with art, flags, songs and sports teams that replaces the sense of self as a citizen and member of a family, religion, class and region.[266] Zahar argues that region and religion are more important markers of self-identify than the nation.[267] Bauder reminds us that nations are not pre-existing but created entities.[268]

Kage was born in Canada but being ethnically Japanese, he grew up in an internment camp during WWII. After the war, the family went to Japan. Attempting to process these difficult experiences, he began to decode his sense of culture, race and identity. He speaks of the myth of Japanese society as homogeneous,[269] caught in self-flattery as being the best in the world with super-nationalistic ideas.[270] He describes national identity as "awareness of the self as belonging to a certain country, a people, a grouping, that is, a spontaneous and subjective element of [being] determined by others, or external conditions."[271] Later, when the family returned to Canada, he says he was caught betwixt his birthland and ancestral land. "We're not Canadians and we're not Japanese—we just look Japanese,"[272] he says.

Identity is experienced emotionally. The Grinbergs explain: "the immigrant in his/her struggle for self-preservation needs to hold onto various elements of his/her native environment, familiar objects, music, memories, and dreams representing different aspects of his native land in order to be able to feel like him/herself."[273] For exiles, the situation is more intense. They often suffer from feelings of insecurity and persecution and a sense of impermanence, of just passing through, along with hopes of return. Their dependence on others can be high. They may lack employment or work in their own field, and experience unfair loss and depersonalization: "It becomes difficult for them to take on any identity other than that of exile."[274] There is sadness, anger, guilt and an identity crisis, along with resistance to newland adaptation and idealization of the homeland. One admitted:

> I confronted the problem of maintaining my identity; I struggled to change it, because when I de-idealized my task, I could accept the 'bad' aspect of my old culture and incorporate the 'good' aspects of the new without completely renouncing my previous identifications.[275]

Race in the form of racial essentialism and reductionism often emerges at the core of identity politics: "Race is a deeply embedded and effective way to group populations globally on biological 'natural' grounds."[276] Race often underlies challenges in global social relations.[277]

Many political refugees who feel safe in newlands maintain intense emotional attachments and engagement with homeland politics. There are three reasons migrants from de-territorialized states are courted and encouraged to promote national interests of homelands:[278]

1) "Human capital upgrading is a development strategy of sending countries that supports not only emigration as a safety valve against poverty and social protest but must also sponsor return migration that imports useful skills and accumulated savings."[279]
2) Remittances from migrants sent under a strong "myth of return" are an important source of capital for many countries that ceases if migrants return or the family leaves for the newland.
3) Migrants function as a domestic political force in the newland to advance homeland economic and foreign policy interests.[280]

In a review of policy reforms in Latin American countries, it was concluded:

> Sending governments do not want their immigrants to return, but rather to achieve a secure status in the wealthy nations to which they have moved and from which they can make sustained economic and political contributions in the name of patriotism and home town loyalty.[281]

Thus, permanent migration of citizens is encouraged along with diasporic identity in newlands. The opposite can also happen when refugees and political exiles suffer cultural, social, political, or physical abuse in the homeland and harbour justice complexes imbued with anger and resentments that prompt vengeful acts and reprisals.[282,283,284]

Identity politics today "has become a master concept that explains much of what is going on globally."[285] The political left is focused on broad economic equality and the interests of marginalized groups, while the right is focused on traditional identity of nation, religion, sect, race and ethnicity.[286] The primary problem of identity politics is the experience of "self as a suffering subject"[287] and of "wounded attachment"[288] to the homeland where the self is "diminished, subjugated, and misrecognized."[289] Identity tied to "a politics of recrimination and rancor" and "culturally dispersed paralysis and suffering" has "a tendency to reproach power rather than aspire to it, to disdain freedom rather than practice it."[290] It suggests Nietzsche's concept of *ressentiment* where rationalized political attitude of suffering is translated into moral superiority and becomes a social virtue. *Ressentiment* actually goes beyond subjective feelings to the need for revenge, with a "fantasized overturning of the entire value system."[291] In fact, "resentment over indignities has become a powerful force,"[292] as "politicized identity mobilized in and through identity politics has an investment in pain"[293]—one's own pain and redress through revenge.

Identity politics[294] based on projections of other cultures and races is problematic.[295] The racialized and colonized are often "parasitically obsessed with the extraneous relation with the colonial power,"[296] which results in "reactive self-perception" and "reactive-identity."[297] It's a "reactive fundamentalism that is foreign-dependent in a negative and contrary form."[298] It can lead to a desire to get even and to seek justice in actions rationalized by "invoking the past and present offenses of the Western world."[299] Sen argues that "decolonization of the mind demands a firm departure from the temptation of solitary identities and priorities."[300]

Migrants' wounded national attachment leads to identity politics that are "more aggressively traditional, and more culturally exclusive and chauvinistic."[301] When "their cherished world becomes more difficult to sustain, as they and their children begin to show symptoms of integration into their adopted land, they become more protective about what they think are their faiths and cultures."[302] Moreover, in attempts to valorize ethnic identity and tradition, it's not uncommon for communities "to objectify women and girls as the preservers of a true tradition, religion or ethnic culture—often expressed in opposition to modernity."[303] Preoccupation of migrants with culture and gender relations is often a political foil that uses women's clothing, hair and personal freedoms and access to education or employment as the expression or essence of their superior way of life.[304] In fact, gender relations may even come to represent a cultural essence to be passed to next generations.[305] As a result, women and girls can be pawns, caught between opposing hegemonic traditionalists.[306,307,308] On one hand are migrants who oppose secularism; on the other, there are host countries that support superficial forms of multiculturalism.[309] An example is how wearing the hijab in France is seen as a "failure of the French Republican system to fully assimilate second and third generation immigrants."[310] Interpreted as evidence of non-integration, it promotes fears of the "growth of fundamentalisms and terrorists"[311] within European society, while it may just be the gender politics of those who feel demasculinized in cultures of equality.

Wounded attachment manifests internally and in migrant relations which may be a reaction to feelings of social dominance. All that can be done, by migrants or other minority groups who feel dominated, is "to accept (willingly or with resignation, submissively or angrily) the dominant definition, or that given by the dominant, of their identity."[312] The reality is that "both parties find themselves caught up in a process of mutual rejection, which is also a process of mutual accusations of rejection."[313] In the case of migrants, their adaptation can become a "subtle game of bluff that is designed to conceal the stigma, or at least to mask its most obvious external signs. They therefore promote a self-image that is as close as possible to a legitimate identity, the dominant identity."[314] It may look like a struggle for self-identity[315] within a newland culture, but for migrants it's a no-win situation of being caught in compromises:

> Sub-proletarians dream of enjoying, simultaneously ... the economic advantages associated with "risk" (advantages that they have discovered thanks to the capitalistic economy), moral and material security, and the solidarity guaranteed them by tradition (advantages specific to the pre-capitalistic social and economic system).[316]

But fundamentally, it's a "contradictory situation one cannot resolve, and which one cannot even escape,"[317] because "the immigrant presence is always marked by its incompleteness; it is an at-fault presence that in itself is guilty. It is a displaced presence [wherein] immigration is an original sin,"[318] says Sayad. Everyone with other-assigned dual-national identity dreams of having a perfectly legitimate identity.[319] One Algerian explains: "once France was in our country—now we are in France's country: that changes everything."[320]

"The search for authenticity has driven many minority groups to speak from a victim position of woundedness, where pain offers a singular, originary [native], and thus irrefutable experience."[321] In fact, the granting of authority and legitimacy is now given only to those who are able to narrate "experiences of pain, hurt and oppression."[322] Thus, the victim has become "the basis of knowledge and moral authority," and all members have to "prove their personal suffering" that celebrates misery and "becomes fetishized as a proof of identity."[323] Victimhood becomes the means of gaining power.[324] Personal pain becomes a "groove of self-repetition and habituated resentment,"[325] that grants privileged identity, authority and power.

Meaders notes migration may change one's geography, but not the inner conflicts of the individual.[326] An authentic newland self-identity requires "restructuring and working though of the old conflicts,"[327] along with 1) emotional distance from the homeland, 2) a new perspective of self gained through 3) new experiences in newlands, and 4) conscious exercise of a new self-expression and identity.[328] Said admits migration led to inner revelations: "The underlying motifs for me have been the emergence of a second self buried for a very long time beneath a surface of often expertly acquired and wielded social characteristic belonging to the self my parents tried to construct."[329] Akhtar concurs saying learning a new language, enables migrants the opportunity for the "acquisition of new identity," and represents a life-saving anchor that allows for "rebirth."[330]

Transnationalism is defined as flows of people, money and/or information that span social networks, organizations, fields and countries.[331] Bauböck explains that migration can lead to transnational citizenship of "overlapping memberships between territorially separated and independent polities."[332] Still, before migrants naturalize and become citizens of newlands, they are citizens of homelands subject to laws of newlands. This creates mismatches between newland and personal polities because, under international law, it entails a right to return to the homeland concurrent with diplomatic protection in the newland.[333] This became an issue recently in Canada, when the Saudi embassy posted bail and gave travel documents to one of its citizens accused of serious crimes, who had been required to surrender his passport.[334]

Belonging

Humans are the "the most social of all social animals—more interdependent, more attached to each other, more inseparable in our behaviours than bees."[335] Belonging is "a personal feeling, the sense of belonging to a certain group, place or social location."[336] Heidegger defines identity as "belonging-together,"[337,338] and a "responding to Being; the essence of humanness."[339] Belonging

> can be the greatest of human gifts. It can give us comfort, identity, companionship, and material support. It can ease our fear and help us feel not so alone on this journey of life. It defines who we are as human beings.[340]

There is a universal emotional human need for belonging and unconditional acceptance.[341] Belonging is not just a need, it's a motivation.[342] In Maslow's hierarchy of human needs, belonging is fulfilled only after physiological and safety needs are met. And belonging is seen as an essential aspect of self-esteem and self-actualization.[343]

It's important to distinguish between "ways of being as identity" and "ways of belonging" or connections.[344] "Identity is constructed through belonging and exclusion,"[345] both assigned membership and choosing to belong.[346] Choice implies "identification"[347] and self-identity.[348] Belonging is relationship with those who matter and in environments where one matters.[349]

Beyond meeting the primary need of emotional attachment, belonging provides access to assets[350] and "emotional closeness, moral support and solidarity which generally arises among members of a group with a common goal,"[351] along with "opportunities for self-promotion as well as access to power and resources."[352] Itself a resource, belonging is "used to draw social demarcations and establish border regimes, the so-called politics of belonging."[353]

"Humans have always lived in groups and these collectivities have had some sense of common belonging ... defined by language, territory and other markers, which have been used to draw boundaries around the group."[354] Although recognition of sameness can create a sense of belonging, it can also create a sense of difference and exclusion. Yet, "loyalty to one's own group is not automatically accompanied by hostility to members of other groups."[355] While identity is spatial and temporal, the social aspect of object-relations "established via projective and introjective identification it helps to create the feelings of belonging."[356]

Migrant identity and sense of belonging are complex, multilayered, full of in-betweenness, ambivalence and uncertainty in "the search for new attachments and new belongings"[357] Attachment, sense of belonging and perceptions of membership take time, as does persistent feelings of not belonging and non-inclusion even after being officially granted citizenship.[358] Not surprising, migrant identities are inherently ambivalent subjected to change.[359]

There are different levels of belonging from relationships to the land, to psychological and social attachments to persons and collectives, political values and identification, as well as politics of citizenship, status and entitlement.[360] Belonging is about identity and "stories people tell themselves and others about who they are (and who they are not)."[361] Such stories can be individual and/or collective. Individual stories of identity are usually about "attributes, body images, vocational aspirations or sexual prowess."[362] Collective identities are about meanings of groups and collectivities of ethnicity, race, nation, culture and religion.[363] Although identities are individually constructed, they can be inherited: "They can relate to the past, to a myth of origin; they can be aimed at explaining the present and, probably above all, they function as a projection of a future trajectory."[364] Constructed stories of belonging are not simply stories; they speak to desire and longing: "Even in its most stable 'primordial' forms, however, belonging is always a dynamic process ... of power relations."[365]

Modern societies are a "series of networks with belonging oriented towards defensive identity-communities and not local, civil societies of nation states"[366] continually in the process of change.[367] Many migrants "put down roots in a host country, maintain strong homeland ties, and belong to religious and political movements that span the globe."[368] Along with globalization, increasing numbers are becoming transnationals which to some degree fragments the sense of identity and belonging.[369,370] Still, transnationalism is not new; it was common in the 19th century. Today, "only five to ten percent of the Dominican, Salvadoran, and Colombian migrants surveyed in the US regularly participated in transnational economic and political activities."[371] They may take part in transnational activities, but don't necessarily identify with transnational groups.[372] In fact, the US is not a melting pot of ethnic assimilation but "cultural pluralism of ethnic groups."[373] They carry symbolic importance; they let people feel ethnic without having to act ethnic all the time and belong to the larger society.[374] The erosion of ethnic identities and loyalties of European descendants was linked to declines in prejudice and discrimination,[375] yet an "ethnic-hum" has survived.[376] In today's globalized world of economics, politics and culture, transnational networks of communities exist of "dense and strong social and symbolic ties."[377] It permits today's migrants to identify and belong to both homelands and newlands, to "participate in social, political, and cultural life in both the host society and the sending state."[378] Their ideas of individual rights are not tied to particular nation states, but are shaped by regional, international and transnational organizations.[379]

Transnational migration is not new: what *is* new is transportation and communication systems. Increasingly, homeland policies encourage enduring long-distance nationalism.[380] In addition to financial remittances are social remittances: "ideas, behaviors, identities, and social capital that migrants export to homeland communities,"[381] innovative "ideas about democracy, health, and community organization."[382] Transnationalism is no longer seen as a "threat to assimilation, and does not take away from migrants' ability to contribute to and be loyal to their host country."[383] Although after arrival migrants tend to be more involved with and identify with familiar homelands, over time with increasing adaptation newlands become more important. In fact, migrants climb two different social ladders.[384] They move up, remain steady, or experience downward mobility in both homelands and newlands.[385] The issue is not whether it's good or bad for migrants to live across national boundaries, those who move and those who stay function "transnationally" in different ways and degrees.[386] The real issues are protection, representation and contribution.[387]

Guibernau speaks of the migrant's "reciprocal commitments,"[388] and feelings of familiarity that evoke "the idea of being and feeling 'at home' where the individual is recognized as 'one of us,' he or she 'matters' and has an identity."[389] Feeling at home and belonging carries the ideas of "a common culture, history, kinship, language, religion, territory, founding moment and destiny,"[390] as well as common symbols and rituals. Important too, are psychological attachments and the emotional pleasure of closeness.[391] Being accepted and belonging can be a "source of anxiety and stress whenever the individual feels inadequate, under-valued, misunderstood or ignored within the group."[392] The shadow side of belonging is ideas of "us and them" that "lead to hostility, intransigence, tribalism, war, oppression and even genocide."[393]

Ignatieff argues that it's necessary to distinguish between inherited and chosen belonging. Ethnic nationalism claims the "deepest attachments are inherited, not chosen,"[394] while modern society is characterized more by chosen memberships. Junger explores tribal bonds of loyalty, sense of belonging and quest for meaning in relationship in hunter-gatherer societies, as well as the importance of initiation rites for adulthood. Recounting early American history, he notes the numbers of white captives of Aboriginal peoples who, after experiencing the cooperative sharing in tribal life, had no desire to return to their inherited, hierarchical colonial societies.[395]

Cultural syncretism is defined as the blending of cultures and convergence among European descendents in the new world where shared values of "family, education, hard work, religiosity and patriotism;" has led to intermarriage and a pan-European identity among European-Americans.[396] It's seen as a new American ethnic group of European ancestry;[397] cosmopolitan identity,[398] and described as fluid, dynamic and open.[399] Ignatieff speaks of the rise of a new political nationalism that holds the "belief that the world's peoples are divided into nations, and that each of these nations has the right of self-determination, either as self-governing units within existing nation states or as nation states of their own."[400] Although people may have many identities, "it is the nation which provides them with their primary form of belonging."[401] The shadow side of nationalism is the "ethic of heroic sacrifice, justifying the use of violence in the defense of one's nation against enemies, internal or external."[402] Still, at its most elemental, Ignatieff argues, nationalism is

> the desire to have political dominion over a piece of land that one loves. Before anything, there must be a fierce attachment to the land itself and a sense that there is nothing else like this, nothing so beautiful, anywhere else in the world.[403]

Further, "nationalism by its very nature defines struggles between peoples as struggles for their honour, identity and soul."[404]

In contrast to anthropological, political and sociological ideas of belonging, depth psychologists speak to the importance to the inner self. Papadopoulos defines home as a "part of the core 'substratum of identity' structured as a 'mosaic.'"[405] Home is a container interconnecting "three, overlapping realms—the intrapsychic, the interpersonal and the socio-political."[406] It enables growth and development of individuals, regulates relations of its members and assists in resolving conflicts, and mediates between the collective home and the outer world, society, culture and socio-political and economic realities.[407] The Grinbergs speak of the individual sense of belonging. In early stages of migration, there's a strong feeling of not belonging anymore to the world one left behind or the world to which one has newly arrived. Feelings of exclusion and loneliness exist until the feeling of belonging emerges, which is "requisite for being integrated into a new country and also for maintaining one's sense of identity."[408] The land "often comes to represent a significant part of a person's sense of identity."[409] And the land and physical architecture is "invested with intense emotional content and tends to persist unmodified as an object of nostalgia and symbol of belonging."[410]

The culture shock of migration is generally a self-limiting crisis,[411] but can become a springboard for psychic disturbances. The Grinbergs recount migration situations where "anxieties can develop pathologically into truly psychotic states"[412] like "paranoia and overt persecutory delusion,"[413] and where the newland is seen as "hostile and dangerous, enmeshed in conspiracies whose object is to hurt or do harm to the subject."[414] Such "disorienting psychosis may cause a person not only to lose his sense of identity but also to become disoriented in time and space."[415] In these situations, dream work is useful and important. At first, there are "recurrent 'evacuative' dreams' that often happen in traumatic neurosis and help to defuse anxiety and guilt."[416] Later dreams are generally more developmental with memories, persons and loved objects, and lead "to greater ego integration."[417] The Grinbergs also underscore the importance of mourning one's former self and the absence of important others and objects, as this permits and "encourages the progressive reestablishment of one's sense of identity."[418] Although, they note, migrants are never likely to fully complete this mourning process, there are steps that permit integration without renouncing either the new or the old and where "ego enrichment is promoted along with the consolidation of what one might call the remodeled sense of identity."[419]

Turner reminds us of the Buddhist view that no life is free from suffering.[420] Migrants have to embrace and deal with the special suffering of migration to truly belong to the newland. It means facing negative emotions, since they tell us where our problems lie.[421] Disappointment can be disguised as boredom or restlessness that forces one to question life's purpose.[422] Impatience reminds us to be cautious.[423] The more difficult emotions make us question ourselves and decisions that can shift into negativity and buyer's regret or seeing migration as wrong, and the self as inadequate or worthless, insignificant, invisible, left out, misunderstood, unimportant and unsupported.[424] "Grief is the response to a broken bond of belonging,"[425] it's also "the expression of healing in motion."[426]

Turner lists the competencies of belonging:[427] 1) commitment and accountability defined as deep devotion and endurance;[428] 2) skills of home-making in a "constant state of learning" and a Zen Buddhist attitude of *shoshin* or beginner's mind of eagerness and openness,[429] 3) emergence and surrender or the capacity to give and receive,[430] and gratitude,[431] a "mentor of belonging."[432] Also to be cultivated are 4) hospitality towards others, 5) rituals of life, and 6) respect for the land and reciprocity with nature.[433]

Place attachment has socio-cultural and biophysical dimensions:[434] 1) personal place identity, 2) place dependency, 3) community social bonding, and 4) environmental place bonding.[435] Warnick sees internal US migration as a virus infecting everyone,[436] resulting in geography-related unworthiness,[437] a form of psychic suffering causing moving-truck wounds.[438] We are cautioned to take personal responsibility for belonging to invest in a place:

Relationships with people are what make you feel most at home ... . Feelings follow action. Happy memories create place attachment ... There's no right town for everyone, just the right town for you right now. Let yourself experience joy for as long as you're there."[439]

Religion, migration and belonging

Religion is "an institutionalized system of beliefs and practices concerning the supernatural realm; spirituality as the personal beliefs by which an individual relates to and experiences the supernatural realm; and faith as the human trust or belief in a transcendent reality."[440] Typically, religions promote a moral code of laws, devotional practices and ritual observances. Historically, some nations attempted to impose religious homogeneity, but the modern western reality is religious pluralism. The demise of religions in modern life has been predicted, yet a plurality of religions play major roles in migration and settlement: "Many of the founders, leaders, and proselytizers of the major world religions have also been migrants [and] have taken along their faiths and practices and adapted them to living in their host societies."[441]

Early American historians, such as Handlin,[442] Herberg,[443] Gordon[444] and recently Cadge and Ecklund[445] have explored US religions. An emerging literature looks at migrant religions and influences of religion in social spheres "not usually thought of as specifically religious, such as workplaces, neighborhoods, local civic and political organizations, childcare centers, recreational facilities, and other aspects of daily life in the United States."[446] Also religion's role in "development and maintenance of transnational relations"[447] has been explored: "Stories of migration found within religious texts offer narratives into which migrants can insert their own migration stories."[448] The stories are paradigmatic; they tell of deportation, exile and life under foreign powers:[449]

> As migrants engage with familiar and new religious texts, they discover resonance with experiences of joy, struggle, hope, and fear in the lives of women and men who have—or are remembered as having—taken these and other journeys before them.[450]

Recitation of epic narratives helps migrants to understand and interpret their own lives and, at the same time, their own migration experiences shed new light on old texts.[451]

Goode sees the absence of theology in interdisciplinary discourse on migration,[452] arguing that "social science without theology does not give us a perspective wide enough to account for the deeper relational and spiritual dimensions of human life that shape, define, and sustain human existence."[453] In rereading the biblical exodus, exile, diaspora, he drafted a four-stage theological model of migration, exile and belonging,[454] offering a "new way of conceptualizing a difficult and contentious global issue."[455] He examines theological concepts of "human dignity, solidarity, communion, and conversion [and justice to] address the negativism, narcissism, nationalism, and nihilism that interfere with building these right relationships."[456]

Religion is a psychological resource, a social support and spiritual companionship in all phases of migration.[457,458] However, for migrants, the practice of homeland religions is not always easy when, for example, religious festivals fall on newland workdays,[459] or when religious symbols become markers of difference[460] and discrimination.[461] Religious organizations provide "traditional healing practices"[462] and healthcare,[463] including establishing hospitals and elder-care facilities. Secular health organizations provide prayer spaces and honour diverse religious practices,[464] and not just health-care facilities: "South Asian Muslim taxi drivers in New York City pray while working, primarily by stopping in restaurants that have created informal prayer spaces."[465] Many faith-based organizations are at the forefront of helping migrant settlement, and are active in political reform and legislative changes:

> Religious voluntary agencies, church-affiliated charities, and congregations have worked with the government to support refugee relief and resettlement—internationally, nationally, at the state level, and locally. They have not only aided refugees in the immediate period after resettlement, but they have also been critical to facilitating refugees' long-term integration.[466]

In 2011, the US Catholic Conference of Bishops called for "solidarity with migrants on the basis of the memory that we too were migrants."[467] Still, a shadow side exists of a "hetero-patriarchal framework of many religious traditions/theologies that make life difficult for migrants who identify as queer or LGBTQI."[468]

Suh explores religion as a primary acculturation agent of American Koreans,[469] which has led to debates about authentic identity.[470] In Korea, Buddhism is the national religion and a marker of Korean identity. However, some see Buddhism as a relic of the past and Christianity as the "marker of a successful American identity."[471] Suh says it's more than a question of identity. The Korean Christian Church creates community through praying, singing and reaching out and supporting opportunities for socializing and business connections.[472] Although the Buddhist temple does not offer opportunities for socializing and business, its teachings are seen by some as the source of wisdom, self-knowledge, self-esteem, open-mindedness, psychological strength and independence which are essential for success in the new world.[473] In contrast, the Christian teachings are criticized as leading to blind faith, weakness of will and dependency.[474]

In summary, ascribed identity is based on physical, social-cultural and national characteristics that a person may cling to for a sense of self and belonging shattered by migration; but these may also liberate with a new personal sense of self and belonging to place, people and land.

Notes

1 Lawler, 2008/2014.
2 Welz, 2005:2–3.
3 Grinberg & Grinberg, 1989:120.
4 Rockefeller, 1992:97.
5 Samuels et al., 1986/2000:107–108.
6 Hyde & McGuinness, 1999:91.
7 Jung, CW7:245; original emphasis.
8 Kalff 2004.
9 Permission granted.
10 Hopcke, 1995:7.
11 Hopcke, 1998:88–89.
12 Hyde & McGuinness, 1999:87.
13 Samuels et al., 1986/2000:50.
14 Ibid.:76.
15 Jacobi, 1959/1974:37.
16 Samuels et al., 1986/2000:135–136.
17 Heidegger, 1927/2008.
18 Ibid.:79.
19 Jung, CW6:757.
20 Ellenberger, 1970:672.
21 Jung, CW6:762; original emphasis.
22 Ibid.:762.
23 Stein, 2006:8.
24 Erikson & Erikson, 1998:65.
25 Goble & Maslow, 1970/1980:25.
26 Rogers et al., 1967:187.
27 Homer, 1946.
28 Papadopoulos, 2002b:13–14.
29 Ibid.:14.
30 Ibid.:15.
31 Ibid.:15.
32 Ainsworth & Bell, 1970.
33 Van Buren & Cooley, 2002:418.
34 Main & Solomon, 1990.
35 Bartholomew & Horowitz, 1991.
36 Hazan & Shaver, 1987.
37 Ibid.:226.
38 Ferenczi & Marshall, 2013.
39 Ibid.:2013.
40 Diener, 1984.

41 Ferenczi & Marshall, 2013.
42 Engbersen et al., 2013.
43 Ibid.:2013.
44 Winnicott, 1986.
45 Ibid..
46 Winnicott, 1971.
47 Winnicott, 1986.
48 Ward et al., 2001:331.
49 Berry, 1997.
50 Portes & Rumbaut, 2006:130–131.
51 Stern, 1973/1985:37.
52 Ibid.:71.
53 Ibid.:102.
54 Ibid.:124.
55 Ibid.:139.
56 Ibid.:162.
57 Lawler, 2008/2014.
58 Carliner, 2000.
59 Ng et al., 2011.
60 Isphording, 2015.
61 Budría et al., 2017.
62 Erikson & Erikson, 1998.
63 Clarkson, 2016:183.
64 Eisenstadt, 1953:34–35.
65 Ng et al., 2011:70.
66 Robert & Gilkinson, 2012:iii.
67 Ibid.:iii.
68 Samuels et al., 1986/2000:26.
69 Ibid.:26–28.
70 Samuels et al., 1986/2000:117.
71 Côté & Levine, 2002.
72 Ibid.:xii.
73 Welz, 2005:2–3.
74 Ibid.:2–3.
75 Bauman, 1995.
76 Beck, 1992.
77 Welz, 2005:4.
78 Côté & Levine, 2002:xi.
79 Welz, 2005:4.
80 Ibid.:19–20.
81 Jung, CW6:741.
82 Ibid.:741.
83 Ibid.:742.
84 Ackers, 2004:45.
85 Ibid.:48.
86 Ibid.:65.
87 Ibid.:65.
88 Ibid.; 66.
89 Ibid.:66.
90 Ibid.:67.
91 Taylor, 1989:x &15.
92 Ibid.:22.

93 Ibid.:22.
94 Ibid.:497.
95 Ibid.:512.
96 Ibid.:509.
97 Lawler, 2008/2014:118.
98 Ibid.; 118.
99 Ibid.:118.
100 Ibid.:118.
101 Rattansi, 2007:117.
102 Ibid.:117.
103 Ibid.:118.
104 Ibid.:118.
105 Bauman, 2004.
106 Rattansi, 2007:89.
107 Côté, 2002.
108 Arnett, 2002.
109 Turkle, 2012:xii.
110 Ibid.:172.
111 Ibid.:172.
112 Ibid.:241.
113 Lobban, 2016:71.
114 Lobban, 2016:75.
115 Ibid.:75.
116 Ibid.:75.
117 Ibid.:75.
118 Connell, 1995:276–277.
119 Ibid.::277.
120 Schechtman, 2011.
121 Olson, 2007.
122 Olson, 1997.
123 Schechtman, 2011.
124 González, 2016:33.
125 Ibid.:48.
126 Basch et al., 2004:221.
127 Ibid.:221.
128 Ibid.:221.
129 Dere, 2019:349.
130 Ibid.:350.
131 Mehta, 1998:133.
132 Ibid.:133.
133 Marcia, 1973:340–354.
134 Grinberg & Grinberg, 1989:130.
135 Ibid.:131–132.
136 Ibid.:131–132.
137 Ibid.:132.
138 Ibid.:132.
139 Ibid.:133.
140 Ibid.:133.
141 Ibid.:133.
142 Ibid.:133.
143 Papadopoulos, 2002b:37.
144 Ibid.:37.

145 Homans, 1979:36.
146 Jung, CW7:160.
147 Smith, 1990:352.
148 Jacobi, 1959/1974:186–187.
149 Mendaglio, 2008:35.
150 Ibid.:35.
151 Ellenberger, 1970:449.
152 Akhtar, 1999/2004:68.
153 Erikson, 1968/1994:66.
154 Ibid.:66–67.
155 Hron, 2009:29.
156 Agier & Fernback, 2008:3–4.
157 Ibid.:4.
158 Ibid.:4.
159 Ibid.:7–8.
160 Ibid.:29.
161 Ibid.:37.
162 Ibid.:59.
163 Ibid.:61.
164 Ibid.:12.
165 Ibid.:, 60.
166 Cohen, 1997/2008.
167 Kenny, 2013:87.
168 Ibid.:2.
169 Ibid.:5–6.
170 Ibid.:9.
171 Hall & Schwartz, 2017:144.
172 Permission granted to quote.
173 Said, 1999:234–4.
174 Ibid.:234–4.
175 Ibid.:234–4.
176 Ibid.:234–234.
177 Tas, 2016:44.
178 Ibid.:42.
179 Ibid.:45.
180 Ibid.:45.
181 Ibid.:48.
182 Ibid.:48.
183 Ibid.:46–47.
184 Ibid.:49.
185 Ibid.:49.
186 Ibid.:50.
187 Ibid.:51.
188 Ibid.:53.
189 Ibid.:53–54.
190 Ibid.:54.
191 Ibid.:57.
192 Ibid.:54–55.
193 Ibid.:54–55.
194 Ibid.:52–53.
195 Said, 2000:185.
196 Ng et al., 2011:93.

197 Ibid.:95.
198 Wihtol de Wenden as quoted in Kinnvall & Nesbitt-Larking, 2011:102.
199 Kuriloff, 2014:2; original emphasis.
200 Brown, 1993.
201 Mishra, 2018:86.
202 Reding, 2017:80.
203 Ibid.:86.
204 Sayad & Macey, 2004:215.
205 Reding, 2017:85.
206 Bauman, 2016.
207 Sayad & Macey, 2004:236.
208 Zahar, 2016:262.
209 Ibid.:282.
210 Hall & Schwartz, 2017:141.
211 Ibid.:144.
212 Lawler, 2008/2014:169.
213 Meaders, 1997:47.
214 Ibid.:52–3.
215 Côté & Levine, 2002:5.
216 Ibid.:3.
217 Ibid.:4.
218 Ibid.:4.
219 Ibid.:4–5.
220 Ibid.:5.
221 Ibid.:5.
222 Winnicott, 1971.
223 Akhtar, 1999/2004:103.
224 Ibid.:144.
225 Ibid.:144.
226 Said, 1999:248.
227 Ibid.:xiii–ix.
228 Ibid.:217.
229 Ibid.:222.
230 Ibid.:222.
231 Ibid.:295.
232 Ibid.:295.
233 Ibid.:295.
234 Bauman & Tester, 2001.
235 Said, 1999:295.
236 Martin, 1982/1988:13.
237 Ibid.:13.
238 Ng et al., 2011:76.
239 Ibid.:76.
240 Sayad & Macey, 2004:251.
241 Ibid.:251.
242 Ibid.:251.
243 Permission granted to quote.
244 Smallwood, 2007:123.
245 Ibid.:126.
246 Ibid.:126.
247 Ibid.:127.
248 Ibid.:127.

Identity and belonging 145

249 Ibid.:127.
250 Ibid.:127.
251 Montero, 1977:51.
252 Ibid.:182–183.
253 Ibid.:182–183.
254 Sen, 2006:113.
255 Sayad & Macey, 2004:267–268.
256 Grinberg & Grinberg, 1989:134.
257 Ibid.:134.
258 Ibid.:134.
259 Bauder, 2011:7.
260 Ibid.:17.
261 Anderson, 1991/2016:6.
262 Ibid.:8–9.
263 Said, 2000:185.
264 Reicher & Hopkins, 2002:222.
265 Ibid .:222.
266 Billig, 1995.
267 Zahar, 2016:262.
268 Bauder, 2011.
269 Kage, 2012:67.
270 Ibid.:117.
271 Ibid.:67.
272 Ibid.:67.
273 Grinberg & Grinberg, 1989:129.
274 Ibid.:160.
275 Ibid.:164.
276 Basch et al., 2004:291.
277 Ibid.:291.
278 Ibid.:270.
279 Bauböck, 2003:709.
280 Ibid.:709.
281 Portes et al., 1999:467.
282 Bauböck, 2003.
283 Østergaard-Nielsen, 2003.
284 Gomez, 2015:18.
285 Fukuyama, 2018b.
286 Furuyama, 2018a.
287 Lawler, 2008/2014:168.
288 Brown, 2002.
289 Lawler, 2014:168.
290 Brown, 1993b:390.
291 Lawler, 2014:168.
292 Fukuyama, 2018b.
293 Brown, 1993b:402–3.
294 Reicher & Hopkins, 2002:222.
295 Sen, 2006:40.
296 Ibid.:89.
297 Ibid.::89.
298 Ibid.:89.
299 Ibid.:89.
300 Ibid.:99.

Identity and belonging

301 Ashis, 1997 quoted in Kinnvall & Nesbitt, 2011:76.
302 Ibid.:76.
303 Ng et al., 2011:70.
304 Yuval-Davis, 1997/2006:46.
305 Ibid.:46.
306 Miller, 2010.
307 Yuval-Davis, 1997/2006.
308 Bayes & Tohidi, 2001.
309 Ng et al., 2011:71.
310 Ibid.:71.
311 Ibid.:71.
312 Sayad & Macey, 2004:256.
313 Ibid.:257.
314 Ibid.:256.
315 Ibid.:256.
316 Ibid.:257.
317 Ibid.:257.
318 Ibid.:283.
319 Ibid.:257.
320 Ibid.:257.
321 Fraser, 1995:68.
322 Ibid.:58.
323 Ibid.:58.
324 Ibid.:58.
325 Ibid.:59.
326 Meaders, 1997:57.
327 Ibid.:58.
328 Ibid.:58.
329 Said, 1999:217.
330 Ackers, 2004:101.
331 Bauböck, 2003:701.
332 Ibid.:700.
333 Ibid.:702.
334 Tutton (2019) p12.
335 Clarkson, 2016:38.
336 Youkhana, 2016:1.
337 Heidegger & Stambaugh 1969/2002.
338 Heidegger, 1969/2002:12.
339 Ibid.:31.
340 Ross & Tartaglione, 2018:212.
341 Rockefeller, 1992:97.
342 Baumeister & Leary, 1995.
343 Maslow, 1962/2010.
344 Schiller et al., 1992.
345 Guibernau, 2013:21.
346 Ibid. 21.
347 Ibid.:21.
348 Ibid.:27.
349 Ibid.:28.
350 Guibernau, 2013:28.
351 Ibid.:28.
352 Ibid.:28.

353 Youkhana, 2016:1.
354 Rattansi, 2007:3.
355 Ibid.:115.
356 Grinberg & Grinberg, 1989:131–132.
357 Krzyżanowski & Wodak, 2008:96.
358 Ibid.:113.
359 Ibid.:114.
360 Yuval-Davis, 2006:199.
361 Ibid.:202.
362 Ibid.:202.
363 Ibid.:202.
364 Ibid.:202.
365 Ibid.:199.
366 Castells, 1996-8.
367 Giddens, 1991.
368 Levitt, 2004.
369 Bauman, 1995/1998.
370 Bauman, 2004.
371 Ibid.:2004.
372 Schiller et al., 1992.
373 Kivisto, 2002:30.
374 Gans, 1979:42.
375 Alba, 1990.
376 Archdeacon, 1990.
377 Faist, 2000:207–208.
378 Kivisto, 2002:39.
379 Kivisto, 2002:39.
380 Levitt, 2004.
381 Ibid.:2004.
382 Ibid.:2004.
383 Ibid.:2004.
384 Ibid.:2004.
385 Ibid.:2004.
386 Ibid.:2004.
387 Ibid.:2004.
388 Guibernau, 2013:32.
389 Ibid.:32.
390 Ibid.:30.
391 Ibid.:33.
392 Ibid.:34.
393 Ross & Tartaglione, 2018:212.
394 Ignatieff, 1993:4.
395 Junger, 2016:33.
396 Waters, 1990:112–113.
397 Alba, 1990:293.
398 Guibernau, 2013:41.
399 Ibid.:42.
400 Ignatieff, 1993:3.
401 Ibid.:3.
402 Ibid.:3.
403 Ibid.:149.
404 Ibid.:165.

405 Papadopoulos, 2002b:17.
406 Ibid.:19.
407 Ibid.:19.
408 Grinberg & Grinberg, 1989:23.
409 Ibid.:80.
410 Ibid.:80.
411 Ibid.:89.
412 Ibid.:88.
413 Ibid.:88.
414 Ibid.:88.
415 Ibid.:88.
416 Ibid.:97.
417 Ibid.:97.
418 Ibid.:97.
419 Ibid.:98.
420 Turner, 2017:108.
421 Ibid.:112.
422 Ibid.:114.
423 Ibid.:117.
424 Ibid.:119.
425 Ibid.:121.
426 Ibid.:122.
427 Ibid.:153.
428 Ibid.:154, 156.
429 Ibid.:164.
430 Ibid.:176–177.
431 Ibid.:182.
432 Ibid.:183.
433 Ibid.:231.
434 Trentelman, 2009.
435 Raymond et al., 2010.
436 Warnick, 2016:244.
437 Ibid.:249.
438 Ibid.:246.
439 Ibid.:257.
440 Saunders et al., 2016:10–11.
441 Ibid, vii.
442 Handlin, 1951/2002.
443 Herberg, 1955/1985.
444 Gordon, 1964.
445 Cadge & Ecklund, 2007:360.
446 Cadge & Ecklund, 2007:371.
447 Ibid.:360.
448 Saunders et al., 2016:19.
449 Ibid.:19.
450 Ibid.:20.
451 Ibid.:20.
452 Groody, 2009:664.
453 Ibid.:664.
454 Ibid.:638, 642.
455 Ibid.:664.
456 Saunders et al., 2016:26.

457 Straut-Eppsteiner & Hagan, 2016.
458 Hagan & Straut-Eppsteiner, 2019.
459 Knott, 2016.
460 Saunders et al., 2016:18.
461 Kassam, 2016.
462 Cadge & Ecklund, 2007:371.
463 Ibid.:371.
464 Ibid.:371.
465 Ibid.:372.
466 Borja, 2018.
467 Ibid.:29.
468 Saunders et al., 2016:26.
469 Suh, 2009:166.
470 Ibid.:167.
471 Ibid.:168.
472 Ibid.:177.
473 Ibid.:169.
474 Ibid.:189.

Chapter 6

Generational differences

Chapter 6 explores attitudes, values and beliefs of 1st-generation migrants (arrivées) in relation to their children, 2nd-generation members born in the newland (*jus soli*) and 3rd-generation members whose parents were born in the newland. Arrivées who migrate as young children and are brought up in the newland (1.5 generation) are usually lumped in with the 2nd generation, as they share similar challenges of living between the two cultures of parental homelands and the newland. Many arrivées claim to have migrated for their children's sake, creating a burden of debt and guilt over parental migration hardships.[1] "Migration changes people and mentalities,"[2] and both the 1st and 2nd generations have to reconcile differences that can also affect 3rd generations.

Arrivées: 1st generation

Whether chosen or forced, 1st-generation migration is initiated by economics (opportunity), self-development (adventure) and/or self-preservation (escape of refugees and exiles).[3] Migrant mindsets are characterized by hope, sometimes alternating with alienation, and in the case of exiles, often despair: "All Americans are immigrants, or recent descendants of immigrants, the experience of being uprooted from a mother country and transplanted to an alien wilderness is in the psychic heritage of us all."[4] And

> most American genealogies go back to dissidents, malcontents, and outcasts, or, alternatively to the rejected, persecuted, and enslaved. Americans have always fancied that the future was theirs, but the lack of a past is a perennial source of cultural inferiority feelings (which we compensate by technological arrogance).[5]

Still, there's symbolic ethnicity and nostalgic allegiance, love and pride in cultural images and parades.[6]

Migration has been described as a "zero-sum game, with finite rights and resources available to a select few."[7] Most migrants would not leave if they felt they had real choices. Instead, they "risk their lives on sardine-packed rickety boats to cross the Mediterranean"[8] for a future that's impossible at home. They usually distinguish between ethnicity and political states:

> In many parts of the world there exist immigrant communities which are cultural and politically committed to continuing to "belong" to their "mother county"—or more specifically to the national collectivity from where they, their parents or their forbearers have come.[9]

This is possible because modern communications enable "intergenerational cultural and linguistic reproduction."[10] Still, there's a difference between diaspora settler communities and political exiles who were "part of political struggles ... and aim 'to go back' the moment the political situation changes."[11] Those who are unable to return often live culturally hybrid lives. Though they may invest energies in newlands, "home" is still where they "feel comfortable and where their nearest and dearest live."[12]

The cultural complexity of the West makes it difficult to speak of any "single" path of migrant integration,[13] as it depends upon reasons for migrating (i.e., chosen or forced), expectations, personal resources, personality and host-country reception. Still, three primary paths have been identified for 1st-generation migrants: 1) *isolationism* and creation of ethnic ghettos, 2) *assimilation* (melting pot), and 3) *adaptation* and selective acculturation (cultural mosaic).

Ethnic ghettos

Isolationism is a response to the stresses, strains and challenges of migration and leads to the creation of ethnic ghettos. Migrants may be in the newland but not part of it, and often they avoid naturalization,[14] depending upon circumstances, their resources, personalities and religious beliefs. Eisen asks: "How could they continue to remain apart *from* American society and culture at the same time they moved to become a full part *of* it?"[15] The reality is "the immigrant world has always been a difficult one, torn between old loyalties and new realities."[16] And "old loyalties die hard because individuals socialized in another language and cultures have great difficulty giving them up as a primary source of identity."[17] First generations may have an "overriding preoccupation with the home country,"[18] true not just for refugees and exiles, because the homeland culture is their primary conditioning—what seems normal and right.

In behavioural psychology, classical conditioning is defined as "learned behaviour" rewarded to encourage it. The earliest experiments with rats and pigeons taught them to press a bar for food pellets. If pellets stopped coming, they stopped pressing the bar. In operant or instrumental conditioning, the timing and schedule of rewards are important. When rewards are reliably consistent—regular in intervals and amount—they reinforce the behaviour, i.e., pressing the bar. When rewards aren't given, the animal quickly stops (technically, the behaviour becomes extinct). When rewards are on a variable schedule or without a regular pattern—sometimes given, sometimes not—hope is created. As a result, the learned behaviour does not become extinct. In humans, gambling is a good example of variable-reward schedules, which results in the hope of success next time, making it difficult to stop.

Application of conditioning theory to migration may not be obvious, but when homeland politics threaten survival, then loyalty to the regime becomes weakened or even extinct, although one may cling to familiar culture, religion and society with hope because of their variable rewards. Beneath homeland tragedies that prompt flight, fight and exile lay memories of past happiness and successes and the hope of returning. It may explain why many refugees and exiles are caught in love-hate relations with both homelands and newlands. There's nostalgia for past rewarding times that are impossible to revive. Not surprisingly, traumas, tragedies and cultural conditioning preoccupy arrivées. Some hold fierce allegiance to homelands and previous "paradises," aching to return. By recreating the homeland, they condition the 2nd generation to homeland languages, cultures and politics and often the desire to return.

Newland diasporic communities "freeze their culture."[19] For instance, the "practice of purdah" is "more extreme and rigid in Bradford than in Bangladesh."[20] In Canada, a Somali youth leader rebuked his community's practice of cultural isolationism: "It's the responsibility of African leaders to show the younger generation that they should be involved in and contribute to the wider, mainstream society ... Staying within their ethnic community does the kids a disservice."[21]

Ethnic "collective memory is not an inert and passive thing, but a field of activity in which past events are selected, reconstructed, maintained, modified, and endowed with political meaning."[22] Some African Americans, as part of an American underclass, identify with an historical idealized homeland they've never seen, with the belief Africa is good because of the absence of a white majority.[23]

From the outside, ethnic enclaves may appear singular and cohesive. Although there's a diverse mix of individuals, often homeland distinctions prevail: class, cultural, regional and linguistic differences and prejudices. An Italian-Canadian recounts:

> People spoke different dialects, their values were different ... they didn't always mix well ... I used to tell people I was from a mixed marriage because my father and immediate family came from the area north of Venice and my mother's family came from a small town between Rome and Naples.[24]

However, when living in a newland ghetto, the ethnic "us versus them" can enable building cohesion and healing ancestral differences.

Ethnic assimilation

Some refugees and exiles are unable to dispel their anger, fear, discomfort, insecurity and angst about forced migration. Even after acquiring newland citizenship, some reshape homeland memories and "reinvent collective memories and myths [into] new myths and mystical atmospheres ... passed between generations."[25] Adaptation is seen as "forsaking their cultural heritage."[26] Sayad says that 1st-generation Algerians in France disapprove of naturalization, seeing it as "a mark and an admission of alienation, as well as an adulteration and denial of one's basic being."[27] Maintaining a homeland accent can represent allegiance. "I will always have an accent in English," one explains; "I have no intention of losing it; my accent is part of who I am."[28]

The American Migration Policy Institute describes three models of ethnic assimilation with differing generational outcomes:[29] 1) classic assimilation, 2) racial/ethnic disadvantage, and 3) segmented assimilation model. In Canada, a fourth model exists: multiculturalism or ethnic pluralism.[30,31,32,33] (See Chapter 7: "Host country.")

Classic assimilation theory: seven stages

In Gordon's theory of seven stages of assimilation,[34,35,36] migrants enter a "straight line" of convergence of greater similarity over time in norms, values, behaviours, and characteristics. First is acquisition of language and culture, followed by "structural assimilation" or closer relations with host societies and intermarriage. Next is identification with newland society and ending of host-society prejudices, discrimination and value conflicts.[37] The seven stages model doesn't account for ethnic rejection, isolationism and/or intergenerational conflicts. It assumes later generations are fully assimilated and intermarry with the host/majority group. Historically, the US claimed to be a melting pot but because full assimilation hasn't occurred, it's more like a salad bowl.[38] Typically the 1st generation remains separated from the mainstream in language and culture differences, but the 2nd generation, newland schooled and acculturated, integrates to a large degree and is only symbolically and ethnically distinct.[39]

Racial/ethnic disadvantage model

Gans says ethnic assimilation is a bumpy course and not a straight line,[40] which led to the racial/ethnic disadvantage model of Glazer and Moynihan,[41] which was in turn updated by Portes and Rumbaut.[42] Here, ethnicity is both a resource and burden because prejudice, discrimination and institutional barriers block employment and social assimilation. Yet migration is still recognized as a "transformative force producing profound and unanticipated social changes in both sending and receiving societies, and also in intergroup relationships within receiving societies, and among the immigrants themselves and their descendants."[43] However, "regardless of their qualifications and experience, recent immigrants generally enter at the bottom of their respective occupational ladders."[44] When discrimination is experienced and anti-ethnic campaigns are mounted, it can stir a sense of common identity, solidarity and "ethnic pride,"[45] as well as "ethnic militancy,"[46] in people who previously may not have been collectively cohesive. The 2nd generation may be captivated by ethnic identity symbols and rallying cries for political solidarity.[47]

Segmented/divergent assimilation model

The segmented/divergent assimilation model argues that American society is so diverse that there's no single assimilation route. Today's 2nd generation faces new adaptation challenges because the racial and ethnic migration after 1960 differs from pre-WWII European migration patterns. In 1990, migrants were 77% non-European: 22.4% Asian, 7.6% Black and 47% Hispanic.[48] The segmented/divergent assimilation model poses three pathways determined by human capital, family structure and modes of incorporation and ethic community resources that affect 2nd and 3rd generations.[49]

The first assimilation pathway is dominated by human capital where the 1st-generation parental "achievement of middle-class status"[50] leads to 2nd-generation achievement of "professional and entrepreneurial occupations and full acculturation."[51] The 3rd generation shows "complete integration into social and economic mainstream."[52] Still, the 1st generation is "strongly oriented toward preserving a strong national identity, which they associate both with community solidarity and with social networks promoting individual success."[53] But the ethnic pride and achievement orientation they instil in their children clashes with their real-life challenges. In Miami, Haitians are "torn between conflicting ideas and values: to remain Haitian they would have to face social ostracism and continuing attacks in school."[54] If they choose to identify with American Blacks, they have to "forgo their parents' dreams of making it in America on the basis of ethnic solidarity and preservation of traditional values."[55] Thus their reality is not assimilation "into mainstream culture but into the values and norms of the inner city."[56] In the past, adopting the outlooks and cultural ways of local people represented the first step of social and economic mobility; today it "leads to the exact opposite,"[57] downward assimilation.

The second pathway is dominated by family structures. The 1st generation has "working-class occupations, with *strong* co-ethnic communities."[58] This leads to 2nd-generation achievement of "selective acculturation, attainment of middle-class status through educational achievement," and in the 3rd generation to "full acculturation and integration into the mainstream."[59] The third path is 1st-generation parental "working-class occupations and *weak* co-ethnic communities."[60] This leads to 2nd-generation "dissonant acculturation and low educational achievement,"[61] and 3rd-generation "stagnation to subordinate menial jobs ... or downward assimilation into deviant lifestyles and reactive ethnicity."[62]

Acculturation: selective and dissonant

Acculturation (adaptation) differs from assimilation in terms of choice, extent of change and time. Some migrants avoid adaptation while others "change flags at the first opportunity."[63] Ethnic adaptation strategies and degree of integration are influenced by structural, cultural and personal context.[64] Structural context refers to newland institutional/formal organizations where adaptation is learning the language and attending educational institutions. Cultural context refers to community activities: religion, art, food, music and events. Personal context entails the individual adopting newland attitudes, values and behaviours, including inter-marriage in the 2nd generation.

Selective acculturation speaks to the 1st generation's "strong parental social capital in the form of stable families and cohesive communities and commonly, but not always fluent bilingualism."[65] It suggests love and respect in parental couples and child-rearing practices rather than "power-over," obedience models with punitive corrections. Important, too, are extended families: in newlands the larger ethnic community may play this role.

Selective acculturation is not always child-centred, even when arrivées insist they came for the children. In a Canadian magazine, a father writes a letter to his newborn daughter saying her name Amna "was built carefully, with great tenderness. Craft and thought and meditation went into choosing it for you."[66] He explains that his last name is long and bulky, yet he wanted it for her and to be a burden so she would feel the "sting of lineage."[67] He explains:

> I was 12 when I came to Canada. I have foundational memories of not just of place but of sense of family ... I have a sense of what Sudan is like: the values and customs and the different way people move ... your blood contains a history of elsewhere.[68]

He says: "blood is a burden" and speaks of battles he's had with his name and predicts she will experience conflict.

> Your job is to fight ... my job is to prepare you for the battle. I will teach you Arabic and I will tell you of your history ... you come from a sturdy tree, strong and resilient and enduring, rooted in the rich soil of history.[69]

In an exploration of the political psychology of globalization, Kinnvall and Paul Nesbitt-Larking found that retreatism by Muslims in the West is "a relatively safe and dignified strategy for first generation immigrants, notably those associated with stronger post-colonial bonds and legitimated extensions of imperial citizenship in France, the Netherlands, and the UK."[70] This is because, beyond the challenge of economic survival, Muslim migrants often deal with racist hostility,[71] fostering a sense of powerlessness that leads to retreat into quiescence.[72] While the 1st and 2nd generations tend to live privately "in a state of relative harmony with the religious, social and national aspects of identity,"[73] the 3rd generation "faces a tension, if not an outright conflict, between the layers of individual, collective and national identity."[74] Thus, it's not surprising the 3rd generation's response to their families is often concealment, especially when parents are rigid about their mainstream friendships and sexuality. This is even more pronounced with homosexuality, resulting in "young people running away from home, living under constant anxiety, getting a new identity, being totally neglected or in some instances, being subjected to violent attacks by family members, even assassinations."[75]

Canadian focus-group members told of struggling between the differing demands of home and mainstream culture. One asked how she would explain this to her family: "I would like to be like you. I would love to follow your way, I love you, but you need to understand that ... I'm dealing with another culture that ... has different expectations of me."[76] They spoke of acquaintances committing suicide over an ethnic identity crisis, but more typically, to protect themselves, they become isolated from the family and community.[77]

The *Persephone syndrome* is characterized by "strong, unresolved emotional attachment to the mother."[78] An over-dependency, it's generally not a problem in mother-daughter relationships until tied migration creates geographic separation. The syndrome is usually experienced by a dutiful daughter in, perhaps, an early arranged marriage, who was never emotionally prepared for separation. Psychological symptoms are "anxiety, depression, psycho-physiologic manifestations, and gross stress reactions, transient psychotic episodes necessitating short hospitalizations."[79]

In *dissonant acculturation*, the 2nd generation abandons the parental homeland language and culture in favour of mainstream society. It leads to "breakdown of intra-family communication and the loss of parent's control over their children."[80] Yet, dissonant acculturation is not only a 2nd-generation issue. Sayad tells of a 64-year-old Algerian 1st-generation migrant who struggled in retirement with being a member of two cultures and feeling he did not fully belong to either.[81] His children in France "regarded him as a foreigner—in his words, 'like an Arab'—even though he had done everything to adopt the lifestyle and mannerisms of the French."[82] In Algiers, his first son who had stayed "looked upon him as a foreigner."[83] Dissonant acculturation does not always lead to *downward assimilation* or lesser status in the 2nd generation. It does, however, put children at risk for it due to "absence or weakening of family support as they confront the external threats and barriers."[84] To deal with these, the children often reject their ethnic family, resulting in a lack of internal and external discipline and inability to achieve. It can lead to deviant lifestyles with heavy alcohol and drug use. When arrivée parents are caught in dissonant acculturation, the 2nd and 3rd generations may adopt *reactive ethnicity* in "an attempt to compensate for their comparatively disadvantaged social status by revitalizing ethnic cultural habits or homeland-oriented identifications."[85] Reactive ethnicity or "holding tight"[86] to traditional practices and beliefs usually emerges from psychological traumas and challenges of migration. *Reactive ethnicity* is also a defence "created by the confrontation with different and frequently harsh realities in the host society."[87]

The 2nd generation

Jung, in *The Complications of American Psychology*, says a nation in the making is a big risk[88]—that the air and soil of a county can change a person, and can actually assimilate them. This is especially true of the 2nd generation, born in the newland.[89] Kobayashu describes the generational differences of Japanese-Canadians. The 1st generation, the *Issei* are seen as "other" with their foreign ways and silences and known as *watari dori* (birds of passage), which symbolizes their journey. The 2nd generation, *Nisei* are seen as ambivalent and caught between the two worlds of homeland and newland. The 3rd generation, *Sansei* are seen as angry and politically active: "The myth of generational difference tends to focus on the different reactions of the three generations to the injustices suffered at that time, the stoicism of the 'birds of passage' against the squawking of the politically activist younger generations."[90] Although the *Issei* are seen as silent, they have a rich tradition of poetry clubs in which they speak their "silence" in syllabic structures of profound images, "expressive of the ascetic mysticism that characterizes much of Japanese art and philosophy."[91] Written in Japanese, it is not well understood by the *Nisei* and not at all by the *Sansei*.[92] Kobayashu cites a few which speak of the feelings and emotions of migration:

"With tears in my eyes
I turn back to my homeland
Taking one last look." (Seijin)
"No hope to go back
Yet I dream of my homeplace,
In sleep returning." (Mutsuko)

"Resolved to become
The soil of the foreign land,
I settle down." (Ryufu)[93]

Migrants arriving as young children, known as the "1.5th generation," face similar challenges to the 2nd generation living under the shadow of parental adaptation struggles. Internalization of external migration challenges can manifest as conflicts within the family. Many 2nd generationers live betwixt and between homeland and newland cultures, feeling pulled in two directions. Due to children's natural language acquisition and cultural adaptation in schools, there is often a role-reversal in families where the children become interpreters and spokespersons for parents.

Often in parental homeland migrant groups, 2nd-generation children struggle with legitimacy: "It's not easy being an outsider is it?" asks "Shappi" Khorsandi, a British-Iranian comedian. "You're never exactly English and you're never exactly like where your family is from. We're sort of stuck in the middle, aren't we?"[94] At the same time, the bicultural 1.5 and 2nd generationers engage in "boundary spanning activities,"[95] and "cultural brokerage"[96,97] for families and communities interpreting newland cultures and languages.[98] An Australian study found language transmission and maintenance of heritage languages was easier when both parents were from the same culture.[99]

Canada has one of the highest ratios of 2nd-generation children. In 2016, over a third (37.5%) of children had at least one arrivée parent.[100] If the current rate of immigration increases, it is estimated by 2036 the percentage of 2nd-generation children could rise to 39–49% of those aged 15 and under:[101] In 2016, "More than one-third spoke only an official [Canadian] language at home compared to 10% of their parents."[102] They bridge cultures, being familiar with the "values and specific cultural practices of their parents' country of origin,"[103] while learning the "values, social norms and official languages of their host country through their school, friends and neighbourhood."[104]

Biculturalism and bilingualism

Biculturalism, belonging to more than one culture, presents challenges and rewards.[105] At one end is anomie, "feeling of disorientation, social isolation and anxiety,"[106] when a person is constantly being "tested" for allegiance to an ethnic group.[107] A Swedish study of 1st-generation migrants found 71% felt they did not belong to either the homeland or newland.[108] A greater sense of belonging occurs when there is full acceptance, respect and learning of multiple languages and cultures.

In the US, 2nd-generation East Indian children attending affluent schools with other South Asians who passively resist Americanization developed four different ways of negotiating their complex social/cultural worlds: 1) *compromised identity*, characterized by cultural alienation from both cultures that carries "high risk of emotional disturbance";[109] 2) *ethnocentric identity* of strong Indian values and being "more comfortable at home than school;"[110] 3) *American identity*, with minimal contact with ethnic Indians and a high likelihood of intermarriage, and 4) *bicultural identity* as Indian-American with flexibility towards music, food and language and strong loyalty to both the US and Indian ethnic groups. In the latter group, their 1st-generation parents were found to be "advanced [in] psychologically coping with their own immigration."[111]

As a child during WWII, Parens narrowly escaped the Nazis.[112] Later, in the US, he explored the challenges children face in cultural conflicts and disharmonies, asking "What burdens does the adolescent experience because of what her immigrant parents feel is unacceptable or undesirable in American culture?"[113] And, "What happens in the family when the parents feel their cultural identity is in jeopardy when they value American culture?"[114] "What about children born in the newland who have acquired ethnic identities?"[115] Parens gives an example of a child who tried to adapt to "two well-defined and conflicting sets of mores and attitudes."[116] He concludes when parents insist on a cultural split, the child's identity can only be that of "not a real American."[117]

Bilingualism is speaking two languages.[118] It's quite natural to speak more than one language, says Arnberg, and is important. Culturally, bilingualism has a broadening role, resulting in less provincialism. Economically, it saves billions on translations. International relations are enhanced and enabled, and bilingualism provides individuals with options to work and live in another place and become acquainted with other peoples.[119] *Alternation* is a bicultural term for those who feel equally at home in more than one culture and are able to respond appropriately to the situation.[120] Bilingualism has positive effects on "brain networks that support language and cognition."[121] "Bilinguals develop a high level of cognitive control that enables them to negotiate the activity of the two languages."[122] They are "more efficient than monolinguals in resolving conflict."[123] And bilingualism is neural protective: "bilinguals present with symptoms of Alzheimer's type dementia 4–5 years later than monolinguals."[124]

Five factors are important in bilingual success: 1) outer reinforcement, 2) pre-programmed structures, 3) active drive to include the second language, 4) active language interaction with care-givers and the wider community, and 5) imitation and modelling.[125] Also helpful are summer language camps, extended visits from those who don't speak the majority language, and visits to the minority-language country.[126] In mixed English-French-speaking Canadian families, Grosjean found children identify with both ethnic groups and both languages and both cultures share equal status.[127] An earlier study[128] reports: "French-English-speaking bilingual children performed better on both verbal and non-verbal intelligence tests than a group of French-speaking monolingual children."[129]

First-generation acculturation challenges

Parental attitudes towards migration, and their mourning and liberation processes, affect their children;[130] their ability to integrate has "significant impact upon their offspring's core self-representation."[131] Adjustment and acculturation of refugees and exiles is more psychologically challenging than for those who chose migration and can choose to return to their homelands. In the US, "roughly one of four migration events is a return to an individual's country of birth."[132]

Second-generation children born early in parental migrations tend to "suffer more than those born when the parents are more advanced in their intrapsychic work of mourning and adaptation":[133]

> what is transmitted to children by their families includes not only the personalities of the actual parents, but also the family, racial and national traditions handed on through them, as well as the immediate social milieu which they represent ... the influences of the past.[134]

Kahn recalls the effects of her parent's migration as a persistent sense of "anxiety my worried parents transmitted to me."[135]

Thorpe speaks of the 1st generation who "left Baghdad in 2006 at the height of the Iraq War—nine years earlier—and had been looking for a safe haven ever since."[136] After years in transit camps, they finally arrived in a newland, "dazed in the abruptness of the transition, looking profoundly lost."[137] What was most difficult was the break-up of the extended family that in the refugee camps had provided close, supportive relationships.[138] And there was the guilt they felt over those abandoned. Arrival meant they were a nuclear family for the first time, and had to start over. First, was the task of figuring out where they were, and who they were in this place? After struggles with identity came questions of where is home?[139] And what does it mean to belong here?[140] One explains: "It would be tough to find a decent place to live that they could afford; it would be difficult to find any kind of job, let alone one they might enjoy," and "learning English would be mind-bogglingly frustrating."[141] There was also the problem of community, of others understanding their story. They struggled with the fear of not being seen, not recognized and being "ghosts."[142] They worried about their children.

The 1.5-generation experiences of the newland are especially influenced by parental attitudes and their need to "insulate themselves and maintain their native culture or alternatively, their desire to become part of the dominant society [and] sometimes the children bear the brunt of their parent's fear of losing their bearing."[143] A new Canadian who arrived at age 8 from Cyprus explains.

> When we first got here my father used to listen to the radio all the time ... he was so worried all the time. My mother used to cry a lot ... I'd come from school, she'd be putting my lunch on the table and she'd be crying and crying.[144]

Although his friends in Cyprus didn't want him to leave, he says "I had to. My country is nice. It is all sunshine. One day, I would like to go back."[145]

Second and even 3rd generationers can be saddled with the dreams of the arrivées.[146] "Experiences, values and traumas are passed between generations in a variety of ways,"[147] says Elovitz. "The dreams of poor immigrants, unfulfilled in their own lives, are often realized by their children and grand-children."[148] Sabelli, a 2nd-generation Argentinian of Italian ancestry in the US says his parents "imprinted in me a sense of social responsibility that eventually led me to oppose a subsequent military dictatorship and forced me to emigrate."[149] His father died when he was 14 years old, yet he "felt I had to save my father's spirit, passing it on to the future. I felt the need to carry out his unfinished mission: to write his book with his message of science and social justice" as these goals are "incompatible with life in Argentina."[150] The 2nd generation also influences the first, playing a vital role of communication between cultures "infusing new patterns and ideas into the old family routines, thereby acculturating the older generation."[151] At the same time, "unfilled dreams of immigrant parents are frequently lived out by their children and grandchildren."[152]

Conflict between generations

The migration challenges of arrivées parents differ from the 2nd generation, who must find a way to reconcile competing demands of traditional families and newland societies. When the parental 1st generation lives in the 2nd generation's adult home, it increases their psychological stress. At the same time, the 1st generation, with limited language acquisition, become dependent and experience psychological malaise.[153]

Internalization of the external migration struggle in the new society often emerges as conflict within families and communities. "The dissonance between the past and the present, the familiar and the strange, often played itself out in the family as disharmony between the old and the young."[154] Portes and Rumbaut list three responses of the 2nd generation to parental ethnicity: 1) "a matter of personal choice," 2) "a source of strength and who will muscle their way up, socially and economically, on the basis of their own communities networks and resources," and 3) "neither a matter of choice nor a source of progress but a mark of subordination."[155] The unfortunate reality of migration today, say Portes and Rumbaut, is many of today's 2nd generation are at risk of becoming part of a "new rainbow underclass [of] inequality and despair in America's inner cities."[156]

Ramanujam speaks of generational clashes among US Asian-Indian migrants. An example is a 2nd-generation woman who married an African American, against the wishes of her parents. She was disowned and estranged until she bore a son and was then invited to visit, but she refused because her husband was not welcome.[157] The problem, Ramanujam says, is due to dependent relations in the Indian culture: "subordinates expect their superior to be sensitive to their needs [and] adopt a paternalistic role."[158] When it doesn't happen, they resort to "passive-aggressive maneuvers."[159] He argues the cultural inflexibility and inability to dialogue and/or communicate personally "adds to the general stress accompanying life in a new environment."[160] Further, the 2nd generation feels they have no social or psychological space, as they are forced to socialize with other Indian families with whom they have no interest:[161] "A main concern of Indian parents is that their children grow up understanding their cultural roots, especially the religious aspects."[162] There is a deep desire for them "to marry within their own community and in the traditional way. Arranged marriages are still the rule. The very few who choose to marry outside the ethnic community, often find outright rejection."[163] In essence, it's an obedience culture that leads to family friction especially in the 3rd generation, raised with western democratic principles and personal freedoms. They complain of interference by grandparents and blaming on both sides which "creates tension in the entire family."[164] The concept of "family cohesion and togetherness is a highly valued ideal among Asian Indians,"[165] whereas in American culture individuality and initiative are ideals: "Fissures in family relations are perceived as failures of the individual family member rather than emanating from the process of acculturation."[166] And families are unable to seek professional help to solve problems because stigma is attached to this kind of action.

The situation differs for Israeli migrants to the US. They may choose to keep a low profile and foster invisibility in the newland to avoid being seen by the ethnic/religious community as "selfish and weak, a failure and a traitor ... defectors who abandoned the Promised Land."[167] Often they carry "anger and guilt for having the burden of 2,000 years of Diaspora imposed upon them by the older generation who helped build the State of Israel."[168]

A review of PTSD in migrants reports "conflicts between generations are common in migrant families, reflecting a gap between the acculturation of parents and children."[169] Arrivées tend to be caught in nostalgic homeland ties and know little and understand less of their children's lives caught up in rapid acculturation and life in two different worlds. It leads to "parent-child arguments and conflicts about friendships, dating, marriage, gender roles, and career choices."[170]

Zahra notes the 1971 European Union agreement went beyond permitting migration for family reunification to let the "Polish government to dump undesirable citizens [who] 'spread recidivist propaganda' along with those 'who burden the country with respect to a poor work ethic, degeneration criminal, alcoholics, chronically ill pensioners, etc.' ... all should be granted visas to the West."[171] While migrant children were struggling to integrate, they were portrayed as victims of opportunistic parents:[172]

> A Kosovar who arrived as a child explained: "You do feel nostalgia about home and you miss it. But deep down, you realise as you walk down a street that this is it, this is pretty much your place, this is the end of the train. For the parents, home will always be over there, but for you, this is it."[173]

Creative writing is one way to deal with emotional crises of migration.[174] The Irish poet, MacGill, reports having been born in the newland to support his parents: "Great care had been taken to drive this fact into my mind from infancy."[175] His parents equating luck with sacrifice would refer to another youth in his situation with condemnation, saying, "He'll never have a day's luck in all his life; he didn't give every penny he earned to his father and mother."[176]

Betwixt and between vs both/and

The migration complex of the 2nd generation is the struggle of "seeing double, and being double."[177] Boulanger reports:

> Those of us who inhabit the hyphenated Space between cultures are hypersensitive to difference: we constantly straddle the gap between one world and the other. For some, that is the gap between their parents' cultural imperative and the larger world in which they live ... We are intimately aware of infinitesimal differences in speech, accent, emphasis in the way a word is said, particular gestures that can give us away or identify us as belonging; we know how to manipulate them, how to appear less alien, how to perform belonging.[178]

An example is given of a 1.5-generation woman plagued by childhood memories of the Oriental world left behind; she struggled with emotional/psychological differences of the two cultures and her chaotic life as the interpreter for illiterate parents who turned to drinking to cope with the demands of migration.[179] For her, successful adaptation meant there was no psychic energy for herself: "I used to have the dream that I was the translator for all the aliens. I helped them fit into this planet, and I helped them understand."[180] Another dream was of "giving birth to twins and having to give one up."[181]

Interviews with youths born in Eastern Europe who migrated to the UK and educated there (i.e., 1.5-generation) reported not being able to remember living in their parental homelands, and weren't fluent in ancestral languages. A 14-year-old spoke of arriving at age 8½:

> It messed something up in my head a bit. I have become a lot more introverted ... I feel like I don't belong anywhere now, as I will never be British or understand the ways of the British, and I don't feel fully Latvian and certainly cannot relate to people there.[182]

Another said: "I would like people to understand that neither country feels like a home to someone like me ... My family doesn't really see me as a Pole and the people here don't see me as a British person."[183]

Beltsiou calls the 1.5 and 2nd generationers "cultural nomads," who may or may not identify with the parental homeland or the newland, and don't feel at home in either place.[184] Although born in France, children of Algerians are legally "vaccinated against deportation,"[185] but socially and culturally they struggle with a migrant mindset:

> I am French despite my Algerian appearance ... I was born here, brought up here, grew up here, was made here ... but deep inside me, I feel myself to be Algerian despite it all, in my heart of hearts. France is just my country. Algeria is my homeland.[186]

Another said with less certainty: "We live here ... but Algeria, that's a complete fiction. It's like the planet Mars. It means we have no *patrie* at a gut level."[187]

In Canada, for many years, language training and educational opportunities were available only for male migrants. The unintended consequence was that migrant mothers were unable to teach their children the newland language. When 2nd-generation children attended school, not knowing either French or English, they experienced culture shock.[188] In Montero's interviews with migrants, one said: "My little girl did not start to speak English until she was five and she started school ... it was difficult for her. We spoke Italian all the time at home ... now if she had her way she wouldn't speak Italian at all."[189] Another claims my "children have a better chance than I did. They are freer."[190] It's because "here they respect you for what you are ... So I've decided that if my children can have a better chance because we live here, I will sacrifice anything I can for them."[191] New citizens recognize that the culture and values are different, yet they admit rebelling: "Sometimes you feel you must resist. And our children are caught between two worlds."[192] An alternate view is presented by Falicov, who speaks of the capacity to find "both/and" solutions, or the best of both worlds by blending in and creating cultural mixes,[193] thus creating the middle path, the resolution of the 2nd-generation migration complex.

Racialization and radicalization

In-depth interviews with 50 young Canadian Muslims explored their identity in the post-9/11 world. They expressed fears of being "stripped of their rights and a lack of ability to assert their religious identities."[194] Also examined were effects of "racialized border practices on identity formation and citizenship depletion among Muslim Canadians,"[195] and other visible minorities perceived as "risky, dangerous, and deviant Others, unable to adapt to Western traditions."[196,197] UK and US, studies documenting racialized practices found they led to greater identification and involvement in ethnic and religious communities.[198] In *The Art of Being Black*[199] and *The Asian Gang: Ethnicity, Identity, Masculinity*,[200] Alexander explores "gangland London—youth wielding weapons, alienated from their families, their community and British society."[201] They're "locked into a cycle of meaningless violence, low self-esteem and self-destruction."[202]

Role reversal or "parentification"

A challenge for 1.5 and 2nd generationers is role reversal or *parentification*, where children become their parents' parents in the newland.[203] It's because the children's adaptation puts them "so far ahead of the parent's progress that key family decisions become dependent on the children's knowledge."[204] During the early, critical period of language acquisition up to age 18, native fluency in language is achieved almost effortlessly,[205] and reinforced in school along with cultural fluency. Migrant parents lacking such opportunities become dependent upon their children to navigate and negotiate the newland.[206,207] It has the potential to undermine parental control and/or prematurely free children from it.[208]

In the US today, "one out of every five children is either an immigrant or has an immigrant parent."[209] In fact, in 2005, the number of migrant children, one of the fastest-growing groups, was estimated to have reached 9 million by 2010.[210] Children may or may not participate in family decision making, but they still experience all stages of migration: abrupt flight (e.g., South East Asians, Bosnians, Somalis, Liberians) and exile and voluntary departures (e.g., South Koreans, Caribbean islanders). They experience loss and worry about those left behind, and encounter persecution, limbo-living in transit camps, depression, survivor guilt and PTSD.[211] Although parents do not mean to harm their children or do it intentionally, there's evidence of negative effects and psychic infection of parents' unresolved frightening and traumatic experiences.[212] Frightening ideation has been found to "alarm the infant via the exhibition of frightened, dissociated, or anomalous forms of threatening behavior."[213] As children age, some of the ways they deal with their own and their parents' fear and anxiety is through role reversal and controlling behaviour toward the parents.[214]

Generational acculturative conflicts bring some migrant families into healthcare.[215] There's a need for services "designed to help immigrants adapt to the new context, value the need to learn the ways of the new culture, and maintain a connection with their old country and culture."[216]

Parental homelands

Von Franz[217] says the 2nd generation is psychically imprinted with parental idealizations and nostalgia for the homeland that produces vicarious identification and yearnings to return. This is found in Hargreaves's work with the *Beurs* (2nd-generation Algerians) born and brought up in France, who carry a deep desire to "return" to Algeria.[218] In France, "school and home were only a few hundred meters apart, in journeying between them; each child migrated daily between profoundly different cultural universes."[219] They experienced a two-way pull of psychological pressure both in desire for 1) peer respect for acculturation, and 2) going "home" to Algeria. Often the family returns during holidays making it an ideal land of deep identity.[220] Yet in Algeria, children may experience a "shock of feeling foreign in a place which from afar was regarded as home,"[221] which triggers a reappraisal of life in France. Baszile remembers how complicated it was for her father to go to his homeland. Neither nostalgic nor romantic, the journey was always shortened: "three days, four days tops, because that's how long he could stand to be home before the ghosts of his boyhood started to haunt him."[222]

One 2nd-generation youth recounts:

> My father talked about his Russian childhood with intense feelings and profound nostalgia. I listened eagerly. The beauty of the Russian landscape, the joys and celebrations of its people, the dreams and sadness (in Russian novels of unrequited love) expressed my father's mourning for his past. They became part of me.[223]

He says he identified so strongly with his "father's longings for his country that I always wanted to go."[224] When it was politically possible to visit his grandmother in Kiev, he went several times and became totally disillusioned: "My father's Russia was dead. It existed only as a part of him, and of other émigrés and their loved ones. Russia existed only as a fantasy of return to everything good that was lost."[225] Another told of her mother's constant stories of Paris and France "full of affection and poetry. She longed to go back, but this was impossible because of the war [and] my mother died without being able to fulfill her dream of returning to France."[226] As a child, unconsciously she identified with her mother's desire to return to France. Her "stories represented a window to a happy, colourful, and free world."[227]

Aldrich speaks of African "slavery migrations" as brutal captures, often facilitated by tribal elders, which created such deep wounds they prevented any clear sense of identity and relation to a homeland. Yet the mythical "return" to Africa translated into a new culture: "the *Créole* language, religious syncretism, and folktale."[228] Likewise, the literature and politics of Césaire and Fanon were "extremists' positions,"[229] that functioned as a return to the homeland. Brown speaks of the mixed feelings of arrivées towards homelands, especially those "seduced by the myth of the American dream, or of the Promised Land,"[230] who felt guilt-ridden about those left behind. In visits, 2nd-generation children and 3rd-generation grandchildren "earned the reputation of being 'spoiled brats' who lacked cultural or linguistic skills and seemingly visited relatives on vacations only to shop or party."[231] The early 1990s return of Czech émigré offspring led to "an estimated 7,000 to 30,000 American expatriates living in Prague, often as business entrepreneurs or artistic bohemians. Many of these foreigners viewed Prague as either an investment opportunity or a cultural commodity."[232] The populace questioned their loyalty to the Czech Republic as a homeland.

Many 2nd-generation youth are consciously aware of differences between parental homelands and their birthland. Sometimes they shoulder feelings of inferiority due to a lack of ancestry and history in the homeland, compounded by parental attitudes of superiority of homeland culture.[233] Others feel socially fraudulent in their attachment and psychological dependence on parental homelands. The solution lies in a special psychological task, Mehta says for the 2nd generation to create transitional (*à la* Winnicott) "third space" for ethnic issues and identity.[234] The ethnic third-space span is uniquely and historically different; it spans inner and outer reality putting to rest the anxieties of the generations.[235] However, insecurely attached children in attempts to "connect" with parents may obliterate the ethnic third space. Those with secure attachment are able to live with a natural ethnic duality and not a pathological split. Further, their cultural/ethnic identity arises from the ego finding expression within the current social and ethnic environment. They describe themselves as living "an American life from 9–5 and an Indian life from 5–9."[236] In their attempt to achieve the best of both worlds, they have "diverse objects for identification,"[237] which can be an enriching and not an alienating experience.

Dellal, born in Australia to Turkish Cypriot parents, says parents don't always understand the struggles of their children:

> Sometimes we'd rather be accepted by our peers than our elders, and integrated but our parents don't understand that. They don't know what you go through on the outside, at school, with your friends, outside of the house and outside the community, and inside the community too.[238]

In France, before the extension of *jus soli* and *jus sanguinis* countries permitted dual citizenship, the 2nd generation was variously called: the "zero" generation, illegitimate, the "following" generation, or the generation of "foreign origins."[239] This makes self-identity problematic, especially for those without strong sense of self that many migrant parents are unable to model.

Separation-individuation issues can emerge in role-reversal families or those with emotionally dependent parents when children become involved in the newland's social-cultural milieu.[240] These can be especially challenging for those with insecurely attached parents who express high levels of anxiety being in an "adopted land."[241] Sometimes, parental envy surfaces of their children's greater opportunities in the newland,[242] or they engage in rivalry with them.[243] Other parents expect continual gratitude from children whom they think don't appreciate the sufferings and sacrifices of migration that made possible their life in the newland. Resolution of such issues is undeniably the parents' responsibility, but many lack the psychological awareness needed to address these problems, or necessary humility to admit their own role in the family conflicts when children are always blamed. This can end up alienating the children. Mehta says rather than developing an integrated and respected core self, arrivées develop a split identity—with "their Indian selves linked to regression and their American selves to progression or vice-versa."[244] Or émigré parents may over-identify with newland children and reject their homeland-selves,[245] or children deny newland identities and develop *reactive ethnicity* of over-identification with ancestral homelands.[246] Alternatively, rejection of ancestral homelands is possible.

Orfanos says the greatest issue facing the Greek-American community is intermarriage— the "final test of assimilation."[247] In 1993, the rate of inter-marriage was almost 50% which later rose to a 2:1 ratio.[248] Despite inter-marriage, there's still evidence of positive ethnic identity in 3rd and 4th generationers.[249] Cultural inter-marriages encourage assimilation: a newland spouse can act as a mentor who "encourages a sense of belonging to the society beyond the family, [and] provides the vehicle for greater integration."[250] And "bilingual children who are equally comfortable with both sets of grandparents [are] indicators of a successful integration of two identities."[251] However, it's not always successful. Kahn writes about four women: one has children and grandchildren described as "100% American":[252] "They have not learned German, never visited Germany, and have remained virtually ignorant of their mother and grandparent's background and personal fate at the hands of the Nazis."[253] Because "the children's organizing cultural context was suburban America,"[254] they know very little about their father's family. Another has a son aged 9, who denies his half-Turkish background, insisting he's "only American."[255] Although his grandmother's family was nominally Muslim, he claims to love Christmas and celebrates it as a non-religious fun time. He's decided he will be "half-Jewish, half-Christian" so he can double all the special holidays.[256]

Newland challenges

Kahn speaks of the importance of ethnic neighbourhoods which are integral to the lives of 2nd-generation children "until at school age, they confront a different reality."[257] An 8-year-old describes her two schools: "the ordinary English school; the Greek school twice a week and Greek Sunday school."[258] Roth's biographical novel[259] and short stories[260] tell of his Austro-Hungarian migrant family's New York move from Brooklyn to an Irish-Italian neighbourhood in Harlem. The move was a dislocation: "the end of my sense of belonging, and with it, my sense of identity."[261] Still, the 2nd generation plays an important role in adaptation and assimilation.[262] Orsi and Alba[263] tell of Italian migrants in the US where "the 2nd generation went to Catholic schools,"[264] while the 3rd generation moved from ethnic enclaves, achieved socio-economic status equivalence[265] and inter-marriage with Protestants:[266] "By the 3rd and 4th generation, they have entered [the] American mainstream [and following from] individual social mobility upward and outward to middle-class they live in ethically mixed areas."[267] Yet, "Italian-American cemeteries remained an expression of enduring family ties across generations and across distances."[268] Although the 1st generation arrived as pious Catholics, the 4th generation was "evenly divided between Catholic and other [with] 18% having no religious affiliation."[269]

Most 2nd generationers recognize and respect parental homelands attitudes and values and still recognize the newland as their primary task. Yet, Egonu tells of a "girl who has never left California but knows the Nigerian national anthem by heart."[270] Some feel frustrated by parental rules and their refusal to permit them to fully engage with the newland:

> I'm eighteen years old and I can't do anything. I can't go out. If I do I have to lie about it. I have to be home around seven or seven-thirty and that's it. I'm not enjoying life. That's why many times my parents and I have arguments.[271]

Sen speaks of the lack of freedom in traditions one has to preserve simply because one is born into it.[272] He compares cultural freedoms arising from the "liberty to question the autonomic endorsement of past traditions [to] unquestioned conservation."[273] Migration permits opportunities "to value living (instead of being restrained by ongoing traditions)."[274] He speaks of freedoms created for 2nd generationers to escape the "tyranny of conformism,"[275] which is achieved through public education and reasoned choice. It permits, he says, the young to "decide for themselves how the various components of their identities (related respectively to nationality, language literature, religion, ethnicity, cultural history, scientific interest, etc.) should receive attention."[276]

Sen quotes Shakespeare: "Some are born great, some achieve greatness, and some have greatness thrust upon them." He argues that "in the schooling of children, it is necessary to make sure that *smallness* is not 'thrust upon' the young, whose lives lie ahead of them."[277] He notes the importance of integration and multiculturalism, and asks "must a person's relation to Britain be *mediated* through the 'culture' of the family in which he or she has been born?"[278] He cautions that the freedoms of "multiculturalism should not lead automatically to giving priority to the dictates of traditional culture over all else."[279] Today, culture and identity are an individual choice: "Human identities can take many distinct forms and people have to use reasoning to decide on how to see themselves, and what significance they should attach to having been born a member of a particular community."[280]

In Canada, 2nd-generation children, except for those from Anabaptist or other religious colonies,[281] attend public schools during the week and on weekends may attend ethnic or religious schools. Generally, they are fluent in both official languages (English and French), as well as their ancestral ethnic language and culture. In the US, "the historical record of all immigrant groups, old and new, show that the politics of the 2nd and successive generations pivot less around issues of class than those tied to a common ethnic origin."[282] Maintaining ethnic ties has network advantages, like "access to sources of working capital, protected markets and pools of labour."[283] Still, "later generations' efforts to maintain a distinct culture have been invariably couched within the framework of loyalty to the US and an overarching American identity."[284]

Sayad speaks of social-cultural domination of migrants. In France, the position of 2nd generationers is in "the field of symbolic power relations [which] is even more dominated and more critical than the position occupied by their parents."[285] Unlike their parents, they cannot delude themselves that they aren't of this land. Nor can they "abandon the game."[286] The only thing they can do is to accept either "willingly or with resignation, submissively or angrily"[287] how they are defined by the dominant culture: "They therefore promote a self-image that is as close as possible to a legitimate identity, the dominant identity."[288] It's a Persona that hides a false self, a symbolic negation of their legitimate identity. In attempts to win "autonomy, self-determination, self-definition,"[289] Sayad says, they are "forced to oscillate between strategies of recognition and strategies of subversion without having the means to implement either,"[290] despite the "dream of all 'immigrants'"[291] to have a dual identity that legitimates them. They're trying to reconcile their dual identity which Sen describes as one of "mutual rejection," along with the

> sub-proletarians dream of enjoying, simultaneously ... the economic advantages associated with 'risk' (advantages that they have discovered thanks to the capitalistic economy), moral and material security, and the solidarity guaranteed them by traditional (advantages specific to the pre-capitalistic social and economic system).[292]

The *Cross-Cultural Coping Scale* measures strategies and differences across cultures and generations. The 2nd and 3rd generations are "reported to utilize more social networking as a coping method as compared to the first-and the mixed-generation groups."[293] In a review of coping mechanisms, sojourners and the least acculturated report

> more areas of stresses and problems (e.g. homesickness, loneliness, etc.) than Chinese-Canadian and European-Canadian students. The latter group also used more positive coping (e.g. more tension reduction and information-seeking), and less passive coping (e.g. wishful thinking and self-blame) than European Canadian students.[294]

A London study of 60 Black Bangladeshi and Black Jamaican youth found that, for them, the civic question was paramount. What kinds of citizen are they becoming? As 2nd generationers, they are legal citizens, yet their "identities are rendered more complex by race and ethnicity, social class and religion or religion and political activism."[295,296] Jamaicans "find that their racial identity is defined by the host community in terms of blackness," while attitudes towards Bangladeshis have been "shaped by Islamophobia" following international political incidents.[297] The biggest problem for both communities is poverty and low educational achievement. Deculturation occurs in 2nd-generation globalized Muslims "attracted to a universalistic and reformed Islam that has to be free from the local cultures that characterized the religion of their parents."[298] Bangladeshis also have not fully embraced British society, but have opted for Muslim as their core identity plus a British or English identity. De Hanas doesn't see them as caught between two cultures, but having embraced a "de-cultured form of universal Islam [and] see themselves in terms of formal rights and opportunities as British citizens."[299] The Jamaicans see "Black" as their primary identity and move easily between cultural worlds.[300] Although civic engagement has more authority for them than radicalization or total assimilation, de Hanas warns, it won't always be the case if these 2nd-generation youth "cannot find meaningful jobs, adequate wages and enjoy social mobility."[301] And it cannot be assumed the 3rd generation will be oriented towards civic engagement.

Gender issues

"Much academic writing about migration has tended to ignore the significance of gender issues,"[302] which are more often discussed in creative literature. Emecheta in *Second Class Citizen* documents the struggles of Nigerian migrant women described as "triply marginalised through their gender, their race and their poverty [and] expected to conform to the traditional values"[303] of their homeland. However, despite the opposition of male relatives, the women manage to educate themselves.[304] Gender is also an issue in the writings of tied migrants—expatriate wives and children. In an early work, Gordon[305] speaks about forced separation from family and friends, and interruption or curtailing of the women's careers. Still, they adapt to a new culture, learn a new language, build new support structures and rely on inner resources. Sometimes, children are sent to boarding schools. A 2018 review of expatriate adjustment found the focus was on adjustment of the worker rather than the family, despite the fact that family members' inability to adjust to foreign environments is cited as "one of the most critical causes of expatriate *failure.*"[306]

For some women, migration brings liberation. In her *Country Girls* trilogy,[307] O'Brien celebrates the escape of young women from the prescribed sex-role drudgeries in the Irish countryside. A recent anthology of American women writers looks at gender/ethnic issues.[308] Roberts-Turner recalls how she was pushed by her grandmother's hope and dreams to rise "above the stereotypes and obstacles"[309] of gender: a struggle they were "faced with the daily Southern indignities of being referred to as gals, girls, niggers and negras, they didn't just struggle to be seen as women, they struggled to be seen as human."[310] Petigara speaks of the great "East-West clash" that lived inside of her following migration: "It had been this very opposition between my beliefs and those of my country, my community—this predetermined fate of all women, so rigid, so stifling-that made me pull away from my own people a long time ago."[311] The problem was, "no one in my family ever asked. They told. Told me how to be married [and] talked at me, not to me."[312]

In an edited volume, Bhattacharya[313] explores the burden of indebtedness young Asian women are made to feel towards their parents for migration sacrifices—a burden that makes it difficult to strive for their own life and identity. Megha discusses the price women pay for perpetual obedience. She realizes that neither she nor her mother can continue to "hold ourselves hostage to some ideal of a sacrificing, pious, grateful, obedient, chaste Indian girls, an idea that many people in India do not subscribe to, and which has if rarely, if ever, described actual women's life."[314] She says "things have changed since we left India in 1993: mothers are different and daughters are too."[315] Dorabji speaks of how cultural expectations of women led to the necessity of the quiet art of subterfuge, a strategy that was passed through generations of women: "We rebel and we are obedient."[316] "I was trained to please, to meet the needs of the family. 'No' was not part of my vocabulary. I was dutifully trying to balance everyone's needs."[317] After living in the West with a different value system, Dorabji found she could no longer play the game and broke the rules:

> I chose honest. I was not soft or sweet. I told my father. *I am not asking for advice.* I made a decision and this is a notification. The subject was closed. I rebelled more in how I told my father my decision than in seeking the separation.[318]

Kundu tells how her "parents had turned our home into the country they remembered, but every morning they were forced to turn me over to the world outside. The second I set foot on school grounds their protective charms dissipated and America took hold."[319] Munaweera examines the negative social relations of migrant culture controlled by gossip and power which the 2nd generation with its western ideals of liberty and freedom rebelled against. Rebellion is necessary, she says, to avoid the tragedy of being suffocated and silenced. The only alternative is the "bittersweet song of the immigrant"[320] she sees in her earlier teen self:

> You may lose family, culture, a sense of belonging. It will be lonely, you will be adrift, the ones you love may not understand what you are becoming. You will lose the village of your father's birth, but you will gain your own pleasure and your own story.[321]

In a 2018 literature review of women's experiences of migration to Canada, Rezazadeh and Hoover, found 1st-generation women face "economic, cultural, linguistic, and systemic barriers that impeded their access to health, social, and economic resources;"[322] but a combination of personal coping skills and support networks eased their transition into Canadian society. "One in five women is born outside Canada,"[323] notes Chui. Their migrations are more challenging because they're often tied-migrants who lack choice or voice. Since 1980, there's been an increase in visible-minority women from developing countries. Generally, they have to learn one or more new languages (English and/or French), seek work and establish social relationships for themselves and their families.[324] Some challenge traditional ethnic gender roles, while others are ambivalent and/or maintain strong identity with ethnic roots important to their sense of identity, well-being and social integration.[325] Das Gupta reports some women though multiple migrations maintain transnational identities in both the homeland and newland.[326] Employment provides them with an alternate sense of identity, even though 1st-generation women are more likely to work in "traditional female jobs at lower wages despite their having education,"[327] since their foreign education and certification are not always recognized. Or they may have issues around language proficiency and lack work experience in the newland. The outcome is a downgrading of their expected career trajectory.[328]

Migrant women are more likely to live in segregated ethnic communities. Because of this, they face an "increased risk for violence because of unequal power relations and differences in gender roles in Canada versus their cultural communities and families."[329] Lacking knowledge of social and health services, along with cultural beliefs, they're made to feel responsible for the violence against them;[330] if they report it, they fear "reprisal by family members."[331] The "stigma and taboo associated with violence"[332] in their ethnic community also promotes non-reporting to maintain the family image: "Gender, ethnicity, immigration status, and class intersect [resulting in] poor health outcomes."[333] This is due partially to cultural pressures to keep sexual and reproductive health matters private, plus a lack of awareness of preventive health and "traditional beliefs about medical care."[334] Following migration, women report "greater autonomy and improved quality of life [and] increased financial independence and greater decision-making powers within the family."[335] Still, there are losses of homeland family, friends, and community and support networks, resulting in social and cultural isolation and depression in the newland.[336] Refugee women are more likely to report poor mental health and help-seeking hindered by language barriers: "Negative attitudes, beliefs, and the stigma associated with mental health issues within their cultures, as well as economic dependence on their spouse strongly influenced their decisions not to seek mental health services."[337]

In Germany, Lucassen says, 2nd-generation women from a Muslim background are restricted in their ambitions by their culture, but generally do better in school and the job market compared to their male peers. This is true too, for 2nd-generation Caribbean women in the UK and for Turkish and Algerian women in France, who do better at school and in the labour market than their male peers.[338] This is despite an internal cultural-discriminatory-gender regime that restricts women and controls them. In cultural enclaves, adolescent girls have less access to the public domain and are socialized to obey rules. Required to stay at home, they do their homework and finish school. As a result, they often gain higher educational qualifications than their ethnic male peers which makes it easier for them to find jobs. Also, girls are less likely than boys to display bad, oppositional and even criminal behaviour.[339]

Second-generation religion

In the West, there's a history of forced abandonment of ancestral Aboriginal religion and cultures, with children placed in cruel religious boarding schools to de-culturate them. These actions drove "a wedge across generations,"[340,341,342,343] and descendants of First Nations and later migrants. Today, reparations are being made by churches and the Canadian government.[344,345]

While Aboriginal religions were denied and practitioners punished, migrant religions were welcomed, transplanted and translated. Eisen speaks of the Jewish exile community where émigrés tried "to remain apart *from* American society and culture at the same time they moved to become a full part *of* it."[346] The 2nd generation found themselves caught between two worlds, an ancient culture to which they did not feel they belonged, and a newland that did not seem to want them. And Judaism as believed and practiced by migrant parents was unappealing to the 2nd generation. In response, Eisen says newland rabbis strove to make Judaism more relevant to newland children and thus, the reformed synagogue emerged.[347]

Iwamura describes Japanese rapid assimilation into mainstream culture making it a model minority.[348] Then, the trials faced during WWII "forged a strong sense of racial-ethnic identity, cultural memory, and social justice that is carried forward"[349] in an annual remembrance in the form of a pilgrimage. The Manzanar, California pilgrimage to the former internment camp has "become a 'sacred' part of the community."[350] It binds and gives "a special sense of meaning and mission that is distinctly religious in nature."[351] It's described as a festival, a political forum and ceremony that's become a "popular" religion of the later generations.[352]

Other religious groups have facilitated adaptation of émigrés while helping to preserve ethnic customs and language, and promoting group solidarity.[353] Some churches provide "housing, food, employment ... and foster networks that often lead to mortgages, housing, jobs, and business opportunities that facilitate social and economic adaptation."[354] Yet for some migrants, their experiences have been one of separation due to the "failure of religious traditions brought from the home country to meet immigrants' needs and the presence of more attractive alternatives."[355]

Yang says the relationship between migration and religion has not been well studied. He quotes an early American sociologist, Herberg (1901–1977), who observed European migrants abandoning everything they had brought from the homeland—language, nationality, culture—except for religion, because this is how they and their children and grandchildren found a place in the US.[356] Another early study by Lazerwitz and Rowitz recall Hansen's 1938 principle of 3rd-generation interest: "What the son wishes to forget, the grandson wishes to remember."[357] This led to *The Three-Generations Hypothesis* of competing interests of migrant generations. It notes "the 2nd generation drops in church attendance while later generations show increases in church attendance."[358] Lenski found the opposite: "the generations show a gradual increase in church attendance which is directly associated with length of time in the United States."[359] Later scholars, Mead, Koenig, Thomas and Gans concur: "there is either a continual decline in church attendance from the foreign-born generation throughout the 3rd generation or no meaningful generational difference."[360] In a re-analysis of early data where gender was taken into account, observable differences were found in 2nd-generation response to religion:

> 1) Protestants of both sexes show an increasing frequency of church attendance with more generations in the United States; 2) Among Catholics, church attendance drops in men who are children of immigrants; 3) Catholic women show no meaningful changes in church attendance for the various generations.[361]

It is hypothesized that "Protestant-Catholic differences stem from the secular orientation of Protestant immigrants."[362]

Kurien studied ways Hinduism in the US has helped migrants from India to negotiate cultural transitions and to assert pride in their heritage at the multicultural table. In contrast, modern "megachurches" promote individualistic faith and praiseful worship services at the expense of ethnic character.[363] Yang studying evangelical Chinese churches reports:

> most members are well-educated professionals who immigrated from Taiwan, Hong Kong, mainland China, and other Southeast-Asian countries. More than half of them have college or graduate degrees; they live in racially-mixed, middle-and upper-middle-class suburbs. The church also has a sizable number of Chinese students attending universities in the region.[364]

He admits "they do not need the church for material support":[365] they need it spiritually. If they fully assimilated to the US, they would be nonreligious because they work in professional environments where "religious expression is discouraged in the highly secularized, private, high-tech companies or government offices."[366] Or they would join local non-ethnic churches rather than driving long distances to an evangelical ethnic church.[367]

Korean evangelical churches emphasize the social needs of members,

Among the majority of Korean immigrants, the religious need (meaning), the social need (belonging), and the psychological need (comfort) for attending the Korean church are inseparable from each other; they are functionally intertwined under the complex conditions of uprooting, existential marginality, and sociocultural adaptation for rerooting.[368]

Akresh says migrants in the US exhibit a robust participation in religious organizations, suggesting that churches play an important role in adjustment following the disruption of migration.[369] Yang says the Chinese community's evangelical churches focus on the "spiritual and psychological needs of the immigrants"[370] with weekly fellowship groups. They "help new immigrants find social belonging ... opportunities for frequent and intimate interactions with compatriots."[371] And "proclaimed teachings help to create a loving and harmonious community where new immigrants can find spiritual peace and psychological ease; church activities and youth programs help to foster a moral environment for nurturing the growing second generation."[372] In fact, "no other type of ethnic Chinese organization or association serves these functions in the way that ethnic Christian churches do."[373]

Generally, it is in the 2nd generation that there's evidence of reactivity against religion. A complex process, it "may include dissatisfaction with home-country religious affiliations"[374] as practiced by parents, but may also arise from "dissatisfaction with the parents themselves and attempts to move away from their traditions."[375] Ethnic religious reactivity seems to point to psychological separation issues. Feeling isolated, along with fears of losing their culture, émigrés may hold more tightly to their children and their culture than if they had remained in the homeland. As a result, they do not facilitate their children's separation and adulthood, an essential step of maturity in the West. In some ethnic groups, socialized with obedience models, the 2nd generation may reactively reject their parents, ethnic culture and religion, or just distance themselves in order to "explore other alternates more consonant with their emotional needs."[376] The opposite can also occur when 2nd generationers bring a broader focus on race and ethnicity to religion.[377]

Religious organizations play important roles in facilitating migration and assisting adaptation. Interestingly, while the US has tended to pressure newcomers to abandon ethnic languages and cultures, this is not the case with their religions.[378] Portes and Rumbaut list the three Rs of religion: Refuge, Respect and Resources.[379] "Traditional beliefs and rituals are a source of comfort and protection,"[380] but émigrés will breaks ties with homeland religions when they fail to meet their needs, or there is a more attractive alternative. Yakushko cautions that religions and spiritual practices can operate as an escape for migrants and religious duties can result in neglect of personal, familiar and social responsibilities.[381]

Herberg is credited with the phrase "cut flower culture" to describe the spiritual rootlessness of modern European and American societies.[382] He sees the 3rd generation returning to the religion of their grandparents, following generational ambivalence, rejection and regret.[383] Ignatieff says the trust put in Herberg's historical generalization relates to the different concerns of the 3rd generation who are not oppressed by an inherited identity, but can choose their own. He asks "What does it mean to be a self in a multicultural society?" And what does it mean when "the very notion of 'the self' is held up to postmodern questioning?"[384]

Cadge and Ecklund see 2nd-generation racial and ethnic identity rooted in religious practices,[385] where they gather "cultural and social capital that leads to economic and educational success."[386] They cite six benefits for adolescents of Asian religious/ethnic communities: 1) protective social networks facilitate educational success and adaptation, 2) the surrogate parental and community support youth at risk of "dangerous and destructive behavior,"[387] 3) networks facilitate moving from working class to middle class,[388] 4) communities supply intangible resources, such as racial and ethnic identities,[389] 5) negotiation of racial and gender constructs that reinforce the image of Asian Americans as model minorities, and 6) a pan-ethnic identity as Asian.[390]

In recent years, there's been an increasing honouring of cultural differences with institutionalized ethnic/religious festivals and holidays in the West. In their annual calendar, Wake Forest University in North Carolina lists 105 official ethnic celebrations.[391] In Canada, there are 10 official ethnic/religious events listed for December. One, the Winter Solstice cites another 8 events for a total of 18 official ethnic/religious celebrations in December.[392] During the rest of the year, many other ethnic/religious festivals are related to seasons of the land.[393]

In summary, many émigrés hold fierce allegiance to their homelands and a deep desire to return that they pass onto newland children. The 2nd generation lives in the shadow of parental adaptation struggles that affects older siblings more than younger ones. Parental attitudes towards newlands and adaptation have significant effects on the core sense of self in 2nd-generation children. Along with their educational/cultural contact in schools, children have a natural advantage in language acquisition that means they quickly adapt and often become cultural brokers for families. They may struggle feeling caught between two worlds. The ideal is finding "both/and" solutions or the best of both worlds. Migration presents special challenges for émigré women, especially those triply marginalized by gender, race and economics and who lack access to education in newlands. Yet, for many women, migration brings liberation, greater autonomy, improved quality of life, financial independence and greater status, with decision-making powers within the family. Religion facilitates adaptation, preserves ethnic customs and language, and promotes group solidarity. For some arrivées, migration permits breaks with heritage religions whose traditions do not meet newland needs and more attractive alternatives are available. Writer Isaac Bashevis Singer in *Love and Exile* says: "I get an occasional urge to write about America, but how can you describe character when everything around is rootless. Among the immigrants the father speaks one language and the son another. Often, the father himself has already half-forgotten his."[394]

Notes

1. Sykes, 2008.
2. White, 1995/2003:1.
3. Tartakovsky & Schwartz, 2001:97.
4. Edinger, 1974:23.
5. Ibid.:23.
6. Hier & Bolaria, 2006.
7. Pailey, 2018:348.
8. Ibid.:348.
9. Yuval-Davis, 1997/2006:12.
10. Ibid.:12.
11. Ibid.:13.
12. Ibid.:13.
13. Portes & Rumbaut, 2006:263.
14. Ibid.:140.
15. Eisen, 2009:224, original emphasis.
16. Portes & Rumbaut, 2006:114.
17. Ibid.:114.
18. Ibid.:114.
19. Yuval-Davis, 1997/2006:46.
20. Ibid.:46.
21. Brunschot, 2011:4.
22. Said, 2000:185.
23. Miles, 1998: 86.
24. Sarti, 2018:12.
25. Ibid.:50.
26. Herberg, 1989:9.
27. Sayad & Macey 2004: 251.
28. Beltsiou, 2016: 99.
29. Brown & Bean, 2006.
30. Herberg, 1989.
31. Kymlicka, 1995,Kymlicka, 1998, Kymlicka, 2001.
32. Taylor, 1989, Taylor, 1992.
33. Wikipedia, Multiculturalism in Canada.
34. Gordon, 1964.
35. Alba, 1990.
36. Nee, 2003.
37. Brown & Bean, 2006.
38. Portes & Rumbaut, 2006:168.

39 Ibid.:168.
40 Gans, 1992.
41 Glazier & Moynihan, 1970.
42 Portes & Rumbaut, 2006.
43 Ibid, xv.
44 Ibid.:58.
45 Ibid.:113.
46 Ibid.:113.
47 Ibid.:148.
48 Portes & Zhou, 1993:77–78.
49 Portes & Rumbaut, 2006:263.
50 Ibid.:265.
51 Ibid.:265.
52 Ibid.:265.
53 Portes & Zhou, 1993:80.
54 Ibid.:80.
55 Ibid.:80.
56 Ibid.:80.
57 Ibid.:80.
58 Portes & Rumbaut, 2006:265; original emphasis..
59 Ibid.:265.
60 Ibid.:265; original emphasis..
61 Ibid.:265.
62 Ibid.:265.
63 Ibid.:140.
64 Kallen, 1982/1995:147–160.
65 Portes & Rumbaut, 2006:267.
66 Abdelmahmould, 2018:66.
67 Ibid.:66.
68 Ibid.:66.
69 Ibid.:66.
70 Ng et al., 2011:100.
71 Ibid.:100.
72 Ibid.:119.
73 Ibid.:100.
74 Ibid.:100.
75 Ibid.:117.
76 Ibid.:119.
77 Ibid.:119.
78 Ibid., 1972.
79 Dunkas & Nikelly, 1972.
80 Portes & Rumbaut, 2006:267.
81 Sayad & Macey, 2004:162.
82 Ibid.:162.
83 Ibid.:162.
84 Portes & Rumbaut, 2006:267.
85 Diehl & Schnell, 2006: 786.
86 Portes & Rumbaut, 2006:325.
87 Ibid.:325.
88 Jung, CG, CW10: 980.
89 Ibid.:968.
90 Kobayashu, 1995:216–217.

91 Ibid.:217.
92 Ibid.:217.
93 Ibid.:219.
94 Khorsandi, 2009:252.
95 Kelly et al., 1994.
96 Landau, 1982.
97 Baptiste, 1993.
98 Birman, 1998.
99 Ibid.:34.
100 Houle & Maheux, 2017.
101 Ibid., 2017.
102 Ibid., 2017.
103 Ibid., 2017.
104 Ibid., 2017.
105 Grosjean, 2010.
106 Arnberg, 1987:14.
107 Ibid.:14.
108 Ibid.:15.
109 Mehta, 1998:134.
110 Ibid.:134.
111 Ibid.:134.
112 Carey, 2018.
113 Parens, 1998:206.
114 Ibid.:206.
115 Ibid.:206.
116 Ibid.:207.
117 Ibid.:208.
118 Grosjean, 2010.
119 Arnberg, 1987:9.
120 Phinney & Devich-Navarro, 1997.
121 Kroll et al., 2014.
122 Ibid., 2014.
123 Ibid., 2014.
124 Ibid., 2014.
125 Arnberg, 1987:53.
126 Ibid.:127.
127 Grosjean, 2010:166.
128 Peal & Lambert, 1962.
129 Arnberg, 1987:22.
130 Akhtar, 1999/2004: 50.
131 Ibid.:50.
132 Azose & Raftery, 2018.
133 Ibid.:50.
134 Elovitz, 1997b: 71.
135 Kahn, 1997b:257.
136 Thorpe, 2017:29.
137 Ibid.:7.
138 Ibid.:25.
139 Ibid.:7.
140 Ibid.:30.
141 Ibid.:134.
142 Ibid.:134.

143 Akhtar, 1999/2004:13.
144 Montero, 1977:178.
145 Ibid.:178.
146 Kahn, 1997b: 278.
147 Elovitz, 1997b:117.
148 Ibid.:117.
149 Sabelli, 1997: 166.
150 Ibid.:166–167.
151 Kahn, 1997b:278.
152 Ibid.:278.
153 Ward et al., 2001:94.
154 Ibid.:279.
155 Portes & Rumbaut, 2001:45.
156 Ibid.:45.
157 Ramanujam, 1997:142.
158 Ibid.:142.
159 Ibid.:142.
160 Ibid.:142.
161 Ibid.:144.
162 Ibid.:145.
163 Ibid.:145.
164 Ibid.:146.
165 Ibid.:146.
166 Ibid.:146.
167 Knafo & Yaari, 1997:221.
168 Ibid.:222.
169 Bustamante et al., 2018:222.
170 Ibid.:222.
171 Zahar, 2016: 263.
172 Ibid.:263.
173 Ibid.:276.
174 Duffy, 1995:21.
175 Ibid.:31.
176 Ibid.:31.
177 Boulanger, 2016:56.
178 Ibid.:56.
179 Ibid.:60.
180 Ibid.:65.
181 Ibid.:65.
182 Tyrrell et al., 2018.
183 Ibid., 2018.
184 Beltsiou, 2016:98.
185 Sayad and Macey, 2004: 253,.
186 Ibid.:251.
187 Ibid.:276–277.
188 My mother's experience.
189 Montero, 1977:152.
190 Ibid.:152.
191 Ibid.:152.
192 Ibid.:162.
193 Falicov, 2003.
194 Nagra & Maurutto, 2016: 165.

195 Ibid.:165.
196 Ibid.:169.
197 Alexander, 2000.
198 Nagra & Maurutto, 2016:184.
199 Alexander, 1996.
200 Alexander, 2000.
201 Ibid.:3.
202 Ibid.:3.
203 Portes & Rumbaut, 2001:51–52.
204 Ibid.:53.
205 Trafton, 2018.
206 Chase, 1999.
207 Yok-Fong, 2013:538.
208 Portes & Rumbaut, 2001:53.
209 Yok-Fong, 2013:541.
210 Pine & Drachman, 2005:538.
211 Ibid.:545.
212 Hesse & Main, 1999:485.
213 Ibid.:483.
214 Hesse & Main, 1999:484.
215 Bustamante et al., 2018:222.
216 Ibid.:222.
217 Von Franz, 1999:7–8.
218 Hargreaves,Hargreaves, 1995:90.
219 Ibid.:91.
220 Ibid.:90.
221 Ibid.:97.
222 Baszile, 2018:2.
223 Marlin, 1997: 247.
224 Ibid.:247.
225 Ibid.:247.
226 Ibid.:248.
227 Ibid.:248.
228 Aldrich, 1995:113.
229 Aldrich, 1995:113.
230 Brown, 2002:197.
231 Ibid.:197.
232 Ibid.:197.
233 Miles 1998: 86.
234 Mehta 1998: 137.
235 Ibid.:156.
236 Ibid.:137.
237 Ibid.:137.
238 Dellal & Zwartz, 2012:242.
239 Wihtol de Wenden, 2012:136.
240 Mehta, 1998:155.
241 Ibid.:157.
242 Ibid.:156.
243 Ibid.:157.
244 Ibid.:160.
245 Ibid.:160.
246 Ibid.:161.

247 Orfanos, 1997:85.
248 Ibid.:85.
249 Ibid.:92.
250 Kahn, 1997b: 217.
251 Ibid.:218.
252 Ibid.:212.
253 Kahn, 1997b: 212.
254 Ibid.:212.
255 Ibid.:213.
256 Ibid.:213.
257 Kahn, 1997b: 277.
258 Montero, 1977:177.
259 Roth, 1934.
260 Roth, 1994.
261 Kahn, 1997b: 278.
262 Alba, 2006.
263 Orsi & Alba, 2009.
264 Alba & Orsi, 2009:45.
265 Ibid.:48.
266 Ibid.:49.
267 Ibid.:33.
268 Ibid.:51.
269 Ibid.:53.
270 Egonu, 2019:330.
271 Ibid.:162.
272 Sen, 2006:116.
273 Ibid.:114.
274 Ibid.:115.
275 Ibid.:117.
276 Ibid.:118.
277 Ibid.:119; original emphasis.
278 Ibid.:158; original emphasis.
279 Ibid.:158.
280 Ibid.:119.
281 Ryan & Millette, 2013/2015.
282 Portes & Rumbaut, 2006:147, 168.
283 Ibid.:64.
284 Ibid.:66.
285 Sayad and Mayce, 2004: 256.
286 Ibid.:256.
287 Ibid.:256.
288 Ibid.:256.
289 Ibid.:256.
290 Ibid.:257.
291 Ibid.:257.
292 Ibid.:257.
293 Kuo, 2014.
294 Ibid., 2014.
295 de Hanas, 2016.
296 Turner, 2016:876.
297 de Hanas, 2016.
298 Ibid.:876.

299 Ibid.:876.
300 Ibid.:877.
301 Ibid.:877.
302 White, 1995/2003:3..
303 Ibid.:11.
304 Ibid.:11.
305 Gordon & Jones, 1999.
306 Sterle et al., 2018:120' original emphasis.
307 O'Brien, 1986.
308 Santana, 2018.
309 Roberts-Turner, 2018:343.
310 Ibid.:342.
311 Petigara, 2018:70.
312 Ibid.:75.
313 Bhattacharya, 2016.
314 Megha, 2016:49.
315 Ibid.:49.
316 Ibid.:59.
317 Dorabji, 2016:63.
318 Ibid.:64.
319 Kundu, 2016: 103.
320 Munaweera, 2106: 129.
321 Ibid.:129.
322 Rezazadeh & Hoover, 2018: 76.
323 Chui, 2011:251.
324 Rezazadeh & Hoover, 2018: 76.
325 Ibid.:77.
326 Das Gupta, 2006.
327 Rezazadeh & Hoover, 2018:79.
328 Ibid.:79.
329 Ibid.:79.
330 Ibid.:79.
331 Ibid.:79.
332 Ibid.:79.
333 Ibid.:80.
334 Ibid.:80.
335 Ibid.:81.
336 Ibid.:81.
337 Ibid.:81.
338 Lucassen, 2005:204.
339 Ibid.:205.
340 Portes & Rumbaut, 2006:348.
341 In Canada, forced assimilation of Aboriginal children was formal policy for many years.
342 Government of Canada, 2019 The Truth and Reconciliation Commission.
343 Wikipedia, 2019n, Canadian Indian residential school system.
344 Royal Canadian Geographical Society with Inuit Tapiriit Kanatami, the Assembly of First Nations, the Métis National Council, the National Centre for Truth and Reconciliation—Indspire, 2019.
345 Aboriginal Healing Foundation, 2006.
346 Eisen, 2009: 334;original emphasis.
347 Ibid.:226.

348 Iwamura, 2009:158.
349 Ibid.:137.
350 Ibid.:137.
351 Ibid.:137.
352 Ibid.:136.
353 Cadge & Ecklund, 2007:362–363.
354 Ibid.:363.
355 Portes & Rumbaut, 2006:326.
356 Herberg, 1960:27–28.
357 Lazerwitz & Rowitz, 1964:530.
358 Ibid.:531.
359 Ibid.:531.
360 Ibid.:531.
361 Ibid.:529.
362 Ibid.:529.
363 Kurien, 2005, 2007, Kurien, 2017.
364 Yang, 1998:239.
365 Ibid.:243.
366 Ibid.:243.
367 Ibid.:243.
368 Hurh & Kim, 1990:31.
369 Akresh, 2011.
370 Yang, 1998:243.
371 Ibid.:245.
372 Ibid.:245.
373 Ibid.:245.
374 Portes & Rumbaut, 2006:327.
375 Ibid.:327.
376 Ibid.:327.
377 Cadge & Ecklund, 2007:363.
378 Portes & Rumbaut, 2006:315.
379 Ibid.:315.
380 Ibid.:326.
381 Yakushko, 2010:271.
382 Eisen, 2009:236.
383 Ibid.:236.
384 Ignatieff, 1993: 243.
385 Cadge & Ecklund, 2007: 369.
386 Ibid.:369.
387 Ibid.:368.
388 Ibid.:368.
389 Ibid.:369.
390 Ibid.:369.
391 Wahl, 2019.
392 Live & Learn, 2017.
393 Sawyer, 2009/2015.
394 Singer, 1984: 261.

Chapter 7

Host country

Chapter 7, "Host country," explores the response of newlands residents to migrants as successful adaptation depends to a large degree upon their reception. Human rights researcher, Hron, says "successful integration takes place when the demands of both immigrant and the host nation are met; these may include economic, affective (psychic), or socio-political demands."[1] Further, "The host environment largely influences what types of hardships immigrants will face, and the types of physical, emotional, and social manifestations of pain they might experience."[2] The American Presidential Task Force on Immigration[3] says there is no "best" migration adaptation of migrants independent of host-country response because success emerges from a balance of social support and pressures to assimilate[4,5,6] amongst fear of strangers.[7,8,9] The US, for instance, has "one international migrant (net) every 47 seconds."[10] Thus, this chapter looks at structures of reception in the newland, attitudes, values and beliefs about migrants, and migrant responses to host countries.

Host countries

Today's five primary countries of immigration or "Settler States" are former colonies: Argentina, Australia, Canada, New Zealand and the US. Migrants are central to their economies. Multiculturalism is the ideology[11] and ethno-relativism is viewed as "progressive thinking."[12] Other countries accept immigrants and refugees seeking asylum, but at the time of writing, the European Union lacked a unified approach and/or policy toward immigration, migrant workers and refugee asylum:

> The arrival of more than one million asylum seekers and migrants to Europe in 2015 exposed serious flaws in the EU asylum system. To respond to the migrant crisis, Parliament has been working on proposals to create a fairer, more effective European asylum policy.[13,14]

According to the UN, in 2017 an estimated 258 million people lived outside their birth country, an increase of 50% from 2000.[15] Acceptance of migrants is evidenced in percentages of naturalized (foreign-born) citizens. In 2019, this amount varied from a low of 1.6% in Japan,[16,17] to 7% in EU countries, 13% in the US,[18] 22% in Canada,[19] and 29% in Australia.[20] Although the actual number of migrants is less in Canada and Australia than in the US, the higher percentages of foreign-born are due to statistical calculations and population size.

Currently, "Europe is a haven of peace and prosperity,"[21] and a destination for refugees. Five million Syrians seeking refuge have fled to neighbouring countries: Jordan, Lebanon and Turkey, and about 2% have embarked by boat for Europe—they are not financially needy: "To get a place on a boat you need to be highly mobile, and sufficiently affluent to pay several thousand dollars to a crook."[22] At issue is finding a better life, but this doesn't always materialize and many become disenchanted with the reality of migration. Previously, social networks mediated migrations, but now Mediterranean *agenti* in mercantilized networks dominate.[23] They facilitate passage but not entrance, so overloaded migrant boats are abandoned in international waters for rescue.[24]

In the EU in 2017, "Germany reported the largest total number of immigrants (917,000); United Kingdom (644,200); Spain (532,000); France (370,000) and Italy (343,400)."[25] Although in terms of sheer numbers, the US still tops the world list with 50 million arrivées, Saudi Arabia, the United Arab Emirates (UAE) and India are major destinations. Asia and the Middle East receive around 30% of the world's migrants (80 million): "In 2015, Asia surpassed Europe as the largest hub of international migrants."[26] Although in the past, South and East Asian countries have been sources of out-migration, they also have considerable internal migration. There's a large "permanent emigration of educated and skilled Singaporeans. Over the past decade, Singapore's multicultural, yet nationalist society, has experienced substantial inflows of Asian and Western professionals, low-skilled migrants from across Southeast Asia, and new immigrants from non-traditional sending countries."[27] There's considerable migration into Hong Kong from other South Asian countries, especially India and Bangladesh. Kawate says, migrants are looking to Asia as the land of opportunity. Thus, Tokyo has a "Korea Town" and "Shin-Okubo is quickly becoming Nepal Town."[28] We are "living on a cosmopolitanized planet with porous and highly osmotic borders and universal interdependence," Bauman reminds us. We're lacking a "'cosmopolitan awareness' to match our cosmopolitan condition."[29]

Nation states and citizens

Nation states and citizenship are based on: 1) "rights of blood" (*jus sanguinis*),[30] where one or more parents is a citizen; 2) "rights of soil" (*jus soli*),[31] which pertain to someone born in the territory, and 3) civic citizenship in Settler States based on eligibility and vows to uphold the laws of the land. From these arise *nationalism* or attitudes towards state and citizenship. Historically in Europe, states have formed "through disputes over borders or consolidation of population groups who had lived in a particular region for centuries"[32] with common ancestry[33] from which it's assumed follows allegiance of heart and soul. These ideas are enshrined in laws, beliefs and expectations. Kohn's pioneering psychological study of nationalism[34] sees it "rooted in religious values, institutions and ideas"[35] of the land and its people. Nationalism is "secularization of a fundamentally religious belief in mankind's salvation through his membership in a particular nation or in a particular class in society, which supposedly leads or represents mankind or is at least of universal importance."[36]

Sen says blood and soil nationalist ideologies are

> now being forced to realize their identity, to create from scratch their "soil" their "blood," their "language," their "ethnicity" [a euphemism for "race"], their "culture," and all the "objective" criteria that can serve as "proofs" of their identity and as reason for laying claim to that identity.[37]

In fact, in many places today, nationalism is a paradox that has become visible: "a sort of 'nationalism without a nation' or 'patriotism without a *patrie*,' or a 'territoriality without a territory;'"[38] and totally "impossible because *jus soli* has not been converted or 'naturalized' into *jus sanguinis.*"[39]

Migrant/host relations

Three types of migrant/host psychological relations have been identified: 1) *retreatism*—hiding/denial/rejection, 2) *essentialism*—intensification of homeland identification and culture used aggressively, and 3) *engagement*— a relationship dialogue continuously in process.[40,41] Portes and Rumbaut define French *jus soli*[42] as a "Republican model"[43] with an ideology of a uniform culture. But practically, Peters says there's no uniform culture, but

> several competing strands: the republican (or Jacobin) tradition (nearest to the civic model), a more statist or 'imperial' element, as well as an 'organic' tradition, relying on Catholic tradition and the identification with a long collective history reaching back to medieval times.[44]

The ideology of "liberty, equality and fraternity are still high in the pantheon,"[45] and the French collective sense of self is reflected in public debates, national symbols, rituals, museum culture, public history and regional cultures, but altogether, they don't add up to a "political identity that is mainly based on the universal values and principles of the French revolution."[46] Present too are pre-Revolution historical images and general "beliefs about the superiority of French culture and civilization."[47] In other words, Peters argues the French republican model is not monocultural, yet there's an expectation of migrants to assimilate into a secularized monoculture.

In Spain,

> conservative sectors took a long time to accept the concept of the nation, but when they did, towards the middle of the 19th century, they gave it a profoundly Roman Catholic content ... Catholicism was the essence of the Spanish nation: being Spanish was one and the same as being Catholic.[48]

More recently the liberal conception of the Spanish nation has triumphed, and "both the Constitution and the Civil Code include *jus soli* and *jus sanguinis* elements in their definition of Spanish citizenship and in regulations to acquire it."[49] Yet, citizenship is not automatic: "Effective legal residence in Spain is the main prerequisite for becoming a Spanish citizen for those without Spanish descent."[50]

In Germany, nationhood is an *ethno-cultural model*[51] based on *jus sanguinis* (blood) or ancestry as the basis and right to citizenship.[52] However, the 1871 unification of former states of the Holy Roman Empire into the present state of Germany was late in comparison to Spain, France and the US,[53,54,55] countries which had the strength and resources to colonize other lands. Peters criticizes comparisons of French republican models of political or civic conceptions of nationhood of "self governing, democratic polity with legal and political equality among its citizen-members"[56] with German "ethno-cultural" conceptions,[57] that still rely "on notions of common genealogy and descent ties, a common history, shared cultural traditions and customs as constitutive elements of the nation or of national identity."[58] He argues for a more multidimensional model of statehood. Lepsius[59] proposes a variable state model arising from the "dominant criteria for 'commonality' or 'equality' between the members of the nation: common descent or shared history, a shared cultural heritage, or membership in a liberal-democratic political community (citizenship), or working-class solidarity."[60] It encompasses "an ethnic conception (*Volksnation*), a cultural conception (*Kulturnation*), a political conception (*Staatsbürgernation*) and a 'class' conception (*Klassennation*)."[61] These four constructs are at the basis of state migration policies, acceptance of migrants and migrant adaptation. They also point to difficulties residents and migrants have in accepting each other and their ideas.

Heath and Tilley in the UK found three competing ideas about what's important to be British: 1) ethnic and civic aspects, 2) only civic aspects, and 3) neither.[62] Those following the ethnic-civic idea want to reduce immigration; remove illegal immigrants, are "more likely to report that they are racially prejudiced, and are less enthusiastic about antidiscrimination laws."[63] Those in the second, civic-only group support multiculturalism.[64] Those "who regard ethnic aspects of national identity as important tend to be rather older than members of our 'civic only' group, whereas the 'neither civic nor ethnic' group tend to be the youngest."[65] It suggests the UK is shifting towards the civic-only concept of national identity.[66]

Historically, EU countries have been "sending-societies" for migration but in recent years, with increasingly ageing populations, they're shifting towards becoming "receiving-societies" of multicultural migrants with a convergence of "policies toward citizenship, cultural practice and social welfare benefits."[67,68] Today, "Europe needs migration economically and demographically."[69] To understand the meaning of migration in the EU, a survey was conducted in eight countries, which reported that "European richness in diversity and the liberal stance on ethnic, linguistic, religious and cultural plurality of European societies are praised on many occasions;"[70] yet, migrants are still treated in ambivalent ways. This is true individually and in official policies that "aim at cultural, linguistic and other coercive assimilation of migrants, rather than supporting integration and diversity."[71] Further, "Fortress Europe excludes many migrants and denies their right to mobility and residence in European countries, while it also makes combating (illegal) migration ... one of the top priorities of the European Union."[72] The result is that migrants who are allowed in "are rarely given the possibility to truly belong to the European societies which are based on obsolete principles of exclusiveness and ethnic homogeneity."[73] At the same time, migrants "provide a convenient scapegoat for society's ills."[74]

Citizenship

Most countries issue visas for short-term visits and renewable short-stay visas for students and migrant workers. Visas can be upgraded to permanent status with potential for citizenship, but this is not automatic. Non-official entrance—often called illegal, but more correctly irregular or undocumented migration—varies from overstaying a visa to clandestine entrance with the help of *agenti*. Migrants often go underground in protective ghettos, or marry for citizenship. Irregular migration is a political football in many countries, with responses varying from accommodation and expectations of assimilation (melting pot), to integration and acculturation in pluralist and multicultural societies (cultural mosaics) and exogamy (intermarriage).

Anderson describes the modern state as "composed of people who share common ideals and (exemplary) patterns of behaviour expressed through ethnicity, religion, culture, or language—that is, its members have shared values ... bound by common experiences."[75] In Settler Societies with multicultural ideals of a common destiny, the nation's future is seen as a collective endeavour.[76] Migrants are recognized as "essential elements in establishment and development"[77] and integration/accommodation is the expectation along with respect for ethno-cultural differences.[78] Kivisto says the "three historic settler states—the US, Canada and Australia—continue to be more heterogeneous than their non-settler state counterparts. On a continuum, the US and Canada are clearly the most ethnically heterogeneous nations while Germany and Japan remain the least heterogeneous."[79]

Citizenship carries obligations: civil, political and social rights, as well as duties.[80] The "first of these rights is basically inherent in legal institutions, the second in political institutions and the third in social services."[81] Further, "the first refers broadly to guarantees of individual liberty and equality before the law; the second to political enfranchisement—the right to vote and to seek political office."[82] The third, "less specific than the other two, comprises a 'modicum of economic welfare and security' and the 'right to share to the full in the social heritage and life of a civilized being according to the standards.'"[83] A good citizen is "the liberal sovereign self: rational, self-owning, and independent, with a moral compass that enables him/her to consider the interests of others."[84] In contrast, the "noncitizen" is an outsider in value-laden and negative terms—foreigner, migrant, refugee, asylum seeker—who does not share the same or "right" values.[85] There are also failed citizens, who are "incapable of, or fail to live up to, liberal ideals."[86] This includes rioters, paedophiles and criminals—feckless, lacking discipline and welfare dependent—but while they cannot be sent away (transported, deported), they *can* be excluded from participation and benefits.[87]

The US defines citizenship as bound not by blood or soil but "shared values of freedom, liberty, and equality" with "rights and responsibilities."[88] Rights include:

> Freedom to express yourself; Freedom to worship as you wish; Right to a prompt, fair trial by jury; Right to vote in elections for public officials; Right to apply for federal employment requiring U.S. citizenship; Right to run for elected office [and Freedom to pursue] life, liberty, and the pursuit of happiness.[89]

Responsibilities include:

Support and defend the Constitution: Stay informed of the issues affecting your community; Participate in the democratic process; Respect and obey federal, state, and local laws; Respect the rights, beliefs, and opinions of others; Participate in your local community; Pay income and other taxes honestly, and on time, to federal, state, and local authorities; Serve on a jury when called upon; and Defend the country if the need should arise.[90]

A similar set of citizenship rights and responsibilities exists for Canada. Rights include "democratic rights (vote); language rights; equality rights; legal rights; mobility rights; freedom of religion; freedom of expression and freedom of assembly and association."[91] Responsibilities are: "To respect the rights and freedoms of others; to obey Canada's laws; to participate in the democratic process, and to respect Canada's two official languages and multicultural heritage."[92]

Attitudes, values, beliefs and policies

Arrivées stir up mixed emotions "ranging from paranoid anxieties to idealization,"[93] says Akhtar, referring to the importance of the host-country reception. A migrant may be "seen as an interloper who would deprive the natives of economic opportunities and life resources, or an unconsciously revered messianic leader who would solve the problems of the existing community."[94] Responses can vary from outright "prejudice and xenophobia on the one hand and excessive kindness followed by disappointment and rejection on the other."[95] Reception depends on: 1) the era of migration, 2) the nature of the existing community, 3) pre-existing ties between homeland and newland, 4) the ethnic diversity of the newland, 5) the "magnitude of cultural differences" and 6) "bodily characteristics of the migrant."[96]

While the migrant may feel his/her identity is endangered, the host may feel their "cultural identity, the purity of its language, its beliefs, and its sense of group identity are also threatened."[97] The psychology of migrant and host country is illustrated in Bion's idea of the "container and contained,"[98] which is "equally applicable to the range of emotional reactions between the person who decides to emigrate and those who stay behind."[99] Interactions between the migrant "with all his baggage and personality traits and the host society can range from enthusiastic acceptance to outright rejection."[100] Kahn notes: "members of the host society harbour a deep ambivalence toward the newcomers similar to the fear, jealousy, and delight with which a newborn sibling is welcomed into the family";[101] "complex personalities and new issues emerge from the crucible of the acculturation process and rich 'transcultural' patterns of living are evidence of the benefits of immigration to both individuals and society."[102]

Bauder identifies five major migration/host issues in Canada: 1) *economic* labour migration,[103] 2) *humanitarianism*, which carries the potential of admission to suspected terrorists, 3) *threats* to national security and social problems destructive to social order and democracy,[104] 4) *culture* and ethnic discrimination represented by Eurocentric hegemony vs ideals of multiculturalism, and 5) *politic*, or the need to avoid offending ethnic communities and fears that multiculturalism will erode sovereignty.[105] These are contrasted with German migration issues where economics is the most important.[106]

Hastie raises a sixth migration/host issue: 6) *justice*, or access of migrants who "formally possess the same employment-related rights on paper as citizen and resident workers, codified in provincial employment standards legislation, and including minimum entitlements."[107] Also to be considered are "the social relations of exploitation"[108] and migrants' "access to their rights in practice."[109] It's a matter of "asserting rights, and by seeking legal remedy or redress where those rights have been violated—that represents the core issue in their ability to access justice."[110] This arises from "a lack of knowledge of legal rights and available resources, or mechanisms for redress,"[111] that permits "abusive treatment and tolerance of it."[112] It's assumed that if migrants knew their rights, they would enforce them but this blames the victim, because the culture of exploitation should not pre-exist their arrival or be part of employment practices. Further, "employer-specific work permits create a distinct disadvantage for migrant workers by producing an exacerbated power imbalance in the employment relationship."[113]

An Italian, 34-country, survey of governments' and individuals' attitudes towards migration identified three categories: 1) "Traditional settlement countries (Australia, Canada, New Zealand and the United States), for which immigration has been a key factor for their establishment and development."[114] 2) "Northern European countries, which have received large inflows of immigrants either due to colonial linkages or to active labour market recruitment policies (France, Germany, the Netherlands, Switzerland, Sweden, the UK, etc.)."[115] 3) "New immigration countries of Western Europe (Italy, Spain, Portugal and Ireland) and of Eastern Europe (Czech Republic and Hungary)."[116] This last group are former countries of emigration, where "strong economic performance has transformed them into net receivers of foreign workers."[117]

A points-system to admit skilled migrants in three Settler Societies accounts for 68% of migrants to Australia; 61% in New Zealand, and 56% in Canada. In contrast, in the US, the dominant reason for immigration is family reunification with only 22% entering in a skills-stream.[118] Until recently, the UK had an open door policy for British Commonwealth citizens.[119] In Germany, Austria and Switzerland, "labour market shortages have been driving migration policies" and admission of temporary guest workers.[120] Most of the OECD (Organization for Economic Co-operation and Development)[121] countries have policies to recruit skilled and highly skilled workers.[122] Recently, Germany issued a "green card" for information technology (IT) professionals, while France has entered into a series of bilateral agreements "to allow foreign young professionals to work in the country."[123] Along with an EU-wide debate about issuing a "skills blue-card" to attract migrants, the Eastern European countries have begun to adopt a market-based migration policy.[124] The "market-based approach to immigration"[125] was first "suggested by Nobel laureate economist, Gary Becker,"[126] and entailed entry visas sold on the international market, with a limited number of free visas for refugees. In this model, "the most skilled, productive persons will be the ones who will gain entry as they will more likely have the money or will have employers willing to pay for their entry."[127] Hence, the market-based approach of "immigration will move towards more skilled and educated persons, who are also individuals who are more likely to work. Family members who enter can still bring in their brothers and sisters and mothers and fathers—but at a price."[128]

Except for migration, "on most issues of public policy ... one can predict the position that individuals will take based on their ideological orientation."[129] But with migration, a wide variation exists in attitudes. The Italian, 34-country, survey reports in "more than twenty high-and middle-income countries, less than ten percent of respondents who gave an opinion about migration were in favour of increasing the number of immigrants to their country."[130] In 2003, the world's countries most open to increased migration were Canada (29%), Israel (27%) and Finland (24%). Less-open countries were, in Eastern Europe—Hungary (2%) and Latvia (2.6%)—and in Western Europe—Portugal (3%), Netherlands (3.7%) and Germany (4%).[131] "In France, only 7.37% of voters welcome increases in migration,"[132] and in the US, only "9.8% of individuals favour higher numbers of immigrants."[133]

Upon arrival, migrants encounter not one, but three different levels of reception: government, societal and communal.[134] At each level, there are three possible outcomes: 1) *exclusion*, which "precludes immigration or forces immigrants into a wholly underground and disadvantaged existence."[135] 2) *Passive acceptance* is legal access to the country without any effort to assist or facilitate settlement and adaptation.[136] 3) *Active encouragement* means that authorities take active steps to facilitate resettlement,[137] and established ethnic communities can also be important facilitators.[138]

In democratic societies, there's a direct relationship between voter attitudes towards migration and existing migration policies: "Countries where the median voter is more opposed to migration tend to implement more restrictive policies."[139] This suggests "that politicians take voters' attitudes towards migrants into account as they formulate their policies."[140] In countries with strong negative attitudes towards migrants, one would expect migration flows to be close to zero, but the reality is continued admission of substantial numbers of foreign workers, which is attributed to pressure-group influence over government policy.[141] "Historically, US labour unions have been a very influential anti-immigration lobby,"[142] but today's demands for specific-skilled workers or labourers in certain industries also drives migration policy. Thus, attitudes and beliefs are driven not just by stereotypes, preconceptions, stubborn intolerance, or irrationality, but also by perceived "direct economic advantages and disadvantages."[143] All are taken into account in migration policies:[144] "Promoting a culture of tolerance can be very effective in shaping attitudes towards globalization."[145]

Prejudice and xenophilia

"Historically, attitudes towards refugees fall along a continuum between compassion and rejection/dehumanization."[146] Today's "xenophobia and/or xeno-racism reflect the fact that, both for individuals and for society, refugees have come to represent the Freudian Uncanny/*das Unheimliche*,"[147] and are viewed with suspicion and fear.[148] Early in 2016 in Germany, the Socio-Economic Panel (SOEP) set up the "Barometer of Public Opinion on Refugees."[149] Although more than half of the respondents associate granting asylum with risks, 81% are in favour, in accordance with international law, of admitting refugees and those fleeing political persecution. Still, the majority feels refugees should return to their homelands when their reasons for leaving change.[150]

In other Western European areas, "opposition to migration has become increasingly politicised."[151] In response, prevention and intervention practices have been sought to reduce intergroup prejudice and hostility.[152] Pioneering research arose amidst the clearing smoke of WWII, the Holocaust and American racial segregation:[153] *The Authoritarian Personality* by Adorno[154] was followed by Allport's *The Nature of Prejudice*;[155] while Cartwright[156] and Jones[157] undertook historical reviews. Recently, Dovidio and colleagues published *The Sage Handbook of Prejudice, Stereotyping, and Discrimination*.[158] They found Right-Wing Authoritarianism (RWA) and Social Dominance Orientation (SDO) to be strongly related, but arising from different values. To explore these concepts, the *dual-process motivational model* (DPM) of ideology and prejudice was developed by Duckitt and Sibley.[159] They found RWA and SDO originate in "different social worldview beliefs, personality trait dimensions, and social environmental influences."[160] This was followed by a meta-analysis of prejudice and its relationship to the Five-Factors Model (FFM) of personality.[161] Known as the Big-Five (acronym OCEAN), they are stable enough from childhood to distinguish individual personalities.[162,163,164,165] Identified in vastly different cultures and languages,[166] it's agreed that OCEAN captures human universals of personality.[167,168] The Five Factors are: 1) Openness to experience —inventive/curious vs consistent/cautious, 2) Conscientiousness—efficient/organized vs easy-going/careless, 3) Extraversion—outgoing/energetic vs solitary/reserved, 4) Agreeableness—friendly/compassionate vs challenging/detached, and 5) Neuroticism—sensitive/nervous vs secure/confident. In a meta-analysis of 71 studies on the relationship between the Big-Five and prejudice, RWA "was predicted by low Openness to Experience but also by Conscientiousness,"[169] while SDO "was predicted by low Agreeableness and also weakly by low Openness to Experience."[170]

Although "personality psychology and sociological research have been separate,"[171] recently three correlates of attitudes towards immigrants have been reported.[172] The first is *socio-economic* (education/income) and *demographic* characteristics (age/gender). The second is *identity, ideology* and *social attitudes*. Third is *interpersonal* experience with migrants.[173] With these three factors in mind, a population-level study of the Big-Five Personality Traits and attitudes towards immigrants was done in the Netherlands. Participants were asked: "Does personality influence attitudes towards immigrants?"[174] If so, "which personality traits are relevant?"[175] The surveyors found "socio-economic and attitudinal factors were more strongly associated with attitudes towards immigrants than personality traits,"[176] and "education and left-right ideology emerge as particularly relevant correlates of attitudes towards immigrants."[177] Unemployed people showed more negative attitudes.[178] In terms of personality traits, they affirmed previous studies in personality psychology that found "agreeableness and openness to experience are the two main personality factors influencing general prejudice levels"[179] and positive attitudes towards immigrants.[180]

An American team found negative attitudes and beliefs of migrant threat related to types of fears: "Security fears affect attitudes towards Muslim immigrants but economic concerns bear on views towards Eastern Europeans. While concern about crime adversely affects sentiment for East Europeans but casts Muslims more positively, cultural threats have the opposite effect."[181]

It's hypothesized that political attitudes develop early in life and the liberalization effects of education fostering egalitarian values and analytic skills translate into positive attitudes towards migrants. But data from a Swiss Household Panel did not show the expected liberalizing effects of education. In fact, when "entering the labour market, the higher educated individuals also become more likely to oppose immigrants."[182] This finding was supported by an American study: "Europeans who compete with immigrants in the labor market have more negative attitudes towards foreigners. In addition, an increased concentration of immigrants in local neighborhoods increases the likelihood of negative attitudes."[183] At the same time, a European Social Survey found generally speaking, "ethnic minorities, urban people, people with higher education and income, as well as people who have work experience abroad are, as a rule, more tolerant towards immigrants in Europe."[184]

Irish sociologists note: "scholars of mass political behaviour have proposed various explanations for why an individual would oppose immigration or support a nativist political movement"[185,186] (*Nativist* being protection of the interests of the native-born).[187] "Contact hypothesis has remained one of the most durable ideas in the sociology of racial and ethnic relations."[188] Other explanations vary from abstract psychological predispositions to xenophobia:[189] "Anomie or alienation, national identity, authoritarianism, cognitive rigidity, pessimism, poor self-efficacy or political powerlessness as well as national pride are all said to cause diverse forms of xenophobic attitudes and nativism."[190,191,192,193,194,195] Micro-theories of nativism and anti-migration attitudes are blamed on "youthfulness, failure to belong to a union, the lack of involvement in one's church, coming from a rural environment, or the lack of contact with immigrants."[196,197,198,199]

To explore attitudes toward migrants in Northern Ireland, three major theories were tested: 1) social contact hypothesis, 2) cultural marginality theory, and 3) economic self-interest theory.[200]

Social contact hypothesis refers to the nature and type of contact with strangers, friends, work colleagues and neighbours, where a "lack of contact with immigrants traditionally stands out as the most commonly evoked factor in explaining nativism and xenophobic attitudes."[201] *Cultural marginality theory* holds that "experiencing marginality or oppression itself creates sympathy for other marginalised or oppressed groups."[202] *Economic self-interest hypothesis* says "political attitudes primarily reflect narrow, material self-interests,"[203] where those who think "they will be disproportionately financially harmed by immigration, such as the lesser educated or the economically weaker classes in a nation, are more likely to oppose immigration and vote for extreme-right parties than their more economically privileged counterparts."[204] The survey found the greatest support for the *social contact hypothesis* for being positive towards migration: over a quarter (27%) had at least one friend from another country, 30% had at least one immigrant work colleague, and 23% lived in an neighbourhood with some or many people of a different ethnic or racial group.[205] "People who have colleagues or friends who have come to live in the UK are indeed more likely to demonstrate pro-immigrant attitudes than those who do not."[206] *Cultural marginality theory* was not found to be a useful predictor as "only a small minority of the adult population (13%) were willing to define themselves as belonging to a discriminated group, Catholics were significantly more likely to do so than Protestants."[207] The authors found that those willing to "describe themselves as being a member of a discriminated group are notably more likely to hold favourable attitudes towards immigrants of a different race or ethnic background than those who do not."[208] *Economic self-interest hypothesis* showed respondents are about equally divided in terms of their views on the UK economy where two-fifths, exactly 40% report that they are "living comfortably on their present income."[209] Those "who are satisfied with the current state of the economy are significantly more likely to express favourable attitudes towards immigrants than those who are not."[210] Further, the vast majority of migrants in Northern Ireland "are concentrated in self-employed businesses such as catering outlets and are thus not in direct competition with the non-immigrant population in terms of their employment practices."[211] Hayes and Dowds concluded that "both social exposure and cultural marginality are the two key explanations, independently important, in predicting pro-immigrant attitudes in Northern Ireland. Of these two theoretical perspectives, however, social exposure stands out as the most consistent explanation of attitudes"[212] towards migrants.

Rather than focus on *xenophobia* (stranger fear), a team of German psychologists[213] wanted to understand *xenophilia* (stranger openness), which is much less studied. We still don't understand prosocial or positive regard for strangers and why "people develop curiosity for other cultures, and or why they engage in cross-cultural exploration, traveling, and contact seeking."[214] Much xenophobia research correlates ethnic ideas of nation and attitudes of "us and them" requiring self-protection, while xenophilia is a historical constant of human societies.[215,216,217,218] Important too is understanding of "the role of personality in adaptive and maladaptive cross-cultural relations in multicultural societies."[219] It's hypothesized that in xenophilia, there's a "complex interplay of multiple factors" including personality traits, individual experiences, social influence from peers or in-group members and cultural values.[220]

The Five-Factors Model of personality suggests xenophilia is partially explained by personality. A Dutch study[221] found high Extraversion and/or high Openness to Experience (endeavour-related) are significantly and positively correlated to multicultural activity, and predictive of an interest in an international career. In contrast, high Emotional Instability and/or High Agreeableness (altruism/cooperation) are negatively correlated.[222] Other studies[223,224,225] report that when "us and them" distinctions are strong, it's "less likely that dispositional empathy—a general tendency to react to another's plight with feelings of compassion and concern—translates into actual helping of an out-group member."[226]

To further explore altruism/cooperation traits in xenophilia and personality, the Six-Factor HEXACO model was used.[227,228] Based on common rather than scientific words of the Big-Five model, the HEXACO trait model adds another dimension, Honesty-Humility (H), to the five traits of Emotionality (E), Extraversion (X), Agreeableness (A), Conscientiousness (C) and Openness to Experience (O).[229,230] These "major personality traits play a significant and unique role in explaining individual differences in xenophilia."[231] Significant correlations were reported "between respondents' gender or respondents' age and the overall attitude measure."[232] Moreover, "endeavor-related traits explained several times more variance in the overall measure of respondents' attitudes toward contact with immigrants than did altruism/cooperation-related traits."[233] In fact, the "major personality traits were significant and direct predictors of xenophilia,"[234] and "individual differences in the levels of endeavor-related personality traits (i.e., eXtraversion, Openness, and Conscientiousness) had a substantially greater power in predicting individual differences in xenophilia than individual differences in levels of altruism/cooperation-related traits (i.e., Honesty-Humility, Emotionality, and Agreeableness)."[235]

Adaptation, assimilation or integration?

"Degrees of acculturation and assimilation trajectories"[236] of migrants "are constrained by different forms of capital their family brought with them and the rate of capital accumulation over time,"[237] says Paat. In other words, cultural adaptation is not simply a matter of attitude and personality, but money. Another perspective is given by Alba and Foner, who explored migrant adaptation in six countries: Canada, France, Germany, Great Britain, the Netherlands and the US .[238] Here, two polar approaches were found: 1) *assimilation* or social-cultural convergence towards the mainstream, and 2) *integration* or accommodation with respect to ethno-cultural differences.[239] A third perspective, found in the US, is *exceptionalism*, a mixture of assimilation and integration.[240] They note the US has historically been perceived as a "uniquely open society, welcoming immigrants and quickly investing them with membership rights [and] mobility into the middle class."[241] Yet Portes and Rumbaut found in the US that ethnicity is more important than class: "The historical record of all immigrant groups, old and new, shows that the politics of the 2nd and successive generations pivot less around issues of class than those tied to a common ethnic origin."[242] This is because maintaining ethnic ties has many advantages, like "access to sources of working capital, protected markets and pools of labour."[243] In fact, ethnicity is so important in the US that ethnic traditions have been institutionalized as festivals and "later generations' efforts to maintain a distinct culture have also been invariably couched within the framework of loyalty to the US and an overarching American identity."[244]

Assimilation

Assimilation means absorption, where one part becomes indistinguishable from the whole. Applied to migration, it refers to culture—language, dress, customs, ideas and religion—where arrivées become indistinguishable from the dominant culture. Although expectations of assimilation are not politically correct in some countries, like Canada, it's assumed in others as a *rite of passage* to citizenship. There are three steps to assimilation:[245] 1)

"Separation (from social relations and from participation in the opportunity structure of the country or culture of origin);"[246] 2) "Marginality (residential, linguistic, economic, especially during the earlier phases of immigration and acute among the first generation),"[247] and 3) "A generation or two after immigration, incorporation into the social structures and cultural codes of the mainstream."[248] Although assimilation is seen as the likely migration outcome over time,[249] it's also recognized as a lengthy, "complex sociological process and not a political and ideological program."[250]

"The dominant narrative of immigration assimilation"[251] says Suárez-Orozco is structured by three assumptions: clean break, homogeneity and progress.[252] Today, a *clean break* is no longer necessary because modern communication and transportation permit easy passage of people, information and goods.[253,254,255] The *homogeneity* assumption is also less likely because today most migrants "are actors in a thoroughly globalized restructured economy that is increasingly fragmented into discontinuous economic spheres."[256] Although the American Founding Fathers envisioned the future as progress, today the *progress* assumption doesn't hold, since the potential for upward mobility no longer exists.[257] In the US's post-industrial economy, the hourglass metaphor no longer holds. At one end there's a "well-remunerated, knowledge-intensive economic sphere that has recently experienced unprecedented growth. On the other is a service economy where low-skilled and semi-skilled workers continue to lose ground in real wages, benefits and security."[258] These two economic poles have been labelled *utopia* (migrants come to thrive) and *dystopia* (migrants come to survive).[259] The latter live in hyperghettos, marginalized districts outside cities, like the *banlieues* in France and the Red and Black Belts in the US.[260] It's not just the US: both sides of the Atlantic have been "hard hit by de-industrialisation, ethnically marked [and] characterised by high unemployment, a concentration of households with low incomes, a very negative stigma, bleak atmospheres."[261]

Western European countries have historically seen themselves as "culturally and ideologically homogenous territories;"[262] actually, they are "deeply divided nationally, socially, and (above all) religiously."[263] In fact,

> Catholics, Protestant and Jews managed to live together but were largely locked in their own worlds and integrated with only the greatest reluctance ... Protestants not only distrusted Catholics because of their allegedly backward and superstitious faith, they thought Catholics also lacked proper feelings of national loyalty.[264]

Further, Lucassen says, there's a stereotype of Roman Catholics' identification and allegiance to the Roman Pope. From this arose a conviction of the Roman conspiracy of Popery and an anti-Catholic backlash in the 19th century,[265] along with the belief that migrants pose a threat because of pre-existing allegiances: "Many think migrants do not want to integrate because they would rather remain faithful to their ethnic community and their home country."[266] The reality is that parental ideas don't always survive subsequent generations: "Children of Algerian immigrants born in France prove to be largely immune to the nationalist passions of their parents, and they take great interest in French culture, notwithstanding the widespread exclusion they experience in French society."[267]

In a global comparison of countries and migration, Kivisto found Germany and France with their "blood-and-soil" nationalisms have the most difficulty accepting multiculturalism. Although the French "appear more open to diversity,"[268] their expectation is one of assimilation where arrivées transform themselves into Frenchmen/women,[269] and republicanism requires "replacing their ethnic identities with that of the French."[270] It's an "aggressive version of assimilation as absorption"[271] that requires giving up one's ethnic past.

A Spanish survey of national identity and the preferred model of integration (assimilation or multiculturalism) of recent mass migrants found 13% of Spanish citizens expressed "passive multiculturalism,"[272] 15% proactive multiculturalism, and 22% spoke of consequent assimilationism, an expectation of subsequent "blending into the larger society and where the state passively contributes to this goal by not spending resources on the preservation of these groups' customs and traditions."[273] In conclusion, "Spanish attitudes are largely aligned with official policy, a policy that can be defined as mildly assimilationist."[274]

Integration and multiculturalism

Lucassen says Canadian political philosophers, Will Kymlicka and Charles Taylor,[275] have started worldwide discussions about the "political and philosophical justification of multiculturalism"[276] that hasn't yet reached Europe. Multiculturalism, or the cultural mosaic,[277] stresses the legal and political accommodation of ethnic diversity.[278] Multiculturalists "argue for transitional identities and ethnic-group consciousness [because they] empower immigrants"[279]

Rather than expecting assimilation, multiculturalism realistically and pragmatically calls for accommodation in a long-term process of generations.[280] Non-homogenous and non-linear, they occur at different speeds in differing domains: economic, social, cultural and political.[281] Adaptation and integration are not one-way processes:[282] They're interactions between migrants and host societies where both parties change[283] and recognize "social cohesion does not require that individual members share identical beliefs."[284] Kymlicka, in an analysis of the rates in which migrants become naturalized citizens, found they "quickly absorb and accept Canada's basic liberal-democratic values."[285] In fact, they "become citizens at rates higher than immigrants to the United States, learn English [and] have contributed to a general leavening of attitudes toward mixed marriages and other cultural issues."[286]

Bertossi notes:

> a national model of integration and citizenship is usually defined as a public philosophy, a policy paradigm, an institutional and discursive opportunity structure or a national cultural idiom. All these concepts attempt to show how social reality is structured by preexisting ideas about a nation's self-understanding.[287]

In a comparison of integration models of French assimilation with Dutch and British multiculturalism, he found France's notion of the Republic is all-encompassing:

> [It] organizes the separation between public and private realms (through a strict color blind approach to ethnicity and race) and between the state and the church (the philosophy of French secularism —*laïcité*), and it underpins the specifically French "political, open definition" of citizenship and immigrant incorporation through nationality.[288]

In contrast are the multicultural ideals of Britain and the Netherlands, which permit ethnic and racial identities and have integration policies aimed "at promoting group-based identities instead of a common citizenship."[289]

Economies are transformed by the turbulence of migration, says Kivisto, i.e., the "massive influx of people from the less-developed nations to the core nations of the capitalist world system,"[290] has produced ethnoscapes or constellations of ethnic groups and patterns of relations in advanced liberal democracies.[291] At the same time has arisen "resurgence of 'ethnonationalism' based on ethnic identity, language, religion, and similar traits,"[292] which has become powerful among members of "nations without states"[293] and prevalent in "Quebec, Scottish and Welsh nationalism and Northern Irish republicans [and] in Spain, the Basque and Catalan movements."[294]

Structural and identificational integration

Structural integration[295] refers to gender and class "measured objectively by mapping social mobility, school results, housing patterns."[296,297] For many years, European countries sought temporary migrant workers— mostly men—for low-wage labour jobs in agriculture and construction.

Twenty years later, the arrival of wives and families was seen as positive because "as long as migrant men wandered in groups and displayed a highly mobile, 'nomadic' lifestyles, as was the case with Italian workers in France, they remained a threat, both economically and socially."[298] Family reunification was welcomed and taken as evidence that the men were settling down. In Germany, the overall image of Italian workers was positive,[299] but in Europe's recent post-industrial economies, 2nd-generation Algerians, Moroccans, Turks and Caribbean islanders have found it difficult to find jobs.[300] Many parents who were laid off in the 1980s remained unemployed and now are seen as poor role models: their children lack opportunity. With poor structural integration, their "real and perceived exclusion, combined with widespread police harassment, [means] many youngsters have openly rebelled against the police [with] serious riots in Britain and France."[301]

Identificational integration is "subjective and refers to the extent to which migrants and their offspring keep regarding themselves as primarily different."[302] It also refers to the "extent that they are viewed as primarily different by the rest of society."[303] In multiculturalism, the ideal of the mosaic is that of "brightly colored bits of ethnicity, culture, racial identity and language embedded side by side to form a portrait of the nation in the same way the dots on a pointillist painting convey a coherent image."[304]

Cultural integration is defined as participation in all or any cultural activities and *personal integration* refers to individual acts, like intermarriage, without forsaking one's cultural heritage. Research shows that "integration may be a slow, gendered and differentiated process, but also that children of migrants gradually become more similar to the established population, both in *structural* and *identificational* respects."[305] Through globalization and migration, it's apparent to the 2nd generation that new lands carry an "attractive cultural model, be it in the sense of popular culture, consumer freedom, human rights or emancipation of women."[306]

Second-generation women often experience discrimination in their families: they are less valued and may have severe restrictions on their freedom and limits to their professional ambitions. Despite this, girls generally do better in school and the labour market than their male peers, especially Caribbean islanders in the UK and, to a lesser extent, Turks and Algerians.[307] Lucassen explains:

> adolescent girls have less access to the public domain and are more socialized to obey rules. They stay at home more, do their homework, finish school and often gain higher qualifications than men and thus have a better starting position on the job market.[308]

They also seem to find jobs more easily than the young men, and are less likely to display oppositional behaviour or engage in criminal acts.[309,310]

Multiculturalism "gives ethnic communities the task to retain and cultivate homeland cultures."[311] While women may be bearers of culture for the next generation, they do not always wish to fully replicate strict patriarchal culture in newlands. This creates ambivalence in many women[312] caught betwixt and between cultures. The shadow side of multiculturalism is found in the lives of women when ethnic cultural norms clash with Western democratic rights, for example, young ethnic women have been murdered over violations of homeland rules.[313]

Role of education in integration

Integration is not an individual responsibility but a societal task that includes education, labour-market access, and participation in mainstream institutions with a sense of belonging, as opposed to an "us and them" dynamic. The primary method of integration of the 1.5 and 2nd generationers is public schooling.[314] France has a nationally funded standardized, centralized education system with expectations of student assimilation.[315] The US expects assimilation too, but its decentralized public-education system, with local economies funding schools, leads to large disparities in the quality of education.[316] Among developed countries, the US also has the shortest educational year, with a cumulative loss of an entire school year over twelve years of public schooling.[317] Germany has the most stratified educational system; the Netherlands also has a highly stratified education system,[318] but its gaps are not as great as German ones.[319]

Mostafa examined student performance in 37 countries with education models ranging from egalitarian to various stratified systems. The former, with centralized funding, are open to all. Stratified education, as in the US, is based on decentralized funding with education and peer relations dependent upon neighbourhood socio-economic status, class and ethnic/migrant mix. Schools differ in terms of resources, class size, and teacher quality plus peer-group orientation. Centrally funded comprehensive, highly egalitarian and homogenous schools (Nordic model) produce more equal outcomes. The Mediterranean model (based on Napoleonic legacies) is centralized with a comprehensive lower secondary system and differentiated upper secondary schools providing little individual choice. Two other models offer little individual choice with high levels of inequality: early-selection stratification systems (German/Japan) and marketization models (UK/US/Japan) showing large community disparities and an elitist private sector.

A Chicago study team made public the School Board scores for local schools and named those schools "on probation" due to poor performance.[320] Public release of the information prompted families to transfer children from probation schools, but poorer families transferred their children at a lower rate. Yet, neither public information nor the transfers actually changed any factors responsible for the school scores.[321]

Families in newlands

Historically, "American social work developed largely around the provision of services to immigrants."[322] Seeing in the 2000 US Census that "one out of every five children is either an immigrant or has an immigrant parent,"[323] Pine and Drachman explored the effects of types of migration—transnational, circular, return, and undocumented—on children. They found the most vital factor to be family's official status: "legal permanent resident, undocumented immigrant, refugee, special immigration juvenile status, and mixed-status families."[324] The last refers to 85% of non-citizen households with children born in the US who are citizens.[325] It leads to inequality and divisiveness within families because the "undocumented status of one member can have a chilling effect on other family members using services, even when they are eligible."[326] The lack of willingness to seek help arises from fears of separation and potential parental deportation.

Often children need psychological help with migration traumas following abrupt flights, exile and negative experiences like "separation from family and friends; withdrawal from a familiar environment; decisions regarding who leaves and who is left behind; experiences of persecution, violence, loss of significant others, or a long wait; and living in limbo prior to departure."[327] Arrival presents issues too for children, especially differences between expectations and the realities of newlands, compounded by survivor guilt and sometimes PTSD.[328]

Pine and Drachman found host-country social factors that affect successful adaptation of children are: the quality of newland reception, degree of cultural distance and number of opportunities. At the personal level, the primary factors affecting children's adaptation are: the degree of cumulative stress, family acculturation levels, inter-generational conflict and changes in family structure:[329] "As men and women shift in their traditional marital roles (particularly when wives are employed and husbands are unemployed or earn less than the wives), marital conflict or dissolution may surface even among cultures where divorce is rare."[330]

In an early Israeli study of absorption of immigrants, Eisenstadt found at the societal level the most important factors was reception and acceptance of émigrés.[331] At the individual level, it was not holding on to the past;[332] learning new roles, transforming primary group values, participation in the wider society;[333] having "patience and hope" and believing in oneself.[334] In terms of family structure, the most important was securing the necessities of life and second was attaining social status compatible with one's own aspirations in relation to newland possibilities: "Attainment of such status is a laborious process fraught with difficulties and insecurity."[335]

Eisenstadt found three different family responses affected adaptation:

1) An *isolated, apathetic family unit* is characterized by disappointment when aspiration and values are not realized and results in extreme negativity and breakdown of internal solidarity.[336] They blame the

newland for false propaganda of hope that induced them to migrate and may alternate acting-out in open aggression against others with periods of apathy and over-identification with their former status and values.[337]

2) *Stable, isolated family units* limit their interaction with the larger society and focus on attainment of economic security and the advancement of their children.[338] Many see fulfilment of their aspirations in their children's accomplishments rather than in their own attainments.[339] Thus, adults show limited transformation because "the family is the main and stable field of expressive and solidarity gratification, and there is little initial disposition to change its pattern (with) strong attachment to the religious values and traditions."[340] Although individuals may wish to have an "accepted place in society,"[341] their focus is not on assimilation. They tend not to connect with social and political organization and show degrees of "anomic, disintegrative behaviour."[342]

3) An *isolated, active stable family unit* holds a positive orientation to the newland. Often, they are an ex-elite family in the homeland, which can result in a weak sense of citizenship in the newland. There is much criticism of bureaucratization and political structures of the newland.[343]

Eisenstadt also found three types of newland ethnic groups:

1) *Cohesive ethnic groups* maintain some of their traditional culture and social relations and an orientation toward occupational changes and wider social and political participation.

2) *Self-transforming cohesive ethnic groups* maintain strong, stable relations with individual migrants and develop formal/informal communication systems. Although they are organized according to traditional social structures, they participate in newland language acquisition, occupational, educational, civic, cultural and political activities.[344] Transformation of individual migrants occurs mainly within the group and social settings that affirms both their homeland and newland.[345]

3) An *instrumentally cohesive ethnic group* is a sub-group comprised of fairly cohesive families who may have migrated together without previous strong homeland associations. Usually, they have modern schooling and are oriented to educational standards, yet live in relative social isolation from the larger culture without much commitment to it.[346]

Women's citizenship

"Women's citizenship has always been mediated," says Anderson.[347] Although wives have been seen as necessary, they have not always been seen as persons with their own rights.[348] In early Canada, women pioneers were not given land grants and were not "persons under the law" until 1929. In 2017, the UN listed the 20 best countries for gender equality: "Iceland, Norway, Finland, Rwanda, Sweden, Nicaragua, Slovenia, Ireland, New Zealand, Philippines, France, Germany, Namibia, Denmark, United Kingdom, Canada, Bolivia, Bulgaria, South Africa and Latvia."[349]

Today in some *jus soli* countries, women are seen as potentially dangerous as mothers of "anchor babies," whose birth permits immediate citizenship and enables sponsoring of extended family who would not otherwise meet the entrance criteria. Some women are victims of sex trafficking and labour exploitation as, until recently, in many countries women have been able to only gain employment as domestic workers, *au pairs* and cleaners, which are positions outside the usual migrant labour channels.[350] Many are consigned to unregulated "reproductive work—mental, physical, and emotional labour,"[351] caring for people, such as children and the homebound elderly, and domestic work, such as cooking and cleaning.[352] With women's work not "fully integrated into the labour market, there is a delicate 'equilibrium of transgression' that means there is widespread informality and illegality in the sector."[353] Also women working *in situ* as "fictive kin,"[354] have been "exempt from the minimum wage."[355] In the UK in 2008, the number of women working in these roles was estimated at 730,000, with evidence that "home-based child and elder care has been growing."[356] In recent years, "over one-third of middle-class dual-career families employed some kind of domestic labour, often paid for with cash, and since the 1990s there has been a growth in the undeclared employment of cleaners."[357]

Many migrants are "imagined as coming from impoverished lands, and this goes along with the idea that there is little one can do to remedy the injustices of the world, but employing a desperate migrant is a small contribution."[358] At the same time, the work of *au pairs* in private homes has not been officially regarded as employment, and as a result, they have not been seen as migrant workers with "immigration controls imposed temporariness as a condition of the *au pair* visa."[359] Anderson says: "the history of the *au pair* visa demonstrates the shifting but mutually dependent nature of citizenship, family, work, and gender, and the attempts to accommodate this within liberal discourses of equality."[360] While the *au pair* visa was originally designed for foreigners working with British families, "the domestic worker visa was designed for non-citizens living and working with non-citizen families."[361] Categorized as *"fictive kin,"* the domestic worker's visa does not permit them to work for other than the specified family, and if she leaves the family, for whatever reason (including abuse), she "los[es] her immigration status and bec[omes] an illegal resident."[362] Not until 2008 in the UK, did domestic workers gain the status of workers, but still this was without standards for wages or benefits. However, it's "not only the domestic worker who is marginalized, but unpaid female labour, the unemployed, the informal worker, and other figures are spectres outside the domain of political economy standards."[363]

The 1995 United Nations Fourth World Conference on Women in Beijing identified critical areas for action: equality, poverty, education, health, reproductive and sexual health, violence, armed conflicts, economic participation and human rights.[364] Specific rights issues are: arranged and child marriages, genital cutting, reproductive rights and honour killings.[365] In *Engaging Cultural Differences*, Shweder, Minow and Markus note intolerance arises when "diverse cultural groups hold contradictory beliefs about appropriate social and family life practices."[366] They ask: "How wide should be the scope of social and legal tolerance?"[367] Exploring differences between communitarian and liberal individualistic approaches to cultural diversity, they question if "people should have direct legal status based on their membership in particular groups?"[368] For instance, liberal individualists seek state neutrality towards individuals and the good life. Here, the purpose of the state and

> justifiable limits on its power—stem from a vision of liberty ensuring individuals freedom to act, to affiliate with subcommunities if they wish (but also the exit from them if they desire); associate with others voluntarily, and express themselves as individuals through choices about religion, culture, and family life.[369]

The authors express suspicion of "ethnography of difference,"[370] or subordinating and ignoring individual rights in favour of ethnic/religious/cultural practices which are more commonly rights issue for women.

Renteln speaks of the "right to culture," defining it in terms of the Canadian Commission for UNESCO: "Culture is a dynamic value system of learned elements and assumptions, conventions, beliefs and rules permitting members of a group to relate to each other and to the world, to communicate and to develop their creative potential."[371] She calls attention to cultural acts that clash with newland laws, and culture being used as a legal defence, like refusing autopsy for evidence because it goes against religious belief;[372] and returning an irregular migrant to a country with oppressive and physically harmful traditions.[373] These issues bring to attention three questions that need to be asked: "1) Is the litigant a member of the ethnic group? 2) Does the group have such a tradition? 3) Was the litigant influenced by the tradition when he or she acted?"[374] Further, "the right to culture is a fundamental human right, but it should be protected only so long as it does not undermine other human rights."[375]

Cultural marriage practices are central to debates around rights of individuals and respect for different customs: polygamy, arranged and forced marriages, and child marriages. Many cultures practice arranged marriages —while in the West, they are technically not "forced" but the degree of freedom and choice is often questionable. Child marriages, contracted before the legal age of majority, raise questions about the rights of children, mothers and the power of parents: "Are the parents the ultimate guardians of their children or merely temporary state agents, subject to state review and control?"[376] And

> does the state's assessment of a child's best interests include the child's membership in a given culture or does it abstract the child from that membership, as if the child had no such connection and was really a "citizen of the world"?[377]

Is multiculturalism bad for women?[378] Okin asks as she looks at laws protecting group rights and privileges over "'personal law'—the laws of marriage, divorce, child custody, division and control of family property, and inheritance."[379] Generally, the latter have greater effects on the lives of women and girls.[380] Important too, are cultural mythologies and ideologies that deny "women's role in reproduction,"[381] along with "appropriations by men of the power to reproduce themselves, characterizations of women as overly emotional, untrustworthy, evil, or sexually dangerous, and refusals to acknowledge mothers' rights over the disposition of their children."[382] And "the servitude of women is presented as virtually synonymous with 'traditions.'"[383] The "most controversial customs—clitoridectomy, the marriages of children or marriages that are otherwise coerced, or polygamy—sometimes explicitly defended as necessary for controlling women."[384] Often older women are "co-opted into reinforcing gender inequality."[385]

Okin gives four examples of cultural defences that violate women's rights: 1) "Kidnap and rape by Hmong men" in "their cultural practice of *zij poj niam* or 'marriage by capture,'"[386] 2) "Wife-murder by migrants from Asian and Middle Eastern countries" where the "wife committed adultery or treated their husbands in a servile way,"[387] 3) "Mothers who have killed their children but failed to kill themselves, and claim that because of their Japanese or Chinese backgrounds the shame of their husbands' infidelity drove them to the culturally condoned practice of mother-child suicide,"[388] and 4) "Clitoridectomy."[389] Okin argues that no arguments for "multicultural group rights has adequately or even directly addressed the troubling connections between gender and culture, or the conflicts that arise so commonly between multiculturalism and feminism."[390]

Reproductive rights are rarely raised in cultural, social and political discussions of nationhood. Yet, the future of all nations depends upon women's reproductive powers. Often there exists unspoken and

> serious conflict between collective national and individual interest in term of the number of children one has. When there are no welfare

structures to look after the elderly and the ill, it is crucial for people to have enough healthy children to support them.[391]

Some states, like China, struggling with over-population, attempted to curb the birth rate, while other countries, decimated by wars, have engaged in demographic campaigns, some providing "rewards" for motherhood, such as maternity leave, child allowances and awards for "heroine mothers" of ten children or more.[392] The child's *right of genetic quality* is never raised. Not only does the state hold interest in women's reproductive powers, social and religious organizations also have positions. In some cases, "the ability of women to control their own bodies is seen as a direct threat to their authority."[393] The Vatican interprets women's control over their own bodies as "a betrayal of sacred religious and customary laws."[394] However, under the UN's 1968 International Conference on Human Rights, reproductive rights are now classified as Human Rights.[395] It's still a contentious issue in some states and religions, and hinders integration of women migrants.

Cultural ceremonies of gender identity and coming-of-age may include genital alterations:[396] "Estimates of the number of contemporary African women who participate in these practices vary widely and wildly between 80 million and 200 million."[397] Although the focus is generally on women, "surveying the world, one finds few cultures, if any, where genital surgeries are performed exclusively on girls, although many cultures perform such surgeries only on boys or on both sexes."[398] Shweder draws attention to the philosopher, John Rawls,[399] to explore the three orientations of liberalism: political, comprehensive and imperial. *Political liberalism* refers to the "minimum ground rules for social cooperation among free and equal citizens in a genuine pluralistic democracy."[400] *Comprehensive liberalism* "is a particular and single-minded doctrine about the proper selection and ordering of values and about ideals for a good life."[401] *Imperial liberalism* holds that

> all social institutions and dimensions of social life (not just political but associational and family life as well) should be ruled by principles of autonomy, individualism and equality—and by the particular ordering of values and ideals of gender identity, sexuality, work.[402]

Further, these liberal values should be "upheld using the coercive power of the state and, if possible, exported to foreign lands, using the coercive powers of international institutions (such as the World Bank the IMF, NATO, and the UN)."[403] Okin argues that, although freedom is the intention of multiculturalism, we should not automatically assume all cultural practices are good and should be supported. We should evaluate them for their effect on individuals, specifically girls and women, as many cultural practices are designed specifically to control them.[404]

The 2nd generation in host countries

Lucassen argues that Europe is more strongly supportive of assimilation than Settler Societies, which are oriented to "pluralistic development with transnationalism, segmented assimilation, and enclave economies."[405] The latter also have a "shared sense of purpose [and] a basic support of the state and its broad directions, its fundamental political structure and a shared willingness to contribute to the common good."[406] He notes it's clear that "integration may be a slow, gendered and differentiated process, but also that children of migrants gradually become more similar to the established population, both in *structure* and *identificational* respects."[407] To date, "the most radical break with the parental homeland is found among children of Algerian migrants who demand to be treated as French citizens."[408] Their contact with parental homeland kin is minimal, even artificial, Lucassen says. In fact, the children are treated as alien by their families and ethnic group because they do not acquire the "cultural and linguistic affinity needed to establish or maintain a meaningful contact."[409] The 2nd generation expresses a mix of feelings. First, regarding their physical and political appearance: "I am Algerian despite my French papers: I am French despite my Algerian appearance … I was born here, brought up here, grew up here, was made here, for here to live here."[410] Next is the feeling that "Deep inside me, I feel myself to be Algerian despite it all, in my heart of hearts, I feel … something tells me that I am Algerian, uniquely Algerian by birth, born into an Algerian family."[411] Then, there is the matter of choice: "I didn't choose to be Algerian or to be French … I went to school in France, in the French mentality, and so on. Is that or isn't that what you call culture?"[412] Finally, there is the reality of belonging: "France is just my country: Algeria is my homeland. You live in a country, work in a county … but you are from a homeland. One can therefore have a country or nationality but belong to a different country or nationality."[413]

The 2nd generation may hold pan-ethnic feelings, but they may be "symbolic ethnicity,"[414] a kind of diasporic identity compatible with integration in the face of day-to-day demands:[415] "Members of minority groups in Britain, as elsewhere in Europe, identify themselves in various ways: sometimes by their families' country of origin, sometimes by colour, often (and perhaps increasingly, especially young Muslims) by religion."[416] However, a 2012 survey shows "for the vast majority, such identifications are not necessarily felt to be in conflict or competition with a sense of Britishness."[417]

Although it is "normal to be American or Canadian and ethnic at the same time,"[418] in Europe, "ethnic identity is often seen as a threat to national cohesion, and ethnic and national identities tend to be cast in a competitive or zero-sum situation."[419] Alba and Foner note the "distinction between assimilation and integration hinges on changes in social boundaries that divide or demarcate individuals and groups on the basis, for example, of ethnicity, race, or religion."[420] In fact, assimilation is more than the right of parity in the labour market and other public institutions: "it encompasses parallel cultural and social changes, possibly on both sides of the minority-majority boundary that brings immigrant-origin individuals close to, or into, a society's mainstream."[421] Over time, these boundaries become less and less salient and "minority persons are accepted as 'just like us' when they are otherwise socially similar to, and intermingle with, members of the native majority."[422] Lucassen speaks of the ongoing linguistic and cultural assimilation process among the 2nd generation who

> in the long run will blend into Western EU societies, adding to it new flavours and colors, as so many migrants have done in the remote and recent past. Europe will be—as it has been for ages already—a multicultural continent.[423]

The major challenge of 2nd-generation children is role reversal: having "moved so far ahead of the parent's progress that key family decisions become dependent on the children's knowledge"[424] thus becoming "their parents' parents."[425] Portes and Rumbaut identify three types of 2nd-generation acculturation:1) *Dissonant/resistant*, where the children adapt while the parents lose control of them because they lack the skills and knowledge to negotiate in new culture,[426] 2) *Consonant*, where learning and abandonment of homeland language and culture occur at the same pace across generations,[427] and 3) *Selective*, where both generations are "embedded in a co-ethnic community of sufficient size and diversity to slow down the cultural shift and promote partial retention of the home language and norms with relative lack of inter-generation conflict."[428] Furthermore, today's newlands are pluralist, fragmented environments, so it is no longer a question of whether the 2nd generation assimilates, rather the more important issue is the challenges they face. This includes educational attainment and career success which depend upon the host country— whether there is racial discrimination, bifurcation of the labour market and growing inequality, and consolidation of marginalized population in the inner city. "Children of Asian, black, mulatto and mestizo immigrants cannot so easily reduce their ethnicity to a level of voluntary decision" as there exists "enduring physical difference and persistent discrimination."[429]

Colonial migrants who "return" to "mother" countries face unique challenges.[430,431,432,433] A special case is the Algerians where 2nd-generation children born in France are considered as *jus sanguinis* or "Algerian children born outside Algerian territory."[434] At the age of majority (16 years), if French nationality has not been granted automatically to 2nd-generation Algerians, they must apply for a resident's permit. Interestingly, automatic citizenship under *jus soli* is seen by some as compulsory naturalization. And within the

French Algerian community, there's been a taboo against citizenship. Sayad sees this as collective "cumulative cultural fear" of French naturalization along with "feelings of guilt or unease."[435] It's experienced as a conflict of rights of citizenship vs membership in the Algerian ethnic community.[436] When a 2nd-generation child is granted French citizenship, it's often treated as a secret, mixed with resignation, satisfaction and fears that the family will be "divided in their nationality. It's feared it will affect family unity believed as the only avenue to ensure superior traditional morality."[437] "We cannot be divided, with some on one side and the rest on the other, some Algerian and the rest French. They all have to be either French or Algerian. It isn't fair."[438] Automatic French nationality is also seen as "taking the children."[439] Yet, when "Frenchness has entered a family" and they realize it is not a total catastrophe and that it will not destroy "cherished relations," their fears are dispersed.[440]

Colonial migrants, even those who confront discrimination and exclusion, usually identify faster with the host societies than other migrants.[441] Religion also plays a strong role in integration. In France, most 2nd-generation Algerians ignore Berber and/or Arabic languages and aren't interested in Islam. They tend to marry within their group, but resist arranged marriages.[442] In the UK, Caribbean migrants embrace British culture and intermarry more than non-Christians, with spouses from Indian, Pakistani and Bangladeshi ethnicities.[443] In the Netherlands, the Surinamese tend not to be devout: the 2nd generation, with African ancestry, have Dutch friends and intermarry at a greater rate than those with Hindu backgrounds.[444]

In Western Europe, the 2nd generation of former guest workers from Muslim countries—Turkey, Morocco and Tunisia—tend to integrate structurally and to marry within their own group: "When the 2nd generation takes over in religious associations and institutions, they generally strive for a more liberal version of Islam than their parents practiced and adapt to the local and national opportunity structures."[445] The lack of a recent tradition of colour slavery as a social organizing principle in Europe, accounts for the more open reception for white and black Muslim migrants than those in the US of African ancestry.[446]

Post-colonial immigrants are "largely acquiescent in terms of their social and citizenship rights;[447] [and] blend in as much as possible and to keep their cultural and religious practices."[448] The 2nd and subsequent generations born and educated in newlands absorb liberal ideologies and are not as compliant as arrivées and may practice "partial concealment."[449] An example is the complex politics of the Muslim veil: "It is not uncommon for community leaders to objectify women and girls as the preservers of a true tradition, religion or ethnic culture—often expressed in opposition to modernity."[450] Daughters may leave home veiled, and, as they near school or work, will remove them, enabling both generations to avoid discussions and internal conflict.[451]

The German guest-worker program, *Gastarbeiter*, has led to Germany becoming a country of permanent residence for many,[452] leading to intergenerational conflict within families due to different relationships to parental homelands. Émigrés tend to maintain close psychological relationships with the homeland and intend to return, while the 2nd generation is oriented towards Germany. The 3rd generation regards Germany as home and the ethnic homeland is a holiday destination. Yet, the German government, under Roman law, defines citizenship as *jus sanguinis,* the right of those with German blood to be citizens. All others are declared "foreign" and naturalization for citizenship requires renunciation of former nationality.[453]

France is burning, not as in the past for religious or political reasons, but social reasons. The 2nd and 3rd generations born in France see themselves as French, while the social message they receive is "they are foremost Arabs, Asians or Muslims."[454] Being socially and politically marginalized, they are susceptible to radical discourses that assert political confrontations between civilizations.[455] In many French outer suburbs or *banlieues*, "Islam has become a social bond for people who live the common experience of marginalization. It provides a sense of history and direction to their lives, giving them a personal location in the global diverse and Western society of France."[456] For example, a woman born and raised in Paris whose parents are from North Africa, says: "Despite being French on paper, I'll always be an Arab, and it's not a simple paper that could change my culture. I was born in France. I have French culture, but I live with Moroccans."[457]

Migrant-host relations

Portes and Rumbaut identify two anti-immigrant ideologies.

1) *Intransigent nativism* "seeks to stop all or most immigration, expel unauthorized immigrants, and put remaining immigrants on notice that they occupy an inferior position, ineligible for the privileges of citizens."[458]
2) *Forced assimilationism* expresses hostility to cultural enclaves and insists on "immersion of foreign children into an English-only environment that 'Made in America' out of them in the course of a single generation."[459] It is believed the only proven way to restore unity and peace is to de-legitimatize the culture and language of migrant parents and instill a sense of inferiority of the linguistic heritage with the expectation that it should be abandoned.[460]

One issue not addressed in anti-immigrants ideologies is the wedge driven between generations and the weakening of parental authority to protect children from dominant cultures.[461] Portes and Rumbaut propose a third solution: 3) *selective acculturation*. They insist this must not be confused with multiculturalism or ethnic enclaves, but involves "acquisition of English fluency and American cultural ways along with preservation of certain key elements of the immigrant culture, of which language is paramount."[462] This "contributes to maintaining channels of communication open across generations keeping youth linked to their community and the material and moral resources that it can provide and providing a cognitive reference point to guide their successful integration."[463]

In response to the reality "as more and more humans cross more and more borders in search of jobs, security and a better future, the need to confront, assimilate or expel strangers strain political systems and collective identities that were shaped in less fluid times,"[464] Harari describes three for-and-against positions of entrance, adaptation and belonging:

1) *Entrance*: the pro-position is that people have a right to go to other lands if they wish, and host countries have a duty to absorb them.[465] The anti-position is that migration is a privilege and favour:[466] countries have the right to choose who enters and to halt migration and to defend themselves from invasions.[467]
2) *Adaptation*: the pro-position is that "Europe itself is extremely diverse, and its native populations have a wide spectrum of opinions, habits and values. This is exactly what makes Europe vibrant and strong,"[468] so migrants have the right to maintain their homeland culture and language. The anti-position is an "obligation to assimilate,"[469] to "embrace at least the core norms and values of the host county, even if that means giving up some of their traditional norms and values."[470] Since many come from cultures of "intolerance, misogyny, homophobia and anti-Semitism [and] Europe cherishes tolerance, it cannot allow too many intolerant people in."[471]
3) *Belonging*: the pro-position is "If the immigrants assimilate to a sufficient degree, over time, they become equal and full members of the host county. 'They' become 'us.'"[472] The anti-position is newcomers should be patient as there is difference between a "personal timescale and collective timescale ... It is hard to expect society to fully absorb foreign groups within a few decades. Past civilization ... all took centuries rather than decades to accomplish this."[473]

Howard argues that it's "unrealistic to expect immigrants and members of ethnic minorities to abandon their family, friends, social networks, languages, beliefs and cultures in order to fully assimilate into the mainstream of the host society."[474] There's no reason for them to do this, and they *don't* do this when "their enclaves can offer a quality of life that is highly competitive with the mainstream. Democracies cannot legally force people to live where they do not want to live to embrace lifestyles that they do not want."[475] While it's true, Duncan says, that "diversity creates unease,"[476] people have to accept this, and "move beyond naive judgments of the newcomer or the host societies. A degree of empathy should be fostered so that both sides are able to understand the other's position."[477]

At the Council of Europe, Farrell and Thirion admit "migrants and minorities too have no desire to see their culture 'calcified' or to live on the sidelines of democracy; rather they want to ensure that what makes them different does not turn into discrimination."[478] The question needing to be asked is about "accommodations that institutions and citizens must make to ensure social cohesion in pluralist societies."[479] The Canadian director of Citizenship and Immigration argues it's "precisely the ability of our social institutions to foster mutually beneficial co-operation in the absence of shared values that constitutes their particular genius."[480] Israeli Harari says each country needs to ask if their migration position is working, rather than blaming newcomers for "not making a sincere effort to assimilate,"[481] and adopting anti-immigrant attitudes that "too many of them stick to intolerant and bigoted world views."[482] The host country has obligations to treat migrants as first-class citizens. Some question if "people from a particular culture have consistently proved themselves unwilling to live up to the immigration deal, why allow more of them in, and create an even bigger problem?"[483] However, it is admitted that host countries have to examine if they're making it difficult to adapt, and if migrants and their descendants even in the 2nd and 3rd generations are being treated as second-class citizens.[484] The reality is likely that neither migrant nor host country is living up to the ideal, fuelling suspicions and resentments in a vicious circle.[485]

Recent legislation in Denmark calls for recognition of migrant "rights and obligations,"[486] and limits the amount of time that 2nd-generation children can be sent to parental homelands for "reeducation."[487] In the US, it is argued that high immigration levels "trigger nationalistic reaction and increasing hostility toward foreigners [seen as] a threat to national culture and the unity of the nation."[488] At the same time, it's recognized that without millions of labour migrants, the US would not be the "strong, vibrant nation that it is."[489] Migrants who have filled "the labor needs of the giant American economy rejuvenate the population and add new energies and diversity to American culture."[490] Without migrants, "the US would come to resemble the profile of rich but aging European societies hobbled by stagnant economies, and a declining population."[491]

Portes and Rumbaut identify five types of migrants where their reception is dependent in large degree who they are, their situation and class of origin:

1) "Sanctioned upper-class refugees coming in the initial waves of a political exodus."[492] They are "elite refugees" who depart before the most traumatic events. Their arrival is characterized by a "favorable public reception and better chances to rebuild their lives in the US, who undergo a fairly rapid process of psychosocial adaption."[493] They have a "highly informed view

of American society—including a realistic awareness of its major problems [and] report high levels of satisfaction."[494] They show effective adaptation.
2) Less common are "former high-status persons who join an unauthorized refugee or labour flow [and] become ghetto service providers, practicing their career clandestinely among their own group or other downtrodden minorities."[495]
3) Not uncommon are "'middleman' merchants and contractors in underground economic activities,"[496] or professionals who arrive illegally or overstay their visa: "Little is known of the mental health and subjective outlook of these groups."[497]
4) More familiar are lower classes of persons arriving at the "tail end of a sanctioned refugee flow."[498] They have experienced chaos, trauma and exile in the homeland. In the newland, they have access to government assistance and ethnic community support and find opportunities for employment and entrepreneurship. The receptive context of their arrival and help-seeking actions gives them a favourable prognosis.
5) "Unsanctioned lower-class escapees from war-torn counties and undocumented immigrant labors"[499] experience poverty-related distress and depression which is compounded by disorientation. They arrive disadvantaged with little education or resources and either without an ethnic community or one that is "too feeble to generate autonomous employment opportunities."[500] They are likely to experience discrimination and downward mobility, and live in dilapidated neighbourhoods in communities of crime and drugs.[501]

In summary, the ancient idea of citizens and nations is based on "rights of blood" (*jus sanguinis*), "rights of soil" (*jus soli*) and, more recently, civic citizenship. Migrants stir up mixed emotions in the newland, ranging from paranoid anxieties to idealization at three levels—government, societal and communal—and elicit three responses: exclusion, passive acceptance, or active encouragement.

Assimilation is social-cultural convergence towards the mainstream, adaptation and integration occurs at different speeds in economic, social, cultural and political domains. Gradually, the 2nd generation, carrying symbolic ethnicity, becomes similar to the established population: it's normal to be American or Canadian and ethnic at the same time.

Notes

1 Hron, 2009:45.
2 Ibid.:46.
3 American Psychological Association, 2012.
4 Phinney, 1990:499–514.
5 Phinney et al, 2001:493–510.
6 Van Oudenhoven et al, 2006:637–651.

7 Kristeva, 1991.
8 Chandler & Tsai, 2001:177–188.
9 Davidov et al, 2008:583–599.
10 US Census 2020.
11 Ward & Masgoret, 2008:227–248.
12 Leong & Ward, 2006:799–810.
13 European Parliament, 2017.
14 BBC News, 2018.
15 Kawate, 2018.
16 Matthews, 2014.
17 Osumi, 2019.
18 United Nations, 2019.
19 Statistics Canada, 2017.
20 Australian Bureau of Statistics, 2019.
21 Collier, 2015.
22 Ibid, 2015.
23 Ahmad, 2010.
24 Specia, 2019.
25 Eurostat, 2019.
26 Kawate, 2018.
27 Yeoh & Lin, 2012.
28 Kawate, 2018.
29 Bauman, 2016:66.
30 Kivisto, 2002:84.
31 Ibid.:84.
32 Alba & Foner, 2015:11.
33 Yuval-Davis, 1997/2006:27.
34 Kohn, 1944/2017.
35 Maor, 2017:3.
36 Kohn, 1964:19.
37 Sen, 2006:258.
38 Ibid.:258.
39 Ibid.:258.
40 Ng et al., 2011.
41 Nesbitt-Larking et al, 2014.
42 Kivisto, 2002:84.
43 Portes & Rumbaut, 2006:339.
44 Peters, 2002:7–8.
45 Ibid.:8.
46 Ibid.:8.
47 Ibid.:8.
48 Medrano, 2005:134.
49 Ibid.:134.
50 Ibid.:135.
51 Alba & Foner, 2015:9.
52 Kivisto, 2002:84.
53 Blackbourn, 1997.
54 Gagliardo, 1980:278–279.
55 Sheehan, 1989.
56 Peters, 2002:4.
57 Ibid.:3.
58 Ibid.:4.

59 Wendt, 2017.
60 Peters, 2002:4.
61 Ibid.:4.
62 Heath & Tilley, 2005:119.
63 Ibid.:119.
64 Ibid.:119.
65 Ibid.:119.
66 Ibid.:124.
67 Alba & Foner, 2015:13.
68 Bejan, 2017:160.
69 Krzyżanowski & Wodak, 2008:96.
70 Ibid.:96.
71 Ibid.:96.
72 Ibid.:96.
73 Ibid.:96.
74 Saunders et al, 2016L 27.
75 Anderson, 2013:3.
76 Ibid.:27.
77 Alba & Foner, 2015:11.
78 Ibid.:7.
79 Kivisto, 2002:87.
80 Anderson, 2013:5.
81 Cekerevac et al, 2018:106.
82 Ibid.:105.
83 Ibid.:105.
84 Anderson, 2013:5.
85 Ibid.:5.
86 Ibid.:6.
87 Ibid.:6.
88 US Department of Homeland Security, 2019.
89 Ibid, 2019.
90 Ibid, 2019.
91 Province of Ontario, 2019.
92 Ibid, 2019.
93 Akhtar, 1999/2004:23.
94 Ibid.:23.
95 Ibid.:23.
96 Ibid.:23.
97 Grinberg & Grinberg, 1989:81.
98 Bion, 1970/1984.
99 Grinberg & Grinberg, 1989:81.
100 Ibid.:81–2.
101 Kahn, 1997b:280.
102 Ibid.:280.
103 Bauder, 2011:64.
104 Ibid.:65.
105 Ibid.:66.
106 Ibid.:67.
107 Hastie, 2017:22.
108 Ibid.:27.
109 Ibid.:22.
110 Ibid.:22.

111 Ibid.:27.
112 Ibid.:27.
113 Ibid.:32.
114 Facchini & Mayda, 2008:659.
115 Ibid.:659.
116 Ibid.:659.
117 Ibid.:659.
118 Ibid.:659.
119 Ibid.:659.
120 Ibid.:659.
121 OECD countries www.oecd.org/about/.
122 Facchini & Mayda, 2008:659.
123 Ibid.:660.
124 Ibid.:660.
125 Becker & Becker, 1997.
126 Hall et al, 2012:214.
127 Ibid.:215.
128 Ibid.:215–6.
129 Ibid.:201.
130 Facchini & Mayda, 2008:655.
131 Ibid.:665.
132 Ibid.:665.
133 Ibid.:665.
134 Portes & Rumbaut, 2001:48.
135 Ibid.:46.
136 Ibid.:47.
137 Ibid.:47.
138 Ibid.:48.
139 Ibid.:695.
140 Ibid.:695.
141 Ibid.:695.
142 Ibid.:656.
143 Guiso, 2008:698.
144 Ibid.:698.
145 Facchini & Mayda, 2008:696.
146 Varvin, 2017.
147 Ibid.:2017.
148 Brewster, 2002.
149 Gerhards, Hans & Schupp, 2016.
150 Ibid.:2016.
151 Hayes & Dowds, 2006:472.
152 Cartwright, 1979:84.
153 Stürmer et al, 2013:833.
154 Adorno et al, 1950.
155 Allport, 1954.
156 Cartwright, 1979.
157 Jones, 1998.
158 Dovidio et al, 2013.
159 Duckitt & Sibley, 2009.
160 Ibid,:98.
161 Sibley & Duckitt, 2008.
162 Digman, 1990.

163 Costa & McCrae, 1992.
164 McCrae & John, 1992.
165 Goldberg, 1993.
166 Allik & McCrae, 2004.
167 Heine & Buchtel, 2009.
168 Schmitt et al, 2007.
169 Sibley & Duckitt, 2008:248.
170 Ibid.:248.
171 Gallego & Pardos-Prado, 2014:94.
172 Ceobanu & Escandell, 2010.
173 Gallego & Pardos-Prado, 2014:82.
174 Ibid.:79.
175 Ibid.:79.
176 Ibid.:89.
177 Ibid.:92.
178 Ibid.:85.
179 Ibid.:92.
180 Ibid.:91.
181 Hellwig & Sinno, 2017.
182 Lancee & Sarrasin, 2015.
183 Gang et al, 2002.
184 Paas & Hakapuu, 2012.
185 Hayes & Dowds, 2006:456.
186 Fetzer, 2000a.
187 Okrent, 2019.
188 Hayes & Dowds, 2006:456.
189 Fetzer, 2000a.
190 Billiet et al, 1996.
191 Hjerm, 1998.
192 Hjerm, 2001.
193 Knudsen, 1997.
194 Lubbers & Scheepers, 2002.
195 Maddens et al, 2000.
196 Adler, 1996.
197 Betz, 1994.
198 Betz & Immerfall, 1998.
199 Lubbers & Scheepers, 2002.
200 Hayes & Dowds, 2006:456.
201 Ibid.:456.
202 Ibid.:457.
203 Ibid.:457.
204 Ibid.:457.
205 Ibid.:464.
206 Ibid.:464.
207 Ibid.:460.
208 Ibid.:464.
209 Ibid.:461.
210 Ibid.:466.
211 Ibid.:472.
212 Ibid.:469.
213 Stürmer et al., 2013.
214 Ibid, 2013.

215 Benet-Martínez & Haritatos, 2005.
216 Ponterotto, 2010.
217 Van der Zee & Van Oudenhoven, 2000.
218 Ibid.:2001.
219 Stürmer et al., 2013:833.
220 Ibid.:833.
221 Van der Zee & Van Oudenhoven, 2000.
222 Stürmer et al., 2013:834.
223 Schlenker & Britt, 2001.
224 Stürmer et al, 2005.
225 Stürmer & Snyder, 2010.
226 Stürmer et al., 2013:834.
227 Ashton & Lee, 2001.
228 Ashton & Lee, 2007.
229 Ashton et al, 2007.
230 Ashton et al, 2004.
231 Stürmer et al., 2013:839.
232 Ibid.:837.
233 Ibid.:839.
234 Ibid.:832.
235 Ibid.:832.
236 Paat, 2013:405.
237 Ibid.:405.
238 Alba & Foner, 2015.
239 Ibid.:7.
240 Lucassen, 2005:8.
241 Alba & Foner, 2015:12.
242 Portes & Rumbaut, 2006:147 &168.
243 Ibid.:64.
244 Ibid.:66.
245 Van Gennep, 1909.
246 Suárez-Orozco, 2002:24.
247 Ibid.:24.
248 Ibid.:24.
249 Lucassen, 2005:17.
250 Ibid.:8.
251 Suárez-Orozco, 2002:25.
252 Ibid,:25.
253 Levitt, 2001.
254 Levitt, 2004.
255 Basch et al, 2004.
256 Suárez-Orozco, 2002:27.
257 Ibid.:29.
258 Ibid.:28.
259 Ibid.:32.
260 Musterd, 2008.
261 Ibid.:2008.
262 Lucassen, 2005:198.
263 Ibid.:199.
264 Ibid.:199.
265 Ibid.:199.
266 Ibid.:200.

267 Ibid.:200.
268 Kivisto, 2002:84.
269 Ibid.:84.
270 Ibid.:84.
271 Ibid.:84.
272 Medrano, 2005:142–143.
273 Ibid.:142–143.
274 Ibid.:143.
275 Stanford Encyclopedia of Philosophy, 2012/2016.
276 Lucassen, 2005:4.
277 Gibbon, 1938.
278 Alba & Foner, 2015:9.
279 Lucassen, 2005:4.
280 Ibid.:19.
281 Ibid.:19.
282 Ibid.:19.
283 Ibid.:19.
284 Duncan, 2012:258.
285 Schneider, 1998.
286 Ibid.:1998.
287 Ibid.:1562.
288 Ibid.:1562.
289 Ibid.:1562.
290 Kivisto, 2002:86.
291 Ibid.:86.
292 Ibid.:87.
293 Ibid.:87.
294 Ibid.:87.
295 Lucassen, 2005:20.
296 Ibid.:19.
297 Kallen 995:147–160.
298 Lucassen, 2005:203.
299 Ibid.:203.
300 Ibid.:204.
301 Ibid.:204.
302 Lucassen, 2005:19.
303 Ibid.:19.
304 Schneider, 1998.
305 Lucassen, 2005:211.
306 Ibid.:201.
307 Ibid.:204.
308 Ibid.:204.
309 Ibid.:205.
310 Herberg E, 1989:9.
311 Yuval-Davis, 2006:47.
312 Ibid.:47.
313 Blatchford, 2012.
314 Alba & Foner, 2015:171.
315 Ibid.:121.
316 Alba & Foner, 2015:173.
317 Ibid.:175.
318 Ibid.:175.

319 Ibid.:183.
320 Rich & Jennings, 2015.
321 Ibid, 2015.
322 Giovannoni, 2004: xi.
323 Pine & Drachman, 2005:541.
324 Ibid.:541.
325 Ibid.:543.
326 Ibid.:543.
327 Ibid.:545.
328 Ibid.:545.
329 Ibid.:546.
330 Ibid.:548.
331 Eisenstadt, 1955:9.
332 Ibid.:116.
333 Ibid.:9.
334 Ibid.:115.
335 Ibid.:139.
336 Ibid.:143.
337 Ibid.:143–144.
338 Ibid.:148.
339 Paat, 2013:405.
340 Eisenstadt, 1955:149.
341 Ibid.:150.
342 Ibid.:151.
343 Ibid.:152.
344 Ibid.:159.
345 Ibid.:160.
346 Ibid.:163.
347 Anderson, 2013:10.
348 Bayes & Tohidi, 2001.
349 Haines, 2007.
350 Anderson, 2013,C8:2.
351 Ibid, C8:3.
352 Ibid, C8:4–5.
353 Ibid, C8:5.
354 Ibid, C8:13.
355 Ibid, C8:6.
356 Ibid, C8:7.
357 Ibid, C8:7.
358 Ibid, C8:11.
359 Ibid, C8:15.
360 Ibid, C8:17.
361 Ibid, C8:17.
362 Ibid, C8:17.
363 Ibid, C8:22.
364 Bayes & Tohidi, 2001:2.
365 Ibid.:2.
366 Shweder et al, 2002:1.
367 Ibid.:1.
368 Ibid.:9.
369 Ibid.:9.
370 Ibid.:9.

371 Canadian Commission for UNESCO, 1977:78–83.
372 Rentlen, 2005:49.
373 Ibid.:49.
374 Ibid.:49–50.
375 Ibid.:66.
376 Shweder et al., 2002a:13.
377 Ibid.:13.
378 Okin, 1999
379 Okin, 1999.
380 Ibid, 1999.
381 Ibid, 1999.
382 Ibid, 1999.
383 Ibid, 1999.
384 Ibid, 1999.
385 Ibid, 1999.
386 Ibid, 1999.
387 Ibid, 1999.
388 Ibid, 1999.
389 Ibid, 1999.
390 Ibid, 1999.
391 Yuval-Davis, 1997/2006:34.
392 Ibid.:30.
393 Ibid.:34.
394 Ibid.:34.
395 Freedman & Isaacs, 1993.
396 Shweder, 2002b:218.
397 Ibid.:218.
398 Ibid.:226.
399 Rawls, 1993,.
400 Ibid.:235.
401 Ibid.:235.
402 Ibid.:235.
403 Ibid.:235.
404 Okin, 1999.
405 Lucassen, 2005:211.
406 Duncan, 2012:262.
407 Lucassen, 2005:211; original emphasis.
408 Ibid.:211.
409 Ibid.:211.
410 Sen, 2006:251.
411 Ibid.:251.
412 Ibid.:251.
413 Ibid.:251.
414 Gans, 1979.
415 Lucassen, 2005:211.
416 Ibid.:211–212.
417 Ibid.:211–212.
418 Alba & Foner, 2015:218.
419 Ibid.:218.
420 Ibid.:219.
421 Ibid.:219.
422 Ibid.:219.

423 Lucassen, 2005:213.
424 Portes & Rumbaut, 2001:51–52.
425 Ibid.:51–52.
426 Ibid.:53.
427 Ibid.:54.
428 Ibid.:54.
429 Ibid.:55.
430 Lucassen, 2005:4.
431 Saada, 2000.
432 Sayad & Macey, 2004.
433 Reding, 2017.
434 Sayad & Macey, 2004:248.
435 Ibid.:249.
436 Ibid.:249.
437 Ibid.:249.
438 Ibid.:249.
439 Ibid.:249.
440 Ibid.:248.
441 Lucassen, 2005:207.
442 Ibid.:207.
443 Ibid.:207.
444 Ibid.:207.
445 Ibid.:207.
446 Ibid.:210.
447 Ng et al., 2011:105.
448 Ibid.:105.
449 Ibid.:112.
450 Ibid.:70.
451 Ibid.:120.
452 Fischer & McGowan, 1995:40.
453 Ibid.:40.
454 Ng et al., 2011:126.
455 Ibid.:126.
456 Ibid.:126.
457 Ibid.:128.
458 Portes & Rumbaut, 2006:346.
459 Ibid.:348.
460 Ibid.:348.
461 Ibid.:349.
462 Ibid.:350.
463 Ibid.:350.
464 Harari, 2018:139.
465 Ibid.:142.
466 Ibid.:142.
467 Ibid.:141.
468 Ibid.:143.
469 Ibid.:142.
470 Ibid.:140.
471 Ibid.:143.
472 Ibid.:140.
473 Ibid.:145.
474 Duncan 2012:265.

475 Ibid.:265.
476 Ibid.:267.
477 Ibid.:267.
478 Farrell & Thirion, 2012:285.
479 Ibid.:285.
480 Biles, 2012:327.
481 Harari, 2018:145.
482 Ibid.:145.
483 Ibid.:146.
484 Ibid.:146.
485 Ibid.:146.
486 Barry & Sorensen, 2018.
487 Ibid.:2018.
488 Portes & Rumbaut, 2006:35.
489 Ibid.:35.
490 Ibid.:35.
491 Ibid.:35.
492 Ibid.:202.
493 Ibid.:202.
494 Ibid.:202.
495 Ibid.:202.
496 Ibid.:202.
497 Ibid.:202.
498 Ibid.:202.
499 Ibid.:201.
500 Ibid.:201.
501 Ibid.:202.

Chapter 8

Summary and conclusions

Migration is as ancient as human life. Although it has been a bit of a "blind spot" in depth psychology, Jung has given us the tools to construct a depth psychology model. The underlying archetype is theorized as the hero.

In the newlands of the Americas—North, Central and South—everyone, including Aboriginal peoples centuries ago, has a personal and/or family history of migration. Ipp recalls "I did not literally flee ... like countless thousands of others, I chose to leave for complex yet compelling reasons."[1] Chosen or voluntary migration permits people to blossom, to find personal freedom and fulfilment, but newland circumstances don't always meet expectations, so resilience is important. Some are well until they migrate when hidden, unresolved issues emerge. Adaptation carries a steep learning curve, demanding living in the now instead of past or imagined futures.

Involuntary migrations range from "tied" family members without voice in decision making, to forced leavings and exile in the chaos of disasters: cultural, environmental, political, or social. It may include experiencing or witnessing traumatic events, resulting in PTSD. Typically, there are huge losses—culture, language, home and loved ones—which may lead to anxieties and fears for others and survivor guilt. When external reality changes demand psychic re-adjustment, Jung says, the whole experience must be fitted into the unconscious: "The world of inner images recedes ... like an inundation and when the waters receded they left a fertile deposit in which that life could thrive, which before had seemed to be impossible."[2] The task of depth psychology is to understand inner experiences and assist in the healing process, so that migration can contribute to one's inner sense of self and psychological growth.

On the journey, migrants encounter archetypal characters with potential for help and/or trauma: mentors, threshold guardians, allies and enemies that may capture, enslave or kill. Each migrant brings language, culture and psychology, in a mix of age, gender, health, race, religion, ethnicity and work history to the newland. All face arrival challenges. For legal migrants, these are waiting times, bureaucracies and recognition. For refugees, it's the uncertainty of asylum and the future. For irregular migrants, there are the risks of capture and deportation.

The challenges pose opportunities for heroic actions and magical powers. Arrival ordeals range from threats of harm and risks of death to peak experiences and euphoria, that can flip into its opposite: disappointment and despair. In classical myth, the treasure is not given, but must be seized, or won. For migrants, seizing the treasure may be the battle for acceptance and remaining open to adaptation and the resolution of losses. Unresolved grief—the Ulysses syndrome—prevents migrants from seizing the treasure. The opposite, *denied* grief, leads to merging with the other, or "cultural localitis." A balance is needed between these two poles to facilitate the emergence of a new reality.

The final three stages of the migrant's journey shift from chaos of the unknown to newland order. Some may end up returning to homelands, or find themselves caught in a psychological complex of persistent longing to return, along with replication of the homeland in the newland. The ease of modern communication and transportation allows migrants to keep in touch with family and friends, while in liberal democracies exists the right to dual and multiple citizenships. Migration success, with the emergence of a new self, is a lengthy process that's neither simple nor linear. "We move forward, but interrupted,"[3] says Ipp:

> We miss the land of our birth, we miss our deep-rooted connectedness to the sights, sounds and smells, and of course, we miss the people, who have formed the very fiber of our being [and] we miss the passion and intensity of our often lunatic countries.[4]

The last stage of the migrant's journey is either return to the homeland or a psychological shift, where the newland becomes a new homeland. Adaptation to newlands requires changes in identity and development of a sense of belonging.

Night dreams assist in the process. Often, dreams are located in a homeland or a previous residence. They can be a mix of homeland and newland places, architecture, music and objects, as well as people and events that help to integrate the two worlds. "Migration does not necessarily destabilise one's sense of identity,"[5] but what can't be avoided is resolution of grief and working through mourning losses, which entails a process of integration of "two countries, two time periods and two social groups … In doing so, a person reorganizes and consolidates his/her sense of identity as someone who remains him/herself despite changes and restructuring."[6]

Jung's alchemical model of psychic transformation helps us understand the needed changes and to identify points where people get stuck. Classically, the stages are *Nigredo* (shadow work), *Albedo* (raising consciousness),

Citrinitas (learning) and finally, *Rubedo* (authenticity and individuation). Also helpful in understanding psychological skill-building are developmental models of infancy: Bowlby's attachment theory, Winnicott's transitional object, Stern's subjective self, and Erikson's life stages.

Voluntary migration is motivated by adventure, self-development and/or economics. When physical and psychological aspects of journeys are not difficult, there's potential for hope and happiness. Involuntary migration is tied to an arbitrary decision maker or necessary for self-preservation. Forced migrations and exile often lead to alienation and depression, along with a preoccupation and allegiance to the political and social conditions of homelands, which hinders adaptation—hidden pathologies may emerge.

Second-generation children live in the shadow of their parents' adaptation issues. The open window of language acquisition until age 18,[7] along with newland educational and cultural opportunities, helps migrant young people to become fluent in their new language and culture. The shadow-side of youthful adaptation is role reversal—acting for their parents as interpreters and cultural brokers with newland institutions.[8] Many arrivées claim they migrated for their children and saddle them with a burden of debt and guilt over their hardships. Unfulfiled parental dreams may be forced onto children, or jealousies can emerge over children's greater opportunities in the newland, leading to dissonance and disharmony. The 2nd generation may be caught betwixt and between two worlds, seeing and being double, as well as finding the capacity for "both/and" solutions in a cultural mix of the best of both worlds. Still, imprinted with parental idealizations and nostalgia for the homeland, the 2nd and even later generations can experience vicarious yearnings to return to an imagined place. Reactive ethnicity or the revitalization of homeland identity to compensate for losses can occur, as well as its opposite, i.e., rejection of parental homelands. Reconciling loss and return may remain an issue for later generations, such as the Dukabour Canadians, whose ancestors had emigrated in 1898, Tolstoy having negotiated their departure amidst persecutions for their beliefs. In 2014, some 4th generationers "returned" to Russia.[9]

The family is greatly affected by the type of migration undertaken and the degree of permanency, be it transnational, circular, return, or undocumented. Family responses are characterized as: 1) apathetic, making no effort to integrate, 2) isolated stable families, who make efforts but don't engage in mainstream culture, and 3) active stable families, who participate in newland culture. Women face special migration challenges being triply marginalized by gender, race and economics. Until recently, in many countries, women were not considered persons under the law, and their citizenship was mediated by male family members. In many places, women's labour has been limited to unregulated domestic and personal care work, which permits them to enter newlands informally under special agreements for *au pairs,* carers, domestic workers and cleaners. Working in situ in private homes, their status as "fictive kin" makes them exempt from minimum wage standards and benefits. Some women find migration brings liberation, autonomy in decision making, improved quality of life, financial independence and greater status. For others, their families lack vision and impede their access to health, social and economic resources. Some are at increased risk of violence. However, greater social control of girls and women in ethnic communities who socialize them to obedience means they are more likely to finish school, gain higher educational qualifications and have better chances in the job market. Special women's issues are arranged and forced marriages, polygamy and genital cutting. Under the UN's 1968 International Conference on Human Rights, reproductive rights are now categorized as Human Rights.

Paramount to successful adaptation is the response of the host country. Traditional ideas of citizenship rights by "blood-and-soil" are challenged by modern democracies' civic citizenship. Attitude studies report that openness to experience and degree of social exposure are good predictors of the newlands' acceptance of migrants. The Six-Factor, HEXACO personality model shows that eXtraversion, Openness and Conscientiousness have power in predicting xenophilia.

Host-country expectations of migrant adaptation vary from assimilation or social-cultural convergence towards mainstream culture to multicultural adaptation models that respect ethno-cultural differences and social cohesion that does not require identical beliefs and behaviours. Akhtar describes settlement as a slowly evolving spiral.[10] The Grinbergs report "migration does not necessarily destablise one sense of identity."[11] What's crucial is sufficient inner resources to cope with the losses,[12,13] and migrants working through the mourning process, integrating the sense of two lands and times, that allows them to reorganize and consolidate their sense of identity as "someone who remains him/herself despite changes and restructuring."[14] Belonging goes beyond possession of land; it's about being seen and understood.[15]

It's unrealistic to expect migrants to abandon family, friends, social networks, languages, beliefs and cultures and to fully assimilate. In multicultural societies, ethnic enclaves offer a high quality of cultural life, so that the migrant's journey is not just about pain and suffering. For many, migration provides opportunities to blossom to be

> sustained by what the new and different world had to offer. The most talented poets, scientists, musicians, painters, professors, actors, and writers among them were able to learn from experience, and, enriched by their experience, trials and tribulations, they produced work that transcended the borders of their adopted countries.[16]

Organized religions play a strong role in migration, both in sponsorships and direct support, as well as in adaptation and preservation of ethnic customs and language. Beyond providing community, some churches/temples foster networks for housing, jobs and business opportunities. Migration also permits breaking with heritage religions, and the adoption of more attractive alternatives or none.

Laub speaks to the role of the analyst working with migrants:

> It is crucial that s/he be aware of the multiplicity of perspective s/he brings with him/herself to what s/he sees to what s/he hears and see in his/her patients. His/her own inner diversity can enhance his tolerance for the many othernesses s/he encounters ... Perhaps it is only through resisting the temptation and the pressure of becoming the same that s/he can listen to the patients as they really are, without succumbing to the generalizing effects of theory and the homogenizing produced by fashion and political correctness.[17]

It's important to acknowledge that the migrant's journey is heroic. Beltsiou says health professionals need to acknowledge that in the counselling room "analytic love can offer asylum in the face of homelessness and ultimately generates a new understanding to come home to."[18] In fact, migration provides the opportunity for both host and migrant to thrive, to learn, to evolve and to deepen their compassion, respect and spirit of generosity.

"Migration, dislocation and various kinds of nomadism are becoming the norm rather than an exception,"[19] says Hoffman. "It sometimes seems that lives rooted in one place and in a sort of narrative continuity are becoming the interesting aberration."[20] We're living in a "perpetually mobile, nomadic, and intermingled world, we also live in an increasingly globalized culture."[21] The heroic acts of migration and adaptation hold treasures of new life and conscious belonging.

Notes

1 Ipp, 2016:52.
2 Jung, 1941/1977, 213.
3 Ipp, 2016:52.
4 Ibid.:52.
5 Grinberg & Grinberg, 1989:134.
6 Ibid.:134.
7 Trafton, 2018.
8 At school, my sister and I were asked to translate.
9 Tertrault-Farber, 2014.
10 Akhtar, quoted in Beltsiou, 2016:107.
11 Grinberg & Grinberg, 1989:134.
12 Ibid.:57.
13 Ibid.:134.
14 Ibid.:134.
15 Boulanger, 2016:66.

16 Grinberg & Grinberg, 1989:165.
17 Ibid.:183–184.
18 Beltsiou, 2016:107.
19 Hoffman, 2016:214.
20 Ibid.:214.
21 Ibid.:215.

Bibliography

Abbas R et al (2015) Comparison of British and French expatriate doctors' characteristics and motivations, *Revue d'epidemiologie et de sante publique*, 63 (1):21–28.
Abdelmahmould E (2018) Dear Amna, *Maclean's Magazine*, September, p66.
Aboriginal Healing Foundation (2006) *Final Report of the Aboriginal Healing Foundation*, Ottawa: Aboriginal Healing Foundation.
Achotegui J (2002) *La Depresión en los Inmigrantes*, Barcelona: Mayo.
Ackers L (2004) Managing relationships in peripatetic careers: Scientific mobility in the European Union, *Women's Studies International Forum*, 27(3):189–201.
Adelman J (2013) *Worldly Philosopher: The Odyssey of Albert O Hirschman*, Princeton, NJ: Princeton University Press.
Adler LL & Gielen UP (2003) *Migration: Immigration and Emigration in International Perspective*, Westport, CT: Praeger.
Adler MA (1996) Xenophobia and ethno-violence in contemporary Germany, *Critical Sociology*, 22: 29–51.
Admin (2016) One third of the immigrants to Canada return home, www.canadaupdates.com/2016/09/09/.
Adorno TW et al (1950) *The Authoritarian Personality*, New York: Harper & Row.
Adzei F & Sakyi E (2014) Drivers of return migration of Ghanaian health professionals, *International Journal of Migration, Health & Social Care*, 10 (2):102–120.
Agier M & Fernback D (trans) (2008) *On the Margins of the World: The Refugee Experience Today*, Cambridge: Polity.
Agier M (2008) *On the Margins of the World: The Refugee Experience Today*, Cambridge: Polity.
Ahmad AN (2010) Pakistanis in Italy: The disenchantments of "living transnationally (v 92, pp161–183) in *Revista CIDOB d'Afers Internacionals*, Barcelona Centre for International Affairs.
Ahmed S (2013) *Uprootings/Regroundings: Questions of Home and Migration*, Oxford: Berg.
Ahrens J et al (2016) Free movement? The onward migration of EU citizens born in Somalia, Iran, and Nigeria, *Population, Space and Place*, 22(1):84–98.
Ainsworth MDS & Bell SM (1970) Attachment, exploration, and separation, *Child Development*, 41(1):49–67.

Ajzen I (2014) The theory of planned behavior (pp438–459), in P Van Lange et al (Eds) *Handbook of Theories of Social Psychology*, London: Sage.

Ajzen I & Fishbein M (1980) *Understanding Attitudes and Predicting Social Behavior*, Englewood Cliffs, NJ: Prentice-Hall.

Ajzen I & Fishbein M (2000) Attitudes and the attitude-behavior relation (v 11, pp1–33) in W Stroebe & M Hewstone (Eds) *European Review of Social Psychology*.

Akhtar M et al (2018) Development of a scale to measure reverse culture shock in fresh foreign degree holders, *Pakistan Journal of Psychological Research*, 33 (1):257–276.

Akhtar S (1995) A third individuation: Immigration, identity, and the psychoanalytic process, *Journal of the American Psychoanalytic Association*, 43:1051–1084.

Akhtar S (1996) "Someday…" and "if only…" fantasies: Pathological optimism and inordinate nostalgia as related forms of idealization, *Journal of the American Psychoanalytic Association*, 44:723–753.

Akhtar S (1998) From simplicity through contradiction to paradox, *International Journal of Psychoanalysis*, 79:241–252.

Akhtar S (1999) The immigrant, exile, and the experience of nostalgia, *Journal of Applied Psychoanalytic Studies*, 1:123–130.

Akhtar S (1999/2004) *Immigration and Identity*, Lanham, MD: Rowman & Littlefield Publishers Inc.

Akhtar S (2007a) The Trauma of Dislocation (pp165–190) in MTH Hooke & S Akhtar (Eds) *The Geography of Meanings*, London: The International Psychoanalysis Library.

Akhtar S (2007b) Prologue (pp1–14) in M Hook & S Akhtar (Eds) *The Geography of Meanings*, London: International Psychoanalytic Association.

Akhtar S & Kramer S (1998) *The Colors of Childhood: Separation-Individuation across Culture, Racial and Ethnic Differences*, London: Jason Aronson Inc.

Akresh IR (2011) Immigrants' religious participation in the United States, *Ethnic and Racial Studies*, 34(4):643–661.

Alba R (1990) *Ethnic Identity*, New Haven, CT: Yale University Press.

Alba R (2006) Bright *vs* blurred boundaries: Second-generation assimilation and exclusion, *Ethnic and Racial Studies*, 28(1):20–49.

Alba R & Foner N (2015) *Strangers No More: Immigration & the Challenge of Integration*, Princeton, NJ: Princeton University Press.

Alba R & Orsi R (2009) Passage in piety: Generational transitions and the social and religious incorporation (pp32–55) in PH Elovitz& & C Kahn (Eds) *Immigrant Experiences*, Madison, NJ: Fairleigh Dickinson University Press.

Alba R et al (2009a) *Immigration and Religion in America*, New York: New York University Press.

Alba R et al (2009b) Incorporation of new religions into American society by European Jews and Arab Muslims (pp191–197) in R Alba et al *Op Cit.* (2009a).

Aldrich R (1995) From Francité to Créolité: French West Indian literature comes home (pp101–124) in King et al (Eds) *Writing across Worlds*, New York: Psychology Press/Routledge.

Alexander CE (1996) *The Art of Being Black*, Oxford: Oxford University Press.

Alexander CE (2000) *The Asian Gang: Ethnicity, Identity, Masculinity*, Oxford: Berg.

Allen R (2010) The bonding and bridging roles of religious institutions for refugees, *Ethnic and Racial Studies*, 33(6):1049–1068.

Allen W et al (2018) Media reporting of migrants and migration (pp191–208) in M McAuliffe & M Ruhs (Eds) *World Migration Report 2018*, Geneva: International Organization for Migration.

Allik J & McCrae RR (2004) Toward a geography of personality traits, *Journal of Cross-Cultural Psychology*, 35(1):13–28.

Allport FH (1920) The Influence of the group upon association and thought, *Journal of Experimental Psychology*, 3(3):159–182.

Allport G (1954) *The Nature of Prejudice*, Boston, MA: Addison Wesley.

Allweiss S & Hilado A (2017) The context of migration: Pre-arrival, migration, and resettlement experiences (p33–56) in A Hilado & M Lundy (Eds) *Models for Practice with Immigrants and Refugees: Collaboration, Awareness, and Integrative Theory*, London: Sage Publications.

Alsaleh M (2018) Things we carry: Storytelling circles, *Pacific Canada Heritage Centre – Museum of Migration Society* (Nov 24).

Aluwihare AP (2005) Physician migration: Donor country impact, *Journal of Continuing Education in the Health Professions*, 25(1):15–21.

American Academy of Religion (2019) *Recommended Reading*, www.aarweb.org.

American Psychological Association (2012) *Presidential Task Force on Immigration. Crossroads: The Psychology of Immigration in the New Century*, Washington, DC: APA.

Amit K et al (2016) The role of leadership in the migration decision-making process, *Journal of Immigrant & Refugee Studies*, 14(4):371–389.

Amit K & Riss I (2010) The duration of migration decision-making, *Journal of Ethnic and Migration Studies*, 39(1):51–67.

Amnesty International (2016) Danger at every turn: Women refugees seeking safety in Europe, www.amnesty.org.uk/blogs.

Amnesty International (2017) Facing walls: USA and Mexico's violations of the rights of asylum-seekers, www.amnesty.org/en/documents/amr01/6426/2017/en/.

Anderson B (1991/2016) *Imagined Communities: Reflections on the Origin and Spread of Nationalism*, Brooklyn, NY: Verso.

Anderson B (2013) *Us and Them? The Dangerous Politics of Immigration Control*, Scholarship Online: ISBN-13: 9780199691593.

Anderson E (2019) The structure of equality, *The New Yorker* (Jan 7):46–55.

Andretta JR et al (2013) Demographic group differences in adolescents' time attitudes, *Journal of Adolescence*, 36(2):289–301.

Andretta JR et al (2014) Predicting educational outcomes and psychological well-being in adolescents using time attitude profiles, *Psychology in the Schools*, 51(5):434–451.

Ang S & Van Dyne L (Eds) (2008) *The Handbook of Cultural Intelligence*, New York: ME Sharpe.

Angel B et al (2010) Effects of war and organized violence on children: A study of Bosnian refugees in Sweden, *American Journal of Orthopsychiatry*, 71(1):4–15.

Anthony M (1990) *The Valkyries: The Women around Jung*: Shaftesbury, Dorset: Element.

Antonovsky A (1987) *Unravelling the Mystery of Health: How People Manage Stress and Stay Well*, San Francisco, CA: Jossey-Bass.

Antonovsky A (1993) The structure and properties of the Sense of Coherence Scale, *Social Science & Medicine*, 36(6):725–733.

Aprile S (2007) Travel, tourism & migration seen through exile (pp28–39) in Geoffroy & Sibley (Eds) *Going Abroad: Travel, Tourism, and Migration. Cross-Cultural Perspectives on Mobility*, Newcastle upon Tyne: Cambridge Scholars Publishing.

Aranda EM (2006) *Emotional Bridges to Puerto Rico: Migration, Return Migration, and the Struggles of Incorporation*, Lanham, MD: Rowman & Littlefield Publishers.

Arango J (2000) Explaining migration: A critical view, *International Social Science Journal*, 52(165): 283–296.

Archdeacon T (1990) Hansen's hypothesis as a model of immigrant assimilation (pp42–63) in P Kivisto & D Blanck (Eds) *American Immigrants and Their Generations*, Urbana, IL: University of Illinois.

Argyle M (1969) The changing role of the professional educator, *Paedagogica Europaea*, 5:72–79.

Arlow JA (1986) The poet as prophet: A psychoanalytic perspective, *Psychoanalytic Quarterly*, 55:53–68.

Arnberg L (1987) *Raising Children Bilingually: The Pre-School Years*, Philadelphia, PA: Multilingual Matters Ltd.

Arnett JJ (2002) The psychology of globalization, *American Psychologist*, 57 (10):774–783.

Arpana G et al (2014) Psychological research on South Asian Americans: A three-decade content analysis, *Asian American Journal of Psychology*, 5 (4):364–372.

Ashton MC et al (2004). A six-factor structure of personality-descriptive adjectives: Solutions from psycholexical studies in seven languages, *Journal of Personality and Social Psychology*, 86(2), 356–366.

Ashton MC et al (2007) German lexical personality factors: Relations with the HEXACO model, *European Journal of Personality*, 21:23–43.

Ashton MC & Lee K (2001) A theoretical basis for the major dimensions of personality, *European Journal of Personality*, 15:327–353.

Ashton MC & Lee K (2007) Empirical, theoretical, and practical advantages of the HEXACO model of personality structure, *Personality and Social Psychology Review*, 11:150–166.

Astor A et al (1982) Physician migration: Views from professionals in Colombia, Nigeria, India, Pakistan and the Philippines, *Social Science & Medicine*, 61 (12):2492–2500.

Åström J & Westerlund O (2011) Sex and migration: Who is the tied mover? *HUI Working Papers 33, HUI Research*: 19–20.

Atwood M (2002) *Negotiating with the Dead*, Cambridge: Cambridge University Press.

Auer C (2007) Emigrant letters in the Scottish Highlands press (1846–1854) (pp40–50) in C Geoffroy & R Sibley (Eds) *Going Abroad*, Cambridge: Cambridge Scholars Publishing.

Ault A (2016) Did Ellis Island officials really change the names of immigrants? www.smithsonian.com.
Australian Bureau of Statistics (2019) *Australia's Population by Country of Birth*, www.abs.gov.au/AUSSTATS/.
Azose JJ et al (2016) Probabilistic population projections with migration uncertainty, *Proceedings of the National Academy of Science (PNAS)*, *1*, 13(23):6460–6465.
Azose JJ & Raftery AE (2018) Estimation of emigration, return migration, and transit migration between all pairs of countries, *Proceedings of the National Academy of Sciences*. doi:10.1073/pnas.1722334116.
Baglay S & Jones M (2017) *Refugee Law* (2nd ed.), Toronto: Irwin Law Inc.
Bailey-Dick M et al (2015) *Finding our Way, Immigrants, Refugees, and Canadian Churches*, Community Based Research www.communitybasedresearch.ca.
Baillot H et al (2014) Reason to disbelieve: Evaluating the rape claims of women seeking asylum in the UK, *International Journal of Law in Context*, 10 (1):105–139.
Bakewell O (2010) Some reflections on structure and agency in migration theory, *Journal of Ethnic and Migration Studies*, 36:1689–1708.
Bandura A (2001) Social cognitive theory, *Annual Review of Psychology*, 52:1–26.
Baofu P (2012) *The Future of Post-Human Migration*, Cambridge: Cambridge Scholars Publishing.
Baptiste DA (1993) Immigrant families, adolescents and acculturation, *Marriage & Family Review*, 19(3–4):341–363.
Barcus H & Halfacree K (2018) *An Introduction to Population Geographies*, London: Routledge.
Bardsley DK & Hugo GJ (2010) Migration and climate change, *Population and Environment*, 32:238–262.
Barenbaum J et al (2004) The psychosocial aspects of children exposed to wars, *Journal of Child Psychology & Psychiatry*, 45(1):41–62.
Barry E & Sorensen MS (2018) In Denmark, Harsh New Laws for Immigrant "Ghettos", *New York Times*, www.nytimes.com/2018/07/01/world/europe/denmark-immigrant-ghettos.html.
Bartholomew K & Horowitz LM (1991) Attachment styles among young adults, *Journal of Personality and Social Psychology*, 61(2):226–244.
Basch L et al (2004) *Nations Unbound: Transnational Projects, Postcolonial Predicaments, and Deterritorialized Nations-States*, Langhorn, PA: Gordon and Breach.
Baszile N (2018) Home going (pp1–5) in D Santana (Ed) *All the Women in My Family Sing*, San Francisco, CA: Nothing But the Truth.
Bates LM & Teitler JO (2008) Immigration and low birth weight in the US, *Center for Research on Child Wellbeing* Working Paper #2008-15-FF, Population Association of America (PAA).
Bauböck R (2003) Towards a political theory of migrant transnationalism, *International Migration Review*, 37(3):700–723.
Bauder H (2011) *Immigration Dialectic: Imagining Community, Economy and Nation*, Toronto: University of Toronto Press.
Bauman Z (1995) *Life in Fragments: Essays in Postmodern Moralities*, Oxford: Blackwell.
Bauman Z (1998) *Globalization: The Human Consequences*, Cambridge: Polity Press.

Bauman Z (2001) Identity in the globalising world, *Social Anthropology*, 9 (2):121–129.
Bauman Z (2004) *Identity: Conversations with Benedetto Vecch*, Cambridge: Polity Press.
Bauman Z (2016) *Strangers at Our Door*, Cambridge: Polity Press.
Bauman Z & Tester K (2001) *Conversations with Zygmunt Bauman*, Cambridge: Polity Press.
Baumeister RF & Leary MR (1995) The need to belong: Desire for interpersonal attachments as a fundamental human motivation, *Psychological Bulletin*, 117 (3):497–529.
Bayes J & Tohidi N (2001) *Globalization, Religion, and Gender*, New York: Palgrave.
Bayraktar N (2016) *Mobility and Migration in Film and Moving Image Art: Cinema beyond Europe*, New York: Routledge.
BBC News (2018b) *Migrant caravan: What is it and why does it matter?* 30 October www.bbc.com/news/world-latin-america-45951782.
Bean FD & Steven G (2003) *America's Newcomers: Immigrant Incorporation and the Dynamic of Diversity*, New York: Russell Sage Foundation.
Beck U (1992) *Risk Society: Towards a New Modernity*, London: Sage.
Becker GS & Becker GN (1997) *The Economics of Life: From Baseball to Affirmative Action to Immigration*, Columbus, OH: McGraw-Hill.
Behera NC (2006) Introduction (pp21–67) in NC Behera (Ed) *Gender Conflict & Migration*, New Delhi: Sage Publications India.
Bejan R (2017) Book Reviews: *Strangers No More: Immigration and the Challenges of Integration in North America and Western Europe*, by R Alba & N Foner (2015) *Social Service Review*, 91(1):159–168.
Beltsiou J (2016) Seeking home in the foreign: Otherness and immigration (pp89–108) in J Beltsiou (Ed) *Immigration in Psychoanalysis: Locating Ourselves*, London: Routledge.
Benet-Martínez V & Haritatos J (2005) Bicultural identity integration (BII): Components and psychosocial antecedents, *Journal of Personality*, 73:1015–1050.
Berger J & Mohr J (1975) *A Seventh Man: A Book of Images and Words about the Experience of Migrant Workers in Europe*, Harmondsworth & Baltimore, MD: Penguin.
Berlin I (1969) *Four Essays on Liberty*, Oxford: Oxford University Press.
Berry JW (1997) Immigration, acculturation and adaption, *Applied Psychology*, 46:5–34.
Berry JW (2001) A psychology of immigration, *Journal of Social Issues*, 57 (3):615–631.
Bertossi C (2011). National models of integration in Europe: A comparative and critical analysis, *American Behavioral Scientist*, 55:1561–1580.
Betz H-G (1994) *Radical Right-Wing Popularism in Western Europe*, London: Macmillan.
Betz H-G & Immerfall S (1998) *The New Politics of the Right*, London: Macmillan.
Bhabha J (2018) *Can We Solve the Migration Crisis?* Cambridge: Polity Press.
Bhattacharya P (2016) *Good Girls Marry Doctors: South Asian American Daughters on Obedience and Rebellion*, San Francisco, CA: Aunt Lute Books.

Bhugra D (2004) Migration, distress and cultural identity, *British Medical Bulletin*, 69(1):129–141.

Bhugra D & Gupta S (2011) *Migration and Mental Health*, Cambridge: Cambridge University Press.

Bickerton D (2008) *Bastard Tongues: A Trailblazing Linguist Finds Clues to Our Common Humanity in the World's Lowliest Languages*, New York: Farrar, Straus & Giroux.

Bidwell P et al (2014) Security and skills: The two key issues in health worker migration, *Global Health Action*, 7:24194.

Biles J (2012) What do you do with a problem like cohesion? (pp246–289) in P Spoonley & E Tolley (Eds) *Diverse National, Diverse Responses: Approaches to Social Cohesion in Immigrant Societies*, Montreal: McGill-Queen's University Press.

Biles J & Frideres J (2012) Conclusions (pp290–312) in J Frideres & J Biles (Eds) *International Perspectives: Integration & Inclusion*, Montreal: McGill-Queen's University Press.

Billiet J et al (1996) Ethnocentrism in the Low Countries: A comparative perspective, *New Community*, 22(3):401–416.

Billig M (1995) *Banal Nationalism*, London: Sage Publications.

Bion WR (1970/1984) *Attention and Interpretation: A Scientific Approach to Insight in Psycho-Analysis and Groups*, London: Tavistock/Karnac Books.

Birman D (1998) Biculturalism and perceived competence of Latino immigrant adolescents, *American Journal of Community Psychology*, 26(3):335–354.

Bjarnason T (2014) Adolescent migration intentions and population change: A 20-year follow-up of Icelandic communities, *Sociologia Ruralis*, 54(4):500–515.

Black J & Mendenhall MJ (1991) The U-Curve adjustment hypothesis revisited, *Journal of International Business Studies*, 22(2):225–247.

Blackbourn D (1997) *The Long Nineteenth Century: A History of Germany, 1780–1918*, Oxford: Oxford University Press.

Blacklock C et al (2014) Exploring the migration decisions of health workers and trainees from Africa, *Social Science & Medicine*, 100:99–106.

Blair G (2015) *The Trumps: Three Generations of Builders and a Presidential Candidate*, New York: Simon & Schuster.

Blatchford C (2012) No honour in "cold-blooded, shameless" murder of Shafia girls, *National Post* (Jan 29). https://nationalpost.com/opinion/jury-reaches-verdict-in-shafia-trial.

Blewett MH (2009) *The Yankee Yorkshireman: Migration Lived and Imagined*, Urbana, IL: University of Illinois Press.

Bloom-Feshbach J et al (1987) *The Psychology of Separation and Loss: The Jossey-Bass Social & Behavioral Science Series*, San Francisco, CA: Jossey-Bass Inc.

Bluedorn AC et al (1999) Polychronicity and the Inventory of Polychronic Values (IPV), *Journal of Managerial Psychology*, 14(3/4):205–231.

Bluedorn AC (2002) *The Human Organization of Time: Temporal Realities and Experience*, Stanford, CA: Stanford University Press.

Blumentritt TL & Van Voorhis CRW (2004) The Million Adolescent Clinical Inventory: Is it valid and reliable for Mexican American Youth? *Journal of Personality Assessment*, 83(1):64–74.

Bochner S (1982/2013) The social psychology of cross-cultural relations (pp5–44) in S Bochner (Ed) *Cultures in Contact: Studies in Cross-Cultural Interactions*, Oxford: Pergamon.

Bonjour S et al (2011) *The Others in Europe*, Bruxelles: Institut D'Etudes Europeennes.

Boothby NG & Knudsen CM (2000) Waging a new kind of war: Children of the Gun, *Scientific American*, 282:60–65.

Borja M (2018) Not all Rosy: Religion and refugee resettlement in the US, *Harvard Divinity Bulletin*, 46(1–2).

Boswell C & Mueser PR (2008) Introduction: Economics and interdisciplinary approaches in migration research, *Journal of Ethnic and Migration Studies*, 34(4):519–529.

Botelho VL & Agergaard S (2011) Moving for the love of the game? International migration of female footballers, *Soccer & Society*, 12(6):806.

Boulanger G (2014) *Wounded by Reality: Understanding and Treating Adult Onset Trauma, Psychoanalysis*, London: Routledge.

Boulanger G (2016) Seeing double, being double: Longing, belonging, recognition, an evasion in psychodynamic work with immigrants (pp53–68) in J Beltsiou (Ed) *Immigration in Psycho-analysis: Locating Ourselves*, London: Routledge.

Bowlby J (1969/1997) *Attachment & Loss*, London: Random House UK.

Boyd M & Pikkov D (2009) *Gendering Migration, Livelihood and Entitlements: Migrant Women in Canada and the United States*, Geneva: United Nations Research Institute for Social Development.

Brett R & McCallin M (1998) *Children: The Invisible Soldiers*, Stockholm: Radda Barnen.

Brettell C (2003) *Anthropology and Migration: Essays on Transnationalism, Ethnicity, and Identity*, Walnut Creek, CA: Altamira Press.

Brettell CB & Hollifield JF (Eds) (2007) *Migration Theory: Talking Across Disciplines*, London: Routledge.

Brewster S (2002) "Das Unheimliche," *The Literary Encyclopedia*, www.litencyc.com/php/sworks.php?UID=5735&rec=true.

Brigden N & Mainwaring C (2016) Matryoshka journeys: Im/Mobility during migration, *Geopolitics*, 21(2):407–434.

British Broadcasting Company (2016) *Migrant Crisis: Migration to Europe Explained in Seven Charts* (March 4), www.bbc.com/news/world-europe-34131911.

Brouillon M (2007) A peculiarly British spirit of adventure (pp132–146) in C Geoffroy & R Sibley (Eds) *Going Abroad: Travel, Tourism, and Migration, Cross-Cultural Perspectives on Mobility*, Cambridge: Cambridge Scholars Publishing.

Brown LA & Sanders RL (1981) Toward a development paradigm of migration, with particular reference to third world settings (pp149–185) in GF de Jong & RW Gardner (Eds) *Migration Decision Making*, New York: Pergamon Press.

Brown O (2008) *Migration & Climate Changes*, Geneva: International Organization for Migration.

Brown SK & Bean FD (2006) Assimilation models, old and new, *Migration Policy Institute*, www.migrationpolicy.org/.
Brown W (1993a) *States of Injury Power and Freedom in Late Modernity*, Princeton, NJ: Princeton University Press.
Brown W (1993b) Wounded attachments, *Political Theory*, 21(3):390–410.
Brown W (2002) *Manhood and Politics: A Feminist Reading in Political Theory*, Lanham, MD: Rowman & Littlefield Publishers.
Browne CV & Braun KL (2017) Away from the islands: Diaspora's effects, *Journal of Cross-Cultural Gerontology*, 32(4):395–411.
Brown-Guillory E (2006) *Middle Passages and the Healing Place of History: Migration and Identity in Black Women's Literature*, Columbus, OH: Ohio State University Press.
Brugha R et al (2016) Passing through: Reasons why migrant doctors in Ireland plan to stay, *Human Resources for Health*, 14:45–54.
Brunschot A (2011) Edmonton's Somalis (pp3–4) in *Seemagazine*, Feb 3–9 www.seemagaine.com.
Brym RJ (1992) The emigration potential of Czechoslovakia, Hungary, Lithuania, Poland and Russia, *International Sociology*, 7:387–395.
Budría S et al, (2017) The impact of host language proficiency across the immigrants' earning distribution in Spain, *IZA Journal of Development and Migration*, 7:12.
Bulman M (2018) Home Office immigration delays nearly double as thousands "left in limbo", *The Independent* (Sept 29).
Burnett A & Peel M (2001) Health needs of asylum seekers and refugees, *British Medical Journal*, 3; 322(7285): 544–547.
Bustamante LHU et al (2018) Stress, trauma, and posttraumatic stress disorder in migrants, *Brazilian Journal of Psychiatry*, 40(2):220–225.
Butalia U (2006) Migration/dislocation: A gendered perspective (pp37–154) in NC Behera (Ed) *Gender Conflict & Migration*, New Delhi: Sage Publications India.
Cadge W & Ecklund EH (2007) Immigration and religion, *Annual Review of Sociology*, 33(1): 359–379.
Cairns E & Dawes A (1996) Children: Ethnic and political violence, *Child Development*, 67:129–139.
Cameron HE (2008) Risk theory and "subjective fear", *International Journal of Refugee Law*, 20(4):567–585.
Campbell J (1949/1973) *The Hero with a Thousand Faces*, Princeton, NJ: Princeton University Press.
Campbell RR & Carkovich L (1984) Turnaround migration as an episode of collective behavior, *Rural Sociology*, 49(1):89–105.
Campese G (2008) Cuantos más?: The crucified peoples at the US-Mexico border (pp271–298) in D Groody & G Campese (Eds) *A Promised Land, A Perilous Journey: Theological Perspectives on Migration*, Notre Dame, IN: University of Notre Dame Press.
Campion P (2003) One nation under God? Religious entrepreneurship and pioneer Latino immigrants in southern Louisiana, *Sociological Spectrum*, 23:279–301.
Campisi E (2016) *Escape to Miami: An Oral History of the Cuban Rafter Crisis*, Oxford: Oxford University Press.

Canadian Commission for UNESCO (1977) *Building Inclusive Communities*, https://en.ccunesco.ca/our-themes/building-inclusive-communities.
Canadian Multiculturalism Act https://en.wikipedia.org/wiki/Canadian_Multiculturalism_Act.
Carens JH (2013) *The Ethics of Immigration*, Oxford: Oxford University Press.
Carey KE (2018) Henri Parens tells story of escape and survival, *Deleo News Network*, County Press.
Carliner G (2000) The language ability of US immigrants: Assimilation and cohort effects, *International Migration Review*, 34(1):158–182.
Carling J (2002) Migration in the age of involuntary immobility, *Journal of Ethnic and Migration Studies*, 28(1):5–42.
Carlson HM & Nilsen EL (1995) Ireland: Gender, psychological health, and attitudes toward emigration, *Psychological Reports*, 76:179–186.
Carpenter S & Meade-Pruitt SM (2008) Does the Twenty Statements Test elicit self-concept aspects that are most descriptive? *World Cultures eJournal*, 16(1).
Carswell K et al (2011) The relationship between trauma, post-migration problems and the psychological well-being of refugees and asylum seekers, *International Journal of Social Psychiatry*, 57(2):107–119.
Cartwright D (1979) Contemporary social psychology in historical perspective, *Social Psychology Quarterly*, 42:82–93.
Cartwright M (2012) Odysseus, *Ancient History Encyclopedia*, www.ancient.eu/odysseus/.
Carvalho AR & Martins FC (2016) A psychological perspective on immigration, *International Journal of Migration, Health & Social Care*, 12(3):216–224.
Casteel SP (2001) Eva Hoffman's double emigration: Canada as the site of exile in "Lost in Translation", *Biography*, 24(1):288–301.
Castells M (1996–1998) *The Information Age: Economy, Society, Culture* (3 volumes), Oxford: Blackwell Publishing Co.
Castles S (2010) Understanding global migration: A social transformation perspective, *Journal of Ethnic and Migration Studies*, 36(10):1568.
Castles S & Miller MJ (1993/2009) *The Age of Migration: International Population Movements in the Modern World* (4th ed.), New York: The Guildford Press.
Castles SH et al (2014) *The Age of Migration: International Population Movements in the Modern World* (5th ed.), Houndsmills, Basingstoke: Palgrave Macmillan.
CBC News (2018) *Ottawa probes birth tourism as new data shows higher non-resident birth rates* www.cbc.ca/news/canada/birth-tourism-new-study-1.4917574.
Cekerevac A et al (2018) Social services for migrants, the case of Serbia, *Croatian and Comparative Public Administration*, 18(1):101–126.
Centre for Community Based Research (2013–2014) *Literature Review: The Role of Churches in Immigrant Settlement and Integration*, http://communitybasedresearch.ca/resources/.
Ceobanu AM & Escandell X (2010) Comparative analyses of public attitudes toward immigrants and immigration using multinational survey data, *Annual Review of Sociology*, 36(1):309–328.
Challiol H & Mignonac K (2005) Relocation decision-making in couple relationships, *Journal of Organisational Behavior*, 26(3):247–274.

Chambers R (2018) Some UK asylum seekers waiting over 20 years for Home Office decisions on their application for asylum, https://immigrationbarrister.co.uk/.

Chandler RC & Tsai Y-M (2001) Social factors influencing immigration attitudes: Analysis of data from the General Social Survey, *The Social Science Journal*, 38:177–188.

Chase ND (1999) Parentification: An overview of theory, research, and societal issues (pp3–34) in ND Chase (Ed) *Burdened Children: Theory, Research, and Treatment of Parentification*, Thousand Oaks, CA: Sage Publications.

Chevalier J & Gheerbrant A (1969/1996) *The Penguin Dictionary of Symbols*, London: Penguin.

Chow ZE (2018) Evaluating the current international legal framework governing the status of refugees in light of contemporary refugee crises, *Singapore Academy of Law Journal*, 30(1):28–69.

Chui T (2011) Chapter 9: Immigrant women (pp251–282) in *Statistics Canada Women in Canada: A Gender-based Statistical Report*, Statistics Canada Catalogue no. 89-503-X.

Church TA (1982) Sojourner adjustment, *Psychology Bulletin*, 91(3):540–572.

Clark WAV & Withers SD (2008) Fertility, mobility and labor-force participation, Unpublished MS, UCLA Department of Geography.

Clarke N et al (2017) Factors influencing trainee doctor emigration in a high income country, *Human Resources for Health*, 15:1–12.

Clarkson A (2016) *Belonging: The Paradox of Citizenship*, CBC Massey Lectures. Toronto: House of Anansi Press.

Cohen R (1997/2008) *Global Diasporas: An Introduction*, London: Routledge.

Coifman KG et al (2007) Does repressive coping promote resilience? *Journal of Personality and Social Psychology*, 92(4):745–758.

Collier P (2015) Refugees, *Social Europe Podcast* (July 15), www.socialeurope.eu/beyond-the-boat-people-europes-moral-duties-to-refugees.

Collins Dictionary (2019) Diaspora, www.collinsdictionary.com/dictionary/english/diaspora.

Collyer M (2005) When do social networks fail to explain migration? *Journal of Ethnic and Migration Studies*, 31(4):699–718.

Connell J (1995) In Samoan worlds: Culture, migration, identity (pp263–279) in R King et al (Eds) *Writing across Worlds: Literature and Migration*, London: Routledge.

Connor P (2017) European asylum applications remained near record levels in 2016, *Pew Research Center, Fact Tank, News in the Numbers*, www.pewresearch.org/fact-tank.

Conroy GP (2016) *Migration Trauma, Culture: Views from British Object Relations Theory*, Lanham, MD: Rowman & Littlefield.

Cooke TJ (2008a) Gender role beliefs and family migration, *Population, Space and Place*, 14(3):163–175.

Cooke TJ (2008b) Migration in a family way, *Population, Space and Place*, 14(4):255–265.

Cooke TJ (2013) All tied up: Tied staying and tied migration within the United States, 1997–2007, *Demographic Research*, 29(30):817–836.

Cornelia M (2017) *Migration, Memory and Diversity: Germany from 1945 to the Present*, New York: Berghahn Books.

Cornelius WA (2005) Controlling "unwanted" immigration: Lessons from the United States, 1993–2004, *Journal of Ethnic and Migration Studies*, 31(4):775–794.

Cornish A (2015) Migrants seek new routes across Europe after Hungary seals border, www.npr.org/2015/09/16/440914056/migrants-seek-new-routes-across-europe-after-hungary-seals-border.

Costa PT & McCrae RR (1992) *Revised NEO Personality Inventory (NEO-PI-R) and NEO Five-Factor Inventory (NEO-FFI) Manual*, Odessa, FL: Psychological Assessment Resources.

Côté JE (2002) *Arrested Adulthood: The Changing Nature of Maturity and Identity*, New York: New York University Press.

Côté JE & Levine CG (2002) *Identity Formation, Agency, and Culture*, Mahwah, NJ: Lawrence Erlbaum Associates Publishers.

Coulter R et al (2012) Partner (dis)agreement on moving desires, *Population, Space and Place*, 18(1):16–30.

Cresswell T (2011) Mobilities I: Catching up, *Progress in Human Geography*, 35:550–558.

Cushman P (2015) A review of contemporary psychoanalysis and the legacy of the Third Reich, *Contemporary Psychoanalysis*, 51(1):176–181.

Cuthbertson C (2018) US border crisis: 100,000 illegal immigrants in 60 days, *The Epoch Times* (Dec 20):1–3.

Dabrowski K (1964/2016) *Positive Disintegration*, Maurice Bassett Publications.

Dahlie H (1985) *Varieties of Exile: The Canadian Experience*, Vancouver: University of British Columbia Press.

Daly M (1978) *Gyn/Ecology*, Boston, MA: Beacon Press.

Dante A (1909–14) *The Divine Comedy* HF Cary (trans) Vol. XX, The Harvard Classics, New York: Collier & Son.

Dao TH et al (2016) *Migration and Development: Dissecting the Anatomy of the Mobility Transition*, Louvain: Institut de recherchs économique at sociales de l'université catholique de Louvain.

Das Gupta T (2006) Twice migrated: Political economy of South Asian immigrants from the Middle East to Canada, *International Journal of the Humanities*, 3:263–274.

DaVanzo J (1983) Repeat migration in the United States: Who moves back and who moves on? *Review of Economics and Statistics*, 65:552–559.

Davidov E et al (2008) Values and support for immigration: A cross-country comparison, *European Sociology Review*, 24(5):583–599.

de Haas H (2014) *Migration Theory Quo Vadis?* Working Papers Paper 100 International Migration MI project paper 24.

de Hanas DN (2016) *London Youth, Religion, and Politics: Engagement and Activism from Brixton to Brick Lane*, Oxford: Oxford University Press.

de Jong GF & Fawcett JT (1981) Motivations for migration (pp13–58) in GF de Jong & RW Gardner (Eds) *Migration Decision Making: Multidisciplinary Approaches to Microlevel Studies in Developed & Developing Countries*, New York: Pergamon Press.

Delisle J (2013) *The Newfoundland Diaspora: Mapping the Literature of Out-migration*, Waterloo: Wilfrid Laurier University Press.

Dellal BH & Zwartz A (2012) Social cohesion: Beyond the theory (pp239–256) in P Spoonley& & E Tolley (Eds) *Diverse National, Diverse Responses: Approaches to Social Cohesion in Immigrant Societies*, Montreal & Kingston: McGill-Queen's University Press.

Demes KA & Geeraert N (2014) Measures matter: Scales for adaptation, cultural distance, and acculturation orientation revisited, *Journal of Cross-Cultural Psychology*, 45(1):91–109.

Denford J (2004) Going away, *Self & Society*, 32(5):11–17.

Denford S (1981) Going away, *International Review of Psychoanalysis*, 59:325–332.

Dere WGW (2019) *Being Chinese in Canada: The Struggle for Identity, Redress and Belonging*, Madeira Park, BC: Douglas & McIntyre.

De Troyes C (1996) *Perceval, the Story of the Grail*, Suffolk: DS Brewer Press.

Deutsche Welle DW (2017) *EU Asylum Applications Drop Drastically in 2017*, www.dw.com/en/eu-asylum-applications-drop-off-drastically-in-2017/a-41976192.

Diaz RM (1983) Thought and two languages: The impact of bilingualism on cognitive development, *Review of Research in Education*, 10:23–54.

Diehl C & Schnell R (2006) "Reactive ethnicity" or "assimilation?" Labor migrants in Germany, *International Migration Review*, 40(4): 786–816.

Diener E (1984) Subjective well-being, *Psychological Bulletin*, 95(3):542–575.

Digman JM (1990) Personality structure: The five-factor model, *Annual Review of Psychology*, 41:417–440.

Dixon TL & Linz D (2000) Overrepresentation and underrepresentation of African Americans and Latinos as lawbreakers on television news, *Journal of Communication*, 50(2):131–154.

Dorabji T (2016) Subterfuge: On how to be obedient while rebelling (pp59–64) in P Bhattacharya (Ed) *Good Girls Marry Doctors: South Asian American Daughters on Obedience and Rebellion*, San Francisco, CA: Aunt Lute Books.

Dossa PS (2004) *Politics and Poetics of Migration: Narratives of Iranian Women from the Diaspora*, Toronto: Canadian Scholars' Press.

Dovidio JF et al (2013) *The Sage Handbook of Prejudice, Stereotyping, and Discrimination*, London: Sage.

Dow HD (2011) An overview of stressors faced by immigrants and refugees, *Home Health Care Management & Practice*, 23(3):210–217.

DPA & Reuters (2018) *Controlled Centers' and Intake Camps: EU Reaches Deal on Migration* (June 29). www.haaretz.com/world-news/europe/.

Drake L et al (2008) Time perspective and correlates of wellbeing, *Time and Society*, 17(1):47–61.

Du Bois WEB (1935/2007) *Black Reconstruction in America*, Oxford: Oxford University Press.

Duckitt J (2001) A dual-process cognitive-motivational theory of ideology and prejudice (pp41–113) in MP Zanna (Ed) *Advances in Experimental Social Psychology*, Cambridge, MA: Academic Press.

Duckitt J & Sibley CG (2009) A dual-process motivational model of ideology, politics, and prejudice, *Psychological Inquiry*, 20(2–3):98–109.

Dueck J et al (2001) *HURIDOCS Events Standard Formats: A Tool for Documenting Human Rights Violations*, Versoix: HURIDOCS.
Duffy P (1995) Literary reflections on Irish migration in the nineteenth and twentieth centuries (pp20–38) in R King et al (Eds) *Writing across Worlds: Literature and Migration*, London & New York: Routledge.
Dummett M (2001) *On Immigration and Refugees*, London & New York: Routledge.
Duncan GR (2018) *Migration to Canada 2018*, Toronto: Carswell.
Duncan H (2012) Immigration, diversity, ethnic enclaves and social cohesion (pp257–268) in P Spoonley & E Tolley (Eds) *Diverse National, Diverse Responses*, Montreal & Kingston: McGill-Queen's University Press.
Dunkas N & Nikelly G (1972) The Persephone syndrome: A study of conflict in the adaptive process of married Greek female immigrants in the USA, *Social Psychiatry*, 7(4):211–216.
Dunne C (2002) *Carl Jung: Wounded Healer of the Soul*, New York: Continuum.
Dupuy HJ (1977) The General Well-being Schedule (pp206–213) in I McDowell & C Newell (Eds), *Measuring Health: A Guide to Rating Scales & Questionnaires*, USA: Oxford University Press.
Dutton D (2009) The promised land, *Newstatesman*, www.newstatesman.com/arts-and-culture/2009/02/landscape-human-art-savannahs.
Duverne A et al (2008) French doctors working in Great Britain, *Revue d'epidemiologie et de sante publique*, 56(5):360–373.
Duyvendak JW (2011) *The Politics of Home: Belonging & Nostalgia*, New York: Palgrave Macmillan Press.
Dyregrov A et al (2002) Children exposed to warfare, *Journal of Traumatic Stress*, 15:59–68.
Durkheim É (1893/1997) *The Division of Labor in Society*, New York: Free Press.
Earley PC & Ang S (2003) *Cultural Intelligence: Individual Interactions across Cultures*, Stanford, CA: Stanford Business Books.
Ebaugh HR & Chafetz J (1999) Agents for cultural reproduction and structural change: Women in immigrant religious institutions, *Social Forces*, 78(2):585–613.
Ebaugh HR & Chafetz J (2000) Dilemmas of language in immigrant congregations, *Review of Religious Research*, 41(4):432–452.
Ebaugh HR & Pipes P (2001) Immigrant congregations as social service providers (pp95–110) in P Nesbitt (Ed) *Religion and Social Policy*, Walnut Creek, CA: Altamira.
Eccles JS & Wigfield A (2002) Motivational beliefs, values and goals, *Annual Review of Psychology*, 53:109–132.
Eck DL (2019) *A New Religious America: How A "Christian Country" Has Become the World's Most Religiously Diverse Nation*, New York: HarperCollins.
Eckersley S (2017) Changing places, changing people: Critical heritages of migration and belonging, *Anthropological Journal of European Cultures*, 26(2):1–5.
Edinger EF (1974) American Nekyia, *Quadrant*, 17(Fall):7–33.
Edinger EF (1985/1996) *Anatomy of the Psyche: Alchemical Symbolism in Psychotherapy*, Chicago, IL: Open Court.
Edinger EF (1992) *Ego and Archetype*, Boston, MA: Shambhala.
Egonu U (2018) African in America (pp329–332) in D Santana (Ed) *All the Women in My Family Sing*, San Francisco, CA: Nothing But the Truth.

Ehrenwald J (Ed) (1991/1997) *The History of Psychotherapy*, Northvale, NJ: Jason Arsonson Inc.
Ehrmann M & Ehrmann B (1948) *The Poems of Max Ehrmann*, Boston, MA: Bruce Humphries Inc.
Eisen A (2009) Choosing closeness in America: The changing faces of Judaism (pp224–245) in R Alba et al (Eds) *Immigration and Religion in America*, New York: New York University Press.
Eisenbruch M (1991) From post-traumatic stress disorder to cultural bereavement: Southeast Asian refugees, *Social Science & Medicine*, 33:673–680.
Eisenstadt SN (1953) Analysis of patterns of immigration and absorption of immigrants, *Population Studies*, 7(2):167–180.
Eisenstadt SN (1955/1975) *The Absorption of Immigrants: The Jewish Community in Palestine and the State of Israel*, Westport, CT: Greenwood.
Eisenstadt SN (1965) Archetypal patterns of youth (pp29–50) in E Erikson (Ed) *The Challenge of Youth*, New York: Anchor Books.
Eisold K (2000) The rediscovery of the unknown, *Contemporary Psychoanalysis*, 36 (1):57–75.
Eissler KR (1978/1998) Biographic sketch (pp10–37) in E Freud et al (Eds) *Sigmund Freud: His Life in Pictures and Words*, New York: WW Norton.
Eliade M (1959) *The Sacred and the Profane*, New York: Harcourt, Brace & Jovanovich Inc.
Ellenberger H (1970) *The Discovery of the Unconscious*, New York: Basic Books.
Elovitz PH (1997a) Patterns and costs of immigration (pp60–70) in PH Elovitz & C Kahn (Eds) *Immigrant Experiences*, Madison, NJ: Fairleigh Dickinson University Press.
Elovitz PH (1997b) Family secrets and lies my parents told me (pp95–117) in PH Elovitz & C Kahn (Eds) *Immigrant Experiences*, Madison, NJ: Fairleigh Dickinson University Press.
Elovitz PH & Kahn C (eds.) (1997) *Immigrant Experiences: Personal Narrative and Psychological Analysis*, London: Associated University Presses.
Emecheta B (1974) *Second Class Citizen*, London: Allison & Busby.
Engbersen G et al (2013) On the differential attachments of migrants from Central and Eastern Europe, *Journal of Ethnic and Migration Studies*, 39(6):959–981.
Erhabor S et al (2013) Migration challenges among Zimbabwean refugees before, during and post-arrival in South Africa, *Journal of Injury & Violence Research*, 5 (1):17–27.
Erikson EH (1950) *Childhood and Society*, New York: WW Norton.
Erikson EH (1958) *Young Man Luther: A Study in Psychoanalysis and History*, New York: WW Norton.
Erikson EH (Ed) (1965) *The Challenge of Youth*, New York: Anchor Books.
Erikson EH (1968/1994) *Identity: Youth & Crisis*, New York: WW Norton.
Erikson EH (1982) *The Life Cycle Completed*, New York: WW Norton.
Erikson EH & Erikson JM (1998) *The Life Cycle Completed*, New York: WW Norton.
Eriksson M & Lindström B (2007) Antonovsky's sense of coherence scale and its relation with quality of life, *Journal of Epidemiology & Community Health*, 61 (11):938–944.

Escobar JI et al (2002) Immigration and mental health: Mexican Americans in the United States, *Harvard Review of Psychiatry*, 8(2):64–72.

Esipova N et al (2010) The world's potential migrants: Who they are, where they want to go, and why it matters? www.imi.ox.ac.uk/files/news/gallup.

Espenshade TS & Calhoun CA (1993) An analysis of public opinion toward undocumented immigration, *Population Research and Policy Review*, 12:189.

Esses V et al (2006) Perceptions of national identity & attitudes toward immigrants & immigration in Canada & Germany, *International Journal of Intercultural Relations*, 30(6):653–669.

European Parliament (2017) *Asylum and Migration in the EU: Facts and Figures*, www.europarl.europa.eu/news/en/headlines/society/20170629STO78630/asylum-and-migration-in-the-eu-facts-and-figures

Eurostat (2019) *Migration and Migrant Population Statistics: Statistics Explained*, https://ec.europa.eu/eurostat/statisticsexplained/.

Ex J (1996) *Adjustment after Migration*, The Hague: M Nijhoff.

Facchini G & Mayda AM (2008) From individual attitudes towards migrants to migration policy outcomes, *Economic Policy*, 23(56):652–713.

Faist T (1997) The crucial meso-level (pp59–90) in T Hammer et al (Eds) *International Migration, Immobility and Development*, Oxford: Berg Publishers.

Faist T (2000) *The Volume & Dynamics of International Migration & Trans-national Social Spaces*, Oxford: Oxford University Press.

Falicov CJ (2003) Immigrant family processes (pp280–300) in F Walsh (Ed) *Normal Family Processes*, New York: Guilford Press.

Falk T (2013) Chinese urbanites are moving back to the countryside, *ZDNet*, www.zdnet.com/article/chinese-urbanites-are-moving-back-to-the-countryside/.

Fang Y (2006) Residential satisfaction, moving intention and moving behaviours, *Housing Studies*, 21(5):671–694.

Farmer P et al (2006) Structural violence and clinical medicine, *PLoS Mediane*, 3: e449.

Farrell G & Thirion S (2012) Social cohesion and well-being (pp269–287) in P Spoonley & E Tolley (Eds) *Diverse National, Diverse Responses*, Montreal & Kingston: McGill-Queen's University Press.

Farwell N (2003) In war's wake, *International Journal of Mental Health*, 32(4):20–50.

Fawcett JT (1989) Networks, linkages, and migration systems, *The International Migration Review*, 23(3): 671–680.

Ferenczi N & Marshall TC (2013) Exploring attachment to the "Homeland" and its association with heritage culture identification, *Plos One* 8(1):e53872.

Fetzer JS (2000a) Economic self-interest or cultural marginality? *Journal of Ethnic and Migration Studies*, 26(1):5–23.

Fetzer JS (2000b) *Public Attitudes toward Immigration in the United States, France and Germany*, Cambridge: Cambridge University Press.

Firat S et al (2017) Results of domestic migration on juvenile delinquency in Adana, Turkey, *Journal of Forensic and Legal Medicine*, 49:81–88.

Fischer R et al (2012) Shelter from the global economic crisis, *Journal of Pacific Rim Psychology*, 6(2):48–56.

Fischer S & McGowan M (1995) From *"Pappkoffer" to* pluralism: Migrant writing in the German Federal Republic (pp39–56) in R King et al (Eds) *Writing Across Worlds*, London: Routledge.

Fischetti M (2016) Pushed out: Violence and disaster are increasing forcing people to flee inside their own county, *Scientific American Online* www.scientificamerican.com/article/more-people-than-ever-are-migrating-because-of-strife/.

Fish J (2011) General well-being schedule in JS Kreutzer et al (Eds) *Encyclopedia of Clinical Neuropsychology*, New York: Springer.

Fisher H et al (2009) Gender differences in the association between childhood abuse and psychosis, *British Journal of Psychiatry*, 194:319–325.

Foa E (1996) *Posttraumatic Diagnostic Scale Manual*, Minneapolis, MN: National Computer Systems.

Foley MW & Hoge DR (2007) *Religion and the New Immigrants*, Oxford: Oxford University Press.

Foner N & Alba R (2008) Immigrant religion in the U.S. and Western Europe, *The International Migration Review*, 42(2):360–392.

Foreign Affairs Canada (2005) *International Child Abductions*, Ottawa: Foreign Affairs Canada.

Fortier A-M (2000) *Migrant Belongings: Memory, Space, Identities*, Oxford: Berg.

Frank RH (2016) *Success and Luck: Good Fortune and the Myth of Meritocracy*, Princeton, NJ: Princeton University Press.

Fraser N (1995) From re-distribution to recognition? *New Left Review*, 212:58–93.

Fray JS (1988) An exploratory study of the culture shock experience of missionary children homecomers, Doctoral dissertation, University of Tennessee, *Dissertation Abstracts International*, 49, 09B, 4063.

Frederiks NT (2016) *Religion, Migration, and Identity*, Leiden: Brill.

Freedman LP & Isaacs SL (1993) Human rights and reproductive choice, *Studies in Family Planning*, 24(1):18–30.

Freud S (1915/1917) Standard Edition of the Complete Psychological Works of Sigmund Freud, *Mourning and Melancholia*, 18:63.

Fried Y & Slowik LH (2004) Enriching goal-setting theory with time, *The Academy of Management Review*, 29(3):404–422.

Frohlick S (2009) Pathos of love in Puerto Viejo, Costa Rica: Emotion, travel and migration, *Mobilities*, 4(3):389–405.

Fujimori A et al (2017) Influences of attachment style, family functions and gender differences on loneliness in Japanese university students, *Psychology*, 8(4):654–662.

Fukuyama F (2018a) *Identity: The Demand for Dignity & the Politics of Resentment*, New York: Farrar, Strauss & Giroux.

Fukuyama F (2018b) Against identity politics: The new tribalism and the crisis of democracy, *Foreign Affairs* (Sept/Oct).

Fuller B & Guerrero A (2018) Commentary: A strong example of heartland values? Immigrant parents, *Chicago Tribune*.

Gagliardo JG (1980) *Reich and Nation: The Holy Roman Empire as Idea and Reality, 1763–1806*, Bloomington, IN: Indiana University Press.

Gallego A & Pardos-Prado S (2014) The Big Five Personality Traits and attitudes towards immigrants, *Journal of Ethnic and Migration Studies*, 40(1):79–99.

Gallo E (2016) *Migration, Masculinities and Reproductive Labour: Men of the Home*, London: Palgrave Macmillan.

Gang IN et al (2002) Economic strain, ethnic concentration and attitudes towards foreigners in the European Union, *IZA Discussion Paper* No. 578.

Gans HJ (1979) Symbolic ethnicity, *Ethnic & Racial Studies*, 2(1):42–52.

Gans HJ (1992) Ethnic invention and acculturation, *Journal of American Ethnic History*, 11(1):42–52.

Gans HJ (1994) Symbolic ethnicity and symbolic religiosity, *Ethnic and Racial Studies*, 17(4):4577–4592.

Gardner RW (1981) Macrolevel influences on the migration decision process (pp59–89) in GF De Jong & RW Gardner (Eds) *Migration Decision Making*, New York: Pergamon Policy Studies on International Development.

Garnett J (2013) *Rescripting Religion in the City: Migration and Religious Identity in the Modern Metropolis*, Farnham, Surrey: Ashgate.

Gartner R & Kennedy L (2018) War and postwar violence, *Crime and Justice: A Review of Research*, 47:1–68.

Gay P (1988/2006) *Freud: A Life for Our Time*, New York: WW Norton.

Gemici A (2011) *Family Migration and Labor Market Outcomes*, New York: Department of Economics, New York University.

Geneva Conventions https://en.wikipedia.org/wiki/GenevaConventions.

Geoffroy C & Sibley R (2007) *Going Abroad: Travel, Tourism, and Migration. Cross-Cultural Perspectives on Mobility*, Newcastle upon Tyne: Cambridge Scholars Publishing.

Gerhards J et al (2016) German public opinion on admitting refugees, *DIW Economic Bulletin*, 21:243–249.

Germain A (2010) *Our Diverse Cities: Quebec*, Ottawa: Metropolis.

Gibbon J (1938) *Canadian Mosaic: The Making of a Northern Nation*, Toronto: McClelland.

Giddens A (1979) *Central Problems in Social Theory*, London: The Macmillan Press.

Giddens A (1991) *Modernity and Self-Identity*, Redwood City, CA: Stanford University Press.

Gilmartin M et al (2018) *Borders, Mobility and Belonging in the Era of Brexit and Trump*, Bristol: Policy Press.

Giovannoni J (2004) Foreword (ppxi–xii) in D Drachman & A Paulino (Eds) *Immigrants and Social Work*, Binghamton, NY: Haworth.

Glazier N & Moynihan DP (1970) *Beyond the Melting Pot*, Boston, MA: The MIT Press.

Glenn G (2002) We have to blame ourselves (pp167–188) in R Papadopoulos (Ed) *Therapeutic Care for Refugees*, Tavistock Clinic Series, London: Karnac.

Goble FG & Maslow HA (1970/1980) *The Third Force: The Psychology of Abraham Maslow*, New York: Pocket Books.

Goenjian AK et al (1997) Outcome of psychotherapy among early adolescents after trauma, *American Journal of Psychiatry*, 154:536–542.

Gok K & Atsan N (2016) Decision-making under stress and its implications for managerial decision-making, *International Journal of Business and Social Research* 6 (3):38–47.

Gold SJ & Nawyn SJ (2013) *Routledge International Handbook of Migration Studies*, London: Routledge.

Goldberg DP et al (1997) The validity of two versions of GHQ in the WHO study of mental illness in general health care, *Psychological Medicine*, 27:191–197.

Goldberg LR (1993) The structure of phenotypic personality traits, *The American Psychologist*, 48(1):26–34.

Goldin I et al (2012) *Exceptional People: How Migration Shaped Our World and Will Define Our Future*, Princeton, NJ: Princeton University Press.

Gomez P (2015) The privilege of protection, *The Magazine of the Writer's Union of Canada*, 43(2):18.

González FJ (2016) Only what is human can truly be foreign: The trope of immigration as a creative force in psychoanalysis (pp15–38) in J Beltsiou (Ed) *Immigration in Psychoanalysis: Locating Ourselves*, London: Routledge.

Goodwin-Gill GS (2001) After the cold war: Asylum and the refugee concept move on, *Forced Migration Review*, 10:14–16.

Gordon E & Jones M (1999) *Portable Roots: Voices of Expatriate Wives*, Brussels: Peter Lang.

Gordon MM (1964) *Assimilation in American Life: The Role of Race, Religion, and National Origins*, Oxford: Oxford University Press.

Gordon MM (1978) *Human Nature, Class, and Ethnicity*, Oxford: Oxford University Press.

Government of Canada (2018) *Immigration-refugees-citizenship*, www.canada.ca/en/immigration-refugees-citizenship/services/refugees.

Government of Canada (2019) *The Truth and Reconciliation Commission*, www.rcaanc-cirnac.gc.ca/eng/1450124405592/1529106060525.

Granberg-Michaelson W (2013) The hidden immigration impact on American churches, *Washington Post* (Sept 23).

Grant T (2009/2018) Immigrants overqualified, earn less, *The Globe & Mail*, www.theglobeandmail.com/report-on-business/immigrants/.

Graphic Science (2016) Pushed out, *Scientific American* (Oct).

Grauer P (2018) BC has the most "anchor babies", *Star Metro Vancouver* (Nov 23).

Greenwood ML & Hart GL (2005) The early history of migration research, *International Regional Science Review*, 26(1):3–37.

Grinberg L & Grinberg R (1984) A psychoanalytic study of migration, *Journal of the American Psychoanalytic Association*, 32(1):13–38.

Grinberg L & Grinberg R (1989) *Psychoanalytic Perspectives in Migration & Exile*, New Haven, CT: Yale University Press.

Grønseth AS (2013) *Being Human, Being Migrant: Sense of Self and Well-being*, New York: Berghahn Books.

Groody DG (2009) Crossing the divide: Foundations of a theology of migration and refugees, *Theological Studies*, 70(3):638–667.

Groody DG & Campese G (2008) *A Promised Land, A Perilous Journey: Theological Perspectives on Migration*, Notre Dame, IN: University of Notre Dame Press.

Grosjean F (2010) *Life with Two Languages: An Introduction to Bilingualism*, Boston, MA: Harvard University Press.

Grosskurth P (1986) *Melanie Klein: Her World and Her Work*, New York: Random House.

Grut L et al (2006) General practitioners' experiences with refugee patients, *Den Norske Laegeforening: Tidsskrift for Praktisk Medicin*, 126(10):1318–1320.

Guarnaccia PJ (1997) A cross-cultural perspective on anxiety disorders (pp3–20) in S Friedman (Ed) *Cultural Issues in the Treatment of Anxiety*, New York: Guilford Press.

Gubhaju B & de Jong GF (2009) Individual *vs* household migration decision rules, *International Migration*, 47(1):31–61.

Guerra JEC (2008) A theology of migration (pp243–270) in D Groody & G Campese (Eds) *A Promised Land, A Perilous Journey: Theological Perspectives on Migration*, Notre Dame, IN: University of Notre Dame Press.

Guibernau M (2013) *Belonging: Solidarity and Division in Modern Societies*, Cambridge: Polity.

Guild E (2009) *Security & Migration in the 21st Century*, Cambridge: Polity Press.

Guiso L (2008) Discussion (pp697–698) in G Facchini & AM Mayda (Eds) From individual attitudes towards migrants to migration policy outcomes, *Economic Policy*, 23(56):652–713.

Gullahorn JT & Gullahorn JE (1963) An extension of the U-Curve Hypothesis, *Journal of Social Issues*, 19(3):33–47.

Gunning IR (1989) Expanding the international definition of refugee, *Fordham International Law Journal*, 13(1):35–85.

Guri T (2015) Motherhood, agency and sacrifice in narratives on female migration for care work, *Sociology*, 49(1):56–71.

Gurieva S et al (2015) Migration as an indicator of people's social and psychological stability, *Psychology in Russia*, 8(1):61–73.

Haag M (2019) Thousands of immigrant children said they were sexually abused in U.S. detention centers, *New York Times*, www.nytimes.com/2019/02/27/us/immigrant-children.

Haberkorn G (1981) The migration decision-making process (pp252–278) in GF de Jong & RW Gardner (Eds) *Migration Decision Making*, New York: Pergamon Policy Studies on International Development.

Haddad YY (2009) The shaping of Arab and Muslim identity in the US (pp246–276) in Haddad YY, Senzai F & Smith JI (eds). *Educating the Muslims of America*, Oxford: Oxford University Press.

Hagan J & Straut-Eppsteiner H (2019) Religion on the move: The place of religion in different stages of the migration experience (pp260–268) in SJ Gold & SJ Nawyn (Eds) *Handbook of Migration Studies*, London: Routledge.

Hagen-Zanker J (2008) *Why do People Migrate?* Working Paper MGSoG/2008/WP002, Maastricht Graduate School of Governance https://mpra.ub.

Haines G (2007) Mapped: The best (and worst) countries for gender equality, *The Telegraph* (Nov 4), www.telegraph.co.uk/travel/maps-and-graphics/.

Hajratwala M (2008) *Leaving India: My Family's Journey from Five Villages to Five Continents*, Boston, MA: Houghton Mifflin.

Hale S & Kadoda G (2016) *Networks of Knowledge Production in Sudan*, Lanham, MD: Lexington Books.

Hall JA & Sharp D (2008) *Marie-Louise Von Franz: The Classic Jungian Tradition*, Toronto: Inner City Books.

Hall JC et al (2012) US immigration policy in the 21st century, *Cato Journal*, 32 (1):201–220.
Hall S & Schwartz B (2017) *Familiar Stranger: A Life between Two Islands*, Durham, NC: Duke University Press.
Halperin S (2004) The relevance of immigration in the psychodynamic formulation of psychotherapy with immigrants, *Applied Psychoanalytic Studies*, 1(2):92–120.
Halseth G & Sullivan L (2003) "The bright lights of the city": Intra-regional migration and the challenge for resource-dependent towns BC, *Geography Research Forum*, 23:138–168.
Handlin O (1951/2002) *The Uprooted* (2nd Ed), Philadelphia, PA: University of Pennsylvania Press.
Hanna SS & Aris ES (2017) *Abducted in Iraq: A Priest in Baghdad*, Notre Dame, IN: University of Notre Dame Press.
Haour-Knipe M (2002) *Moving Families: Expatriation, Stress and Coping*, London: Routledge.
Harari YN (2018) *21 Lessons for the 21st Century*, London: Jonathan Cape.
Harding ME (1933/1970) *The Way of All Women*, New York: Putnam Publishing.
Hargreaves A (1995) Perceptions of place among writers of Algerian immigrant origin in France (pp89–100) in R King et al (Eds) *Writing across Worlds*, London: Routledge.
Hargreaves A (2010) Third-generation Algerians in France, *The French Review*, 83 (6):1290–1299.
Harris A et al (2013) LPN Perspectives of factors that affect nurse mobility in Canada, *Nursing Leadership*, 26:70–78.
Harris N (2007) The economics & politics of the free movement of people (pp33–50) in A Pécoud & P De Guchteneire (Eds) *Migration without Borders*, New York: UNESCO & Berghahn Books.
Hart J (2008) *Years of Conflict: Adolescence, Political Violence and Displacement*, New York: Berghahn Books.
Hashemnezhad H et al (2013) Sense of place and place attachment, *International Journal of Architecture and Urban Development*, 3(1):5–13.
Hastie B (2017) The inaccessibility of justice for migrant workers, *Windsor Yearbook of Access to Justice*, 34 (2):20–39.
Haug S (2008) Migration networks and migration decision-making, *Journal of Ethnic and Migration Studies*, 34(4):585–605.
Hayes BC & Dowds L (2006) Social contact, cultural marginality or economic self-interest? *Journal of Ethnic and Migration Studies*, 32(3):455–476.
Hazan C & Shaver P (1987) Romantic love conceptualized as an attachment process, *Journal of Personality and Social Psychology*, 52(3):511–524.
Heath AF & Tilley JR (2005) British national identity and attitudes towards immigration, *International Journal on Multicultural Societies*, 7(2):119–132.
Hébert GA et al (2018) An agent-based model to identify migration pathways of refugees (pp45–58) in L Perez et al (Eds) *Agent-Based Models and Complexity Science in the Age of Geospatial Big Data*, Cham: Springer.
Heidegger M (1927/2008) *On Being and Time*, London: Routledge.
Heidegger M & Stambaugh J (1969/2002) *Identity and Difference*, Chicago, IL: University of Chicago Press.

Heine SJ & Buchtel EE (2009) Personality: The universal and the culturally specific, *Annual Review of Psychology*, 60(1):369–394.
Hellwig T & Sinno A (2017) Different groups, different threats: Public attitudes towards immigrants, *Journal of Ethnic and Migration Studies*, 43(3):339–358.
Hendel T & Kagan I (2011) Professional image and intention to emigrate among Israeli nurses, *Nurse Education Today*, 31(3):259–262.
Heptinstall E et al (2004) PTSD and depression in refugee children, *European Child Adolescent Psychiatry*, 13:373–380.
Herberg E (1989) *Ethnic Groups in Canada: Adaptations and Transitions*, Scarborough: Nelson.
Herberg W (1955/1985) *Protestant-Catholic-Jew: An Essay in American Religious Sociology*, Chicago, IL: University of Chicago Press.
Hermansson AC et al (2002) The mental health of war-wounded refugees, *Journal of Nervous and Mental Disease*, 190(6):374–380.
Hermansson AC & Timpka T (1999) "How do you feel?": A self-rating scale for measuring well-being in refugees, *Transcultural Psychology*, 36(5):317–328.
Hesse D & Main M (1999) Second-generation effects of unresolved trauma in non-maltreating parents, *Psychoanalytic Inquiry*, 19(4):481–540.
Hesse D & Main M (2006) Frightened, threatening, and dissociative parental behavior in low-risk samples, *Development and Psychopathology*, 18(2):309–343.
Hier SP & Bolaria BS (2006) *Identity and Belonging: Rethinking Race and Ethnicity in Canadian Society*, Toronto: Canadian Scholars' Press.
Higson-Smith C & Bro F (2010) Tortured exiles on the streets, *Intervention*, 8(1):14–28.
Hill A (2018) The Briefing: Migration: How many people are on the move around the world. *Guardian*, Sept 10, 2018, www.theguardian.com/news/2018/sep/10/migration-how-many-people-are-on-the-move-around-the-world
Hillman J (1975) *Revisioning Psychology*, New York: Harper & Row.
Hinds D (1966/2001) *Journey to an Illusion: The West Indian in Britain*, London: Bogle-l'Ouverture Press.
Hirschman A (1970) *Exit, Voice & Loyalty*, Boston, MA: Harvard University Press.
Hirschman C (2004) The role of religion in the origins and adaptation of immigrant groups in the United States, *International Migration Review*, 38(3):1206–1233.
Hirschman C et al (1999) *Handbook of International Migration: The American Experience*, New York: Russell Sage Foundation.
Hitchcott N (2006) *Calixthe Beyala: Performances of Migration*, Liverpool: Liverpool University Press.
Hjälm A (2014) The "Stayers": Dynamics of lifelong sedentary behaviour in an urban context, *Population Space & Place*, 20(6):569–580.
Hjerm M (1998) National identities, national pride and xenophobia: A comparison of four Western countries, *Acta Sociologica*, 41(24):335–347.
Hjerm M (2001) Education, xenophobia and nationalism, *Journal of Ethnic and Migration Studies*, 27(1):37–60.
Hodes M (2001) Health needs of asylum seekers and refugees, *British Medical Journal*, 323(7306):229.
Hoffman E (1994) *The Drive for Self: Alfred Adler & the Founding of Individual Psychology*, Reading, MA: Addison-Wesley.

Hoffman E (2016) Out of exile: Some thought on exile as dynamic condition (pp211–216) in J Beltsiou (Ed) *Immigration in Psychoanalysis: Locating Ourselves*, London: Routledge.

Hoffman HS (1996) *Amorous Turkeys and Addicted Ducklings*, Sarasota, FL: Authors Cooperative.

Hollenbach D (2016) The rights of refugees: Who is responsible for people forced into flight? *America*, 214(1):14–17.

Holman EA & Silver RC (1998) Getting "stuck" in the past, *Journal of Personality and Social Psychology*, 74(5):1146–1163.

Holmes TH & Rahe RH (1967) The social readjustment rating scale, *Journal of Psychosomatic Research*, 11(2):213–221.

Holpuch A (2019) US to remove limit on how long immigrant children can be detained, *The Guardian* (Aug 17).

Holtz TH (1998) Refugee trauma *versus* torture trauma, *Journal of Nervous and Mental Disease*, 186(1):24–34.

Homans P (1979) *Jung in Context*, Chicago, IL: University of Chicago Press.

Homer (1946) *The Odyssey*, Harmondsworth, Middlesex: Penguin.

Hondagneu-Sotelo P (1994) *Gendered Transitions: Mexican Experiences of Immigration*, Oakland, CA: University of California Press.

Hopcke RH (1995) *Persona: Where Sacred Meets Profane*, Boston, MA: Shambhala.

Hopcke RH (1998) *A Guided Tour of the Collected Works of CG Jung*, Boston, MA: Shambhala.

Hopper T (2018) Canada will soon have more illegal border crossers than Syrian refugees, *National Post* (May 1).

Horwood C et al (2018) *Mixed Migration Review 2018*, Geneva: Mixed Migration Centre.

Houle R & Maheux H (2017) Children with an immigrant background, *Statistics Canada*.

Howe S (2003) Britishness and multiculturalism (pp3–46) in R Cuperus et al (Eds) *The Challenge of Diversity*, Innsbruck: Studienverlag.

Hron M (2007) The Czech émigré experience of return after 1989, *Slavonic and East European Review*, 85(1):47–78.

Hron M (2009) *Translating Pain: Immigrant Suffering in Literature & Culture*, Toronto: University of Toronto Press.

Hua A (2005) Diasporic and cultural memory (pp191–208) in V Agnew & (Ed) *Diaspora, Memory and Identity*, Toronto: University of Toronto Press.

Hubert G (1994) Symbolic ethnicity and symbolic religiosity, *Ethnic and Racial Studies*, 17(4):4577–4592.

Hugo GJ (1981) Village-community ties, village norms, and ethnic and social networks (pp186–224) in GF De Jong & RW Gardner (Eds) *Migration Decision Making*, New York: Pergamon Press.

Human Rights Watch (2003) *Trapped by Inequality: Bhutanese Refugee Women in Nepal*, www.hrw.org/reports/2003/nepal0903/.

Human Rights Watch (2017) *In Custody: Police Torture and Abductions in Turkey* (Oct 12), www.hrw.org/report/2017/10/12/custody/police-torture-and-abductions-turkey.

Humphries N et al (2013) A cycle of brain gain, waste and drain—a qualitative study of non-EU migrant doctors in Ireland, *Human Resources for Health*, 11:63.
Hurh WM & Kim KC (1990) Religious participation of Korean immigrants in the United States, *Journal for the Scientific Study of Religion*, 29(1):19–34.
Husain S (1997) *The Goddess*, Alexandra, VA: Time-Life Books.
Hyde M & McGuinness M (1999) *Introducing Jung*, Duxford, Cambridge: Icon Books.
Ibrahim Y & Howarth A (2018) Review of humanitarian refuge in the United Kingdom, *Politics & Policy*, 46(3):348–391.
Idemudia ES et al (2013) Migration challenges among Zimbabwean refugees before, during and post-arrival in South Africa, *Journal of Injury & Violence Research*, 5(1):17–27.
Ignatieff M (1993) *Blood & Belonging: Journeys into the New Nationalism*, Toronto: Viking.
International Crisis Group (2018) *Mexico's Southern Border*, www.crisisgroup.org.
International Justice Center (2018) *Asylum & the Rights of Refugees*, https://ijrcenter.org.
Ipp H (2016) Nell—A bridge to the amputated self: The impact of immigration on continuities and discontinuities of self (pp41–52) in J Beltsiou (Ed) *Immigration in Psychoanalysis*, London: Routledge.
Iredale R & D'arcy B (1992) *The Continuing Struggle: Refugees in the Australian Labour Market*, Canberra: Australian Government Publication Service.
Isphording IE (2015) *What Drives the Language Proficiency of Immigrants?* Germany: IZA.
Iwamura JN (2009) Critical faith: Japanese Americans and the birth of a new civil religion (pp135–165) in RD Alba et al (Eds) *Religion and Immigration in America*, New York: New York University Press.
Jacobi J (1959/1974) *Complex Archetype Symbol in the Psychology of C.G. Jung*, Princeton, NJ: Princeton University Press.
Jacoby M (1985) *Longing for Paradise*, Boston, MA: Sigo Press.
Jaffe PG et al (2003) Vicarious trauma in judges, *Juvenile and Family Court Journal*, 54(4):1–9.
Jain A (2005) Is arranged marriage really any worse than Craigslist? *New York* (Mar 25).
Jamieson L (2000) Migration, place and class, *Sociological Review*, 48(2):203–224.
Janis IL & Mann L (1979) *Decision Making: A Psychological Analysis of Conflict, Choice, and Commitment*, New York: Free Press.
Janmaat JG (2006) Popular conceptions of nationhood in old and new European member states, *Ethnic and Racial Studies*, 29(1):50–78.
Janoff-Bulman R (1992) *Shattered Assumptions*, New York: Free Press.
Jarrett JL (1997) *Jung's Seminar on Nietzsche's Zarathustra*, Princeton, NJ: Princeton University Press.
Jedwab J (2012) Identities, interest, and immigration integration in the 21st century (pp274–290) in J Frideres & J Biles (Eds) *International Perspectives: Integration & Inclusion*, Montreal & Kingston: McGill Queen's University Press.
Jenkinson C et al (2001) An assessment of the construct validity of the SF-12 summary scores across ethnic groups, *Journal of Public Health Medicine*, 23:187–194.

Jensen ER (2019) personal communications.

Jensen PM (2016) *Artist Emily Carr & the Spirit of the Land*, London: Routledge.

Jensen PM (2018) American & Canadian cultural complexes, *Jung Journal*, 12 (2):91–108.

Jensen PS & Shaw J (1993) Children as victims of war, *Journal of the American Academy of Child and Adolescent Psychiatry*, 32:697–708.

Johnson NC (2012) Global journeys: From transnationalism to diaspora, *Journal of International and Global Studies*, 4(1):41–58.

Jones E (1953–1957) *The Life and Work of Sigmund Freud* (3 vols), New York: Basic Books.

Jones EE (1998) Major developments in five decades of social psychology (vol 1, pp3–57) in DT Gilbert et al (Eds) *The Handbook of Social Psychology* (4th ed.), Boston, MA: McGraw-Hill.

Jones L & Kafetsios K (2002) Assessing adolescent mental health in war-affected societies, *Child Abuse and Neglect*, 26:1059–1080.

Jones S, et al (2018) Human-trafficking prevention is not sexy, *Journal of Human Trafficking*, 4(3):231–255.

Judson DH (1990) Human migration decision-making, *Behavioral Science*, 35 (4):281–289.

Jung CG (1941/1977) *Post Script to the Vision Seminars, Spring 1977*, Zurich: Spring Publications.

Jung CG (1950/1989) *The Symbolic Life, (Collected Works of C.G. Jung, Volume 18)*, Princeton, NJ: Princeton University Press.

Jung CG (1953/1993) *Psychology and Alchemy (Collected Works of C.G. Jung, Volume 12)*, Princeton, NJ: Princeton University Press.

Jung CG (1954/1985) *The Archetypes and the Collective Unconscious (Collected Works of C.G. Jung, Volume 9i)*, Princeton, NJ: Princeton University Press.

Jung CG (1954/1985) *Practice of Psychotherapy (Collected Works of C.G. Jung, Volume 16)*, Princeton, NJ: Princeton University Press.

Jung CG (1955/1970) *Mysterium Coniunctionis (Collected Works of C.G. Jung, Volume 14)*, Princeton, NJ: Princeton University Press.

Jung CG (1956/1990) *Symbols of Transformation (Collected Works of C.G. Jung, Volume 5)* Princeton, NJ: Princeton University Press.

Jung CG (1958/1977) *Two Essays on Analytical Psychology (Collected Works of C.G. Jung, Volume 7)*, Princeton, NJ: Princeton University Press.

Jung CG (1960/1969) *The Structure and Dynamics of the Psyche (Collected Works of C.G. Jung, Volume 8)*, Princeton, NJ: Princeton University Press.

Jung CG (1961/1989) with A Jaffé (Ed) & R & C Winston (trans) *Memories, Dreams, Reflections*, New York: Random House.

Jung CG (1964) *Civilization in Transition, Collective Works (Collected Works of C.G. Jung, Volume 10)*, Princeton, NJ: Princeton University Press.

Jung CG (1967/1983) *Alchemical Studies (Collected Works of C.G. Jung, Volume 13)*, Princeton, NJ: Princeton University Press.

Jung CG (1971/1990) *Psychological Types (Collective Works of C.G. Jung, Volume 6)*, Princeton, NJ: Princeton University Press.

Jung CG (1998) *Jung's Seminar on Neitzsche's Zarathustra*, Princeton, NJ: Princeton University Press.
Jung E (1957/1981) *Animus and Anima: Two Essays*, Dallas, TX: Spring Publications.
Jung E & von Franz M-L (1960/1970) *The Grail Legend*, Princeton, NJ: Princeton University Press.
Junger S (2016) *Tribe: On Homecoming and Belonging*, Toronto: HarperCollins.
Juni S (2016) Survivor guilt: A critical review from the lens of the Holocaust, *International Review of Victimology*, 22(3):321–337.
Kage T (2012) *Uprooted Again: Japanese Canadians Move to Japan after World War II*, Victoria, BC: Ti-Jean Press.
Kagitcibasi C (1987) Alienation of the outsider: The plight of migrants, *International Migration*, 25(2):195–210.
Kahn C (1997a) Four women: Immigrants in cross-cultural marriages (pp199–220) in PH Elovitz & C Kahn (Eds) *Immigrant Experiences*, Madison, NJ: Fairleigh Dickinson University Press.
Kahn C (1997b) Conclusion (pp274–284) in PH Elovitz & C Kahn (Eds) *Immigrant Experiences*, Madison, NJ: Fairleigh Dickinson University Press.
Kahn C (2017) A brief introduction to mass migration: Then and now, *The Psychoanalytic Review*, 104(Special Issue: Mass Migration):643–660.
Kalff D (2004) *Sandplay: A Psychotherapeutic Approach to the Psyche*, Hot Springs, AZ: Temenos Press.
Kallen E (1982/1995) *Ethnicity & Human Rights in Canada*, Oxford: Oxford University Press.
Kandel W & Massey DS (2002) The culture of Mexican migration, *Social Forces*, 80(3):981–1004.
Kaplan M & Marks G (1990) Adverse affects of acculturation, *Social Science & Medicine*, 30(12):1313–1319.
Karpathakis A (2001) Conclusion: New York City's religions (388–394) in T Carnes & A Karpathakis (Eds) *In New York Glory: Religions in the City*, New York: New York University.
Kassam Z (2016) The challenges of migration & the construction of religious identities (pp91–121) in JB Saunders et al (Eds) *Intersections of Religion and Migration Issues at the Global Crossroads*, New York: Palgrave McMillan.
Kawate J (2018) Migrants look to Asia, the new land of opportunity: More workers turn east as US and Europe shut their doors, *Nikkei Asian Review*, https://asia.nikkei.com/Economy/Migrants.
Keely C (1992) The resettlement of women and children refugees, *Migration World*, 20(4):14–18.
Kelly JG et al (1994) Creating social settings for diversity thesis (pp452–464) in E Trickett et al (Eds) *Human Diversity: Perspectives on People in Context*, San Francisco, CA: Jossey Bass.
Kelly M (2013) *Onward Migration: The Transnational Trajectories of Iranians Leaving Sweden*, Sweden: Department of Social and Economic Geography, Uppsala University.

Kennan J & Walker JR (2012) *Modeling Individual Migration Decisions*, Madison, WI: University of Wisconsin-Madison and the National Bureau of Economics Research Inc. (NBER).

Kenny K (2013) *Diaspora: A Very Short Introduction*, Oxford: Oxford University Press.

Keung N (2018) World's displaced population hit record in 2017: UN, *Star Metro Vancouver* (July 19).

Khoo S-E et al (2008) Which skilled temporary migrants become permanent residents and why? *International Migration Review*, 42 (1):93–226.

Khorsandi S (2009) *A Beginner's Guide to Acting English*, Croydon: Ebury Press.

Kim JH & Min PG (Eds) (2001) *Religions in Asian America: Building Faith Communities*, Lanham, MD: AltaMira Press.

King James (2014) Psalm 137, *The Holy Bible*, www.kingjamesbibleonline.org.

King R et al (1995) Preface (ppix–xvi) in R King et al (Eds) *Writing Across Worlds*, London: Routledge.

King S & Winter A (2013) *Migration, Settlement and Belonging in Europe, 1500–1930s: Comparative Perspectives*, New York: Berghahn Books.

Kingsley P (2016) *The New Odyssey: The Story of Europe's Refugee Crisis*, London: Guardian Books.

Kinnvall C & Nesbitt-Larking P (2011) *The Political Psychology of Globalization: Muslims in the West*, Oxford: Oxford University Press.

Kira IA et al (2017) Screening for psychopathology using the Three Factors Model of the Structure of Psychopathology, *Psychology*, 8(14):2410–2427.

Kivisto P (2002) *Multiculturalism in a Global Society*, Oxford: Blackwell Publishers.

Kivisto P (2014) *Religion and Immigration Migrant Faiths in North America and Western Europe*, Cambridge: Polity Press.

Klabunde A & Willekens F (2016) Decision-making in agent-based models of migration, *European Journal of Population*, 32:73–97.

Klein M (1921–1945) *The Collected Writings of Melanie Klein*, London: Hogarth Press.

Kleiner H (1970) On nostalgia, *Bulletin of the Philadelphia Association for Psychoanalysis*, 20:11–30.

Klingman A (2002) Children under stress of war (pp359–380) in A La Greca et al (Eds) *Helping Children Cope with Disasters and Terrorism*, Washington, DC: APA Books.

Knafo D & Yaari A (1997) Leaving the Promised Land: Israeli immigrants in the US (pp221–240) in PH Elovitz & C Kahn (Eds) *Immigrant Experiences*, Madison, NJ: Fairleigh Dickinson University Press.

Kniveton D et al (2008) *Climate Change and Migration, Migration Research Series 33*, Geneva:International Organization for Migration.

Kniveton DR et al (2011) Agent-based model simulations of future changes in migration flows for Burkina Faso, *Global Environmental Change*, 21(S1):S34.

Knott K (2016) Living religious practices (pp71–90) in JB Saunders et al (Eds) *Intersections of Religion and Migration Issues at the Global Crossroads*, New York: Palgrave McMillan.

Knudsen K (1997) Scandinavian neighbours with different character? Attitudes towards immigrants and national identity in Norway and Sweden, *Acta Sociologica*, 40(3):223–243.

Kobayashu A (1995) Birds of passage or squawking ducks: Writing across generations of Japanese-Canadian literature (pp216–228) in R King et al (Eds) *Writing across Worlds*, London: Routledge.

Kohls RL (2001) *Survival Kit for Overseas Living* (4th ed.), Boston, MA: Nicholas Brealy.

Kohn H (1944/2017) *The Idea of Nationalism: A Study in Its Origins and Background*, London: Routledge.

Kohn H (1964) *Living in a World Revolution*, New York: A Trident Press Book.

Koikkalainen S & Kyle D (2016) Imagining mobility: The prospective cognition question in migration research, *Journal of Ethnic & Migration Studies*, 41(5):759–776.

Krabbendam L & van Os J (2005) Schizophrenia and urbanicity: A major environmental influence-conditional on genetic risk, *Schizophrenia Bulletin*, 31:795–799.

Krahn H & Gartrell JW (1981) Social mobility in a Canadian single-industry community, *Canadian Journal of Sociology*, 6(3):307–324.

Krahn H et al (1981) The quality of family life in a resource community, *Canadian Journal of Sociology*, 6(3):307–324.

Kristeva J (1991) *Strangers to Ourselves*, New York: Columbia University Press.

Kroll JF et al (2014) Two languages in mind, *Current Directions in Psychological Science*, 23(3):159–163.

Krzyżanowski M & Wodak R (2008) Multiple identities, migration and belonging (pp95–114) in CR Caldas-Coulthard & R Iedema (Eds) *Identity Trouble*, London: Palgrave Macmillan.

Kuhn MT & McPartland TS (1954) An empirical investigation of self-attitudes, *American Sociological Review*, 19:68–76.

Kulu H (1998) Ethnic return migration, *International Migration*, 36(3):313–336.

Kundera M & Asher L (trans) (2003) *Ignorance*, New York: Harper Perennial.

Kundu S (2016) Modern mythologies (pp101–107) in P Bhattacharya (Ed) *Good Girls Marry Doctors: South Asian American Daughters and Obedience and Rebellion*, San Francisco, CA: Aunt Lute Books.

Kuo BCH (2014) Coping, acculturation, and psychological adaptation among migrants, *Health Psychology & Behavioral Medicine*, 2(1):16–33.

Kuo BCH & Gargi R (2006) Development of the Cross-Cultural Coping Scale, *Measurement and Evaluation in Counselling and Development*, 39:161–181.

Kurien P (2005) Being young, brown, and Hindu: The identity struggles of second generation Indian Americans, *Journal of Contemporary Ethnography*, 34:434–469.

Kurien PA (2007) *A Place at the Multicultural Table: The Development of an American Hinduism*, New Brunswick, NJ: Rutgers University Press.

Kurien P (2017) *Ethnic Church Meets Megachurch*, New York: New York University Press.

Kuriloff E (2012) History means interpretation, *Contemporary Psychoanalysis*, 48(3):367–393.

Kuriloff EA (2014) *Contemporary Psychoanalysis & the Legacy of the 3rd Reich*, London: Routledge.

Kuzio T (2002) The myth of the civic state, *Ethnic and Racial Studies*, 25(1):20–39.

Kwong K et al (2009) Factors associated with reverse-migration separation among a cohort of low-income Chinese immigrant families in New York City, *Social Work in Health Care*, 48(3):348–359.
Kymlicka W (1995) *Multicultural Citizenship*, Oxford: Clarendon.
Kymlicka W (1998) *Finding Our Way: Rethinking Ethnocultural Relations in Canada*, Oxford: Oxford University Press.
Kymlicka W (2001) *Politics in the Vernacular: Nationalism, Multiculturalism, and Citizenship*, Oxford: Oxford University Press.
La Vecchia-Mikkola VJ (2013) *Longing to Return and Spaces of Belonging, Serial B, Humaniora*, University of Turku, Finland.
Laghi F et al (2009) Suicidal ideation and time perspective in high school students, *European Psychiatry*, 24(1):41–46.
Lancee B & Sarrasin O (2015) Educated preferences or selection effects? A Longitudinal analysis of the impact of educational attainment on attitudes towards immigrants, *European Sociological Review*, 31(4):490–501.
Landau J (1982) Therapy with families in cultural transition (pp552–572) in M McGoldrick et al (Eds) *Ethnicity and Family Therapy*, New York: Guilford Press.
Langerberg S & Wesseling H (2016) Making sense of Weick's organising, *Philosophy of Management*, 15(3):221–240.
Laoire CN et al (2011) *Childhood and Migration in Europe*, London: Routledge.
Laor N & Wolmer L (2002) Children exposed to disaster (pp925–937) in M Lewis (Ed) *Child and Adolescent Psychiatry: A Comprehensive Textbook*, Philadelphia, PA: Lippincott Williams & Wilkins.
Laub D (2016) On leaving home and the flight from trauma (pp169–184) in J Beltsiou (Ed) *Immigration in Psychoanalysis*, London: Routledge.
Laventure L (2017) Central American corridor a dangerous route for migrants heading to Canada, *CBC News*, Feb 22, www.cbc.ca/news/world/.
Lawler S (2008/2014) *Identity: Sociological Perspectives*, Cambridge: Polity Press.
Lazerwitz B & Rowitz L (1964) The Three-generations hypothesis, *American Journal of Sociology*, 69(5):529–538.
Le Bon G (1895/2009) *Psychology of Crowds*, Southampton: Sparkling Books.
Leander K & de Haan M (2015) *Media & Migration*, London: Routledge.
Lee C (2009) Theories of immigration, *Journal of Human Behavior in the Social Environment*, 19(6):663–674.
Lee CS et al (2012) On the cognitive benefits of cultural experience, *Applied Cognitive Psychology*, 26(5):768–778.
Lee E & Moon M (2013) Korean nursing students' intention to migrate abroad, *Nurse Education Today*, (12):1517–1522.
LegalLine.ca (2018) Who qualifies as a refugee in Canada? www.legalline.ca/legal-answers/who-qualifies-as-a-refugee-in-canada/.
Lemming G (1992) *The Pleasures of Exile*, Ann Arbor, MI: University of Michigan Press.
Leong C-H & Ward C (2006) Cultural values and attitudes toward immigrants and multiculturalism, *International Journal of Intercultural Relations*, 30(6):799–810.
Levin AP & Greisberg S (2003) Vicarious trauma in attorneys, *Pace Law Review*, 24(1):245–252.

Levitt P (2001) *The Transnational Villagers*, Berkeley, CA: University of California Press.
Levitt P et al (2003) International perspectives on transnational migration, *International Migration Review*, 37(3):565–568.
Levitt P (2004) Transnational migrants, *Migration Policy* (Oct 1).
Levy-Warren M (1987) Moving to a new culture (pp300–315) in J Bloom-Feshbach et al (Eds) *The Psychology of Separation and Loss*, San Francisco, CA & London: Jossey-Bass Inc.
Lewicka M (2014) In search of roots (pp49–60) in LC Manzo & PD Wright (Eds) *Place Attachment*, London: Routledge.
Lewin BD (1946) Sleep, the mouth, and the dream screen, *Psychoanalytic Quarterly*, 15:419–434.
Li FL et al (1996) Migrating to learn and learning to migrate, *International Journal of Population Geography*, 2(1):51–67.
Liao P-S (2001) Contextual analysis of rural migration intention, *International Journal of Comparative Sociology*, 42(5):435.
Lichtenberg JD (1989) *Psychoanalysis and Motivation*, Hillsdale, NJ: Analytic Press.
Lin AC (2009) Muslim, Arab &American (pp277–296) in R Alba et al (Eds) *Immigration and Religion in America*, New York: New York University Press.
Linderman P & Brayer-Hess M (2002) *Realities of Foreign Service Life*, Bloomington, IN: Writers Club Press.
Lineth HU et al (2018) Stress, trauma, and posttraumatic stress disorder in migrants, *Brazilian Journal of Psychiatry*, 40:220–225.
Live & Learn (2017) 10 multicultural holiday celebrations you may not be aware of, https://livelearn.ca/article/about-canada/9-multicultural-holiday-celebrations/.
Livermore DA (2011) *The Cultural Intelligence Difference*, New York: AMACOM.
Livni E (2016) Trees please: The Japanese practice of "forest bathing", *Quartz* (Oct 12).
Lobban G (2016) The immigrant analyst (pp69–86) in J Beltsiou (Ed) *Immigration in Psychoanalysis*, London: Routledge.
Loisos P (2002) Misconceiving refugees? (pp41–56) in RK Papadopoulos (Ed) *Therapeutic Care for Refugees: The Tavistock Clinic Series*, London: Karnac.
Long JC (2014) Diasporic families, *Annals of the Association of American Geographers*, 104(2):243–252.
Longo V et al (2017) The scales of general well-being (SGWB), *Personality and Individual Differences*, 109(April):148–159.
Looker D & Naylor T (2009) "At risk of being rural?" *Journal of Rural & Community Development*, 4(2):39–64.
Losi N (2006) *Lives Elsewhere: Migration and Psychic Malaise*, London: Karnac.
Loughry M (2003) *Psychosocial Concepts in Humanitarian Work with Children*, Washington, DC: National Academies Press.
Lovell DM (1997) Psychological adjustment among returned overseas aid workers, Unpublished PhD Thesis, University of Wales, Bangor.
Lowry C (2000) Mental health interventions for war affected children, *Children in Adversity*, www.childreninadversity.gov/.
Lubbers M & Scheepers P (2002) French Front National voting, *Ethnic and Racial Studies*, 25(1):120–149.

Lubkemann SC (2008) Involuntary immobility, *Journal of Refugee Studies*, 21 (4):454–475.
Lucassen L (2005) *The Immigrant Threat*, Urbana & Chicago, IL: University of Illinois Press.
Lukić V (2016) Understanding transit asylum migration, *International Migration*, 54 (4):31–43.
Lyons K (2018) Revealed: Asylum seekers' 20-year wait for Home Office ruling, *The Guardian* (Aug 17).
Lysgaard S (1955) Adjustment in a foreign society, *International Social Science Bulletin*, 7:45–51.
Machel G (2001) *The Impact of War on Children*, London: Hurst & Company.
Macksoud M et al (1993) Traumatic war experiences and their effects on children (pp625–633) in JP Wilson & B Raphael (Eds) *International Handbook of Traumatic Stress Syndromes*, New York: Plenum.
Maddens B et al (2000) National identity and attitude towards foreigners in multi-national states, *Journal of Ethnic and Migration Studies*, 26(1):45–60.
Madianou M & Miller D (2011) *Migration & New Media*, London: Routledge.
Madison G (2006) Existential migration, *Existential Analysis*, 17(2):238–260.
Madison G (2010) *Existential Migration*, Saarbrücken, Germany: Lambert Academic Publishing.
Magdol L (2002) Is moving gendered? *Sex Roles*, 47:553–560.
Magnan M-O (2006) *To Stay or Not to Stay: Migrations of Young Anglo-Quebecers*, Montréal: Institut national de la recherche scientifique (INRS).
Main M & Solomon J (1990) Procedures for identifying infants as disorganized/disoriented during the Ainsworth Strange Situation (pp121–160) in MT Greenberg et al (Eds) *The John D. And Catherine T. MacArthur Foundation Series on Mental Health and DevelopmenT. Attachment in the Preschool Years*, Chicago, IL: University of Chicago Press.
Malgady RG (1996) The question of cultural bias in assessment and diagnosis of ethnic minority clients, *Professional Psychology: Research and Practice*, 27 (1):73–77.
Manchandra R (2006) Contesting "Infantalisation" of Forced Migrant Women (p205–226) in NC Behera (Ed) *Gender Conflict & Migration*, New Delhi: Sage India.
Manzo L & Devine-Wright P (Eds) (2013) *Place Attachment*, London: Routledge.
Maor Z (2017) Hans Kohn: The idea of secularized nationalism, *Nations and Nationalism*, 23(4):1–21.
Maphosa F (2007) Remittances and development, *Development in Southern Africa*, 24(1):123–136.
Marcia JE (1973) Ego-identity status (pp340–354) in M Argyle (Ed) *Social Encounters*, Westminster: Penguin.
Marcia JE (2014) From industry to integrity, *Identity*, 14(3):165–176.
Marcus AP (2009) Brazilian immigration to the United States and the geographical imagination, *Geographical Review*, 99(4):481–498.
Marlin O (1994) Special issues in the analytic treatment of immigrants and refugees, *Issues in Psychoanalytic Psychology*, 16:7–16.

Marlin O (1997) Fleeing towards the new and yearning for the old (pp241–254) in PH Elovitz & C Kahn (Eds) *Immigrant Experiences*, Madison, NJ: Fairleigh Dickinson University Press.
Marsella AJ & Ring E (2003) Human migration and immigration (pp3–22) in L Adler & U Gielen (Eds) *Migration: Immigrants and Emigration in International Perspective*, Westport, CT: Greenwood Press.
Marshall TH (1964) *Class Citizenship & Social Development*, Garden City, NY: Doubleday.
Martin R (1982/1988) Truth, power, self (pp9–15) in L Martin et al (Eds) *Technologies of the Self: A Seminar with Michel Foucault*, Amherst: University of Massachusetts Press.
Martin SF (1991) *Refugee Women*, London: Zed Books.
Marx K (1984/1975) *Early Writings*, Harmondsworth: Penguin.
Maslow AH (1954/1987) *Motivation and Personality*, New York: Harper & Row Publishers.
Maslow AH (1962/2010) *Toward a Psychology of Being*, Eastford, CT: Martino Fine Books.
Mason G & Lelitro D (2018) Voyages into the Unknown, *Journal of Psychological Therapies*, 2(1):41–47.
Massey D, et al (1993) Theories of international migration: A review and appraisal, *Population and Development Review* 19(3):431–466.
Matthews C (2014) Can immigration save a struggling, disappearing Japan? *Fortune*, http://fortune.com/2014/11/20/japan-immigration-economy/.
McAuliffe M et al (2018) Understanding migration journeys from migrants' perspectives (pp171–190) in M McAuliffe & M Ruhs (Eds) *World Migration Report 2018*, Geneva: International Organization for Migration.
McAuliffe M & Ruhs M (2017) Report overview: Making sense of migration in an increasingly interconnected world (pp1–12) in M McAuliffe & M Ruhs (Eds) *World Migration Report 2018*, Geneva: International Organization for Migration (IOM).
McAuliffe M & Ruhs M (2018) Migrants: A global overview (pp13–42), *World Migration Report 2018*, Geneva: International Organization for Migration.
McConnan I & Uppard S (2001) *Children – Not Soldiers: Guidelines for Working with Child Soldiers and Children Associated with Fighting Forces*, London: Save the Children Fund.
McCrae RR & John OP (1992) An introduction to the five-factor model and its applications, *Journal of Personality*, 60(2):175–215.
McGinley E (2013) *Enduring Migration through the Life Cycle*, London: Karnac Books.
McHugh KE (1985) Reasons for migrating, *Sociology & Social Research*, 69(4):585–589.
McInerney JT (1997) Irish emigration as banishment (pp118–138) in PH Elovitz & C Kahn (Eds) *Immigrant Experiences*, Madison, NJ: Fairleigh Dickinson University Press.
McKay MT et al (2017) Temporal focus clusters differ meaningfully in terms of anxiety and depressive symptomatology, *Psychiatry Research*, 257:283–285.

McNally RJ (1996) Assessment of posttraumatic stress disorder in children, *Journal of School Psychology*, 34:147–161.
Meaders NY (1997) The transcultural self (pp47–59) in PH Elovitz & C Kahn (Eds) *Immigrant Experiences*, Madison, NJ: Fairleigh Dickinson University Press.
Meaders NY (2011) A story of adaptation told from ego-psychological perspectives, *International Forum of Psychoanalysis*, 20(4):242–249.
Meaders NY (2018) The Japanese psychology of resignation, *akirame*, and the writings of Kawabata, *International Forum of Psychoanalysis*, 28(1):47–54.
Médecins Sans Frontières (MSF) (2017) *Forced to Flee Central Americans Northern Triangle: A Neglected Humanitarian Crisis*, www.msf.org/sites/msf.org/files/msf_forced-to-flee-central-americas-northern-triangle.
Medrano JD (2005) Nation, citizenship and immigration in contemporary Spain, *International Journal on Multicultural Societies*, 7(2):133–156.
Megha C (2016) Daughter of mine (pp45–49) in P Bhattacharya (Ed) *Good Girls Marry Doctors*, San Francisco, CA: Aunt Lute Press.
Mehta P (1998) The emergence conflict, and integration of the bicultural self: Psychoanalysis of an adolescent daughter of South-Asian immigrant parents (pp131–168) in S Akhtar & S Kramer (Eds) *The Colors of Childhood: Separation-Individuation across Culture, Racial and Ethnic Differences*, London: Jason Aronson Inc.
Mendaglio S (2008) *Dabrowski's Theory of Positive Disintegration*, Tucson, AZ: Great Potentials Press Inc.
Menjívar C (2001) Latino immigrants and their perceptions of religious institutions, *Migraciones Internacionales*, 1:65–88.
Merriam-Webster.com *Localitis* www.merriam-webster.com/dictionary/localitis.
Merritt DL (1991) Spirit in the land, spirit in animals, spirit in people, *EcoJung.com*, www.dennismerrittjungiananalyst.com/Spirit_in_Land.htm.
Mihi-Ramirez A & Kumpikaite V (2013) The whys and wherefores of student international migration, *Economics & Management*, 18(2):351–359.
Miles C (1998) Mothers and others: Bonding, separation-individuation, and resultant ego development in different African-American cultures (pp81–112) in S Akhtar & S Kramer (Eds) *The Colors of Childhood: Separation-Individuation across Culture, Racial and Ethnic Differences*, London: Jason Aronson Inc.
Millender E & Lowe J (2017) Cumulative trauma among Mayas living in Southeast Florida, *Journal of Immigrant & Minority Health*, 19(3):598–605.
Miller EM (2019) An entire Lutheran denomination has declared itself a "sanctuary church body," signaling support for immigrants, *Washington Post, Religion News Service* (Aug 8).
Miller JC (2004) *The Transcendent Function: Jung's Model of Psychological Growth through Dialogue with the Unconscious*, Albany: State University of New York Press.
Miller KA & Boling BD (1990–1991) Golden streets, bitter tears: The Irish image of America during the era of mass migration, *Journal of American Ethnic History*, 10 (1/2):16.
Miller KE & Billings DL (1994) Playing to grow, *American Journal of Orthopsychiatry*, 64:346–356.

Miller SE (2010) The hegemonic illusion? Traditional strategic studies in context, *Security Dialogue*, 41(6):639–648.
Millon T & Davis RD (1993) The Millon adolescent personality, *Journal of Counselling & Development*, 71(5):570–574.
Min PG (1992) The structure and social functions of Korean immigrant churches in the United States, *International Migration Review*, 26:1370–1394.
Mincer J (1978) Family migration decisions, *Journal of Political Economy*, 86(5):749–773.
Mirksy J & Kaushinsky F (1989) Migration and growth, *Adolescence*, 24(95):725–740.
Mishra P (2018) The great protestor: Ghandi for the age of post-truth politics, *The New Yorker* (Oct 26):82–86.
Montero G (1977) *The Immigrants*, Toronto: James Lorimer & Co.
Montgomery E (1998) Refugee children from the Middle East, *Scandinavian Journal of Social Medicine*, 54(54):1–152.
Morais JM (1986) *Homesickness, Loss of Sacred Place*, CG Jung Institute Zurich thesis.
Morgan C et al (2010) Migration, ethnicity, and psychosis, *Schizophrenia Bulletin*, 36(4):655–664.
Morgan C & Fisher H (2007) Environment and schizophrenia, *Schizophrenia Bulletin*, 33(1):3–10.
Morgan G et al (2017) Exploring the relationship between post-migratory stressors and mental health for asylum seekers and refused asylum seekers, *Transcultural Psychiatry*, 54(5–6):653–674.
Morrison T (2017) *The Origin of Others*, Cambridge, MA: Harvard University Press.
Morse CE & Mudgett J (2018) Happy to be home: Place-based attachments, family ties, and mobility among rural stayers, *Professional Geographer*, 70(3):260–269.
Mostafa T (2015) *Social Stratification and Educational Inequalities*, London: London Institute of Education.
Mueller J et al (2011) Mental health of failed asylum seekers as compared with pending and temporarily accepted asylum seekers, *European Journal of Public Health* 21(2):184–189.
Mulder TJ et al (2002) *Evaluating Components of International Migration*, Population Division Working Paper #62, U.S. Census Bureau.
Munaweera N (2016) The only dates are the ones you eat and other laws of an immigrant girlhood (pp121–129) in P Bhattacharya (Ed) *Good Girls*, San Francisco, CA: Aunt Lute Books.
Musterd S (2008) Banlieues, the hyperghetto and advanced marginality, *City*, 12(1):107–114.
Nagra B (2017) *Securitized Citizens: Canadian Muslims' Experiences of Race Relations and Identity Formation Post–9/11*, Toronto: University of Toronto Press.
Nagra B & Maurutto P (2016) Crossing borders and managing racialized identities, *Canadian Journal of Sociology*, 41(2):165–194.
Nahirny VC & Fishman JA (1965) American immigrant groups, *Sociological Review*, NS-13:311–326.
Nash D (1991) The course of sojourner adaptation: A new test of the U-Curve hypothesis, *Human Organization*, 50(3):283–286.

National Geographic Partners (2018) *Genographic Project/Map of Human Migration*, https://genographic.nationalgeographic.com/human-journey/.
Ndeti K (1981) At home but alien (pp264–277) in L Eitinger & D Schwartz (Eds) *Strangers in the World*, Bern: Hans Huber Publishers.
Nee V (2003) *Remaking the American Mainstream: Assimilation and the New Immigration*, Cambridge, MA: Harvard University Press.
Nehru J (1936/1956) *An Autobiography*, London: Bodley Head.
Neistat A (2008) *Recurring Nightmare: State Responsibility for "Disappearances" and Abductions in Sri Lanka*, New York: Human Rights Watch.
Nentwich MM et al (2015) Staying and working at home or considering migrating, *Der Ophthalmologe: Zeitschrift Der Deutschen Ophthalmologischen Gesellschaft*, 112(5):429–434.
Nesbitt-Larking P et al (2014) *The Palgrave Handbook of Global Political Psychology*, London: Palgrave Macmillan.
Newbold KB (1996) Internal migration of the foreign-born in Canada, *International Migration Review*, 30(6):728–747.
News BBC (2018a) *Migration to Europe in Charts*, www.bbc.com/news/44660699.
News Desk (2018) Immigrants heading to America more educated than natives, *The Express Tribune, World* (Dec 19).
Ng E et al (2011) Official language proficiency and self-reported health among immigrants to Canada, *Health Reports, Statistics Canada*, Catalogue no. 82-003-X.
Ngabo G (2016) Toronto the diverse: BBC study declares city most diverse in the world, *Metro News* (May 16).
Nogle JM (1994) Internal migration for recent immigrants to Canada, *The International Migration Review*, 28(1):31–48.
Noh S et al (2006) *Korean Immigrants in Canada: Perspectives on Migration, Integration, and the Family*, Toronto: University of Toronto Press.
Norris FH & Hamblen JL (2004) Standardized self-report measures of civilian trauma and PTSD (pp63–102) in JP Wilson et al (Eds) *Assessing Psychological Trauma and PTSD*, New York: Guilford Press.
O'Brien, D (1968) *The Conscience of James Joyce*, Princeton, NJ: Princeton University Press.
O'Brien E (1986) *The Country Girls Trilogy and Epilogue*, New York: Farrar Straus Giroux.
Oberg K (1960) Cultural shock: Adjustment to new cultural environments, *Practical Anthropology*, 7(4):177–182.
Okin SM (1999) *Is Multiculturalism Bad for Women?* Princeton, NJ: Princeton University Press.
Okrent D (2019) *The Guarded Gate: Bigotry, Eugenics and the Law that Kept Two Generations of Jews, Italians, and Other European Immigrants Out of America*, New York: Scribner.
Oliver-Smith A (2009) Introduction: Development-forced displacement and resettlement (pp3–24) in A Oliver-Smith (Ed) *Development & Dispossession*, Santa Fe, NM: School for Advanced Research Press.
Olson E (1997) *The Human Animal: Personal Identity without Psychology*, Oxford: Oxford University Press.

Olson E (2007) *What are We? A Study in Personal Ontology*, Oxford: Oxford University Press.

Orfanos SD (1997) The Greek-American dance of continuity and integration (pp75–94) in PH Elovitz & C Kahn (Eds) *Immigrant Experiences*, Madison, NJ: Fairleigh Dickinson University Press.

Orgler H (1963) *Alfred Adler: The Man and His Work*, New York: Liveright.

Orsi RA & Alba R (2009) Passages in piety: Generational transitions and the social and religious incorporation of Italian Americans (pp32–55) in AJ Alba & J DeWind (Eds) *Immigration and Religion in America*, New York: New York University Press.

Orsillo SM (2001) Measures for acute stress disorder and posttraumatic stress disorder (pp255–307) in MM Antony & SM Orsillo (Eds) *Practitioner's Guide to Empirically Based Measures of Anxiety*, New York: Kluwer Academic/Plenum.

Ossman S (2013) *Moving Matters: Paths of Serial Migration*, Stanford, CA: Stanford University Press.

Østergaard-Nielsen E (2003) The politics of migrants' transnational political practices, *International Migration Review*, 37(3):760–786.

Ostrovsky Y et al (2008) *Internal Migration of Immigrants*, Statistics Canada, Analytical Studies Branch Research Paper Series.

Osumi M (2019) Number of foreign residents in Japan rose 6.6% in 2018, *The Japan Times*, www.japantimes.co.jp/news/2019/03/22/.

Otto R (1917/1923/1970) *The Idea of the Holy*, Oxford: Oxford University Press.

Ozcurumez S & Aker DY (2016) What moves the highly skilled and why? Comparing Turkish nationals in Canada and Germany, *International Migration*, 54 (3):61–72.

Özden Ç & Schiff M (2006) *International Migration, Remittances, and the Brain Drain*, Washington, DC: World Bank and Palgrave Macmillan.

Paas T & Hakapuu V (2012) Attitudes towards immigrants and the integration of ethnically diverse societies, *Eastern Journal of European Studies*, 3(2):161–176.

Paat Y-F (2013) Understanding motives for migration in working with immigrant families, *Journal of Human Behavior in the Social Environment*, 23(4):403–412.

Pacella BL (1980) The primal matrix configuration in R Lax et al (Eds) *Rapprochement: The Critical Sub-phase of Separation-Individuation*, London: Jason Aronson.

Pailey RN (2018) In a world obsessed with passport tiers (pp346–349) in D Santana (Ed) *All the Women in My Family Sing*, San Francisco, CA: Nothing But the Truth.

Pajo E (2018) *International Migration, Social Demotion, and Imagined Advancement*, New York: Springer.

Papadopoulos RK (2002a) The other other: When the exotic other subjugates the familiar other, *Journal of Analytical Psychology*, 47:163–188.

Papadopoulos RK (2002b) Refuges, home and trauma (pp9–39) in RK Papadopoulos (Ed) *Therapeutic Care for Refugees*, London: Karnac Books.

Papadopoulos R & Hulme V (2002) Transient familiar others (pp139–166) in R Papadopoulos (Ed) *Therapeutic Care for Refugees*, London: Karnac Books.

Parens H (1998) The impact of the cultural holding environment on psychic development (pp201–230) in S Akhtar & S Kramer (Eds) *The Colors of Childhood*, London: Jason Aronson.
Park RE (1928) Human migration and the marginal man, *American Journal of Sociology*, 33:881–893.
Paskievich J (2008) *My Mother's Village* (film), National Film Board of Canada.
Passel JS (2018) *Estimates of Unauthorized Immigrants in the United States*, Washington, DC: Pew Research Center.
Peal E & Lambert WE (1962) The relation of bilingualism to intelligence, *Psychological Monographs: General and Applied*, 76(27):1–23.
Pécoud A & De Guchteneire P (2007) Introduction: The migration without borders scenario (pp1–30) in A Pécoud & P De Guchteneire (Eds) *Migration without Borders*, New York: UNESCO & Berghahn Books.
Pei-Shan L (2001) Contextual analysis of rural migration intention, *International Journal of Comparative Sociology*, 42(5):435.
Perez-Foster R et al (1996) *Reaching across Boundaries of Culture and Class*, Northvale, NJ: Jason Aronson.
Peters B (2002) A new look at "national identity", *European Journal of Sociology*, 43(1):3–32.
Peterson J (2018) *12 Rules for Life: An Antidote to Chaos*, Toronto: Random House Canada.
Petigara P (2018) This is how you do (pp69–76) in D Santana (Ed) *All the Women in My Family Sing*, San Francisco, CA: Nothing But the Truth.
Petrescu RM et al (2011) Descriptive analysis of the international migration phenomenon in Romania between 1991 & 2008, *Annals of Faculty of Economics*, 1(1):288.
Petrič J (1995) Sunday too far away (pp162–171) in R King et al (Eds) *Writing Across Worlds*, London: Routledge.
Petschauer PW (1997) Rediscovering the European in America (pp29–46) in PH Elovitz & C Kahn (Eds) *Immigrant Experiences*, Madison, NJ: Fairleigh Dickinson University Press.
Pew Hispanic Center (2006) *2006 National Survey of Latinos*, www.pewhispanic.org/2006/07/13/2006-national-survey-of-latinos/.
Pham P et al (2007) *Abducted: The Lord's Resistance Army and Forced Conscription in Northern Uganda*, Berkeley, CA: Berkeley-Tulane Initiative for Vulnerable Populations.
Phinney J (1990) Ethnic identity in adolescents and adults, *Psychological Bulletin*, 108(3):499–514.
Phinney J, et al (2001) Ethnic identity, immigration and well-being, *Journal of Social Issues*, 57(3):493–510.
Phinney JS & Devich-Navarro M (1997) Variations in bicultural identification among African American and Mexican American adolescents, *Journal of Research on Adolescence*, 7(1):3–32.
Piaget L (1937/1952) *Origins of Intelligence in Children*, New York: International Universities.
Pine BA & Drachman D (2005) Effective child welfare practice with immigrant and refugee children and their families, *Child Welfare*, 84(5):537–562.

Pinedo M et al (2018) Deportation and mental health among migrants who inject drugs along the US–Mexico border, *Global Public Health*, 13(2):211–226.
Plato A (1928/1990) *The Theaetetus of Plato*, Indianapolis, IN: Hackett Publishing Company.
Poirier F & Piquet M (2007) Afterwords: Travel tales (pp203–207) in C Geoffroy & R Sibley (Eds) *Going Abroad: Travel, Tourism, and Migration*, Newcastle upon Tyne: Cambridge Scholars Publishing.
Ponterotto JG (2010) Multicultural personality, *The Counseling Psychologist*, 38:714–758.
Poot J et al (2016) The gravity model of migration, *Regional Science* IZA DP No. 10329.
Porter J (1965) *The Vertical Mosaic*, Toronto: University of Toronto Press.
Portes A et al (1992) Mental illness and help-seeking behavior among Mariel Cuban and Haitian refugees in south Florida, *Journal of Health & Social Behavior*, 33(4):283–298.
Portes A (1996) *The New Second Generation*, New York: Russell Sage Foundation.
Portes A et al (1999) The study of transnationalism, *Ethnic and Racial Studies*, 22(2):217–237.
Portes A et al (2005) Segmented assimilation on the ground: The new second generation in early adulthood, *Ethnic and Racial Studies*, 28:1000–1040.
Portes A et al (2017) Commentary on the study of transnationalism, *Ethnic and Racial Studies*, 40(9):1486–1491.
Portes A & Rumbaut RG (2001) *Legacies: The Story of the Immigrant Second Generation*, Los Angeles, CA: University of California Press.
Portes A & Rumbaut RG (2005) Introduction: The second generation and the children of immigrants, *Ethnic and Racial Studies*, 28(6):983–999.
Portes A & Rumbaut RG (2006) *Immigrant America: A Portrait* (3rd ed.), Los Angeles, CA: University of California Press.
Portes A & Zhou M (1993) The new second generation, *Annals of the American Academy of Political and Social Science*, 530:74–96.
Potter M (2015) "Recipe for disaster" Haitian human smuggling on the rise, *NBC News*, www.nbcnews.com/news/world/recipe-disaster-haitian-human-smuggling-rise.
Poudel C et al (2018) Exploring migration intention of nursing students in Nepal, *Nurse Education in Practice*, 29:95–102.
Powell KM (2015) *Identity and Power in Narratives of Displacement*, London: Routledge.
Power MJ (2003) Development of a common instrument for quality of life (pp145–163) in A Nosikov & V Gudex (Eds) *Developing Common Instruments for Health Surveys*, Amsterdam: IOS Press.
Pratt AV (1985) Spinning among fields: Jung, Frye, Levi-Strauss and feminist archetypal theory (pp93–136) in E Lauter & CS Rupprecht (Eds) *Feminist Archetypal Theory*, Knoxville, TN: The University of Tennessee Press.
Presbitero A (2016) Culture shock and reverse culture shock, *International Journal of Intercultural Relations*, 53:28–38.
Press R (2017) Dangerous crossings, *Africa Today*, 64(1):3–27.

Pritchard R (2010) Re-entry trauma, *Journal of Studies in International Education*, 15 (1):93–111.
Province of Ontario (2019) What are my rights and responsibilities as a Canadian citizen? https://settlement.org/ontario/immigration-citizenship.
Punamaki RJ (2002) The uninvited guest of war enters childhood, *Traumatology*, 8:45–63.
Puppa FD (2018) Ambivalences of the emotional logics of migration and family reunification, *Identities: Global Studies in Culture & Power*, 25(3):358.
Qin D (2008) Doing well *vs* feeling well, *Journal of Youth & Adolescence*, 37 (1):22–35.
Quero HC (2016) Embodied (dis)placements: The intersections of gender, sexuality, and religion in migration studies (pp151–171) in JB Saunders et al (Eds) *Intersections of Religion and Migration Issues at the Global Crossroads*, New York: Palgrave McMillan.
Quinn S (1987) *Mind of Her Own: The Life of Karen Horney*, New York: Summit Books.
Quiroga J & Jaranson JM (2005) Politically-motivated torture and its survivors, *Torture*, 16(2–3):1–96.
Rabin N (2018) Understanding secondary immigration enforcement, *Journal of Law & Education*, 47(1):1–40.
Rajan S et al (2015) *Migration, Mobility and Multiple Affiliations: Punjabis in a Transnational World*, Cambridge: Cambridge University Press.
Rajasingham-Senanayake D (2006) Between Tamil and Muslim (pp172–204) in NC Behera (Ed) *Gender Conflict & Migration*, New Delhi: Sage Publications India.
Ramanujam BK (1997) The process of acculturation among Asian-Indian immigrants (pp139–147) in PH Elovitz & C Kahn (Eds) *Immigrant Experiences: Personal Narrative & Psychological Analysis*, Madison, NJ: Fairleigh Dickinson University Press.
Ramji-Nogales J (2017) Migration emergencies, *Hastings Law Journal*, 68 (2):609–655.
Ramos C (2018) Onward migration from Spain to London in times of crisis, *Journal of Ethnic and Migration Studies*, 44(11):1841–1857.
Rapport N & Dawson A (1998a) *Migrants of Identity*, Oxford: Berg.
Rapport N & Dawson A (1998b) Migrants of identity: Perceptions of home in a world of movement (p23) quoted in JW Duyvendak *The Politics of Home*, New York: Palgrave Macmillan.
Rath A (2015) Thousands arrive at Austrian border, bused through Hungary, *Weekend All Things Considered* (NPR) (Sept 5), www.npr.org/2015/09/05/437873832/thousands-arrive-at-austrian-border-bused-through-hungary.
Rattansi A (2007) *Racism*, Oxford: Oxford University Press.
Ravenstein EG (1885) The laws of migration, *Journal of the Statistical Society of London*, 48(2):157–236.
Rawls J (1993) *Political Liberalism*, New York: Columbia University Press.
Raychaudhury AB (2006) Women after partition (pp155–174) in NC Behera (Ed) *Gender Conflict & Migration*, New Delhi: Sage Publications India.

Raymond C et al (2010) The measurement of place attachment: Personal, community, and environmental connections, *Journal of Environmental Psychology*, 30(4):422–434.
Reding MJ (2017) *Yesterday's Colonization and Today's Immigration: Abdelmalek Sayad, 1957–1998*, Master's Thesis in History, University of Oregon.
Redwood-Campbell L et al (2003) How are new refugees doing in Canada? *Canadian Journal of Public Health/Revue Canadienne De Sante Publique*, 94(5):381–385.
Reich D (2018) *Who We are & How We Got There*, New York: Pantheon Books.
Reicher S & Hopkins N (2002) Psychology and the end of history, *Political Psychology*, 2(2):383–407.
Reichlová N (2005) Can the theory of motivation explain migration decisions? *Working Paper UK* FSW-IES no. 97.
Rentlen A (2005) The use and abuse of the cultural defense, *Canadian Journal of Law and Society*, 20(1):47–67.
Rezazadeh MS & Hoover ML (2018) Women's experiences of immigration to Canada, *Canadian Psychology/Psychologie Canadienne*, 59(1):76–88.
Rich PM & Jennings JL (2015) Choice, information, and constrained options, *American Sociological Review*, 80(5):1069–1098.
Richardson J (2007) Migration, *Foresight*, 9(5):48–55.
Rigaud K et al (2018) *Groundswell: Preparing for Internal Climate Migration*, Washington, DC: World Bank, https://openknowledge.worldbank.org/handle/10986/29461.
Roazen P (1985) *Helene Deutsch*, Piscataway, NJ: Transaction Publishers.
Robert A-M & Gilkinson T (2012) Mental health and well-being of recent immigrants in Canada, *Citizenship and Immigration Canada*, www.canada.ca/content/dam/ircc/migration/.
Roberts D (2013) Stressed Chinese leave cities, head for the countryside, Bloomberg Business Week Reports.
Roberts-Turner R (2018) When life is a crystal stair (pp342–345) in D Santana (Ed) *All the Women in My Family Sing*, San Francisco, CA: Nothing But the Truth.
Rockefeller SC (1992) Comment (pp87–98) in C Taylor (Ed) *Multiculturalism & the Politics of Recognition*, Princeton, NJ: Princeton University Press.
Rogers CR et al (1967) *Person to Person, the Problem of Being Human*, Lafayette, CA: Real People Press.
Rokeach M (1973) *The Nature of Human Values*, New York: Free Press.
Rosenberg JS (2016) *Mean Streets*, New York: Women's Refugee Commission.
Ross HJ & Tartaglione J (2018) *Our Search for Belonging*, Oakland, CA: Berrett-Koehler Publishers Inc.
Roth H (1934) *Call it Sleep*, New York: Robert O Ballou.
Roth H (1994) *Shifting Landscape*, New York: St Martin's Press.
Rothe EM et al (2002) Post traumatic stress disorder among Cuban children and adolescents after release from a refugee camp, *Psychiatric Services*, 53(8):970–976.
Rothman DJ (1982)The uprooted, *Reviews in American History*, 10(3):311–319.
Rousseau C et al (2002) The complexity of determining refugeehood, *Journal of Refugee Studies*, 15(1):43–70.
Rowe S (2002) *Home Place*, Edmonton: NeWest Press.

Royal Canadian Geographical Society with Inuit Tapiriit Kanatami, the Assembly of First Nations, the Métis National Council, the National Centre for Truth and Reconciliation–Indspire (2019) *Redress and Healing | Indigenous Peoples Atlas of Canada*, https://indigenouspeoplesatlasofcanada.ca/article/redress-and-healing/.

Rudmin FW (2009) Constructs, measurements and models of acculturation and acculturative stress, *International Journal of Intercultural Relations*, 33(2):106–123.

Ryan J & Millette D (2013/2015) Hutterites, *The Canadian Encyclopedia*, www.thecanadianencyclopedia.ca/en/article/hutterites.

Ryan L (2007) Migrant women, social networks and motherhood, *Sociology*, 41:295–312.

Ryce-Menuhin J (1987) An extended model of the infant self (pp163–195) in N Schwartz-Salant & M Stein (Eds) *Archetypal Processes in Psychotherapy: The Chiron Clinical Series*, Wilmette, IL: Chiron Publications.

Saada E (2000) Abdelmalek Sayad and the double absence, *French Politics, Culture & Society*, 18(1):28–47.

Sabelli HC (1997) Becoming Hispanic, becoming American (pp158–179) in PH Elovitz& & C Kahn (Eds) *Immigrant Experiences*, Madison, NJ: Fairleigh Dickinson University Press.

Sabini M (2002) *The Earth Has a Soul: CG Jung's Writings on Nature*, Berkeley, CA: North Atlantic Books.

Sačer S et al (2017) Determinants of choice of migration destination, *International Journal of Sales, Retailing & Marketing*, 6(1):48–60.

Sachs E et al (2009) Entering exile, *Journal of Traumatic Stress*, 21(2):99–208.

Said EW (1999) *Out of Place*, New York: Alfred Knopf.

Said EW (2000) Invention, memory, and place, *Critical Inquiry*, 26(2):175–192.

Sakamoto I & Zhou YR (2005) Gendered nostalgia (pp209–229) in V Agnew (Eds) *Diaspora, Memory, Identity*, Toronto: University of Toronto Press.

Salgado de Snyder VN et al (1996) *Dios y el Norte*: The perceptions of wives of documented and undocumented Mexican immigrants to the United States, *Hispanic Journal of Behavioral Science*, 18(3): 283–296.

Sam DL et al (2008) Immigration, acculturation and the paradox of adaptation in Europe, *European Journal of Developmental Psychology*, 5(2):138–158.

Samuels A (1985) *Jung and the Post-Jungians*, London: Routledge & Kegan Paul.

Samuels A et al (1986/2000) *A Critical Dictionary of Jungian Analysis*, London: Routledge.

Samuels A (1993) *The Political Psyche*, London: Routledge.

Sandiford P & Kerr R (1926) Intelligence of Chinese and Japanese children, *Journal of Educational Psychology*, 17(6):366–367.

Sanna LJ et al (2003) Rumination, imagination, and personality (pp105–124) in EC Chang & LJ Sanna (eds.) *Virtue, Vice, and Personality*, Washington, DC: American Psychological Association.

Santana D (2018) *All the Women in My Family Sing*, San Francisco, CA: Nothing but the Truth.

Santric-Milicevic MM et al (2014) First-and fifth-year medical students' intention for emigration and practice Abroad, *Health Policy*, 118(2):173–183.

Sarti D (2018) The city's Italian immigrants saw their share of hardship, *The Georgia Straight* (June 7–14):12.

Saunders D (2018) The real reasons why migrants risk everything for a new life elsewhere, *The Globe & Mail*, April 24, 2015 (Updated May 12, 2018).

Saunders JB et al (2016) *Intersections of Religion and Migration Issues at the Global Crossroads*, New York: Palgrave McMillan.

Sauter MB (2018) Population migration, *USA Today*, www.usatoday.com/35801453.

Sawyer AC (2009/15) Festivals, *The Canadian Encyclopaedia*, www.thecanadianencyclopedia.ca/en/article/festivals.

Sayad A & Macey D (trans) (2004) *The Suffering of the Immigrant*, Cambridge: Polity Press.

Scarpa F (1995) Friulian emigrant literature (pp141–161) in R King et al (Eds) *Writing Across Worlds*, London: Psychology Press Routledge.

Schaffar A et al (2016) The determinants of elderly migration in France, *Papers in Regional Science*, 98(2):951–972.

Schär BHR & Geisler R (2008) *Theological Reflections on Migration*, Brussels: Churches' Commission for Migrants in Europe (CCME).

Schechtman M (2011) The biological approach: Personal identity, in *Routledge Encyclopaedia of Philosophy*, London: Taylor and Francis.

Scheineson A (2009) China's internal migrants, *Council on Foreign Relations*, www.cfr.org/backgrounder/chinas-internal-migrants.

Scheutz A (1945) The homecomer, *American Journal of Sociology*, 50(5):369–376.

Schick M et al (2018) Changes in post-migration living difficulties predict treatment outcome in traumatized refugees, *Frontiers in Psychiatry*, 9:476.

Schiller NG et al (1992) From immigrant to transmigrant, *Anthropological Quarterly*, 68(1):48–65.

Schlenker BR & Britt TW (2001) Strategically controlling information to help friends, *Journal of Experimental Social Psychology*, 37:357–372.

Schmidle N (2015) Ten borders: One refugee's epic escape from Syria, *The New Yorker* (Oct 26):42–53.

Schmidt S et al (2006) The EUROHIS-QOL 8-item index, *European Journal of Public Health*, 16(4):420–428.

Schmitt DP et al (2007) The geographic distribution of Big Five Personality Traits, *Journal of Cross-cultural Psychology*, 38(2):173–212.

Schneider H (1998) Canada: A mosaic, not a melting pot, *Washington Post*, July 15, www.washingtonpost.com/archive/politics/1998/07/05/canada-a-mosaic-not-a-melting-pot/.

Schultz T (1961) Investment in human capital, *The American Economic Review*, 51(1):1–17.

Schupman E (2007) *Native Words, Native Warriors*, Washington, DC: National Museum of the American Indian & the Smithsonian Institute https://americanindian.si.edu/education/codetalkers/html/chapter5.html.

Schwab-Stone M et al (2001) Cultural considerations in the treatment of children and adolescents, *Child and Psychiatric Clinics of North America*, 10:729–743.

Schwartz SH (1992) Universals in the content and structure of values (vol 25, pp1–69) in M Zanna (Ed) *Advances in Experimental Social Psychology*, San Diego, CA: Academic Press.

Schwartz SH (2012) An overview of the Schwartz Theory of basic values, *Online Readings in Psychology and Culture*, 2(1), doi:10.9707/2307-0919.111.
Schweitzer R et al (2006) Trauma, post-migration living difficulties, and social support as predictors of psychological adjustment in resettled Sudanese refugees, *Australian New Zealand Journal of Psychiatry*, 40(2):179–187.
Scott JA (1996) *Dante's Political Purgatory*, Philadelphia, PA: University of Pennsylvania Press.
Scully JA et al (2000) Life event checklists, *Educational & Psychological Measurement*, 60(6):864–876.
Seeberg ML & Goździak EM (2016) *Contested Childhoods: Growing up in Migrancy*, Cham: Springer International Publishing.
Segal UA & Mayadas NS (2005) Assessment of issues facing immigrant and refugee families, *Child Welfare*, LXXXIV(5):563–583.
Seiter JS & Waddell D (1989) The intercultural reentry process, Paper presented at the *Annual Meeting of the Western Speech Communication Association* (Spokane, WA, Feb 17–21).
Selby SP et al (2009) Resilience in re-entering missionaries, *Mental Health, Religion & Culture*, 12(7):701–720.
Selby SP et al (2011a) Cross-Cultural re-entry for missionaries, *Omega*, S2 (4):329–351.
Selby SP (2011b) *Back Home*, Doctoral thesis, University of Adelaide, Australia.
Sen A (1988) Freedom of choice, concept and content, *European Economic Review*, 32(2–3):269.
Sen A (1999) *Development as Freedom*, New York: Anchor Books.
Sen A (2006) *Identity and Violence*, New York: WW Norton.
Serrano Diaz de Otalora M, et al (2011) Acculturation stress in immigrant population, migratory mourning and associated co-morbidities, *European Psychiatry*, 201, 26 (Sl):476.
Shay S (2017) *Israel and Islamic Terror Abductions, 1986–2016*, Chicago, IL: Sussex Academic Press.
Sheehan DV et al (1998) The Mini-International Neuropsychiatric Interview (M.I.N.I), *Journal of Clinical Psychiatry*, 59(S) 20:22–33.
Sheehan JJ (1989) *German History, 1780–1866*, Oxford: Oxford University Press.
Shelley RM (2002) *The Ulysses Syndrome*, Cambridge, MA: Academic Press.
Shihadeh ES (1991) The prevalence of husband-centered migration, *Journal of Marriage and the Family*, 53:432–444.
Shipp AJ et al (2009) Conceptualization and measurement of temporal focus, *Organizational Behavior and Human Decision Processes*, 110:1–22.
Shoichet CE (2018) Forget conspiracy theories about migrants, *Sun* (Nov 4).
Shweder R et al (2002a) Introduction: Engaging cultural differences (pp1–16) in R Shweder et al (Eds) *Engaging Cultural Differences*, New York: Russell Sage Foundation.
Shweder RA (2002b) What about female genital mutilation? (pp216–251) in R Shweder et al (Eds) *Engaging Cultural Differences*, New York: Russell Sage Foundation.
Sibley CG & Duckitt J (2008) Personality and prejudice, *Personality and Social Psychology Review*, 12:248–279.

Silove D et al (1997) Anxiety, depression and PTSD in asylum-seekers, *British Journal of Psychiatry*, 170:351–357.
Simpson P & French R (2006) Negative capability and the capacity to think in the present moment, *Leadership*, 2(2):245–255.
Singer IB (1984) *Love and Exile: An Autobiographical Trilogy*, New York: Farrar, Straus &Giroux.
Sipos D et al (2018) The attrition and migration behaviour among Hungarian radiographers, *Global Journal of Health Science*, 10(1):1–10.
Skeldon R (2013) *Global Migration*, New York: United Nations.
Sly DF & Wrigley JM (1985) Migration decision making and migration behavior in rural Kenya, *Population and Environment: Behavioral and Social Issues*, 8 (1–2):78–97.
Small M (2009) Why did humans migrate to the Americas, *Live Science*, www.livescience.com/7640-humans-migrate-americas.html.
Smallwood D (2007) The integration of British migrants in Aquitaine (pp119–131) in C Geoffroy & R Sibley (Eds) *Going Abroad, Travel, Tourism, and Migration*, Newcastle upon Tyne: Cambridge Scholars Publishing.
Smart A (2018) Footprints found in BC confirmed as earliest known of their kind in North America, *The Globe & Mail*, www.theglobeandmail.com/canada/britishcolumbia.
Smelser NJ (1962) *Theory of Collective Behavior*, Glencoe, IL: Free Press.
Smith B (1988) *Foundations of Gestalt Theory*, Munich: Philosophia Verlag.
Smith CD (2014) Modelling migration futures, *Climate and Development*, 6:77–91.
Smith D & King R (2012) Editorial introduction, *Population Space & Place*, 18 (2):127–133.
Smith EJ (2006) The strength-based counseling model, *The Counseling Psychologist*, 34:13–79.
Smith EL (1990) Descent to the underworld (pp351–364) in K Barnaby & P D'Acerino (Eds) *CG Jung and the Humanities*, Princeton, NJ: Princeton University Press.
Smith TL (1957) *Revivalism and Social Reform in Mid-19th Century America*, New York: Abingdon Press.
Smith TL (1978) Religion and ethnicity in America, *American Historical Review*, 83 (5):1155–1185.
Soon JJ (2012) Home is where the heart is, *Journal of Ethnic and Migration Studies*, 38(1):147–162.
Specia M (2019) Hundreds of migrants stranded in Mediterranean in standoff over aid ships, *New York Times* (Aug 12).
Spoonley P & Tolley E (2012) *Diverse National, Diverse Responses: Approaches to Social Cohesion in Immigrant Societies*, Montreal & Kingston: McGill-Queen's University Press.
Srinivasan KY (1990) Exodus to cities and quality of life, *Ministry of Information and Broadcasting*, 34(14–15):21–27.
Stahl RY (2015) A Jewish America and a Protestant civil religion: Will Herberg, Robert Bellah, and mid-twentieth century American religion, *Religions*, 6:434–450.
Stanford Encyclopedia of Philosophy (2012/2016) Multiculturalism, https://plato.stanford.edu/entries/multiculturalism/.

Statistics Canada (2016) *Internal Migration in Canada, 2013/2014 to 2014/2015* www150.statcan.gc.ca/n1/pub/91-209-x/2016001/article/14650-eng.htm.

Statistics Canada (2017) *Number and Proportion of Foreign-born Population in Canada*, 1971–2036 www.statcan.gc.ca/eng/dai/btd/othervisuals/other006.

Statistics Canada (2018a) *From East to West* www.statcan.gc.ca/.

Statistics Canada (2018b) *Report on the Demographic Situation in Canada: Internal Migration*, www150.statcan.gc.ca/n1/daily-quotidien/180605/dq180605c-eng.htm.

Steer RA et al (1997) Further evidence for the construct validity of the Beck Depression Inventory-II with psychiatric outpatients, *Psychological Reports*, 80 (2):443–446.

Stein M (2006) *The Principle of Individuation*, Wilmette, IL: Chiron Publishers.

Sterle MF et al (2018) Expatriate family adjustment, *Frontiers in Psychology*, 9:1207.

Stern D (1973/1985) *The Interpersonal World of the Infant*, New York: Basic Books.

Stewart E & Shaffer M (2015) *Moving On? Dispersal Policy, Onward Migration and Integration of Refugees in the UK*, Glasgow: University of Strathclyde.

Stewart LA et al (2010) An initial report on the results of the pilot of the computerized mental health intake screening system (CoMHISS), *Correctional Service of Canada*.

Steyn I (2009) Reasons for migration and cultural distance in South African women's migratory adjustment experiences, *Edith Cowan University*, https://ro.ecu.edu.au/theses_hons/1169.

Stievano A et al (2017) Indian nurses in Italy, *Journal of Clinical Nursing*, 26 (23–24):4234–4245.

Stillman S (2007) *Migration and Mental Health*, Washington, DC: The World Bank.

Stillman S (2018) No refuge: For some immigrants, deportation is a death sentence, *The New Yorker* (Jan 15):32–43.

Stockdale A (2014) Unravelling the migration decision-making process, *Journal of Rural Studies*, 34:161–171.

Stockdale A (2017) From "trailing wives" to the emergence of a trailing husbands' phenomenon, *Population, Space & Place*, 23:e2022.

Stockdale A & Haartsen T (2018) Putting rural stayers in the spotlight, *Population, Space & Place*, 24(4):e2124. doi:10.1002/psp.2124.

Stonequist EV (1937) *The Marginal Man*, New York: Scribner/Simon & Schuster.

Stor W (2014) Kony's child soldiers, *The Telegraph* (Feb 12).

Straut-Eppsteiner H & Hagan J (2016) Religion as psychological, spiritual, and social support in the migration undertaking (pp49–70) in JB Saunders et al (Eds) *Intersections of Religion and Migration Issues at the Global Crossroads*, New York: Palgrave.

Strohschein L (2012) I want to move, but cannot: Characteristics of involuntary stayers, *Journal of Aging Health*, 24(5):735–751.

Stürmer S et al (2005) Pro-social emotions, *Journal of Personality and Social Psychology*, 88:532–546.

Stürmer S et al (2013) Psychological foundations of xenophilia, *Journal of Personality and Social Psychology*, 105(5):832–851.

Stürmer S & Snyder M (2010) Helping "us" versus "them" (pp33–58) in S Stürmer & M Snyder (Eds) *The Psychology of Prosocial Behavior*, Oxford: Wiley & Blackwell.

Suárez V & Van Cleave RG (2001) *American Diaspora*, Iowa City: University of Iowa Press.
Suárez-Orozco MM (2002) Everything you ever wanted to know about assimilation but were afraid to ask (pp19–42) in R Shweder et al (Eds) *Engaging Cultural Differences*, New York: Russell Sage.
Suh SA (2009) Buddhism, rhetoric and the Korean American community (pp166–197) in R Alba et al (Eds) *Immigration and Religion in America*, New York: New York University Press.
Sunderland J (2016) *The Mediterranean Migration Crisis, Why People Flee, What the EU Should Do*, New York: Human Rights Watch.
Surawski N et al (2008) Resisting refugee policy: Stress and coping of refugee advocates, *The Australian Community Psychologist*, 22:16–29.
Sussman NM (2001) Repatriation transitions: Psychological preparedness, cultural identity, and attributions among American managers, *International Journal of Intercultural Relations*, 25:109–123.
Sussman NM (2002) Repatriation transitions, *International Journal of Intercultural Relations*, 25:109–123.
Sussman NM (2010) *Return Migration and Identity*, Hong Kong: Hong Kong University Press.
Syed NA, et al (2008) Reasons for migration among medical students from Karachi, *Medical Education*, 42(1):61–68.
Sykes S (2008) *A Story of Reefs and Oceans, A Framework for the Analysis of the "New" Second Generation in Canada*, Discussion Paper, Ottawa: Policy Research Initiative, Government of Canada.
Sylvie A (2007) Travel, tourism and migration seen through exile (pp28–39) in C Geoffrey & R Sibley (Eds) *Going Abroad*, Newcastle upon Tyne: Cambridge Scholars Publishing.
Tabor AS et al (2015) International migration decision-making and destination selection among skilled migrants, *Journal of Pacific Rim Psychology*, 9(1):28–41.
Tajfel H & Dawson JL (1965) *Disappointed Guest*, Oxford: Oxford University Press.
Tak YL et al (2012) Resilience as a positive youth development construct, *Scientific World Journal*, Article ID 390450, doi: 10.1100/2012/390450.
Tarricone I et al (2011) Research perspectives in transcultural psychiatry for young psychiatrists, *European Psychiatry*, 26(Suppl):1797.
Tartakovsky E & Schwartz SH (2001) Motivation for emigration, values, wellbeing, and identification among young Russian Jews, *International Journal of Psychology*, 36(2):88–99.
Tas L (2016) How international law impacts on statelessness and citizenship, *International Journal of Law in Context*, 12(1):42–62.
Taylor C (1989) *Sources of the Self: The Making of the Modern Identity*, Cambridge, MA: Harvard University Press.
Taylor C (1992) *Multiculturalism & and the Politics of Recognition*, Princeton, NJ: Princeton University Press.
Taylor JE & Fletcher PL (2001) Remittances and development in Mexico: The new labour economics of migration, *Rural Mexico Research Project 2*.
Tertrault-Farber G (2014) Tolstoy's Canadian Doukhobors return to Russia over 100 years after fleeing, *Moscow Times* (Oct 2).

Thapan M (2005) *Transnational Migration and the Politics of Identity*, New Delhi: Sage India.

The Associated Press (2018) Waits for citizenship applications stretch to 2 years, *Twin Cities, Pioneer Press* (Oct 28), www.twincities.com/2018/10/28.

The Economist (2018) Immigrants to America, www.economist.com/united-states/2017/06/08/immigrants-to-america-are-better-educated-than-ever-before.

The Guardian (2018) Global migration figures higher than previously thought, www.theguardian.com/world/2018/dec/24/.

Thober J et al (2018) Agent-based modeling of environment-migration linkages, *Ecology and Society*, 23(2):41.

Thomas E (2008) Mental health and attitudes towards returning to the country of origin in refugees from Yugoslavia, *Zeitschrift Fur Klinische Psychologie Und Psychotherapie*, 37(2):112–121.

Thorpe H (2017) *The Newcomers*, New York: Scribner.

Tilson D et al (2009) *Recognizing Success*, Report of the Standing Committee on Citizenship and Immigration, House of Commons, www.credentials.gc.ca.

Tönnies F & Loomis CP (trans) (1887/1940) *Fundamental Concepts of Sociology (Gemeinschaft Und Gesellschaft)*, New York: American Book Company.

Torstar News (2017) Immigration on the rise, *Metro News* (Jan 26).

Tötösy de Zepetnek S, et al (2013) Perspectives on identity, migration, and displacement, *CLCWeb*, https://docs.lib.purdue.edu/clcweblibrary/perspectivesonmigrationanddiaspora/.

Trafton A (2018) Cognitive scientists define critical period for learning language, *MIT News Office* (May 1).

Trentelman CK (2009) Place attachment and community attachment: A primer grounded in the lived experience of a community sociologist, *Society & Natural Resources*, 22(3):191e210.

Triandafyllidou A (1998) National identity and the "other", *Ethnic and Racial Studies*, 21(4):593.

Triandafyllidou A (2008) The governance of international migration in Europe and North America, *Journal of Immigrant & Refugee Studies*, 6(3):281–296.

Triandis H (2009) *Fooling Ourselves*, Westport, CT & London: Praeger.

Tucker C et al (2013a) Migration decision-making among Mexican youth, *Hispanic Journal of Behavioral Sciences*, 35(1):61–84.

Tucker C et al (2013b) Rural parents' messages to their adolescent sons and daughters to leave their home communities, *Journal of Adolescence*, 36(5):963–970.

Tumang PJ & de Rivera J (2001) *Homelands, Women's Journeys across Race, Place and Time*, Emeryville, CA: Seal Press.

Turkle S (2012) *Alone Together*, New York: Basic Books.

Turner BS (2016) Book review DeHanas DN: *London Youth, Religion, and Politics*, *British Journal of Sociology*, 69(3):876–877.

Turner RH & Killian LM (1987) *Collective Behavior* (3rd ed.), Englewood Cliffs, NJ: Prentice-Hall.

Turner T-P (2017) *Belonging*, Salt Spring Island, BC: Her Own Press.

Tutton M (2019) Call for tighter bail rules after Saudi sex-crime suspect vanishes, *Star Metro Vancouver* (Jan 21):12.

Tyldum G (2014) Motherhood, agency and sacrifice in narratives on female migration for care work, *Sociology*, 49:56–71.
Tyrrell N et al (2018) Belonging in Brexit Britain, *Population Space & Place*, 25(1): e2205.
Uhlenberg P (1973) Non-economic determinants of non-migration, *Rural Sociology*, 38(3):297.
UNESCO (2018) *Displaced Person / Displacement, Social & Human Sciences*, www.unesco.org/new/en/social-and-human-sciences/themes/international.
UNICEF (2016) *The Growing Crisis for Refugee and Migrant Children*, UNICEF.
UNICEF (2018) *Data Brief. Children on the Move: Key Facts and Figures*, UNICEF.
United Nations (1948) *The Universal Declaration of Human Rights*, www.un.org/en/universal-declaration-human-rights/.
United Nations (1984) *Convention against Torture and Other Cruel, Inhuman or Degrading Treatment or Punishment* (10 December), https://treaties.un.org/.
United Nations (2017a) Population Facts, www.un.org/en/development/desa/population/publications/pdf/.
United Nations (2017b) *Sustainable Development: 244 Million International Migrants Living Abroad*, www.un.org/sustainabledevelopment/blog/2016/01/.
United Nations (2018a) *United Nations Convention against Transnational Organized Crime and the Protocols Thereto*, www.unodc.org/unodc/en/organized-crime/intro/UNTOC.html.
United Nations (2018b) *The Crime of Trafficking in Persons*, www.unodc.org/unodc/en/human-trafficking-fund/human-trafficking-fund_projects.html.
United Nations (2019) *Department of Economic and Social Affairs, Population: International Migration*, www.un.org/en/development/desa/population/migration/index.asp.
United Nations, Department of Economic and Social Affairs (2017) *The International Migration Report 2017*, www.un.org/development/desa/publications/international.
United Nations High Commission for Refugees (1994) *Refugee Children: Guidelines on Protection and Care*, Geneva: UNHCR.
United Nations High Commissioner for Refugees (2018) *States Parties to the 1951 Convention relating to the Status of Refugees and the 1967 Protocol* www.unhcr.org/3b73b0d63.pdf.
University of Miami (2018) *The Cuban Rafter Phenomenon*, http://balseros.miami.edu/.
UN Refugees and Migrants (2018) *Global Compact for Migration* https://refugeesmigrants.un.org/migration-compact.
Urry J (2007) *Mobilities*, Cambridge: Polity.
US Census (2020) U.S. and World Population Clock, www.census.gov/popclock/
US Department of Homeland Security (2019) *Citizenship Rights and Responsibilities*, www.uscis.gov/citizenship/learners/citizenship-rights-and-responsibilities.
Van Blerk L & Ansell N (2006) Imagining migration, *Geoforum*, 37(2):256–272.
Van Buren A & Cooley E (2002) Attachment styles, view of self and negative affect, *North American Journal of Psychology*, 4(3):417–430.
Van der Ven E et al (2015) Testing Odegaard's selective migration hypothesis, *Psychological Medicine*, 45(4):727–734.

Van der Zee KI & Van Oudenhoven JP (2000) The multicultural personality questionnaire, *European Journal of Personality*, 14:291–309.
Van der Zee KI & Van Oudenhoven JP (2001) The multicultural personality questionnaire, *Journal of Research in Personality*, 35:278–288.
Van Gennep CAK (1909) *The Rites of Passage*, Chicago, IL: University of Chicago Press.
Van Ginneken J (2003) *The European Institute for the Media Series. Collective Behavior and Public Opinion*: Mahwah, NJ: Lawrence Erlbaum Associates Publishers.
Van Oudenhoven JP et al (2006) Patterns of relations between immigrant & host societies, *International Journal of Intercultural Relations*, 30(6):637–651.
Van Reisen M & Mawere M (2017) *Human Trafficking and Trauma in the Digital Era, the Ongoing Tragedy of the Trade in Refugees from Eritrea*, Bamenda, Cameroon: Langaa RPCIG.
Vanstone WH (1982) *The Stature of Waiting*, London: Longman and Todd.
Varty A (2019) Mark Takeshi McGregor and Liam Hockley explore unsettling sounds of displacement for Vancouver New Music, *The Georgia Straight* (Feb 7–14/2019:15).
Varvin S (2016) Asylum seekers and refugees, *Psyche-Zeitschrift Fur Psychoanalyse Und Ihre Anwendungen*, 70(9–10):825–855.
Varvin S (2017) Our relations to refugees, *American Journal of Psychoanalysis*, 77:59.
Vasileva K (2012) Nearly two-thirds of the foreigners living in EU member states are citizens of countries outside the EU-27, *Eurostat, European Commission*, https://ec.europa.eu/eurostat/documents/3433488/5584984/KS-SF-12-031-EN.PDF/be48f08f-41c1-4748-a8a5-5d92ebe848f2.
Vega WA et al (1984) The prevalence of depressive symptoms among Mexican Americans and Anglos, *American Journal of Epidemiology*, 120:5–607.
Vega WA & Rumbaut RG (1991) Ethnic minorities and mental health, *Annual Review of Sociology* 17:351–383.
Ventevogel P et al (2007) Properties of the Hopkins Symptom Checklist-25 (HSCL-25), *Social Psychiatry & Psychiatric Epidemiology*, 42(4):328–335.
Vickers P (2017) International immigration and the Labour Market, *Office for National Statistics*, www.ons.gov.uk/peoplepopulationandcommunity/populatio nandmigration/internationalmigration/articles/migrationandthelabourmarketuk/2016.
Vilhelmson B & Thulin E (2016) Environment as a multifaceted migration motive, *Population Space & Place*, 22(3):276–287.
Vogler C (1998/2007) *The Writer's Journey* (3rd ed.), Sheridan Books (online).
Volkan VD & Zintl R (1993) *Life after Loss*, New York: Macmillan.
Von Franz M-L (1995) *Shadow and Evil in Fairy Tales*, Boston, MA: Shambhala.
Von Franz M-L (1996) *Dreams: A Study of the Dreams of Jung, Descartes, Socrates, and Other Historical Figures*, Boston, MA: Shambhala.
Von Franz M-L (1999) *Archetypal Dimensions of the Psyche*, Boston, MA: Shambhala.
Von Lersner U et al (2008) Mental health of refugees following state-sponsored repatriation from Germany, *BMC Psychiatry*, 8:88.
Wacquant LJ & Wilson WJ (1989) The cost of racial and class exclusion in the inner city, *Annals of the American Academy of Political and Social Sciences*, 501(1):826

Wahl A (2019) *Calendar of Ethnic Holidays*, American Ethnic Studies, Wake Forest University, https://aes.wfu.edu/calendar-of-ethnic-holidays/.
Walck C (2003) Using the concept of land to ground the teaching of management and the natural environment, *Journal of Management Education*, 27 (2):205–219.
Waldinger R & Feliciano C (2004) Will the new second generation experience downward assimilation? Segmented assimilation re-assessed, *Ethnic and Racial Studies*, 27(3):376–402.
Wallace PM et al (2010) A review of acculturation measures and their utility in studies promoting Latino health, *Journal of Behavioral Science*, 32(1): 37–54.
Walls NE & Bell S (2011) Correlates of engaging in survival sex among homeless youth and young adults, *Journal of Sex Research*, 48(5):423–436.
Walsh SD & Shulman S (2007) Splits in the self following immigration, *Psychoanalytic Psychology*, 24(2):355–372.
Walzer C et al (2009) *Out of Exile*, San Francisco, CA: McSweeneys Books.
Ward C et al (1998) The U-Curve on trial: Adjustment during cross-cultural transition, *International Journal of Intercultural Relations*, 22(3):277–291.
Ward C et al (2001) *The Psychology of Culture Shock* (2nd ed.), Hove, East Sussex: Routledge.
Ward C & Masgoret AM (2008) Attitudes toward immigrants, immigration, and multiculturalism in New Zealand, *International Migration Review*, 42 (1):227–248.
Warner L & Srole L (1945) *Social Systems of American Ethnic Groups*, New Haven, CT: Yale University Press.
Warnick M (2016) *This Is Where You Belong: The Art & Science of Loving the Place You Live*: New York: Viking.
Wasuge M (2018) *Youth Migration in Somalia*, Heritage Institute for Policy Studies, Mogadishu, Somalia, www.heritageinstitute.org.
Waters M (1990) *Ethnic Options*, Berkeley, CA: University of California Press.
Wehr G (1987) *Jung: A Biography*, Boston, MA: Shambhala.
Weick K (2015) *The Social Psychology of Organizing* (2nd ed.), New York: McGraw-Hill.
Weill Cornell Medicine Center (2019) *Grief Intensity Scale*, https://endoflife.weillcornell.edu/research/grief-intensity-scale.
Weiss DS & Marmar CR (1996) The impact of event scale – revised (pp399–411) in J Wilson & TM Keane (Eds) *Assessing Psychological Trauma and PTSD*, New York: Guilford.
Weist K (2016) *Women and Migration in Rural Europe*, Houndsmills, Basingstoke: Palgrave Macmillan.
Welz F (2005) Rethinking identity, *The Society, an International Journal of Social Sciences*, 1:1–25.
Wendt C (2017) Introduction to Lepsius' concept of institutional theory (pp1–21) in C Wendt (Ed) *Max Weber and Institutional Theory*, Cham: Springer.
Werneke U et al (2000) The stability of the factor structure of the General Health Questionnaire, *Psychological Medicine*, 30(4):823–829.
White P (1995/2003) Geography literature and migration (pp1–19) in R King et al (Eds) *Writing across Worlds*, London: Psychology Press/Routledge.

WHO Assist Working Group (2002) The alcohol, smoking and substance involvement screening test (ASSIST): Development, reliability and feasibility, *Addiction*, 97:1183–1194.
Wihtol de Wenden C (2002) Integration and citizenship, *Asian and Pacific Migration Journal*, 11(4):529–533.
Wihtol de Wenden C (2012) The immigrant 2nd generation and urban unrest in France (pp133–150) in PH Spoonley & E Tolley (Eds) *Diverse National, Diverse Responses*, Montreal & Kingston: McGill-Queen's University Press.
Wikipedia (2018a) *Asylum in the United States*, https://en.wikipedia.org/wiki/Asylum_in_the_United_States.
Wikipedia (2018b) *Medusa*, https://en.wikipedia.org/wiki/Medusa.
Wikipedia (2019a) *Air India Flight 182*, https://en.wikipedia.org/wiki/Air_India_Flight_182.
Wikipedia (2019b) *Albert Camus*, https://en.wikipedia.org/wiki/Albert_Camus.
Wikipedia (2019c) *Canadian Indian residential school system*, https://en.wikipedia.org/wiki/Canadian_Indian_residential_school_system.
Wikipedia (2019d) *Central American Migrant Caravans*, https://en.wikipedia.org/wiki/Central_American_migrant_caravans.
Wikipedia (2019e) *Chain Migration*, https://en.wikipedia.org/wiki/Chain_migration.
Wikipedia (2019f) *Critical Period*, https://en.wikipedia.org/wiki/Critical_period.
Wikipedia (2019g) *Cultural Intelligence*, https://en.wikipedia.org/wiki/Cultural_intelligence.
Wikipedia (2019h) *Frantz Fanon*, https://en.wikipedia.org/wiki/Frantz_Fanon.
Wikipedia (2019i) *Lot's Wife*, https://en.wikipedia.org/wiki/Lot%27s_wife.
Wikipedia (2019j) *Multiculturalism in Canada*, https://en.wikipedia.org/wiki/Multiculturalism_in_Canada.
Wikipedia (2019k) *Positive Disintegration*, https://en.wikipedia.org/wiki/Positive_disintegration.
Wikipedia (2019l) *Protocol to Prevent, Suppress and Punish Trafficking*, https://en.wikipedia.org/wiki/Protocol_to_Prevent,_Suppress_and_Punish_Trafficking.
Wikipedia (2019m) *Survival Sex*, https://en.wikipedia.org/wiki/Survival_sex.
Wikipedia (2019n) *Translations*, https://en.wikipedia.org/wiki/English_translations_of_Homer.
Williams P (2007) Foreword (ppxvii–xx) in M Hooke & S Akhtar (Eds) *The Geography of Meanings*, London: The International Psychoanalysis Library.
Wilson JP & Raphael B (1993) *International Handbook of Traumatic Stress Syndromes*, New York: Springer Science + Business Media, LLC.
Winnicott DW (1953) Transitional objects and transitional phenomena, *International Journal of Psychoanalysis*, 34:89–97.
Winnicott DW (1963/1965) The development of the capacity for concern (pp73–82) in *The Maturation Process and the Facilitating Environment*, New York: International Universities Press.
Winnicott DW (1971) *Playing and Reality*, Middlesex, England: Penguin.
Winnicott DW (1986) *Home Is Where We Start From*, Middlesex, England: Penguin.
Winnicott DW (2016) *The Collected Works of D.W. Winnicott*, edited by I Caldwell & HT Robinson, Oxford: Oxford University Press.
Wohlleben P (2016) *The Hidden Life of Trees*, Vancouver, BC: Greystone Books.

Wolman T (2007) Human space, psychic space, analytic space, geopolitical space, in MTS Hooke & S Akhtar (Eds) *The Geography of Meanings*, London: Karnac Books.

Wong DFK et al (2003) Mental health and social competence of Mainland Chinese immigrant and local youth in Hong Kong, *Journal of Ethnic and Cultural Diversity in Social Work*, 12(1):85–110.

Wong DFK & Song HX (2008) The resilience of migrant workers in Shanghai China, *The International Journal of Social Psychiatry*, 54(2):131–143.

Wood LCN (2018) Impact of punitive immigration policies, parent-child separation and child detention on the mental health and development of children, *BMJ Paediatrics Open*, 2(1):e000338.

Wroughton l (2018) U.S. to sharply limit refugee flows to 30,000 in 2019, *Reuters* (Sept 17), www.reuters.com/article/us-usa-immigration.

Xi J & Hwang SS (2011) Unmet expectations and symptoms of depression among the Three Gorges Project Resettlers, *Social Science Research*, 40(1):245–256.

Yakushko O (2008) The impact of social and political changes on survivors of political persecutions in rural Russia and Ukraine, *Political Psychology*, 28(1):119–130.

Yakushko O (2010) Stress and coping strategies in the lives of recent immigrants, *International Journal for the Advancement of Counselling*, 32:256–273.

Yakushko O & Chronister KN (2005) Immigrant women and counselling, *Journal of Counseling & Development*, 83(3):292–298.

Yang F (1998) Chinese conversion to evangelical Christianity, *Sociology of Religion*, 59(3):237–257.

Yazdi K (2019) *Displacement II*, https://soundcloud.com/user-529844759/displacement-ii.

Yeoh B & Lin W (2012) Rapid growth in Singapore's immigrant population brings policy challenges, *Migration Policy Institute*, www.migrationpolicy.org/article/rapid-growth.

Yok-Fong P (2013) Understanding motives for migration in working with immigrant families, *Journal of Human Behavior in the Social Environment*, 23:403–412.

Youkhana E (2016) "Belonging," *InterAmerican Wiki: Terms - Concepts - Critical Perspectives*, www.uni-bielefeld.de/cias/wiki/b_Belonging.html.

Young-Bruehl E (1988//2008) *Anna Freud: A Biography* (2nd ed.), New Haven, CT & London: Yale University Press.

Young-Eisendrath P (1992) Gender, animus & related topics, in N Schwartz-Salant & M Stein (Eds) *Gender & Soul in Psychotherapy*, Wilmette, IL: Chiron Clinical Series.

Yuval-Davis N (1997/2006) *Gender and Nation*, London: Sage.

Yuval-Davis N (2006) Belonging and the politics of belonging, *Patterns of Prejudice*, 40(3):197.

Zahar T (2016) *The Great Departure*, New York: WW Norton.

Zalinsky W (1974/2016) Self-ward bound? *Economic Geography*, 50(2):144–179.

Zambelli P (2018) Paradigm shifts: Towards a new model for refugee status determination in Canada, *UBC Law Review*, 51(1):228–270.

Zapf MK (1991) Cross-cultural transitions and wellness, *International Journal for the Advancement of Counselling*, 14(2):105–119.

Zheng R (2017) China's internal migrants, *The Monsoon Project*, https://themonsoonproject.org/2017/10/02.

Zheng X & Berry JW (1991) Psychological adaptation of Chinese sojourners in Canada, *International Journal of Psychology*, 26:451–471.

Zhou M & Bankston C (1998) *Growing Up American*, New York: Russell Sage Foundation.

Zhu G (1990) A probe into reasons for international migration in Fujian Province, *Chinese Journal of Population Science*, 2(3):229–246.

Zieck M (2018) Refugees and the right to freedom of movement, *Michigan Journal of International Law*, 39(1):19–116.

Zilo M (2018) Asylum-seeker surge at Quebec border choking Canada's refugee system, *The Globe & Mail* (Sept 12).

Zimbardo PG & Boyd JN (1999) Putting time in perspective, *Journal of Personality and Social Psychology*, 77(6):1271–1288.

Zimbardo PG & Boyd JN (2008) *The Time Paradox*: New York: Free Press.

Zimbardo PG & Boyd J N (1999) Putting time in perspective: A valid, reliable individual-differences metric, *Journal of Personality and Social Psychology*, 77 (6):1271–1288.

Zimmerman I (2002) Trauma and judges, *Canadian Bar Association Annual Meeting* (Aug 13).

Index

abductions (kidnapping) 42, 43, 44, 58, 210
Aboriginal peoples viii, 135, 175, 229
acculturation 3, 95, 98–99, 112, 115, 151, 154, 155–157, 160, 163, 192, 193, 206, 215
adaptation ix, 2, 3, 4, 26, 67, 75, 76, 77, 82, 86, 88, 89, 91, 92, 94, 95, 96, 98, 99, 102, 111, 113, 115, 119, 124, 125, 126, 131, 151–158, 164, 165, 169, 175, 177, 178, 179, 187, 190, 195, 200, 202, 206, 216, 218, 229, 230, 231, 232, 233
adopted land 69, 88, 95, 126, 127, 131, 168, 232
Adorno 196
Afghans 55
Africa / Africans x, 5, 6, 14, 16, 17, 20, 21, 23–24, 27, 28, 30, 37, 41, 54, 56, 59, 61, 103, 118, 121, 152, 162, 167, 208, 211, 214, 215
African-Americans / Blacks 32, 61, 103, 117, 152, 154, 162, 171, 172, 201, 213, 214
agenti 188, 190, 191
aid workers 90
Ajzen and Fishbein 19
Akhtar viii, 67, 74, 76, 116, 132, 193, 232
Akresh 177
Alaska 5, 27
Alba and Foner 200, 212
alchemical model of change 96–98, 230
Aldrich 167
Alexander 165
Algeria / Algerian 31, 69, 123, 126, 127, 132, 153, 156, 164, 166, 167, 174, 202, 204, 212, 213, 214

alienation 10, 67, 85, 91, 94, 122, 123, 137, 150, 153, 159, 198, 231; *see also* feelings
allies 3, 54, 60, 229
Allport 196
alterity / otherness 116, 117, 118, 127, 233
America / Americans *see* USA
American dream / ideal 11, 28, 167
American Migration Policy Institute 153
American Naturalization Act 75
American Presidential Task Force on Immigration 187
analytic love 233
anarchists 63
Anatomy of the Psyche 96
ancestors xii, 5, 67, 119, 231
Anderson 128, 192, 207, 208
anti-immigrant ideologies 55, 215
Arango 34
Arcadia 10
archetype / archetypal ix, x, xii, 9, 10, 11, 66, 78, 54, 111, 115, 229
Argentina 13, 19, 29, 110, 161, 187
Arnberg 167
Arnett 117
arrival ix, 3, 22, 30, 40, 55, 59, 62, 63, 66–78, 82, 85, 90, 93, 113, 115, 135, 160, 187, 194, 204, 206, 216, 218, 229, 230
arrivées/émigrés i, 4, 32, 67–69, 70, 74, 75, 87, 88, 150, 151, 152, 155, 161, 163, 167, 168, 175, 178, 179, 188, 193, 200, 202, 214, 215, 231
Art of Being Black, The 165
art 10, 110, 119, 129, 155, 157, 165, 173
A Seventh Man 75

Asia / Asians 14, 17, 18, 20, 21, 23, 24, 30, 32, 127, 157–158, 159, 163, 165, 178, 188, 211, 213, 215
Asian Gang, The 165
assimilation 3, 4, 16, 70, 83, 85, 92, 94, 99, 118, 134, 135, 151, 153–155, 157, 168, 169, 172, 175, 185, 190, 191, 200, 201, 202, 203, 205, 207, 212, 213, 215, 218, 232
Åström and Westerlund 36
asylum 6, 7, 13, 26, 33, 34, 35, 37, 38, 39, 40, 41, 42, 55, 69, 70, 71, 73, 74, 93, 187, 192, 196, 230; *see also* refugees
attachment 4, 7, 10, 11, 12, 15, 26, 34, 40, 57, 84, 86, 91, 94, 111–113, 115, 129–138, 156, 167, 207, 231
attitudes 4, 7, 17, 19, 32, 38, 70, 83, 85, 86, 95, 96, 97, 98, 101, 113, 120, 127, 150, 155, 159, 160, 167, 169, 171, 174, 187, 189, 193–200, 202, 203, 217
Atwood 85
Ault 75
au pair 208
Australia 5, 6, 13, 22, 61, 76, 90, 93, 110, 113, 168, 187, 188, 192, 194
Austro-Hungarian 169
Authoritarian Personality, The 196

Bangladesh / Bangladeshi 22, 24, 32, 62, 152, 171, 188, 214
banlieues (France) 201, 215
Barometer Public Opinion on Refugees 196
Basque 203
Bauböck 99, 132
Bauder 12, 129, 194
Bauman 12, 14, 117, 123, 126, 188
Becker 195
Behera 43, 59
Belgium 75
belonging i, 1, 2, 4, 5, 13, 66, 67, 76, 88, 93, 94, 98, 110, 111, 116, 119, 122, 128, 129, 132. 133–140, 158, 163, 169, 173, 177, 198, 205, 211, 216, 230, 233
Beltsiou 59, 164, 233
Berger and Mohr 75
Berlin, Isaiah 13
Berlin wall 55
Bertossi 203
betwixt and between 4, 98, 129, 158, 163, 205, 231
Beurs 166

Bhattacharya 173
Biblical references 2, 67, 68, 75, 98, 139
bicultural / bi-national 15, 107, 124, 139, 158, 159
Big-Five personality (OCEAN) 196–197
bilingual / bilingualism 155, 158–160, 169, 170
Billig 129
Bion 86, 193
birth tourism 22, 208
Blacks 32, 154, 171, 172; *see also* African-Americans
Bluedorn 85
Bolivia 208
Bosnia 165
Boulanger 163
Bowlby 4, 94, 111, 112, 231; *see also* attachment
Brazil 24, 27, 29, 60
Brief Acculturation Orientation Scale 95
Brief Perceived Cultural Distance Scale 95
Brief Sociocultural Adaptation Scale 95
Brief Psychological Adaptation Scale 95
bright lights hypothesis 14, 30
Britain *see* UK
British Psychoanalytical Society 86
Brown 87, 123, 167
Buddhism 66, 102, 137, 139
Bulgaria 207
Burnett and Peet 72

Cadge and Ecklund 138, 178
call to adventure 2, 12, 13, 18, 26, 94, 150, 231
Cambodia 72
Cameron 39
Cameroon 23
Campbell, Joseph ix, 74
Campese 55
Campisi 60
camps refugee / transit 3, 33, 34, 39, 55, 71, 73, 120, 121, 123, 160, 166
Camus 68
Canada / Canadian i, ix, xii, xiii, 5, 13, 17, 18, 22, 27, 28, 29, 30, 32, 34, 35, 38, 39, 43, 57, 59, 60, 63, 70, 71, 73, 76, 82, 84, 87, 88, 89, 92, 93, 95, 100, 101, 110, 113, 115, 118, 127, 128, 129, 133, 151, 152, 153, 154, 156, 157, 158, 159, 161, 163, 164, 165, 170, 173, 174, 175, 178, 187, 188, 192, 193, 194,

195, 200, 201, 203, 207, 208, 209, 212, 218, 231
Canadian Citizenship and Immigration 217
Canadian Commission for UNESCO 209
Canadian Group of Seven artists viii
Canadian Population Health Survey 34
Carens 73
Caribbean 6, 165, 174, 204, 214
Carr (artist) i, viii, ix, 87
Cartwright 196
Catalan 203
Catholics / Catholicism 100, 101, 102, 169, 170, 176, 189, 190, 200
Central American 11, 31, 54, 61, 62, 114, 229
Césaire 167
Charon 58
children / adolescents / youths i, 4, 10, 11, 12, 16, 17, 18, 19, 22, 23, 24, 26, 27, 29, 30, 36, 39, 40, 42, 43, 44, 56, 61, 70, 72, 74, 75, 77, 78, 84, 89, 93, 94, 102, 103, 112, 116, 119, 122, 123, 125, 127, 131, 150, 152, 155, 156, 157, 158, 159, 160, 161, 163, 164, 165, 166, 167, 168, 170, 172, 174, 176, 177, 178, 202, 204, 205, 206, 207, 208, 210, 211, 212, 213, 214, 215, 216, 217, 231
China (Hong Kong) 23, 30, 31, 37, 70, 93, 115, 118, 176, 188, 211
Chow 38
Christian 100, 102, 116, 139, 140, 169, 177
Chui 173
churches / temples 4, 70, 100, 102, 175, 176, 177, 233
citizens ix, 4, 6, 13, 22, 33, 38, 69, 82, 92, 96, 98, 99, 121, 125, 127, 129, 130, 132, 133, 163, 165, 171, 172, 188, 190, 191–193, 194, 202, 203, 206, 208, 210, 212, 215, 217, 218
citizenship 4, 22, 25, 27, 30, 32, 34, 69, 73, 75, 82, 92, 96, 99, 100, 110, 118, 119, 122, 132, 134, 153, 156, 165, 168, 188, 189, 190, 191, 192, 193, 199, 203, 207–211, 213, 214, 215, 232
Clark and Withers 36
Clarkson, Adrienne 115
class 22, 29, 116, 118, 129, 154, 162, 169, 170, 171, 172, 174, 176, 178, 189, 190, 200, 203, 205, 208, 217, 218

clean break 201
climate change 20, 37, 61, 96
co-ethnic communities 154, 213
Coifman 86
Cold War (1947–1962) 12, 58
Colombia 17, 24, 62, 134
Columbus complex 12
complexes viii, 3, 5, 10, 12, 25, 26, 27, 34, 41, 66–67, 78, 88, 114, 117, 119, 124, 125, 131, 134, 159, 163, 165, 230
Complications of American Psychology, The 157
conditioning 151–152
conflict 36, 39, 56, 88, 93, 115, 155, 156, 159, 210, 212, 214
coniunctio 96, 97
Connell 118
Conrad 88
consciousness xi, 21, 23, 28, 34, 54, 66, 69, 83, 92, 94, 96, 97, 110, 111, 117, 123, 124, 132, 167, 201, 230
Cooke 36
Cooper's refugee camp 61
coping mechanisms 84, 86, 171
Côté 117
Council of Europe 217
Country Girls 172
Croatia 39, 54
creative illness 120
Cross-Cultural Coping Scale 171
Cuba / Cubans 35, 60, 62
culture ix, 14, 28, 29, 57, 67, 70, 72, 77, 83, 84, 85, 89, 90, 91, 95, 96, 99, 111, 103, 117, 124, 126, 127, 128, 129, 131, 134, 136, 150, 151, 153, 154, 156, 159, 161, 162, 164, 165, 170, 173, 175, 177, 189–190, 194, 196, 201, 205, 207, 209, 210, 213, 214, 215, 216, 217, 232
cultural 4, 11, 13, 15, 18, 20, 21, 22, 26, 27, 29, 33, 40, 41, 42, 59, 60, 66, 70, 72, 76, 77, 82, 84, 86, 89, 90, 91, 92, 93, 94, 95, 96, 97, 98, 99, 100, 101, 103, 112, 113, 115, 116, 118, 119, 121, 122, 123, 124, 125, 126, 127, 128, 130, 131, 134, 135, 136, 137, 140, 150, 151, 152, 153, 154, 155, 157, 158, 159, 161, 162, 163, 164, 165, 166, 167, 168, 169, 170, 171, 172, 173, 174, 175, 176, 177, 178, 190, 191, 192, 193, 197, 198, 199, 200, 201, 202, 203, 204, 205, 206, 207, 209, 210, 211, 212, 213, 214, 215, 216, 218, 229, 230, 231, 232

cultural localitis 3, 66, 70, 99, 230
cultural mosaic 136, 151, 202, 204
Cultural Quotient Scale (CQ) 91
culture shock/shock 70, 71, 72, 76, 83, 84, 86, 89, 90, 91, 99, 128, 136, 164, 166
"cut flower culture" 178
Cyclops 55
Cyprus 161
Czech Republic 12, 58, 72, 87, 88, 167, 194

Dabrowski 92, 120
Dahlie 85
Daly 2
Dante 5
Darién Gap 62
Das Gupta 174
DaVanzo 18
decision-making 2, 5, 10, 14–21, 23, 26, 35, 40, 42, 59, 70, 83, 91, 92, 97, 119, 167, 173, 229, 231, 232
deficiency model 11, 19
de Hanas 172
de Hass 13, 14
de Jong and Fawcett 13
developmental psychology 94, 111–114, 115, 120, 124–125, 137, 231
diasporic 1, 4, 32, 33, 82, 92, 99, 118, 119, 120–125, 130, 139, 151, 152, 162, 212
discrimination 22, 27, 32, 33, 61, 74, 87, 88, 93, 100, 118, 134, 139, 153, 154, 191, 194, 196, 202, 213, 214, 217, 218; *see also* prejudice
displaced 7, 26, 28, 36–42, 121, 132; *see also* exiles/refugees
dissociative mechanisms 77, 83
diversity 100, 102, 191, 193, 202, 209, 213, 216, 217, 233
DNA 5, 10, 118
Dominican 134
Dorabji 173
double consciousness 94, 117, 163
Dovidio 196
Dow 40, 76
downward mobility 83, 101, 135, 154, 155, 157
dreams x, 6, 9, 11, 18, 26, 28, 66, 88, 118, 121, 127, 128, 129, 132, 137, 156, 157, 161, 164, 166, 167, 171, 172, 230, 231

dual citizenship 30, 82, 110, 124, 168, 230
dual-career couples 35, 36, 208
Duckitt and Sibley 196
Dukabour 231
dumping of unwanted 6, 163
Duncan 216
Dunkas and Nikelly 86
Duyvendak ix, 28

earth has soul 10, 89, 136, 189
Eastern Europe 27, 37, 45, 55, 58, 88, 124, 164, 195, 197
economic self-interest 198–199
Edinger 96
education 16, 23, 24, 27, 29, 32, 69, 82, 87, 92, 93, 101, 131, 170, 174, 197, 205
egalitarian 35, 197, 205
ego 4, 7, 66, 68, 84, 94, 96, 97, 110, 111, 114, 116, 120, 126, 137, 167
Egonu 169
Eisen 151, 175
Eisenstadt 206, 207
elixir/treasure 3, 4, 66, 74, 75, 76, 82, 230
Elovitz 161
El Salvador 11, 31, 27, 134
Emecheta 172
Emerson 92
enemies 3, 38, 54, 60, 136, 229
Engaging cultural differences 209
engagement (political) 129, 189
England *see* UK
epic narratives 54, 138
Erickson 1, 4, 111, 114, 115, 231
Eritrea/Eritrean 61, 93
essentialism 129, 189
Estonia 87
Ethics of immigration, The 73
Ethiopia 23, 62, 77
ethnicity 6, 33, 39, 40, 57, 68, 70, 87, 92, 99, 100, 101, 102, 103, 113, 115, 118, 123, 126, 129, 130, 131, 134, 136, 150, 151, 152, 153, 154, 155, 156, 157, 158, 159, 160, 161, 162, 165, 167, 168, 169, 170, 171, 172, 174, 175, 176, 177, 178, 179, 189, 190, 191, 192, 193, 194, 195, 197, 198, 199, 200, 201, 202, 203, 204, 205, 207, 209, 212, 213, 214, 215, 216, 218, 231, 232
euphoria 3, 67, 230
European Social Survey 197

European Union (EU) ix, 1, 6, 11, 17, 19, 21, 22, 24, 25, 27, 28, 31, 32, 33, 36, 39, 45, 55, 61, 62, 63, 70, 71, 75, 88, 94, 95, 100, 112, 124, 128, 131, 134, 136, 154, 163, 175, 178, 187, 188, 189, 191, 194, 195, 196, 197, 198, 201, 202, 203, 204, 212, 213, 214, 216, 217
exceptionalism 200
exile 2, 4, 5, 11, 29, 36, 39, 41, 42, 59, 63, 67, 72, 83, 85, 88, 89, 92, 98, 99, 121, 122, 125, 129, 136, 139, 152, 165, 175, 179, 206, 218, 229, 231; *see also* refugee; displaced persons
exit 40, 44, 71, 78

Falicov 165
families 15, 16, 17, 18, 19, 20, 21, 22, 23, 24, 26, 27, 28, 29, 30, 31, 32, 33, 34, 35, 36, 40, 42, 43, 44, 58, 59, 61, 69, 70, 71, 72, 75, 76, 78, 84, 86, 88, 90, 93, 95, 97, 100, 111, 115, 116, 119, 125, 126, 129, 130, 152, 154, 155, 156, 157, 158, 159, 160, 161, 162, 163, 164, 165, 166, 168, 169, 170, 172, 174, 194, 200, 204, 205, 206–207, 208, 209, 210, 211, 212, 213, 214, 215, 229, 230, 231, 232
Fanon 167
Farrell and Thirion 217
"fatherland" 112
feelings (happy) 3, 11, 29, 34, 75, 77, 82, 87, 90, 92, 94, 95, 96, 113, 121, 137, 138, 150, 152, 167, 172, 192, 206, 207, 231
feelings (unhappy) ix, xi, xii, 2, 22, 26, 32, 37, 39, 40, 41, 42, 55, 60, 67, 68, 72, 73, 74, 76, 77, 83, 84, 85, 86, 88, 89, 90, 94, 95, 100, 101, 113, 115, 119, 120, 121, 122, 123, 124, 125, 126, 129, 130, 133, 135, 137, 138, 153, 156, 157, 158, 160, 161, 162, 166, 168, 173, 174, 206, 217, 218, 229, 231
Figure-Ground Gestalt 94
Finland 82, 195, 208
Five-Factors Model (FFM) of personality 196, 199
Flaubert 63
forced labour/prostitution 43–44, 45
forced migration 5, 9, 14, 21, 22, 61, 68, 76, 83, 98, 100, 112, 121, 122, 125, 153, 161, 172, 229, 231; *see also* tied-migration

Foucault 126
France 13, 25, 26, 31, 54, 59, 63, 69, 75, 123, 126, 127, 131, 132, 153, 156, 164, 166, 167, 168, 170, 174, 188, 189, 190, 194, 195, 200, 201, 202, 203, 204, 205, 208, 212, 213, 214, 215
fraudulent families 74
freedom 6, 11, 12, 13, 26, 32, 33, 34, 36, 58, 59, 66, 89, 92, 117, 118, 121, 123, 126, 128, 130, 170, 173, 192, 193, 204, 209, 210, 211, 229
Freud 38, 116, 120, 196
Frohlick 88
Fuentes 61
fundamentalism 131
future 7, 12, 17, 27, 28, 32, 33, 40, 58, 59, 66, 67, 68, 71, 75, 82, 85, 86, 88, 123, 134, 150, 151, 161, 192, 201, 210, 216, 229, 230

Gallup Poll 11, 12
Gans 153, 176
Gartner and Kennedy 38
General Well-Being Scale 72
generations 4, 150–187; 1st generation 4, 150–156, 160–169, 173, 177; 1.5 generation 150, 158, 160, 163, 165, 205; 2nd generation 4, 131, 150, 151, 153, 152, 154, 155, 156, 157–161, 163–165, 166, 167, 168, 169, 170, 171, 173, 174, 175–179, 200, 204, 205, 212–215, 217, 218, 231; 3rd generation 131, 154, 156, 157, 162, 169, 172, 176, 178, 215
genetics 93, 211
Geneva Convention 37, 38, 252
gender 6, 15, 19, 21, 22, 35, 68, 77, 86, 116, 118, 131, 163, 172, 174, 176, 178, 188, 200, 203, 208, 210, 211, 229, 230
geographic 5, 28, 67, 84, 86, 103, 115, 118, 128, 156, 169
Germany 7, 13, 17, 25, 27, 34, 41, 44, 57, 89, 169, 174, 188, 190, 192, 194, 195, 196, 200, 202, 204, 205, 208, 215
Ghana 27
Ghandi 123
ghettos 151–153, 191, 201
ghost (trails, villages) 62, 75
Giddens 87
Glazer and Moynihan 153
Global Code of Practice on International Recruitment of Health Personnel 23

globalization 6, 83, 91, 99, 116, 117, 134, 155, 171, 196, 201, 204, 233
God: Gods and Goddesses 9, 10, 57, 68, 75, 90, 96, 102
Gok and Atsan 19
González 118
Goode 138
Goodwin-Gill 71
Gordon 138, 153, 172
Granberg-Michaelson 100
great allegory of life 66
"Great Awakening" 117
Greece x, 10, 58, 86, 121, 156, 168, 169
grief 3, 59, 66, 68, 88, 90, 115, 124, 137, 230; *see also* feelings
Grief Intensity Scale 284
Grinbergs 94, 119, 128, 129, 136, 137, 232
Grosjean 159
guardians 54, 58, 125, 210, 229
Guatemala 11, 31, 61
Guibernau 135
guilt (survivor guilt) 32, 83, 84, 87, 88, 99, 114, 129, 137, 150, 160, 162, 166, 167, 206, 214, 229, 231
Guinea slave trade 54

Hague Convention 43
Haiti / Haitians 35, 43, 118, 154
Hall 67, 68, 83, 91, 121, 124
Halperin 93
Handlin 138
Hansen's principle 176
Harari 216, 217
Harris viii
Hastie 194
Haug 15
Hawaiian 27
Hayes and Dowds 199
health services 23, 24, 25, 39, 41, 70, 72, 139, 174, 232
health status 21, 35, 36, 37, 39, 41, 61, 68, 69, 70, 72, 78, 90, 92, 93, 94, 115, 126, 135, 174, 209, 218, 229
healthcare providers i, 24, 25, 30, 77, 82, 101, 233
Heath and Tilley 191
Heidegger 111, 133
Herberg 103, 138, 175, 178
hero archetype ix, xii, 2, 3, 5, 9, 12, 57, 60, 66, 68, 70, 74, 96, 99, 136, 230, 233
HEXACO six-factor model 199, 232

hijab 100, 131, 152, 214
Hinduism 10, 176, 214
Hirschman 95, 100
Hodes 72
holding environment 94, 126
Holocaust 19
Holy Grail 12
Homans 120
Homecomer Culture Shock Scale 91
homeland 3, 9, 10, 11, 12, 13, 14, 15, 16, 18, 19, 22, 23, 24, 25, 26, 27, 28, 30, 31, 34, 35, 39, 42, 57, 58, 59, 60, 61, 62, 69, 69, 70, 82, 83, 84, 85, 86, 88, 90, 91, 94, 95, 96, 98, 99, 111, 115, 118, 120, 121, 122, 126, 130, 135, 136, 137, 138, 151, 156, 158, 159, 160, 161, 163, 164, 166, 167, 170, 173, 174, 175, 177, 202, 204, 208, 213, 214, 215, 229, 233
Homer, Iliad and the Odyssey 82, 91, 96
homesickness 67, 68, 70, 171
homogeneity 33, 138, 191, 201
homosexuals *see* LGBTQI
Honduras 11, 31, 61, 62
host countries i, 2, 3, 4, 7, 13, 70, 72, 78, 91, 95, 96, 100, 112, 113, 118, 124, 126, 131, 134, 135, 138, 151, 153, 157, 158, 171, 187–218, 232
hourglass metaphor of society 201
Howard 216
Hron 85, 88, 187
human potential movement 117
human rights 6, 33, 36, 37, 42, 58, 62, 71, 73, 187, 204, 209, 232
humour 95, 127
Hungary 23, 194, 195

Ibrahim and Howarth 38
Iceland 23, 208
identity i, 1, 2, 3, 4, 5, 28, 38, 42, 87, 91, 92, 93, 98, 100, 102, 110–140, 154, 156, 159, 160, 165, 167, 168, 170, 171, 172, 174, 178, 189, 190, 191, 193, 202, 204, 211, 212, 230, 231, 232
Ignatieff 135, 136, 178
Illegal/irregular migration 14, 22, 43, 44, 55, 56, 62, 70–74, 75, 78, 93, 121, 124, 191, 206, 208, 209, 230
India 5, 21, 22, 24, 30, 31, 32, 36, 38, 42, 43, 57, 58, 61, 67, 82, 90, 98, 103, 159, 162, 167, 168, 173, 176, 188, 214
individualism 92, 116, 117, 211

individuation 12, 111, 168, 231
inferiority xii, 67, 114, 150, 167, 215
instinct xi, xii, 3, 9, 115
integration 33, 66, 71, 76, 82, 90, 92, 94, 97, 99, 100, 111, 115, 119, 123, 124, 127, 128, 131, 137, 139, 151, 154, 155, 169, 170, 174, 187, 191, 192, 200, 202, 203, 204, 205, 211, 212, 213, 214, 216, 218, 230
intent-to-migrate 10, 12–14, 16, 19, 22, 23, 24, 25
intent-to-return 16, 22, 24, 25, 69, 82, 83, 86, 87, 88, 89, 94, 115, 123, 124, 152, 167, 231; *see also* return
intent-to-stay 23, 135
internal migration ix, 20, 28, 29, 30, 85, 95, 137, 18
internally displaced persons (IDP) 26, 37, 38
inter-generational conflict 153, 161–163, 168, 170, 206, 213, 214, 215
International Policy Institute for Counter Terrorism 42
internationalists/internationalism 82, 83
International Migration Institute 2
International Organization (IOM) 7, 56
International Social Survey 13
Ipp 229, 230
Iran 33, 59
Iraq / Iraqis 54, 55, 82, 122, 123, 160
Ireland/Irish 11, 21, 22, 24, 25, 26, 32, 54, 56, 92, 95, 163, 169, 172, 194, 198, 199, 203, 208
Islam 100, 171, 172, 214, 215; *see also* Muslim
isolation/isolationism 30, 32, 67, 77, 93, 114, 138, 151, 153, 174, 207
Israel/Israeli 21, 24, 32, 42, 57, 67, 93, 98, 162, 195, 206, 217; *see also* Judaism
Issei generation 157
Italy 18, 22, 25, 55, 56, 59, 82, 84, 152, 161, 164, 169, 188, 194, 195, 204
Iwamura 175

Jacoby 67
Jamaica / Jamaican 67, 68, 171, 172
Janis and Mann 16
Janoff-Bulman 90
Japan 10, 18, 32, 59, 63, 86, 88, 124, 129, 157, 175, 188, 192, 210
Jensen, ER 90
Jones 196

Jordan 188
journal: *Population, Space & Place* 34
journey (heroic journey of migration) i, ix, 2, 3, 5, 9, 21, 28, 40, 54–63, 68, 71, 72, 74, 75, 82, 93, 120, 125, 133, 138, 149, 166, 229, 230, 231, 232, 233
Joyce 95
Judaism 44, 100, 103, 121, 169, 175, 201
Jung, CG / Jungian ix, x, xii, xiii, 3, 5, 9, 10, 23, 54, 66, 67, 93, 96, 110, 111, 115, 116, 120, 157, 229, 230
Junger 135
Juni 84
jus sanguinis 4, 168, 188, 189, 190, 202, 213, 215, 218
jus soli 4, 22, 75, 150, 168, 188, 189, 190, 202, 208, 213, 218
justice 23, 91, 92, 130, 131, 139, 157, 161, 175, 194, 208

Kage 18, 59, 63, 129
Kahn 160, 169, 193
Kant xii, 9
Kawate 188
Kennan and Walker 18
Kent State Emotion, Stress & Relationships Lab 86
Kenya 17, 23
Khorsandi 158
Kingsley 55
Kinnvall and Nesbitt-Larking 155
Kivisto 92, 192, 202, 203
Knafo and Yaari 11, 57, 85
Kobayashu 157
Koenig 176
Kohls 91
Kohn 189
Kohut 123
Konstanz Psycho-trauma Research and Outpatient Clinic 41
Korea 102, 139, 165, 176–177
Kosovar 163
Kulu 87
Kundera 72
Kundu 173
Kurds / Kurdish 122, 123
Kurien 176
Kuwait 31
Kymlicka 202

labour unions 196
Laos 72

Latvia 195, 208
Laub 233
Lazerwitz and Rowitz 176
Lebanon 188
Lenski 176
Lepsius 190
Levy-Warren 83, 84
LGBTQI 139, 156
Liberians 165
Libya 56, 61
life-stages 111, 114, 124–125, 231
Linhartová 88
literature 2, 4, 26, 36, 41, 85, 101, 138, 167, 173
Lobban 117
London Medical Foundation for the Care of Victims of Torture 72, 77
loss xi, xii, 2, 3, 19, 22, 23, 28, 39, 41, 60, 66, 67, 68, 72, 73, 76, 83–84, 85, 86, 88, 89, 90, 94, 100, 101, 115, 119, 120, 121, 122, 123, 124, 126, 128, 129, 166, 174, 179, 206, 229, 230
love 29, 67, 91, 93, 98, 116, 137, 150, 152, 156, 173, 233
Love and Exile 72, 98, 179
Lucassen 174, 201, 202, 204, 212, 213

MacGill 163
Madison 90
Magdol 36
Malaysia 31
Manchandra 38
Manzanar pilgrimage 175
Marcus 60
marginalized 92, 102, 122, 130, 178, 201, 208, 213, 215, 231
market-based migration policy 195
Marlin 58
marriage 4, 14, 16, 18, 26, 32, 33, 43, 77, 86, 92, 98, 152, 155, 156, 163, 168, 169, 209–210, 214
Marshall 92
Maslow 19, 93, 111
mass migrations 32, 43, 58, 59, 61
massacre 39
McAuliffe 56
McInerney 11
Mead 176
Meaders 86, 124, 132
Médecins Sans Frontières 62
media stereotypes 27, 28, 59, 69
Mediterranean 21, 31, 56, 59, 151, 188

Medusa 67–68
Megha 173
Mehta 167, 168
mental health 37, 61, 69, 72, 74, 76–77, 83–84, 90, 93–94, 115, 174, 189
mental maps 10, 84
mentor 3, 54, 57–58, 63, 137, 168, 229
Mexico/Mexicans 26, 27, 55, 56, 57, 61, 62, 74
Middle East 5, 25, 42, 55, 103, 121, 188, 210
Migration phases and stages: Phase 1, pre-migration 9–53; Stage 1, the ordinary world 9–11; Stage 2, call to adventure (voluntary) 12–33; Stage 3, refusing the call (stayers and involuntary migrants) 34–45; Phase 2, the journey 54–65; Stage 4, meeting the mentor 57–59; Stage 5, the crossing 59–60; Stage 6, tests, allies, enemies 60–62; Stage 7, the approach (inmost cave) 62–63; Phase 3, post-migration (arrival) 66–81; Stage 8, ordeal at arrival 67–80; Stage 9, possession of the treasure 74–78; Phase 4, post-migration (home) 82–109; Stage 10, the road back 82–90; Stage 11, resurrection 91–95; Stage 12, the hero's return 96–100
Mincer 19
missionaries 90
Modarressi 59
Mohr 75
money 17, 18, 43, 55, 57, 67, 70, 75, 132, 195, 200
Montero 17–18, 57, 70, 84, 89, 127, 164
Morais 67
Morocco/Moroccans 56, 123, 204, 214, 215
Mostafa 205
Motherland/mother country 57, 112, 151
mourning 74, 77, 83, 126, 128, 137, 160, 166, 230, 232
Mozambique 77
multiculturalism ix, 4, 27, 33, 75, 90, 92, 99, 110, 118, 127, 128, 131, 153, 170, 176, 178, 191, 192, 193, 194, 199, 202, 203, 204, 205, 210, 211, 213, 216, 232
Munaweera 173
Muslim 101, 102, 103, 139, 155, 156, 165, 169, 171, 172, 174, 197, 212, 214, 215; *see also* Islam

Mutsuko 157
My Mother's Village 88
myth xi, 12, 17, 54, 62, 67, 74, 83, 129, 130, 134, 157, 167, 230

name changes 75
Namibia 208
Nationalism 122, 123, 129, 135, 136, 139, 189, 203
nation states 4, 6, 92, 118, 128, 134, 135, 136, 157, 187, 188–189, 190, 199, 204, 217
nativism 198, 215
naturalization 69, 127, 151, 153, 188, 213, 214, 215
Nature of Prejudice, The 196
Nazi 12, 59
Nehru 98
Nekyia (night-sea journey) 120
Nepal / Nepalis 14, 24, 31, 62, 90, 188
Nesbitt-Larking 155
Netherlands / Dutch 76, 93, 123, 156, 194, 195, 197, 199, 200, 203, 205, 214
newland i, 4, 26, 33, 63, 66, 68, 69, 70, 82, 83, 84, 85, 86, 87, 88, 89, 91, 92, 95, 96, 97, 98, 99, 100, 102, 110, 112, 113, 114, 115, 118, 119, 120, 125, 127, 129, 130, 132, 137, 139, 150–160, 163, 164, 169–175, 179, 187, 193, 206–207, 209, 218, 230, 231
New Economics of Labour Migration (NELM) 15
New York Declaration for Refugees and Migrants 69
New Zealand 13, 21, 22, 110, 121, 187, 194, 208
Nicaragua 208
Nietzsche 126, 130
Nigeria / Nigerians 24, 33, 169, 172
Nisei generation 157
North Africa 61, 215, 217
North America *see* Canada, USA
Norway 27, 89, 90, 208

obedience cultures 114, 155, 162, 173, 177, 232
Oberg 90
object-relations psychology 134
O'Brien 172
Odysseus 54, 55, 57, 82, 83, 86, 91, 96, 100, 111; *see also* Homer
OECD 195

Okin 210, 211
Orfanos 168
Ovid 85

Paat 200
Pakistan 24, 32, 43, 58, 59, 214
Panama 62
Papadopoulos 7, 42, 136
Parens 159
parentification / role reversal 158, 165–166, 168, 213, 231
participation mystique 111, 116
Paskievich 88–89
passports 43, 55, 73
peace-building 38
peasants 18, 69, 87, 127
Penelope 86, 91
Percival 12
Persian Gulf 54
Persephone syndrome 86, 156
Perseus 67, 68
persona 4, 59, 110
Peters 189, 190
Peterson 10, 96
Petigara 172
Petschauer 57, 89
Philippines 208
Philosopher's stone 98
Pine and Drachman 206
pioneers 1, 21–22, 207
Plato xii, 9
Poirier and Piquet 54
Poland 13, 128, 163
Polynesia 5
Portes and Rumbaut 69, 85, 153, 161, 162, 177, 189, 200, 213, 215, 217
Portugal 22, 194, 195
poverty 7, 11, 26, 31, 38, 59, 77, 85, 130, 171, 172
power 5, 9, 11, 13, 21, 44, 57, 58, 68, 97, 100, 117, 122, 130, 131, 132, 133, 135, 155, 170, 173, 174, 194, 200, 209, 210, 211, 232
prejudice 4, 19, 22, 27, 32, 33, 61, 74, 87, 88, 93, 100, 118, 134, 139, 153, 154, 193, 194, 196–200, 204, 213, 214, 217, 21
Press 59, 61
professionals i, 23, 24, 25, 30, 76, 82, 139, 218, 232
projection 67, 96, 134
Prometheus 75

Promised Land 11, 32, 67, 162, 167
Protestants 100, 169, 176, 198, 201
psychoanalysis 1, 66, 116, 117
psychology ix, 1, 5, 7, 14, 20, 85, 94, 111, 121, 123, 151, 155, 193, 197, 229
Psychology of Culture Shock, The 70, 99
psychopathology 2, 41, 73, 86, 93, 98, 136, 168
PTSD (post-traumatic stress disorder) 2, 41, 73, 76, 77, 83, 84, 88, 93, 162, 166, 229
Pueblo chief, Mountain Lake xi
push-pull factors 16, 26, 27, 30, 54, 126

Québec 203

Rabin 56
race/racialization 37, 38, 57, 68, 71, 92, 99, 118, 128, 129, 130, 131, 134, 153–154, 156, 162, 165, 172, 175, 177, 178, 189, 196, 198, 203, 213, 229, 231; *see also* prejudice
Ramji-Nogales 56
Rattansi 117
Rawls 211
reasons-for-leaving 14, 16, 17–18, 24, 25–27, 29–31, 39–40, 53, 67, 82, 118, 229
Reding 123
refugee children 40, 42, 61, 72, 93
refugees 7, 13, 33, 34, 36–43, 54, 56, 61, 63, 69, 70–73, 74, 76, 77, 88, 93, 102, 115, 121, 123, 129–130, 139, 152, 153, 187–188, 196, 217
refusal to adapt 88, 124, 125, 131, 159, 165, 207
Regional Mixed Migration Secretariat 62
Reichlová 19
religion 4, 9, 37, 38, 40, 57, 68, 71, 95, 99, 100–103, 115, 129, 130, 131, 134, 135, 138–140, 152, 170, 171, 175–179, 192, 203, 214, 229, 232
remittances 14, 15, 16, 22, 27, 28, 31, 60, 130, 135
Renteln 209
resignation 62, 86, 131, 171, 214
resilience 56, 61, 86, 90, 94, 114, 229
return i, 3, 6, 18, 26, 27, 31, 37, 39, 41, 54, 58, 69, 70, 71, 75, 80, 82, 85, 86, 87, 88, 89, 90, 91, 96, 122, 125, 130, 133, 151, 160, 167, 198, 206, 213, 230, 231

Rezazadeh and Hoover 173
Riding Mountain National Park 9
rights 4, 6, 14, 23, 33, 36–37, 40, 70–71, 73, 117, 121, 133, 135, 165, 172, 188, 192–194, 204, 209–210, 211, 214, 218, 232
rites 3, 115, 135, 137
Roberts-Turner 172
Rogers 111
Rokeach 13
Romania 44
Roth 169
Rudmin 95
Rwanda 208
Ryufu 158

Sabelli 29, 161
Sačer 55
Sage Handbook of Prejudice, Stereotyping, and Discrimination, The 196
Said 121, 126, 132
Sandplay 110
Sansei generation 157
Saudi Arabia/Arabs 31, 61, 62, 103, 188, 215
Sayad 31, 87, 123, 127, 128, 132, 153, 156, 170, 171, 214
scales (cultural / psychological) 91, 95, 99, 171
Scandinavia 32, 41
Schechtman 118
Scheutz 89
Schopenhauer xii, 9
Schultz 18
Schwartz 13
Scientific American 36
Scotland 29, 54, 60, 92, 203
Seijin 157
self 4, 12, 13, 26, 28, 29, 56, 68, 70, 74, 83, 85, 90, 92, 93, 94, 95, 96–98, 110–114, 115–116, 118, 119, 124–126, 129, 130, 132, 133, 136, 137, 165, 168, 171, 178, 192, 198, 231
Sen 128, 131, 170, 171, 189
sending-societies 191
Sense of Coherence Scale 238
separation 4, 25, 43, 61, 67, 86, 94, 95, 96, 97, 111, 112, 115, 121, 156, 172, 173, 175, 177, 201, 203, 206
Serbia/Serbian 25, 39
settler states 151, 187, 189, 192, 194, 212

shadow xii, 6, 22, 60, 67, 97, 119, 135, 136, 158, 178, 205, 230, 231
Shakespeare 170
Shay 42
Shweder 211
Shweder, Minow and Markus 209
Simpson and French 86
Singer 72, 98, 179
slavery 43, 44, 167, 214
Sly and Wrigley 17
smuggling 21, 22, 42–44, 55, 56, 58, 59, 62, 63, 73, 74
Socrates 5
Somalia / Somalians 19, 21, 31, 33, 62, 152, 165
social cohesion 202, 217, 232
social contact 198
sojourner 9, 20, 90, 95, 118, 171
Slovenia 208
South Asia 20, 54, 127, 139, 159, 176, 188
South / Latin America 5, 6, 20, 22, 54, 61, 62, 76, 115, 130, 229
Spain 13, 33, 56, 89, 188, 190, 194, 202, 203
Sri Lankan 76
stateless 122, 123
stayers 2, 3, 9, 14, 34–35
Stella matutina 97
Stern 4, 111, 113–114, 231
Stockdale 35
Straits of Gibraltar 61
structural integration 203–205
students 22–25, 90, 96, 171, 176, 191
Suárez-Orozco 201
Sudan 61, 155
Suh 139
Sumatra–Andaman earthquake 37
survival sex 56, 71
Sweden 33, 34, 36, 76, 93, 158, 194, 208
Switzerland 25, 76, 194
symbol x, xi, 12, 68, 83, 90, 135, 136, 139, 153, 154, 189
Syria / Syrians 34, 54, 55, 56, 62, 122, 188

Taiwan 23, 29, 176
Tanzania 69
Tas 122
Tausk 116
Taylor 92, 117, 202
temporary workers 69, 71, 75–76, 82, 194, 203

The Uprooted 100
Thomas 176
Thoreau 10, 92
Thorpe 160
Three-Generations Hypothesis 176
threshold guardians 54, 58–59, 63, 229
tied-migration 2, 21, 35–36, 156, 172, 173, 229
Tolstoy 231
torture / persecution 11, 37, 38, 41–42, 55–56, 59, 62, 71–72, 74, 77, 83, 166, 198, 206
traditional xi, 4, 26, 30, 35, 36, 57, 62, 77, 101, 116, 117, 125, 127, 130, 131, 139, 154, 157, 161, 162, 170, 171, 172, 174, 206, 207, 214, 216
trafficking 4, 6, 42–43, 44, 45, 58, 61, 208
transformation 3, 96–98, 117, 124, 207, 230–231
transnational 27, 45, 76, 83, 132, 134–135, 138, 174
Triandis 91
trickster / shape-shifter 60, 74
Tunisia 214
Turkey 27, 34, 58, 93, 123, 168, 169, 174, 188, 214
Turkle 11
Turner 137

Ukraine 88–89
Ulysses syndrome 3, 66, 77, 230
uncanny other (*Unheimliche*) 38, 196
UNICEF 40
United Arab Emirates (UAE) 31, 188
United Kingdom (UK) ix, 15, 21, 22, 23, 24, 25, 26, 33, 34, 35, 45, 73, 93, 127, 156, 164, 165, 174, 191, 194, 199, 205, 208, 214
United Nations (UN) 37, 40, 41, 43, 44, 70, 121, 209, 211, 232
United States (USA) x, xi, 5, 6, 7, 11, 12, 13, 26, 28, 32, 35, 36, 37, 38, 44, 54, 56, 57, 58, 63, 69, 70, 71, 72, 73, 74, 75, 90, 91, 95, 96, 98, 100, 101, 110, 113, 118, 121, 123, 124, 126, 134, 135, 137, 128, 138, 139, 150, 151, 152, 153, 154, 159, 161, 162, 165, 167, 168, 169, 170, 172, 173, 175, 176, 177, 178, 179, 187, 192, 194, 195, 196, 197, 200, 201, 203, 205, 206, 212, 214, 216, 217, 218
U-shaped model 77, 90

USSR / Russia 6, 7, 29, 87, 89, 98, 166–167, 231
utopia vs dystopia 201

Varvin 38
vicarious trauma 74
victim 43, 44, 123, 132, 194
Vietnam 72, 102
visa 11, 14, 31, 55, 63, 69, 73, 163, 191, 195, 208
Vogler 68
Volkswagen Germans 124
von Franz xii, 5, 67, 166

Wake Forest University 178
Wales 92, 203
war/war zones 17, 36, 38, 39, 40, 41, 43, 55, 59, 71, 72, 89, 93, 96, 121, 129, 135, 167, 218
Warnick 137
Wasuge 19
watari dori 157
W-shaped culture-shock model 90
Winnicott 4, 57, 94, 111, 112–113, 126, 167
women 4, 14, 22, 24, 27, 28, 32, 35, 36, 39, 43, 44, 56, 58, 71, 73, 77, 86, 94, 101, 115, 123, 131, 169, 172, 173–174, 178, 204, 205, 207–211, 214, 231–232
work 5, 12, 14, 17, 18, 21, 22, 23, 24, 25, 26, 27, 29, 30, 31, 32, 35, 36, 45, 55, 69, 71, 74, 75, 76, 89, 90, 91, 94, 119, 127, 129, 139, 159, 163, 174, 187, 190, 191, 194, 195, 196, 198, 200, 201, 204, 208, 209, 215; *see also* professionals
World Bank 12, 20, 211
World Health Organization (WHO) 23
World War I (WWI) 6
World War II (WWII) 11, 18, 37, 44, 59, 63, 70, 87, 89, 112, 120, 129, 154, 159, 175, 196
wound of return 86, 89, 90, 91, 111, 126, 166

xenophilia 4, 196–200, 232
xenophobia 69, 87, 193, 196, 198, 199

Yakushko 177
Yang 175, 176, 177
Yemen 62
Yugoslavia 39

Zahar 11, 39, 45, 72, 88, 129, 163
Zimbabwe 16, 56
Zimbardo time perspective 85